MW01125840

Nahum Bogner

AT THE MERCY OF STRANGERS
The Rescue of Jewish Children with Assumed Identities in Poland

This publication was supported by a grant
from the following organizations:

The Conference on Jewish Material Claims Against Germany

Claims Conference   ועידת התביעות
The Conference on Jewish Material Claims Against Germany

The Memorial Foundation for Jewish Culture
The Adelson Family Charitable Foundation

Nahum Bogner

# AT THE MERCY
# OF STRANGERS

The Rescue of Jewish Children with
Assumed Identities in Poland

Yad Vashem ★ Jerusalem ★ 2009

Nahum Bogner

*At the Mercy of Strangers*

*The Rescue of Jewish Children with Assumed Identities in Poland*

Translated from the Hebrew by Ralph Mandel

*Language Editor:* Asher Weill

© 2009 All rights reserved to Yad Vashem
P.O.B. 3477, Jerusalem 91034, Israel
publications.marketing@yadvashem.org.il

ISBN 978-965-308-331-8

Typesetting: Judith Sternberg

Printed in Israel by Offset Shlomo Nathan Press
2009

*To the children who were saved from that conflagration*
*To their rescuers who took their life in their hands*
*And to those who devoted themselves to returning them*
*to their people*

Yes, little girl, yes, slender hands,
Yes, you may cry now, now yes you can.
Yes, angel denuded of hair and eyebrows,
Yes, now it's permitted, now it's allowed.
Now the night at long last is clear and serene,
Now Uncle Jozef Kremer has departed the scene.
Now the radio has counted the numbers so steep
Of what they did to you, poor little sheep.
You were very well trained and complied
And in the darkness you never once cried
And even (lest anyone hear!)
You teethed without shedding a single tear
And about it all, it all, it all
At long last there is a written protocol
Collated and stapled together, my sweet --
And now at long last, yes, you may weep.

Natan Alterman
The Seventh Column, October 19, 1945

*Translated by Vivian Eden*

# Contents

# Preface

The fate of Jewish children in the Holocaust is one of the most deeply moving subjects in the story of modern Jewish martyrdom. The children were the most vulnerable of all the groups, and only a few of them survived. Yet even in those dark times, their desperate effort to cling to life astonished the adult population. The children's life in the ghettos, and the struggle to save them, is a highly charged issue which cries out from the depths of the chronicles and diaries of the Holocaust era. After the war, Jews the world over were spellbound by the fate of the few children who survived and what they had experienced during the course of their rescue. In the unvarnished, unembellished language of children, free of introspection, they told their stories and described what they had endured. Some of their stories were published immediately after the war, and many more testimonies were added over the years, in the form of diaries and memoirs by the children and their rescuers.

Surprisingly, despite the abundant documentation that is now available, little research has been devoted to this topic. A few studies have been written regarding the rescue of Jewish children in Nazi-occupied countries, and they deal mainly with the outer circle of the rescue efforts — that is, with the rescuers, both Jews and non-Jews, who operated within the framework of what can be referred to as institutionalized rescue by underground movements and operatives. Scant attention has been paid to the ordeals undergone by the children themselves. Their shattering rescue experiences and their path back into Jewish society have been neglected and have often faded into oblivion.

Since the end of the 1960s much has been written about the impact of the Holocaust on the second generation of survivors, although the latest psychological data led to no substantive conclusions. In contrast, the problems of the first generation children during the Holocaust were gradually forgotten, seeming to vanish as though they had never been. Israel absorbed thousands of child survivors, many of them orphans who were rescued under assumed identities, but their stories, surprisingly, were rarely made known to the public. The powerful impact of these stories was seen in the emotional response of viewers to Israel Television documentary films about the rescue of Jewish children in Poland that were broadcast in recent years.

Of the approximately 1.5 million Jewish children who perished in the Holocaust, about sixty percent were Polish. Only a small fraction of Poland's Jewish children survived the Nazi occupation. A few survived the war in hiding places of various kinds or with adults in the forests. However, the majority of the children who survived did so individually, under assumed identities, with Christian families, in monasteries and convents, and on farms in rural areas.

The present work deals with the children in Poland who lived under assumed identities and who were rescued after the war and were able to return to Jewish society. I was attracted to this subject by the unprecedented experiences that the children underwent. At its heart was the abrupt severance from their familiar social surroundings when their parents placed them in the hands of strangers; their need to adopt and internalize a false identity at an early age; and their dependence on the mercy of the surrogate "parents." They lived a life of unremitting fear and anxiety, heightened by uncertainty about what the future held for them. After the war, both their relatives and Jewish institutions undertook great efforts to restore the children to the Jewish fold — a far from simple task. It soon became apparent that the manner of their rescue had left a deep imprint on them which continued to weigh heavily even after they were able to return to their true identity. These children, with their dual identity, their experiences with their rescuers, and their road back to their families and Jewish society, lie at the core of this book.

Methodologically, this subject presented a daunting challenge, as it must be based largely on the testimonies and memories of those who were children at the time. Moreover, the background of the rescue of Jewish children in wartime Poland lies almost exclusively within the intimate, private, non-establishment realm, under conditions of extreme pressure, verging on the brink of catastrophe.

In vain, then, will we search for authentic contemporary documentation regarding the thoughts and feelings of the child or its parents as they smuggled the child out of the ghetto and placed him or her in the custody of a Christian foster family; nor can we know what sort of an agreement was reached concerning the future. In the prevailing circumstances almost nothing was committed to writing. Consequently, we must resort to oral documentation collected after the war and to the literature of memoirs. Every historian is aware of the limitations of such sources, but in this case there is no other recourse. Nevertheless, rigorous textual criticism must be applied, as it must with all forms of historical documentation. The alternative would have been to allow these riveting human experiences to be forgotten.

Most of the research for this book was done at the International Institute for Holocaust Research at Yad Vashem in Jerusalem, and I am deeply beholden to all those who assisted me. The book had its genesis in a joint initiative which I undertook with my friend and mentor, Prof. Yisrael Gutman, the institute's first director. Prof. Gutman invited me to become a research fellow in the institute, and together we drew up the plan for this study. Throughout my years in the Institute he followed the progress of the research keenly and urged me to complete it, and for this I owe him heartfelt thanks. I am also grateful to Esther Aran, the institute's first administrative director; to Hadassah Modlinger and Yehudit Kleinman from the Yad Vashem Archives; to Eva Feldenkreis, the archivist of the Ghetto Fighters' Museum in Kibbutz Lochamei Haghettaot; to Neta Sivan, the archivist of Kibbutz Gan Shmuel, and to the staff of the other archives who located the material I requested. Special thanks are due to Dr. Bella Gutterman and Avital Saf, from the Yad Vashem publications department, and to the language editor of the original Hebrew version, Sigal Adler, who dealt with the production of the book with never-failing amiability. I would also like to express my appreciation to Ralph Mandel who translated the book into English and to the editor, Asher Weill, who edited the complete manuscript and prepared it for press.

And finally, my deep appreciation to my wife, Neta, who was the first to read the manuscript: to her I owe boundless thanks for her comments and stylistic corrections.

N.B.
February, 2009

# CHAPTER ONE

# Difficulties of Rescue in Poland

On the eve of the Second World War, the Jewish population of Poland numbered approximately 3.3 million,[1] of which, according to different estimates, about ten percent survived the conflagration. Most of the survivors had been refugees in the Soviet Union, to where they were deported by the Soviet authorities or to where they had fled in the summer of 1941 when the Germans invaded in Operation Barbarossa. Many of them returned to Poland after the war.[2] In Poland itself few Jews survived. By the middle of June 1945, a month after the end of the war, a total of 55,509 Jews had registered with the Jewish committees that were established for that purpose around the country. That number included all the Jews who had survived in Poland itself,[3] either by posing as non-Jews or by the grace of their Christian neighbors, and several thousand who fought with the partisans or hid in the forests, as well as those who survived the ordeal of the concentration camps.[4]

Notably, there were very few children among the survivors. Before the war there had been nearly one million Jewish children below the age of fourteen in Poland.[5] It is estimated that no more than some 28,000 of them survived — about three percent.[6] Of these, only some 5,000 had lived throughout the war in Poland itself, and most of them had lost one or both of their parents.[7] This horrifically low number attests to the overwhelming difficulties

---

1   Jacob Lestschinsky, *Crisis, Catastrophe and Survival* (New York: Institute of Jewish Affairs of the World Jewish Congress, 1948), p. 60.

2   Lucjan Dobroszycki, *Survivors of the Holocaust in Poland* (Armonk, New York: M.E. Sharpe, 1994), pp. 18–22.

3   Ibid., p. 68.

4   Yisrael Gutman, *The Jews in Poland after World War II* (Hebrew) (Jerusalem: Zalman Shazar Center, 1985), p. 12.

5   Lestschinsky, *Crisis*, p. 61.

6   Report of the Central Jewish Committee of Poland, Jan.1, 1946-June 30, 1946, Warsaw, 1947 (Yiddish).

7   *Sprawozdanie wydzial opieki nad dzieckiem C.K.Ż w P. na rok 1946*, Archiwum Żydowskiego Institutu Historycznego (AŻIH), (CKŻ, WO).

which were entailed in rescuing children during the war in German-occupied Poland. It is, above all, the loss of the children that brings home the full impact of the tragedy that befell Poland's Jews in the last chapter of their life in a country which had been their homeland for centuries. Polish Jewry, which constituted the overwhelming majority of the Jewish people in Europe, was dealt a mortal blow with the almost total annihilation of its younger generation.

Germany's rapid conquest of Poland in September 1939, which launched the Second World War, severed the potential escape routes of the millions of Jews who were caught in the Nazi pincers with no hope of escape. The only rescue options available to them were in Poland itself, under the protection of their Christian neighbors, but these options turned out to be very limited. Three main factors combined to eliminate almost entirely the possibility of Jews surviving in Poland:

(a)   The draconian occupation regime installed by the Nazis.
(b)   The brutal and systematic extermination policy undertaken against Poland's Jews, who in the eyes of the Nazis represented the essence of ethnic and religious Jewry and, as such, the source of the world's evil.
(c)   The hostile attitude of much of the Christian population — both the Poles, and even more the Ukrainians — toward their Jewish neighbors, and their consequent indifference to their plight.

The occupation regime in Poland was the harshest imposed by the Germans and bore no resemblance to the regimes introduced in Western Europe — for example, in France, Belgium, and Holland. The Nazis considered occupied Poland to be *debellatio* — a state which had ceased to exist politically and legally. In practice, the occupiers arrogated to themselves the right to rule the country without restraint. The Nazis were determined to destroy Poland's social and economic fabric, so as to prevent the Poles from ever renewing their national life. From the outset of the occupation, their goal was to systematically eradicate the Polish elites: the intelligentsia, members of the liberal professions, such as the clergy, doctors, officers, businessmen, civil servants, and in general everyone who was suspected of being a potential enemy of the Reich. The destruction of the country's economic life led to a steep decline in the living standard of the occupied population. Poland was intended to provide *Lebensraum* ("living space") for the Third Reich as it spread eastward. Ideologically, the Nazis considered the Poles to be racially inferior, like the other Slavic peoples: only a small minority would be assimilated with the

Germans, while the majority were destined to become laborers in the service of the masters.

Immediately after the invasion of Poland, the Germans unleashed a reign of terror and brutality against the entire population. Roundups on the streets in which innocent passersby were seized and deported for forced labor in Germany became commonplace. Suspected "wanted" persons were hunted down and arrested mercilessly. The transportation and communications systems were subject to the continuous supervision of the German police, who relentlessly searched crowded trains for possible subversive elements and black-market smugglers. Tens of thousands of Polish citizens were thrown into concentration camps without trial.

Most frightening of all, though, was the indiscriminate collective punishment which the Germans imposed on the civilian population in the wake of attempted resistance. Warsaw, the capital and political center of Poland, became a hunting ground to uncover suspected anti-German activity, and the blood of citizens who were executed in full public view ran in the streets.[8]

At the same time, the Nazis adopted a divide-and-rule policy, inciting the Christian population against the Jews by feeding it virulent and primitive antisemitic propaganda in the press, on the radio, in exhibitions, and in films which portrayed the Jews as exploiters and parasites and as disease-carrying vermin that must be exterminated.

Beset by the economic crisis and the severe shortage of basic commodities, many Poles lost their moral values. Hitherto honest and decent citizens seized Jewish property without compunction. The Jews were viewed as "deceased on leave" whose fate was sealed and therefore did not need to be shown any consideration. Instances are recorded of Christians who stopped repaying their debts to Jews when the deportations began, in the hope that sooner or later the creditors would fall into the Germans' net. In most cases Christians refused to return to Jews items which they had been given for safekeeping, claiming that the Germans had taken them, that they had been stolen, or citing similar excuses. Jewish assets effectively became a springboard for extortion and denunciation: Poles who wanted to be rid of undesirable property claimants had no compunction in denouncing them to the authorities.[9]

8  Jan Tomasz Gross, *Polish Society Under German Occupation* (Princeton: Princeton University Press, 1979), pp. 42–91.
9  Emanuel Ringelblum, *Polish-Jewish Relations During the Second World War* (Jerusalem: Yad Vashem, 1974), pp. 77–78.

In this lawless and violent atmosphere, the Jews, deprived of legal-judicial status and thus unprotected, were at the mercy of the arbitrary rule of the German occupation authorities, the police and the SS. Every uniformed German was at liberty to inflict injury and abuse on the Jews. From the first day, the entry of the Germans into Poland was accompanied by anti-Jewish measures involving plunder, indemnities, arbitrary collective taxes in the form of cash and valuables, hostage-taking, beatings, torture, humiliation, roundups of Jews for forced labor, desecration of religious artifacts, burning of synagogues, and murder.[10]

In contrast to their policy in the occupied countries of Western Europe, in Poland the Germans immediately began to separate the Jews from their Christian neighbors. Every Jew from the age of ten had to wear an identifying badge of shame — a white ribbon with a blue Star of David on the arm in the territory of the *Generalgouvernement* (the German occupation regime in most of Poland), or a yellow patch with the word *Jude* ("Jew") on it in black lettering in the territories annexed to the Reich. Jews were forbidden to change their place of residence and to enter certain streets and squares. Their movement outside their place of residence was restricted and they were barred from using the roads or trains. Each such prohibition was underlined by a stern warning that violators were liable to severe punishment.[11] The isolation of the Jews was completed with their confinement in ghettos. An order issued by Hans Frank, the governor of the Generalgouvernement, on October 15, 1941, sentenced to death any Jew who left the ghetto without permission, as well as Christians who aided or sheltered them. Similar orders were issued by the local governors throughout Poland in 1942 as part of the *endlösung* — the "Final Solution," the Nazi euphemism for the systematic annihilation of the Jews.[12]

It should be emphasized that the Nazis introduced the death penalty for Christians who dared to aid Jews only in Poland and Eastern Europe. They refrained from taking such a drastic step in countries such as Belgium and France and elsewhere in Western Europe.[13]

10  Philip Friedman, *Roads to Extinction: Essays on the Holocaust* (New York: Jewish Publication Society, 1980), pp. 215–216.
11  Yitzhak Arad, Yisrael Gutman, Abraham Margaliot, eds., *Documents on the Holocaust* (Jerusalem, Yad Vashem, 1988), pp. 178–182.
12  Władysław Bartoszewski and Zofia Lewin, eds., *Righteous Among Nations* (London: Earls Court Publications, 1969), pp. 632–643.
13  Teresa Prekerowa, *Konspiracyjna Rada Pomocy Żydom w Warszawie 1942–1945* (Warsaw: Państwowy Instytut Wydawniczy, 1982), p. 43.

There is no doubt that this draconian measure deterred many Christians from helping Jews who managed to escape from the ghettos and camps and who sought shelter on the Aryan side. Nevertheless, despite the brutal occupation regime, the Poles might have been expected to display greater consideration for their Jewish neighbors, given their common enemy. In practice, few Poles, and even fewer Ukrainians, were willing to risk offering help to the Jews in their desperate time of need. The Polish historian, Teresa Prekerowa, who carried out research regarding the help the Polish population gave the Jews during the Holocaust, and had no interest in underplaying the numbers, estimates that between 160,000 and 360,000 people, or no more than about two percent of the Polish public, were actively involved in aiding the Jews. Prekerowa herself lived throughout the war in Poland, helped Jews, and knew first-hand the dangers this entailed. Equally familiar with the frame of mind among the Polish public and its attitude toward the Jews, she concludes with regret: "Faced with the Nazi plans for the total extermination of the Jews, we were powerless. The only effective form of rescue was that offered by individuals, with or without the support of political parties or aid organizations… I believe that the scope of rescue could have been much broader."[14]

The relations between Poles and Jews during the war are a painful and controversial issue, particularly in the light of the fact that fully eighty-eight percent of Poland's Jewish community perished. Although this subject has been extensively dealt with by historians and commentators, Jews and Poles alike, it continues to generate powerful emotions often based on misunderstandings and prejudice. Moreover, the majority of the 250,000 Polish Jews who survived in Poland after the war soon left as part of the massive *Bricha* movement — the underground exodus of Jews from Eastern Europe to displaced persons (DP) camps in Western Europe, on their way to Palestine — Eretz Israel.

The driving factor in this process was the vicious anti-Jewish atmosphere which prevailed in liberated Poland and which reached its peak on July 4, 1946, with the pogrom perpetrated in the city of Kielce, and the killing of hundreds of Jewish survivors by the end of that year. The persecution of the Jews continued after the Communists assumed power in Poland; indeed, by

---

14  Teresa Prekerowa, "The Just and the Passive," *Yad Vashem Studies*, vol. XIX (1988), pp. 370–371.

the end of the 1960s, the Communist regime had brought about the almost total expulsion of the Jews from the country.[15]

To understand the Polish attitude toward their Jewish neighbors during the Holocaust, it is necessary to examine the relations between the Poles and the Jews from the late nineteenth century to the beginning of the twentieth century. Traditional Christian antisemitism had been rife in Poland for generations but without adopting the extreme forms it took elsewhere in Europe. On the contrary: Poland, which had long been multi-ethnic, took pride in its tolerant approach to minorities. The country's rulers acted as generous hosts towards the Jews, and allowed them to manage their affairs autonomously. However, the situation took a turn for the worse following the establishment of the new Polish state after the First World War.

Tellingly, Poland's renewed independence was from the outset accompanied by anti-Jewish pogroms which swept the country, even though the Jews supported the new state and Jewish soldiers took part in the Polish war of independence.[16] Antisemitism flourished in Poland between the wars, becoming an element of Polish culture, and rendering the lives of the Jews intolerable. The "Jewish question" was no marginal issue but a central theme in Polish national life and, as a political problem, remained high on the public agenda until the outbreak of the Second World War and even in its course. Unlike the Western democracies, pluralism did not strike roots in the new Poland. Polish nationalism, which evolved in the nineteenth century, before the emergence of the new Poland, was grounded in the concept of an ethnic state based on ties of blood and religion and the collective memory of the people. The left-wing parties and liberal circles opposed antisemitism on grounds of principle, and argued that the Jewish question must be resolved through assimilation. However, the right-wing parties and their representatives — the National Democrats, or *Endecja* — who had a dominant influence in the country before the Second World War, maintained that the Jews were an alien element and could not be integrated into Polish society. The Jews, they maintained, could never become ordinary citizens because they were totally different from the Poles, foreign to the Polish spirit and culture, and indeed, to the very spirit of Europe. The Endecja held the Jews to be a

---

15 Yisrael Gutman, "'Polish Jewry in the Holocaust," in Yisrael Bartal and Yisrael Gutman, eds., *The Broken Chain: Polish Jewry through the Ages* (Hebrew) (Jerusalem: Zalman Shazar Center, 1997), vol. I, p. 485.

16 Celia Stopnicka Heller, *On the Edge of Destruction; Jews of Poland Between the Two World Wars* (New York: Columbia University Press, 1977), pp. 47–53.

grave threat to the integrity of Polish society and therefore looked askance at their efforts to assimilate. In their eyes, the Jews were outcasts who clung to a depraved and incorrigible way of life. The conclusion they drew from this fundamentally racist outlook was that after the Jews were expelled from the country, the Poles would be able to breathe a sigh of relief.[17]

In 1935, following the death of Marshal Jozef Pilsudski, the revered leader who was the progenitor of the new Poland and who exercised a moderating influence on the nation's hostile attitude toward the Jews, his successors adopted a virulently anti-Jewish policy and in both the domestic and international spheres used every possible means to induce the Jews to emigrate. The traditional antisemitic approach of the Catholic clergy, whose advocacy of nationalism had a profound impact on the Church's adherents, heightened the extreme anti-Jewish climate whose origins lay in ethno-nationalism. From every pulpit and platform, priests preached against the Jews, accusing them of corrupting Polish values by disseminating atheism and Communism.[18]

Despite the generations-long contribution of the Jews to Poland's economic and cultural development, most Poles considered them to be inferior. The Poles' social, religious, and economic life was redolent with antisemitism. Devout Catholics, they did not differentiate between being Polish and being Catholic. Thus, in contrast to the countries of central and western Europe, in Poland the concept of "a Pole of the Mosaic faith" was untenable. The Poles viewed the Jews stereotypically, as both inferior and threatening. This unconditionally negative attitude was reflected in both the Polish language and in Polish folklore, which contained few neutral references to Jews as such. In Polish, the very term *żyd* ("Jew") carries a negative connotation fraught with images which evoke repulsion among both the uneducated masses and the educated elites. Expressions such as "dirty as a Jew," "calculating like a Jew," and "as noisy as a synagogue," to mention just a few, became commonplace in everyday discourse amongst the Poles themselves and in their interactions with the Jews.

In the inter-war period, multi-national Poland suffered from problems relating to minorities, who accounted for more than a third of the population. The Ukrainians, the Belorussians, and the Germans in Poland wanted to disengage from the country. The Jews were the only minority who did not pose a threat to Poland's integrity, wishing only to be treated as equal citizens.

---

17  Ezra Mendelson, "Polin," in Jacob Tsur, ed., *The Diaspora: Eastern Europe* (Hebrew) (Jerusalem, Keter, 1976), pp. 187–188.
18  Heller, *Edge of Destruction*, pp. 109–114.

Nevertheless, the Poles, despite brutal confrontations with the Germans and Ukrainians, considered them "locals" (*tutejszy*) capable of being assimilated into the dominant society, and treated them differently from the Jews. The Jews, on the other hand, were "aliens" (*obcy*), even though their history in Poland was almost as old as Poland itself.[19]

In September 1939, the Poles found themselves in the same predicament as the Jews, fighting for their lives against a common enemy — Nazi Germany. Suddenly the Poles understood that antisemitism served Hitler's goals. The previously antisemitic press ceased incitement against the Jews, and even the most rabid antisemites understood that the Jews could be allies in the struggle against the common enemy.[20] This conciliatory attitude kindled hope among the Jews but soon dissipated. Immediately following the German conquest, the Poles, even before they had recovered from the shock of defeat, reverted to their old ways as though nothing had happened. Emanuel Ringelblum, the historian of the Warsaw Ghetto, who followed closely the development of Polish-Jewish relations, wrote at the time:

After the German invasion, there was a revival of antisemitism in the full sense of the term. It was manifested in the relief work carried out by the NSV (National-Socialist Social Welfare). In the public squares, enormous NSV trucks distributed free bread and soup... to the starving population of Warsaw. For the first few days, the Jews were not excluded from this relief. But this was primarily for the sake of the films that were being made in the newly-conquered capital. On Muranowski Square I witnessed how the Jews who had been given free bread and soup for the sake of the filming were immediately afterwards beaten up by German soldiers and how the queue, which the Germans themselves had caused to be formed, was made to disperse. The antisemitic mob would pick out the hungry Jews standing in line before the NSV trucks and would point out who was a *Jude* — the one German word the hooligans learned at once. Very soon round-ups began for various military formations that needed skilled workers for jobs of various kinds. As the Jews were not yet wearing special badges, it was difficult for the German bloodhounds to distinguish between Jews and non-Jews. The antisemitic scum came to their aid and obligingly pointed out the Jews to the Germans. Thus

19  Ibid., pp. 48–76.
20  Ringelblum, *Polish-Jewish Relations*, pp. 23–24.

was the first bond sealed between the Polish antisemites and the Nazis. The platform that united them was, as usual the Jews.[21]

Afterwards, some Poles tried to explain the attitude towards the Jews during the Nazi occupation by alleging that the Jews had been disloyal to the defeated Poles in the eastern districts, had greeted the Soviet conquerors enthusiastically and had collaborated with them. (During this period, both the Soviet Union and Nazi Germany, which had divided the Polish homeland between them, were considered enemies of Poland.) Despite this understandable viewpoint, its exponents ignored the situation in which the Jews found themselves after the conquest of Poland. Given the possibility of either German occupation or Soviet occupation, the vast majority of the Jews naturally favored the latter, particularly as they had no good reason to identify with Poland, which regarded them as undesirable.[22]

In fact, though, the indifference to the fate of the Jews predated the rumors of their behavior in the Soviet-occupied eastern districts. More than 100,000 Jews were members of the Polish army in the campaign of September 1939; about 30,000 fell in the fighting and 60,000 were captured by the Germans. Despite this, and with no connection to the Jews' warm welcome of the Soviet forces, their Polish comrades-in-arms turned their backs on them the moment they were taken captive and harassed and humiliated them in front of their German captors.[23]

A particularly harsh fate befell the more than one million Jews who were trapped in the eastern districts, where the population was largely Ukrainian, following the withdrawal of the Soviet forces in the summer of 1941. Ukrainian antisemitism is deeply rooted and generations old. Almost invariably, social and political crises in these regions spawned mass violence against the Jews. In the 1930s, the bad relations between Ukrainians and Jews were further exacerbated by the influence of ultra-nationalist Ukrainian agitators, who hoped that Nazi Germany would help them create an independent Ukrainian state. They forged ties with Nazi Germany and in practice adopted the Nazi policies towards the Jews. Even after the split in the extreme wing of the Ukrainian national movement (OUN), between the supporters of Andrei

21  Ibid., pp. 37–38.
22  Gutman, "Polish Jewry in the Holocaust," p. 489.
23  "Jewish POW among Poles and Germans," in Joseph Kermish, ed., *To Live with Honor And Die with Honor: Selected Documents from the Warsaw Ghetto Underground Archives* (Jerusalem: Yad Vashem, 1986), pp, 215–221, 227, 230.

Melnyk and those of Stepan Bandera over cooperation with the Germans, both wings remained united in their abhorrence of Jews.

As part of the preparations for the invasion of the Soviet Union, the German army established two Ukrainian units, *Nachtigal* and *Roland*, which were active in the wave of anti-Jewish pogroms that the Nazis instigated in the summer of 1941, immediately after seizing the eastern districts of Poland. The pogroms, perpetrated by nationalist mobs that were whipped into a frenzy by educated members of the local leadership, swept up in their wake people who were considered moderate and conservative. The pretext for the rampages was that the Jews had abetted in the murder of Ukrainian prisoners by the Soviet security services (NKVD) before their withdrawal. The Jews were also accused of having supported the Soviet regime from 1939 to 1941. The Ukrainians, though disappointed when the Germans eradicated all signs of their independent statehood and arrested Stepan Bandera, continued to pursue the goal of annihilating all the Jews in their districts. Thousands of young Ukrainians enlisted in the German Auxiliary Police and operated together with the Nazis in the murder of Polish Jews. It is precisely against the background of this active collusion in the murder of the Jews and the identification of the majority of the Ukrainian population with these actions, that the few who for humanitarian and religious reasons secretly assisted the persecuted Jews, deserve to be cited.[24]

Unlike the Ukrainians, the Poles did not collaborate with the Nazis. The Polish nation takes pride in its tenacious, suffering-ridden stand against the Germans and in its stubborn fight against them on all fronts. The defeat of September 1939, resulting in the fourth partition of Poland, did not break the Polish spirit. Although the country was dismantled, the nation did not accept the defeat. Many Poles continued to fight for their freedom and for the liberation of their country, wherever they were. Their resolve was manifested concretely in the establishment in London of a Polish government-in-exile, and the organization of the Polish army outside the country and its integration into the British and Soviet forces. Despite the reign of terror which the Germans unleashed in Poland, no public figure — such as Vidkun Quisling in Norway and his like elsewhere in occupied Europe — collaborated with the Nazi occupiers.

From the outset of the occupation, an extensive underground movement was organized in Poland, which was subordinate to the government-in-exile. The underground was led by the *Delegatura* (the government delegate's office

---

24 Friedman, *Roads to Extinction*, pp. 176–208.

at home), a political body parallel to the government-in-exile, which was effectively deputy to the prime-minister-in-exile. The Delegatura established a kind of underground state in occupied Poland, with its own armed force, the *Armia Krajowa* or AK (the "Home Army,") which spearheaded the national struggle against the occupation. However, even though the government-in-exile, which sought to obtain every possible drop of sympathy among free-world public opinion for the Polish cause, co-opted two Jewish delegates to its National Council (akin to a parliament-in-exile), the Delegatura in Poland took no similar action. This omission reflects the true nature of the main Polish underground movement — which purported to represent and defend all the country's citizens, including the minorities — and particularly its attitude toward Poland's Jewish citizens. Indeed, until the end of 1941 the Delegatura ignored the problems of the Jews altogether and in practice excluded them from the country's citizenry.[25] As such, its political leadership reflected the prevailing mood among the Polish majority. The Delegatura's approach is reflected vividly in its reaction to the incarceration of nearly half a million Jews in a ghetto in the heart of the capital, Warsaw. A message sent by the Delegatura at the end of 1940, upon the ghetto's establishment, to the government-in-exile in London, stated:

> The ghetto issue is part of the Jewish question in general. Of course Polish society does not approve of the methods which the occupier applies against the Jews. But it would be a great mistake to suppose that Polish antisemitism belongs to the past. Antisemitism persists in all strata of the population, but it has assumed a different form. Although Polish public opinion disapproves of violence against the Jews, it would most emphatically refuse to tolerate the return of the Jews to their prewar positions and influence. The Jews have lost their supremacy: in particular in industry and in the wholesale trades. Polish society will never agree if the Jews ever try to regain the foothold they have lost. The government shows poor comprehension of this attitude: the best proof being the recent radio message of Minister Stanczyk which expressed a commitment to granting equal rights to Jews in liberated Poland. In Poland, the message left a very unfavorable impression. It was resented even by working-class elements belonging to the Polish Socialist Party.[26]

---

25 Yisrael Gutman and Shmuel Krakowski, *Unequal Victims: Poles and Jews During World War II* (New York: Holocaust Library, 1986), pp. 41, 57, 143–144.
26 Ibid., p. 60.

In 1942, when the Germans set about systematically annihilating the Jews throughout Poland, the underground leadership knew about their methods as the very annihilation was taking place. This information, which reached the Delegatura leadership through the countrywide underground cells, was more accurate and more comprehensive than the reports that were reaching the Jews in the ghettos. Although neither the underground nor the Polish public could have prevented the murder of the Jews even had they wanted to, they could at least have warned the Jews in the ghettos and the camps what lay in store for them, so that they could try to escape and save themselves. The underground leadership could also have tried to persuade the Christian population to show mercy to fleeing Jews who were seeking shelter, and not rob or denounce them. Until the autumn of 1942, apart from reporting to the government-in-exile regarding the fate of the Jews, the Polish underground did nothing to assist them. The only question that engaged the underground's leadership, even as the annihilation of Poland's Jews reached its horrific peak, was their emigration after the war.[27]

It was not until September 17, 1942, a week after the conclusion of the mass *Aktion* in the Warsaw Ghetto, which lasted almost two months, when more than 250,000 Jews were transported to their death in Treblinka, that the Directorate of Civil Resistance published in the underground's main information organ, *Biuletyn Informacyjny*, a protest in the name of the Polish people condemning the crimes of the Nazis against the Jews.[28] Also at this time, an organization called Żegota was created under the Delegatura's auspices, to assist Jews who succeeded in escaping to the Aryan side. This organization is discussed in detail in Chapter Five, but suffice it to say here that it was too little and too late. Other than the voice of protest and the activity of Żegota on behalf of Jews who were in hiding in the Aryan areas, the Polish underground did little for the country's Jewish citizens. More than forty years later, a number of Polish intellectuals berated themselves for the frightening indifference that had been demonstrated by the majority of the Polish public, including the underground, toward their Jewish neighbors in their hour of need. With courage and intellectual integrity, Halina Balicka-Kozłowska, who was active in the underground and whose family helped rescue Jews, wrote:

> Only a few considered defending Jews as one of the manifestations of the struggle against the occupier. Resistance to the Germans was uni-

27  Ibid., pp. 69–70.
28  Ibid., p. 74.

versally regarded as a matter of Polish honor... In contrast, the rescue of Jews was usually seen as a purely private matter. There were occasions when members of the underground were reproached for sheltering Jews since, so the argument went, they thereby exposed other partisans to risk and jeopardized apartments needed by the underground... There is also another very painful issue: many more Jews could have been saved if Poles had not been afraid of Poles. For it is not true that Jews had to be hidden only from German eyes; they sheltered themselves both from death at the hands of the Germans and from the eyes of the Poles who were present in places beyond the reach of the Germans, or even the *Volksdeutsche*.[29]

The cries of protest by enlightened circles in Polish society against turning over the Jews to the enemy, and the activity of the few people of conscience who risked their lives to save Jews, was of no avail in the face of the indifference of the majority of the Christian population toward the Jews, even when it was clear that few of them would survive. The mood among ordinary Poles was described with disappointment by an employee of the Warsaw Municipality, a patriot and a believing Catholic, to Shmuel Breslav, one of the leaders of the Warsaw Ghetto underground:

> First, it needs to be understood that the incarceration of the Jews gave the Poles numerous material advantages... Imagine a shopkeeper who was able to be rid of a Jewish competitor more agile than he, a concierge in a Jewish house who invaded a five-room apartment that was emptied of Jews on Marshalkovska Street, a fat butcher woman who wrapped herself in a fur coat that had belonged to Jews, and so on and so forth — the examples are legion. The conscience of all those who gained from the separation of the Jews is not very pure. They are reflecting fearfully about the period after the war, when all these good things will end. Frequently one hears people conversing: "But sir, what will happen when all the Jews breach the walls? What will they do to us? It's frightening to think about it." Everyone keeps repeating this without thinking, as though there was really something threatening them. The result of this psychosis is that the reports about the expulsions are received with a certain relief. This too should be known, because the rabble that has

---

29  Shmuel Krakowski, "Relations between Jews and Poles during the Holocaust — New and Old Approaches in Polish Historiography," *Yad Vashem Studies,* vol. *XIX* (1988), pp. 318–321.

become corrupt in the wake of the war is weaving dreams for itself, with the usual Polish lack of logic, and connecting the blows to the Germans with the settling of accounts with the Jews.[30]

This popular mood was ultimately manifested politically. At the end of 1943, the Office of Information and Propaganda of the AK Supreme Command issued a secret internal document summing up the attitude towards the Jewish question of the thirteen main political groups that were subject to Delegatura authority. Nine of the groups espoused a clear anti-Jewish platform, calling for the Jews to emigrate; one group even advocated their liquidation. Only four groups were in favor of granting the Jews equal rights after liberation. By this time the overwhelming majority of Poland's Jews were no longer among the living.[31]

Another body, apart from the underground, which could have helped temper the anti-Jewish mood among the Christian population and encouraged assistance to the Jews, particularly the rescue of children, was the Catholic Church. The Church has always been one of the major centers of power in Poland. Polish nationalism and Catholicism exist in a symbiotic relationship. During the lengthy period from Poland's partition and loss of independence at the end of the eighteenth century, until the establishment of the new Polish state in 1918, the Catholic Church was the bastion of nationalism around which the Polish people rallied in their struggles for independence. Once independence was achieved, Catholicism effectively became the state religion. The Episcopate — the senior hierarchy of the Church — which numbered forty-one cardinals, archbishops, and bishops,[32] enjoyed high prestige and wielded great influence among the Polish people. During the bitter period which followed the defeat of September 1939, the Church remained one of the nation's sources of comfort, and the Church establishment was an organic part of the national resistance movement. The bishops, who were in close touch with the people, could have had recourse to both overt and covert ways to encourage the masses of believers to come to the aid of the Jews, or at least to save Jewish children, but they did nothing. Ringelblum, who tried to emphasize every humanitarian gesture by the Poles toward the Jews, and commended the nobility of spirit of those who tried to rescue Jews, wrote bitterly about the clergy's attitude toward the persecuted Jews:

---

30  Shmuel Breslav, "Poles and Jews," *Yalkut Moreshet* (Hebrew), vol. XI, (1969), pp. 103–105.
31  Gutman and Krakowski, *Unequal Victims*, p. 107.
32  Zenon Fijałkowski, *Kosciół Katolicki na Ziemiach Polskich w Latach Okupacii Hitlerowskiej* (Warsaw: Książka i Wiedza, 1983), p. 36.

The Polish clergy has reacted almost with indifference to the tragedy of the slaughter of the whole Jewish people. Before the war, while the Polish clergy was distinguished for its remarkable antisemitic attitude… the clergy in Western Europe fought racialism and antisemitism as being opposed to Christian teaching, which does not recognize higher and lower races. A significant part of Catholic clergy in the West fought Fascism on the grounds that it was against the principles of the Christian religion. The Polish clergy at that time remained neutral on the problem of antisemitism, and to some extent this neutrality constituted approval of the steadily increasing pogroms and excesses… One could hardly expect any serious help from a clergy like this in the present war, if it gave no help at a time when it was still possible to do so. It was in line with the Dutch Church's prewar attitude towards the Jews that they should behave with the heroism we have heard about in its defense of the Jews during the present war… A similar stand was taken by the French Catholic clergy… In Belgium, money was collected during church services for the benefit of Jewish children…[33] In Poland, this West European attitude was found only in exceptional cases among the Polish clergy.[34]

Ringelblum's criticism of Polish clergy is undoubtedly too sweeping. He also erred in likening the status of the clergy in Poland to its counterpart in occupied western Europe. The situation of the church in Poland was immeasurably more difficult than in France, Belgium, and the Netherlands. In Poland, the Germans did not hesitate to attack the Catholic Church and take measures against members of the clergy who were suspected of engaging in subversive activity against the occupation authorities. Nor, in Poland, did the cassock provide immunity. The Nazis persecuted the Polish clergy, whom they perceived as being part of the national elite, and a part of the Polish intelligentsia. The history of Catholic martyrdom in Poland tells of thousands of priests, monks, and nuns who were incarcerated in concentration camps and paid with their lives for conducting activities which in the German view exceeded

33  On the involvement of the Church hierarchy in rescuing Jews in Western European countries, see: Michael R. Marrus and Robert O. Paxton, *Vichy France and the Jews* (New York: Basic Books, 1981, pp. 270–279; Josef Michman, "The Problem of the Jewish War Orphans in Holland," in Yisrael Gutman and Adina Drechsler, eds., *She'erit Hapleta, 1944–1948: Rehabilitation and Political Struggle* (Jerusalem: Yad Vashem, 1990), pp. 187–209; Mark Van Den Wijngaert, "Belgian Catholics and the Jews During the German Occupation 1940–1944," in Dan Michman, ed., *Belgium and the Holocaust: Jews, Belgians, Germans* (Jerusalem: Yad Vashem, 1998), pp. 225–233.
34  Ringelblum, *Polish-Jewish Relations*, pp. 206–208.

their ecclesiastical mission. Moreover, the threat of the death penalty for any-one who dared to help or rescue Jews applied equally to the clergy. Neverthe-less, many acts of rescue are known in which priests took part, some of whom indeed paid with their lives. Father Urbanowicz, from Brisk, was shot by the Germans in June 1943 for helping Jews. For committing a similar "crime," the rector of the Clerical Academy in Warsaw, Roman Archutowski, was de-ported to Majdanek and did not return.[35] Many more testimonies could be cited concerning members of the clergy who risked their lives to provide flee-ing Jews with false birth and baptismal certificates, which were then lifesav-ing documents. The literature of memoirs and testimonies contain moving accounts of priests who helped Jews in the Aryan areas and sheltered them in institutions under their supervision or referred them to monasteries where they found a haven.

Halina Ashkenazy was a young girl when she arrived in the Praga sub-urb of Warsaw, alone and frightened, without papers, and sought help from Father Michał Kubacki in the Basilica Church. He was her last hope. She was exhausted and faint when she arrived at the church. Kubacki took her to his room, fed her, provided her with a baptismal certificate, and found her work in the kitchen of Charitas, a charity institution, until she could be placed in a convent. His assistant, Father Stanek, collected a solitary little Jewish girl from the street — she had been evicted from the home of her would-be res-cuer — and, at the risk of his life, hid her in the church.[36]

But these acts of rescue were personal initiatives, carried out at the dic-tat of each priest's conscience and faith, not the result of policy or directives from above. Ringelblum was thus right concerning the senior clergy, who were supposed to serve as an example and source of inspiration for those serving under them and for the masses of believers. What is glaringly obvi-ous in the behavior of the senior clergy in Poland during the occupation is their persistent silence concerning the rescue of Jews. Some historians of the Catholic Church in Poland have tried to defend its leaders, maintaining that despite their perilous situation they were among the first to intercede with the Germans on behalf of the Jews, even before the establishment of Żegota. Often cited in this connection is the Archbishop of Kraków, Prince Adam Sapieha, who was considered the supreme spiritual authority in Poland dur-

35  Philip Friedman, *Their Brothers' Keepers* (New York: Holocaust Library, 1978), p. 126.
36  Halina Ashkenazy-Engelhard, *I Want to Live* (Hebrew) (Tel Aviv: Moreshet and Sifriat Poalim, 1976), pp. 72–80.

ing the war. However, an examination of the facts reveals that he was only interested in converts and that Jews as such did not concern him.

On October 30, 1940, Archbishop Sapieha asked Count Adam Roniker, the president of the Polish Relief Organization (*Rada Główna Opiekuńcza* — RGO), to try to persuade the occupation authorities to exempt Jewish converts to Christianity from wearing the ribbon with the Star of David and from having to reside in the ghetto along with the Jews. In a letter to Roniker he wrote, "They are being greatly wronged by being forced to live among a public which they abandoned of their own free will, which is hostile to them, and among whom they feel alienated. I request that you raise this painful problem with the authorities. As a bishop, I cannot ignore their complaints. Passionately I protect these partners to our faith who expect the support of the Church."[37]

There are some who argue that Sapieha's failure to intervene on behalf of all the Jews was based on a realistic appraisal of the situation. To do so, this argument maintains, would have demonstrated hopeless naïvety, as in any event, the Jews were doomed.[38]

However, the point is not the senior clergy's intercession on the Jews' behalf, which would indeed have been useless. In fact, even their pleading for the converts was of no avail, because under the Nazi racial laws they were still considered Jews, even though they had been baptized, and so were subject to the same restrictions and fate as all the Jews.[39] Where the Polish Catholic leaders failed gravely was in not conveying a positive message to the millions of adherents to the faith which might have prompted them to help Jews. The German occupation caused suffering not only for the Jews but for the Poles as well — their religious life, too, was under assault — but this changed nothing in the attitude of the senior clergy towards the Jews. Even as thousands of Catholic intellectuals, priests, and monks were being tortured and murdered in concentration camps, the Church establishment's traditional hatred of the Jews continued to seethe, as though nothing had happened. Even though the Jews were already incarcerated in ghettos and isolated from the rest of Polish society, in the eyes of the senior clergy, they still constituted a major threat

37 Fijałkowski, *Kosciól Katolicki*, pp. 199–200.
38 Zygmunt Zielinski, "Activities of Catholic Orders on behalf of Jews in Nazi-Occupied Poland," in Otto Dov Kulka and R. Mendes-Flohr, eds., *Judaism and Christianity under the Impact of National Socialism* (Jerusalem: Zalman Shazar Center, 1987), p. 382.
39 Emanuel Ringelblum, *Diary and Notes from the Warsaw Ghetto: September 1939 — December 1942* (Hebrew) (Jerusalem: Yad Vashem and Ghetto Fighters' House, 1992), p. 238.

to Catholic Poland, and were perceived as the destroyers of the social fabric. Thus, not only was rescuing Jews not seen as a goal for which risks should be taken, it was a propitious opportunity to be rid of them once and for all, which could be seen as a blessing. This attitude is apparent in a church report, in which the Jewish question occupied a central place. This report was transmitted in the summer of 1941 from occupied Poland to the government-in-exile in London:

> ... With regard to the Jewish matter, it must be said that with the grace of God the Germans have made a good start. If we ignore the troubles that the Germans have inflicted and continue to inflict on our country, they have shown that it is possible to liberate Polish society from the Jewish affliction. They have shown the way we must follow. Of course with less cruelty and brutality, but with consistency. It can be said that the finger of God was involved here, that the occupiers took it on themselves to resolve this burning problem, which the Polish people would never have been able to do because of its merciful heart, its unsystematic approach, and its inability to muster the strength needed. It is clear to everyone that this is a burning issue, as the Jews are causing untold harm to our religious and national life. Not only are they sucking the nation's marrow and preventing its economic development, but because of them our villages and cities are losing their Catholic character. They are the source of the demoralization of our society. They are corrupting our public life. It is they who are mainly responsible for the spread of prostitution and pornography. Because of them our people have turned to drink, and they are corrupting the youth. They inculcate immoral and un-Catholic messages into our literature and art. They always join forces with everyone who can do harm to the Church and Poland, in order to weaken and humiliate them. Remarkably, even today, though they are under the lash of the Germans, they hate the Poles more than the Germans and dream of taking revenge on us for the wrongs done to them. According to the most authoritative people here, the Jewish problem in Poland, which will surface again, will have to be dealt with differently. Our goal must be to ensure, in an international forum, their immigration to their own country overseas. Until then they will have to be completely isolated from our society.[40]

40  Sprawozdanie Kościelne, June 1, 1941-July 15, 1941, Yad Vashem Archives (YVA), O.25/89.

This report was composed at the height of Operation Barbarossa, when German forces were streaming eastward into the Soviet Union, and the future of European Christian civilization and of the Polish people was completely unclear. Yet in this bleak period the urgent question which preoccupied the Catholic establishment in Poland was the solution of the Jewish question. Even though the report was written in occupied Poland, which was fighting for its life, its authors, self-styled custodians of grace and mercy, displayed not one iota of compassion for the persecuted Jews — indeed, what is apparent is a sense of satisfaction at what the Jews were undergoing at the hands of the Germans. Despite their own suffering, the Polish writers see the German conquerors as the instruments of God's wrath, sent to do unto the Jews what the Poles were incapable of doing themselves.

A notable exception on behalf of the Jews was the head of the Ukrainian Uniate (Greek Catholic) Church in Eastern Galicia, Metropolitan Andrei Szeptycki of Lvov. Before the war, the Uniate Church in Poland, which is affiliated with the Vatican, had about three million Ukrainian adherents, most of them antisemitic nationalists who took an active part in the annihilation of the Jews in Eastern Poland. Yet their spiritual shepherd was vehemently opposed to the participation of his flock in the murder of Jews. A complex figure, Szeptycki was an ecumenicist who sought to unite the Christian world and espoused a positive attitude toward the Jews. For decades he was on friendly terms with rabbis and public figures in the Galician Jewish community and was highly regarded by the Jewish public for his humanitarian stance. In 1941, with the German occupation of Galicia, Szeptycki found himself facing a moral dilemma. On the one hand, he initially welcomed the Germans, regarding them as a buffer against rapidly spreading communist atheism and hoping they would grant the Ukrainians political independence; at the same time, he opposed the murder of the Jews, in which many Ukrainians were taking part. Szeptycki tried to persuade the Ukrainian population to desist from these acts in both written and oral pastoral letters. In November 1942, he issued his famous pastoral letter, which took its title from the fifth commandment: "Thou shalt not kill." Although it does not mention the Jews specifically, its timing, as the annihilation of Galician Jewry was reaching its height, indicates that this was its principal intent.[41]

---

41 Shimon Redlich, "Szeptycki and the Jews in World War II" (Hebrew), *Shvut,* vol. 13, 1989, pp. 7–17; David Kahane, *Lvov Ghetto Diary* (Amherst: University of Massachusetts Press, 1990), pp. 120–125, 157–162.

It is impossible to know what effect, if any, Szeptycki's exhortations had on his Ukrainian flock, but he at least tried to bring his full influence to bear. To his credit, he also practiced what he preached, opening the institutions under his authority to Jews. He instructed his brother, the Ihumen (abbot) Kliment Szeptycki, the head of the monasteries of the Studite order, and the Ihumenia (mother superior) Iosefa, who headed the order's convents, to provide Jews, and especially Jewish children, with shelter in their institutions.[42]

Every Jew who succeeded in escaping to the Aryan side needed the help of the local Christian population to meet their most basic needs: a place of refuge, food, documents, and everything that could make existence possible in conditions of all-pervasive fear. In the absence of such assistance, Jews stood virtually no chance of surviving, even adults who were normally capable of providing for themselves. The situation was infinitely more critical for children, who could not fend for themselves. However, in the light of the bitter relations between Jews and Christians in Poland, which became even more aggravated during the occupation, only a minuscule fraction of the Jews had any chance of finding a Christian household that would be willing to hide their whole family or at least one of the children.

Nevertheless, it should be emphasized that for a Christian family to shelter a Jew, whether an adult or a child, entailed, in addition to substantial physical danger, a considerable economic burden. Feeding another person over a lengthy period in conditions of a chronic shortage of basic foodstuffs was extremely difficult. The standard of living of the majority of the Polish population, which was not high to begin with, declined drastically during the occupation. This was particularly felt in the cities, where many families were compelled to seek aid from welfare organizations.[43] Consequently, most of the Christians who sheltered Jews, even the more sensitive among them who empathized with the Jews' plight, requested payment in return for their help.[44] This is also one of the reasons why it was almost impossible for complete Jewish families to find shelter on the Aryan side. Therefore parents tried to arrange a haven at least for their children, while they remained in the ghetto in order to raise the necessary funds for supporting the children's subsistence on the Aryan side. Frequently parents despaired from the outset of the possibility of getting to the Aryan side to join their children, as they lacked

---

42  Kahane, *Lvov Ghetto Diary*, pp. 57–59.

43  Gross, *Polish Society*, pp. 98–100.

44  Vladka Meed, *On Both Sides of the Wall* (Tel Aviv: Ghetto Fighters' House and Hakibbutz Hameuchad 1972), p. 239.

the means. The cost of looking after a Jewish child in the summer of 1942 in Poland was quite high — 100 zlotys a day. Only affluent parents could afford this, the more so as the sheltering families frequently demanded payment in advance, in case the parents were deported, leaving no one to cover the child's upkeep. Tens of thousands of zlotys were needed to pay for sheltering a child on the Aryan side,[45] an amount that was well beyond the means of all but a few Jewish families.

The perception of the Polish Christian population who perceived the Jews as rich was incorrect in regard to the majority of the Jews even before the war, and certainly after its outbreak. Indeed, even wealthy Jews lost most of their assets immediately upon the German conquest and were left destitute when they were herded into the ghetto. Few Jews possessed the means to find shelter on the Aryan side for the whole family, or even for their children. Few had managed to save foreign currency or valuables for a time of trouble and hide them securely. Those who lacked the means and the appropriate connections within the Christian society were forced to look on broken-hearted as the children — often the first to be taken — went to their death in the frequent Aktions in the ghettos.

All told, a deeply melancholy picture emerges from contemporary sources and postwar testimonies concerning the rescue of Jews in Poland. Fear of the occupiers, deeply-rooted antisemitism among the Polish masses, the demonstrative hostility of the political establishment and the senior church hierarchy — institutions which did not shed their prewar conceptions — toward the Jews, and the breakdown in morality which affected large segments of the population because of the war's hardships, combined to create a cynical Darwinist climate among the Poles, which substantially reduced the number of people who were willing to risk their lives to save Jews. Ringelblum, who closely observed the development of the relations between Poles and Jews from the start of the occupation until the spring of 1944, when Poland was virtually bereft of Jews, and who wrote a comprehensive work on the subject in his hiding place with a Polish family on the Aryan side, tried to refute the sweeping accusation — which was already then being voiced in some Jewish circles — that the Poles displayed satisfaction at the plight of the Jews and that there were few who agonized over the destruction of Polish Jewry.[46] Yet after taking note of the few idealists within the different classes of

45  Ringelblum, *Polish-Jewish Relations*, p. 140.
46  Ibid., pp. 1–2.

Polish society who had come to the rescue of the Jews, he too finally reached a gloomy conclusion:

> The Polish and Jewish peoples have lived together on the same soil for a thousand years. What did our neighbors do, at the moment when the invader, armed from head to foot, attacked the most defenseless people of all, the Jews? When the victims of Nazis fled from the ghettos to the so-called Aryan side, were they afforded asylum despite the prevailing terror, or was asylum provided only if amply paid for and then withdrawn when the funds were insufficient? ... The Polish people and the government of the Republic of Poland were incapable of deflecting the Nazi steam-roller from its anti-Jewish course. But it is legitimate to pose the question as to whether the attitude of the Polish people befitted the enormity of the calamities that befell the country's citizens. Was it inevitable that the Jews, looking their last on this world as they rode in the death trains speeding from different parts of the country to Treblinka or other places of slaughter, should have had to witness indifference or even joy on the faces of their neighbors? In the summer of 1942, when carts packed with captive Jewish men, women and children moved through the streets of the capital, did there really need to be laughter from the wild mobs resounding from the other side of the ghetto walls, did there really have to prevail such blank indifference in the face of the greatest tragedy of all time?[47]

---

47  Ibid., pp. 7–8.

CHAPTER TWO

# Children Hidden with Christian Families

## How the Children Reached Families

The escape of Jews from the ghettos to the so-called "Aryan side" in order to seek shelter among the Christian population actually began only after the mass-extermination Aktions which devastated the ghettos the length and breadth of Poland in 1942. Yet even then, it was not an option that was available to everyone. If there were Jews who had previously considered leaving the ghetto in order to find a haven under an assumed identity, they were now deterred from taking this course — not only due to lack of means but primarily for fear that their Christian neighbors would denounce them to the Germans. The frame of mind among the Jews in the ghetto before the Aktions is described in the diary of Calel Perechodnik, who was among those who finally abandoned the ghetto and tried to save themselves on the Aryan side:

> If the only and direct means of salvation for escape from the ghetto is by securing a *Kennkarte* — or in the worst case, a birth certificate — and residence in a Polish neighborhood, no one is thinking of this... Jews — even if they have a grasp of the dreadful situation — did not do this for several reasons. On the one hand, the gendarmes impressed on them the certainty that leaving the ghetto was equivalent to a sentence of death, and on the other, they were gripped by a terrible fear of the Poles. The Jews were afraid of being robbed in the Polish neighborhoods and of being handed over to the gendarmes. And although one could hide from the gendarmes — after all, there weren't so many of them in the street — how could one hide from the Poles who could easily recognize Jews?[1]

---

1    Calel Perechodnik, *Am I a Murderer? Testament of a Jewish Ghetto Policeman* (Boulder: Westview Press, 1996), p. 22.

The mass deportations of the Jews from the ghettos and their subsequent murder exacerbated the situation. In order to deter Christians from assisting Jews, the Germans adopted a primitive carrot-and-stick method: anyone who dared shelter Jews in their home faced the death penalty, while those who turned them over to the authorities were promised a reward. In the prevailing atmosphere of terror, this method proved quite successful. Indeed, the hostile attitude of the majority of the local Christian population toward their Jewish neighbors grew even more acute as the campaign of annihilation intensified. Ringelblum, himself in hiding on the Aryan side, described the unfolding situation in the cities and villages throughout Poland:

> For Jews hiding in the countryside, this proves to be a difficult matter, as in small towns and particularly in the villages everybody knows everybody else — a stranger arouses curiosity. The Germans know very well that after every "resettlement" action, some Jews would be seeking refuge with Christian neighbors or in the nearby countryside. To clear the surrounding area of Jews, the Germans would employ two methods: that of rewards and that of threats. Financial rewards were put on the head of every Jew captured, in addition to which the clothes and belongings of those captured were also handed over to the captors. In Western "Little Poland"… for example, 500 zlotys and a kilogram of sugar were the reward for every Jew captured. These tactics resulted in success for the Germans. Large numbers of the local population turned Jews over to the Germans, who shot the "criminals." In Volhynia, three liters of vodka were given for every Jew denounced. Vodka as a reward for denouncing Jews was repeated in other provinces as well. Besides rewards, the Germans also utilized a system of punishments for hiding Jews. Posters threatening capital punishment for this "crime" appeared with the start of every "liquidation action" against the Jews in any given locality.
>
> These threats and rewards, however, did not always achieve the desired effect. In small towns where Jews had lived together with the Christian population in harmony for centuries, Jews found refuge with Polish neighbors, friends and acquaintances with whom they had been friendly for years and even for generations. A peasant or a burgher would give a Jewish fugitive shelter. However, the length of time that was possible to go on hiding a Jew depended on two things — the German terror and the surrounding atmosphere. Where the environment had been infected with antisemitism before the war, hiding Jews presented great difficulties, and denunciations by antisemitic neighbors were more to

be feared than the German terror. But this terror was intensified day by day.[2]

Fear of being seized by the Germans and the pervasive sense of foreboding made the ghettos a death trap for most of the Jewish inmates. Nevertheless, they clung to life in the hope that by some miracle the war would suddenly come to an end and they would survive. In the prevailing atmosphere of dread and apathy, only a small minority of the Jews in the ghetto had any chance of finding shelter with Christian families on the Aryan side. The fortunate few who found help were mainly well-to-do people who had managed to keep some of their assets, or practitioners of the liberal professions[3] — doctors, lawyers, large-scale merchants — who had been well-integrated into pre-war Polish society. They belonged to a narrow social class and had close ties with Christian friends who remained loyal and stayed in touch with them even during the anguished period of the ghetto.

The first deportations were concentrated on the so-called "unproductive elements:" the elderly, the sick and the children. Already in the spring of 1942, when Operation Reinhardt — the systematic annihilation of Polish Jewry — was launched, rumors spread in the ghettos that the first to be taken to the slaughter would be children aged under ten and adults of sixty and above.[4] Did parents who heard these rumors try to find Christian families which would shelter their children before the Aktion and thus save them? The few contemporary sources that we have do not show such a tendency. People heard the appalling rumors but seem to have been paralyzed. On March 10, 1942, four months before the great deportation from the Warsaw Ghetto, the father of one little girl wrote in his diary, "Once more fear for the fate of the children. Vague but definite and constantly repeated rumors are arriving that the children are being slaughtered in their masses. Children up to ten… Parents who encounter one another look into each other's eyes with the question: Did you hear, is it true? And whisper in secret — How old is your child? And up to what age are they in danger?"[5]

Ruth Cyprys, who was the mother of a three-year-old girl and was an energetic woman with good connections among the Polish intelligentsia in Warsaw, found work in Schultz's "safe shop" in the ghetto (a workshop that manufactured winter clothing for the Wehrmacht). Like many of her friends,

2    Ringelblum, *Polish-Jewish Relations*, pp. 137–138.
3    Ibid., p. 96.
4    Ringelblum, *Diary and Notes*, p. 379.
5    Ruben Ben-Shem, "Warsaw Ghetto Diary" (Hebrew), *Masua*, vol. 10 (1982), p. 39.

she too hoped that her work document would provide her and her daughter immunity from deportation. However, they were placed on a transport to Treblinka. Unable to bear the thought of parting from her little girl, Ruth jumped off the death train with her and returned to Warsaw. It was only following the intervention of Polish friends that she agreed to part with the girl and hide her with a Polish family.[6]

Cyprys was among the few fortunate inmates of the ghetto who had both the right connections in Polish society and the means required for survival on the Aryan side. The indifference of the majority of the Christian population toward the fate of their Jewish neighbors, particularly the elderly, the women, and the children among them, who were being led to slaughter, did not encourage parents to seek a haven for their children. In the autumn of 1942, immediately after the great deportation from the Warsaw Ghetto, Vladka Meed, an activist in the Bund, the Jewish socialist party, and an emissary of the Jewish underground on the Aryan side, set out on a mission on behalf of the Bund. One of her tasks was to find shelter with Polish families for the children of Bund activists. However, her efforts to persuade Poles to take in Jewish children, even for full payment, fell mostly on deaf ears. With disappointment tinged with bitterness, she describes in her memoirs the callous disregard shown by the majority of the Poles to the fate of the Jewish children:

> During the winter of 1942–1943, the Poles had welcomed with open arms the first trainloads of Polish [i.e. Christian] children evacuated from the eastern section of the Zamość region. At that time, Gentile women had gone running to the sealed railroad cars with bread and clothing for the shivering children. However, the same Poles remained utterly indifferent to the fate of the Jewish children, their ghetto neighbors. Relatively few were kindhearted, even fewer were prepared to harbor a Jewish child for pay. The vast majority of the Polish population was completely unconcerned.[7]

But the truth is that, apart from the difficulty of finding Christian families willing to shelter Jewish children as the end loomed in sight, many parents were reluctant to part with their children and place them in the hands of strangers. One man, Calel Perechodnik, from Otwock, a town near Warsaw,

---

6   Ruth Altbeker Cyprys, *A Jump for Life*, (New York: Continuum, 1997), pp. 46–53, 108–112.

7   Meed, *On Both Sides of the Wall*, p. 139.

one of the few who had both the means and the necessary connections with Poles outside the ghetto, considered saving his young daughter by placing her in the custody of a Christian family, but for some reason took action too late. After the girl and her mother were sent to their death, he tried to explain his failure and what deterred parents like him from trying to save their children:

> At the time I thought that it would be good if my daughter Aluśka, a beautiful two-year-old, blond with blue eyes, could be given to Poles to be brought up. I was ready to pay a year of money in advance... In the event of our death, I would be certain that our daughter would be adopted, if only because of our estate, of which she would be the only heir. Most Jews at that time were of the opinion that the small children should share the lot of their parents and that it was not right to leave orphans in the world. I thought that if my daughter was delivered to the right people, she would still be able to live a good life. The property would assure her of independence as well of an opportunity for a proper upbringing. Aside from that, I thought that it is easier for parents to die when they know that they leave somebody after them and that their family will not be completely wiped out. In my opinion it was up to me to find responsible people to whom I could entrust the fate and future of my child. This was well thought-out and had a 100 percent chance of succeeding, but it was necessary to do it quickly... As for leaving the baby in a home for foundlings, this was discussed, but the matter was dropped. My daughter, petted and pampered, was too precious for that. On the other hand, no one thought that the danger was that near and immediate.[8]

Perechodnik attributed his failure to save his daughter mainly to a Polish mediator's delay in arranging a haven for her with a Polish family in another city. Yet his words show that he, like many other parents in the same situation, was unable to part with his child and that day after day went by with various excuses — amounting to self-deception — until the opportunity was missed. We can well understand his hesitation. In the atmosphere of terror prevailing in the doomed ghettos, not all parents were willing to send their children to the Aryan side, even when the possibility existed. Indeed, some parents were unwilling to part with their children under any circumstances, and even when the potential for rescue occurred, they decided to link the child's fate

---

8  Perechodnik, *Am I a Murderer?* pp. 22–23.

with their own, believing that the child would not survive without them in the Gentile world.

After the great deportation from the Warsaw Ghetto, Bund activists on the Aryan side succeeded in locating a Polish family which was willing to shelter the only son of the Bund leader, Shmuel Zygielbojm, but without the boy's mother. When Vladka Meed tried to persuade Manya, the mother, not to delay, she declined, saying, "I can't do it, believe me. I can't part with him. My son has no one but me now. I must guard him as the apple of my eye. Together we have endured the misery brought on us by the Germans. No, he would perish without me... Whatever is fated for me will also be the fate of my son. We have been through so much together. Perhaps we will succeed in surviving after all — or we will perish together," she concluded in a whisper. No one tried further to persuade her. She did not hand over the boy and they both died during the ghetto uprising.[9]

Manya Zygielbojm's reaction to the possibility that she would have to part with her son seems to be a natural response by a mother who believed that a child's place at such a time was at his parents' side, as only they could see to his needs and protect him. A child is the family's most precious asset, and in times of distress it is only natural for parents to want to keep their children close to them. But conditions changed rapidly when the mass murders began and parents realized that they were unable to protect their children. Only then did a feverish search begin for Christian families to shelter the children — but, as noted, there were few such families to be found.

Even in normal times, there are not many families which would be willing to take in a strange child; all the more so in wartime and against the background of the traditional enmity between Christians and Jews in Poland. Sheltering a Jewish child was fraught with tangible risks for a Christian family. It was not easy to hide a child for a protracted period in an attic or a closed cellar, although there were such cases. The option of raising the child openly within the family as a foster child was akin to a time-bomb, requiring the child's partial legalization and foisting on him an assumed identity accompanied by a credible cover story that the child would have to learn.

During the Nazi occupation, every person was required to carry identification papers and be prepared to identify himself to every official. Children were not exempted: they had to carry a certificate declaring their identity

---

9   Meed, *On Both Sides of the Wall*, pp. 140–141. In 1940, Zygielbojm fled from Warsaw to London, where he committed suicide in 1943 to protest the annihilation of European Jewry.

and their national-religious affiliation. A Jewish child living in Christian surroundings under an assumed identity needed a Christian birth certificate.
Such documentation was obtainable from the parish churches, in which local
births and deaths were registered, or from professional forgers who specialized in producing false papers in return for high payment. Few of the parish
priests were willing to take the risk of issuing false birth certificates to Jews.
In any event, as Jews rarely had direct ties with priests, they needed the help
of a Christian go-between who, on various pretexts, could more easily obtain
a certificate, ostensibly for a family member.[10] In some cases, priests took the
risk of issuing a birth certificate in the name of a deceased Christian child
for a Jewish child who was being sheltered by a Christian family. Such documents were known as "death certificates" (*Umarlanki*).[11] Other priests agreed
to issue a birth certificate on condition the child was baptized.[12]

However, obtaining a Christian birth certificate was not the primary difficulty and was not the major obstacle that blocked the rescue of children.
The fact is that not all the Jewish children who were placed in the custody of
Christian families under assumed names possessed Christian birth certificates. Moreover, the certificate as such did not guarantee the child's safety. Indeed, rescuers who lived in remote rural areas far from the centers of government often preferred not to secure a Christian birth certificate for the child
they were sheltering so that as few people as possible would delve into his or
her past and the risk of someone denouncing them to the authorities would
be lessened. The greatest source of danger was curious neighbors who might
go to the Germans with their suspicions. Accordingly, a plausible cover story
had to be devised to explain the child's sudden appearance.

For a Jewish child to live with a Christian family under a false identity
and without arousing suspicion, he needed to have the "right" appearance.
In other words, an Aryan look — light, smooth hair, blue eyes, a turned-up
nose — which few Jewish children possessed. Few Christian families were
willing to shelter a child who had dark, curly hair, a semitic nose, and dark
eyes, as he or she would immediately be assumed to be Jewish. Still, the Germans were unlikely to discover the presence of a Jewish child in a Christian
family solely because of his appearance. The primary danger, as we have seen,
lay with neighbors who might denounce the foster family to the authorities.

10  Testimony of Zofia Boczkowska, YVA, M.31/239.
11  Altbeker Cyprys, *A Jump for Life*, p 114.
12  Testimony of David Danieli, Institute of Contemporary Jewry, Oral History Division,
    Hebrew University of Jerusalem (OHD), (68)53.

Their motivation might be simple antisemitism, envy of the sheltering family for receiving various benefits for hiding the child, revenge in the wake of a previous dispute with the sheltering family, and so forth. The many testimonies of rescuers and those they saved indicate that in most cases the Germans learned of the presence of Jews hiding on the Aryan side from local Christians who had denounced the families. Jewish girls who adopted an assumed identity had a better chance of survival, as virtually all the Jewish boys were circumcised. As Ringelblum notes:

> The circumcision of Jewish boys is a major obstacle to finding them refuge on the Aryan side. The number of uncircumcised boys is very small. Pressure from religious parents and relations, together with judicial difficulties with the Jewish community and municipal authorities, were so great that very few parents, even the most progressive ones, would not have their boys circumcised. One simply was not given a birth certificate and the child would be exposed to humiliations and difficulties in school.[13]

At the end of 1942, when it was clear that the children were doomed, some parents in the Warsaw Ghetto tried to obscure their children's circumcision by means of surgery. Certain physicians in Warsaw specialized in these reverse operations, which became a goldmine for those involved, particularly for the mediators between the surgeons and the Jews. However, although most such operations succeeded in the case of adults, this was not so with children.[14]

In general, the Jews in Poland could readily be identified. They differed from the Christians in their outer appearance, names, customs, speech, and body language. The majority of the Jews spoke Yiddish, and even though they might also be fluent in Polish, they often had a telltale Jewish accent. For the most part they lived in different streets and neighborhoods. A Jewish child could well reach maturity without having any genuine social contact with his Polish peers, even if they attended the same school. Nor did the occupation draw the two populations closer. On the contrary: the isolation of the ghetto distanced the Jews from their Christian neighbors even more so, and even from those with whom they had ties in the past. Hence the small number of children who found shelter in Christian homes. As noted, those with the "right" appearance who were raised in assimilated families which could afford to pay for their care stood a better chance.

---

13  Ringelblum, *Polish-Jewish Relations*, pp. 145–146.
14  Jonas Turkow, "Children of the Ghetto" (Hebrew), *Dapim: Studies of the Holocaust and Jewish Resistance*, vol. I (1969), p. 264; Altbeker Cyprys, *A Jump for Life*, pp. 160–161.

The age of most of the children who were hidden with Christian families ranged from infancy to twelve. Children of twelve and more were considered, in the terms of that era, fully-fledged youths and so had to fend for themselves in times of acute danger, just as did the adults. Moving a Jewish child from the ghetto to a Christian family on the Aryan side was a complex, obstacle-strewn process, which was usually carried out under pressure. Often it was done at the last minute, during an Aktion, under the very noses of the Germans. Advance planning was thus not possible, and the preparations that were made ahead of the act of handing over the child were usually insufficient, as it was impossible to know what obstacles would suddenly arise when the child was smuggled out of the ghetto. A rescue attempt that was planned and initiated by a Jewish family was usually preceded by direct or indirect negotiations with the Christian family, in which the terms of payment for the child's upkeep would be agreed on together with compensation for the risks entailed. Payment was generally made in cash, in local or foreign currency, or in the form of jewelry, clothing, household utensils, furniture, bedding, and the like. In some cases a promise was made in an agreement that after the war, if the child survived, the real estate holdings of the family would be transferred to the foster family.

In June 1943, during the liquidation of the Buczacz Ghetto, the Klonicki-Klonymus family fled to the fields of a nearby village, hoping to find shelter in the home of one of the local peasants. At this time the last Jews of Galicia were being annihilated and the region was declared *Judenrein* — free of Jews. Every Jew who was caught was murdered immediately. The young parents wandered with their infant son in the fields, hounded by Ukrainian peasants who blackmailed them, threatening to turn them over to the Germans. Finally they reached the home of their former maidservant and asked her to give shelter at least to their son. The woman promised to look into the matter and consulted with the *soltys*, the village headman, who advised her to take in the boy, because after the war he would be redeemed for a large amount of money. The parents gave the woman all the material goods they had with them, which were worth an estimated 8,000 zlotys, and another 2,000 zlotys and fifteen dollars in cash. This was definitely not a small payment for a first installment, but they were also willing to undertake to transfer to her their share of the family property after the war, on condition that she would rescue their child.[15]

---

15  Aryeh Klonicki, *The Diary of Adam's Father* (Jerusalem: Ghetto Fighters' House and Hakibbutz Hameuchad, 1973), pp. 25–37, 65.

Even when a Christian family promised its longtime Jewish friends a haven in their home in return for advance payment according to an agreement, there was no guarantee that at the moment of truth the friendship would meet the test. Some panicked at the last minute, fearing the risks involved, but having already accepted payment tried to disavow the commitment at the first opportunity, citing various excuses for their refusal.

In April 1943, shortly before the outbreak of the Warsaw Ghetto uprising, Hana Avrutzky, an eleven-year-old girl from Warsaw, was sent by her parents to a Polish friend of the family on the Aryan side. The plan was for her parents to join her soon after. Ahead of her arrival the friend was given a large sum of money and undertook to obtain Aryan papers for the whole family and prepare a place for them to hide in his home. When Hana arrived, the friend said he was astonished that she had come alone. She told him that the rest of the family would arrive in a few days and that until then "Father said you have to make all the arrangements and prepare the hiding place." When they failed to arrive, the man told her that they would never come. Hana insisted that they would and went to wait for them by the opening to the underground passage through which they were supposed to get to the Aryan side. After waiting in vain she returned, utterly exhausted, to "Mr. Alexander," her father's friend, who now informed her that the plans had changed and that he would not be able to shelter her, as by doing so, he would endanger his family. He gave her a little money and sent her out into the street.[16]

In the terms of that period, Hana was already a big girl and was able to reach the Aryan side on her own. Younger children, though, needed the help of adults. Numerous stratagems were adopted to smuggle children out of the ghetto; each case had its own rationale and no escape resembled another. Frequently a third party, Jewish or Christian, who possessed a transit permit, was involved. Some small children were moved in crates and backpacks. It was particularly difficult to take out toddlers, who were liable to begin crying at a critical moment and thus bring disaster on themselves and on those who were trying to smuggle them out. To avert this danger, very young children were dosed with sleeping pills.[17]

Alfred Mazeh, a boy from an affluent Warsaw family, had the "right" appearance, making it possible to walk on the Aryan side without arousing suspicion that he was Jewish. The problem was to get him through the ghetto

---

16  Testimony of Hana Avrutzky, YVA, O.3/5737.
17  Leib Garfunkel, *The Destruction of Kovno's Jewry* (Hebrew) (Jerusalem: Yad Vashem, 1959), p. 153.

gate. Alfred, who was aged about six when he was smuggled out, remembers that one day a woman he did not know came to their apartment in the ghetto and she was given two suitcases. One contained expensive household goods, the other, watches. His mother told him that the lady would take him with her and promised that she and his father would join him in a few days. As a *Volksdeutsche* — a Pole of German origin — the woman was not subjected to a search. She took Alfred through the gate with no special problem after telling the German gendarmes that he was her son.[18]

Yet not even the most fortunate of the children, whose parents had managed to find them a decent foster family on the Aryan side, could be certain that the family would be able to shelter them indefinitely — and not because of any evil intentions. Danger lurked everywhere and there were constant surprises. In many cases, a Christian family who had taken in a Jewish child was compelled to transfer him elsewhere at very short notice — to another family, a convent, or an orphanage of the RGO, the Polish relief organization — because of the danger of informers.

After one of the Aktions, the mother of Leah Blumenkrantz, from Tarnów, asked Janina Walęga, a Pole who was a good friend, to save their daughter Leah, who was aged five. Walęga hid Leah in her home, where her parents also lived. During the day, when the adults were out of the house, Leah remained in the sealed attic; in the evening she joined the family. The Walęgas were a cultured family and treated Leah well. However, she was bored by being alone in the house. One day she got tired of her enforced prison and decided to peek out of the window to see what was going on outside. Suddenly she noticed a woman looking at her from the house across the way and waving a threatening finger at her. Leah understood that she had done something wrong and told the family. After talking it over among themselves, they decided that it was essential to get Leah out of the house quickly, for fear the neighbor would inform on them. Janina Walęga took Leah to an acquaintance, an elderly woman who lived in Przemyśl, in the hope she would agree to take her in. But the woman refused, shouting, "I don't want any *żydowka* [Jewess] here." Having no other choice, Walęga placed Leah in the first convent that agreed to accept her.[19]

As the Aktions intensified, the lives of the children who remained in the ghetto became increasingly intolerable. Their parents forbade them to

18  Testimony of Alfred Mazeh, OHD, (68)1.
19  Leah Fried-Blumenkrantz, "Lilka the Convent Girl" (Hebrew), *Edut*, vol. 10 (1994), pp. 71–83.

leave the house and adopted various ruses to conceal them. The children were compelled to hide for days at a time in crowded, stifling places, without seeing the light of day or breathing fresh air. They lived in constant fear that they would be seized, torn away from their parents, and sent to an unknown destination. The younger children, too, felt instinctively the tension in the air and the danger that lurked at every step. It is thus not surprising that many of them were prepared to move to the Aryan side even without their parents. The temptation to be able to go into the street and walk in the garden in the fresh air, was difficult to resist. But when the moment of parting with their parents arrived, the children underwent severe crises which they did not soon overcome, even if the survival instinct was paramount.

Martha Elbinger was five or six when she was smuggled out of the Warsaw Ghetto to the Aryan side. She had already lost her mother in an earlier Aktion and only her father remained with her in the ghetto. She remembers parting from him and the rest of the family without crying, because she instinctively understood that this was the way she would remain alive. When her aunt brought her to the home of her Polish rescuers, the Rogala family, which lived in the placid Żolibórz district of Warsaw, she immediately felt safe and protected, and waited impatiently for her aunt to leave because she was afraid that because of her she would be caught.[20]

However, not all the children reacted like Martha at the moment of parting. The transfer of a child to strangers was one step in the process of the dissolution of the family unit in a situation of mortal danger. Abruptly the child's last bulwark, which had provided security and warmth, was torn asunder. Separation from the parents left the child hanging by a thread. It is not surprising, then, that the separation was accompanied by deep anxiety on the part of both the child and the parents. Some children were afraid to leave their parents and refused vehemently to move to the Aryan side, preferring to die with them.[21]

Sometimes the children's resistance could only be overcome by subterfuge, by telling them all manner of tales to distract them before they were placed in the custody of strangers. They were given various excuses and told that the separation would be brief and that mother and father would soon join them. Anyone who reads the testimonies of survivors who were children during the Holocaust will be struck by the harshness of the experience of parting from parents, which marked them indelibly. Even children as young

20 Testimony of Martha Elbinger, YVA, M.31/3674.
21 Ringelblum, *Polish-Jewish Relations*, pp. 140–141.

as five or six who had few memories of home — in some cases they could not even remember their parents' faces — carried with them the moment of part- ing for years. Older children recall the event in vivid detail.

Nina Drucker was an only child. After her mother was murdered in one of the first Aktions in Lvov, she was left alone with her father, to whom she was deeply attached. A doctor, he managed to make contact with a Polish woman from aristocratic circles who, in return for a service he had done her, was ready to take care of Nina. Nina was about seven when her father left her with Olga Zawadzka. This did not come as a surprise to the girl; her father had prepared her as well as he could for the move to the home of her new guard- ian and for the conditions she could expect there. He helped her to become familiar with her new assumed name and explained to her that the woman she would be living with would be her aunt. As the time to part approached, he bought her a red ball, and Olga Zawadzka arrived, supposedly to take her to a day camp. Although Nina later forgot many of the events of that period, the moment of parting with her father remained engraved in her memory as though it had happened the day before: "The last image I recollect of my father is of him accompanying me on the street with that Polish woman. I gave her my hand and immediately called her auntie. My father turned away from us and walked in the opposite direction. His face looked terrible, the face of an elderly man, crying. That is the last image I have of my father."[22]

For most of the children who survived, this moment of parting was the last time they saw their parents, and the parting became a landmark in their lives, after which a different life seemingly began. Over time they forgot many details from the past, but they seemed to make a special effort to remember at least the faces of their parents, which became increasingly blurred in their memories. Gerta Zilber, from Lvov, was nine when her father placed her in the custody of a Christian family in a village near Tarnów , which had agreed to hide her in return for payment. Although she does not remember the name of the village — she was there only briefly — she does remember how her supposed rescuers treated her cruelly, took her clothes for themselves, and decided to get rid of her. The woman of the family forcibly put her on a train that took her to Przemyśl. From the train station she was taken by a prosti- tute to a convent in the guise of a Polish orphan. Forty years later she related that at night she would lie awake in bed, trying not to forget the faces of her parents. "I remember so well how I would lie there with open eyes in order not to forget what mother looked like, what father looked like. At some stage,

22 Testimony of Noa Libes (Nina Drucker), OHD, (68)13.

very gradually, mother's image became blurred, but I remembered father's the whole time."[23]

Not all the children who were rescued by Christian families reached them at the parents' initiative and by prior arrangement. Some were left along highways, on the doorstep of a house, or by the wall of a convent, in the hope that a merciful passerby would take them in out of pity. Decades later, in their testimonies, some of these survivors still expressed unconcealed anger at those who had abandoned them when they were small and helpless. Even though many years had gone by and they possessed a mature understanding of the circumstances, a conscious feeling of abandonment still remained.

Hanna Batista was about five when she and her mother were compelled to leave the monastery in Częstochowa where they had found refuge, after someone had denounced them. In her despair, the mother determined to drown herself in the river. First, however, she sought to save little Hanna by sending her to a Polish woman of her acquaintance in the hope that she would take her in. Hanna recalls clearly how she and her mother arrived at the bridge over the river which cuts through the city, and how her mother gave her a note and sent her to a woman, telling her she would soon follow. "I stood there completely indifferent and listened to what she told me. She did not hug or kiss me. I have a suspicion that maybe she did not love me. It is hard for me to come to terms with that. She sat down next to me so she would see my face and told me what I had to do. She gave me a note and slice of bread with jam wrapped in a cloth and said: Guard this, because it is the last slice of bread. We have no more. I heard her and went. Afterwards I learned that she had jumped from the bridge but did not drown but only broke a leg. Later the Germans killed her." Hanna arrived at the woman's home but was refused entry. Finally she was rescued by a family she did not know, who brought her up.[24]

In their memoirs, survivors rarely mention the parents who had abandoned them on the brink of annihilation, but that such cases occurred is revealed in many testimonies and unpublished diaries.[25] Probably in their anguish and in the extreme conditions at the time, when parents were compelled to abandon a child by the roadside, they did not contemplate his long-term future; at that moment their only thought was that he should survive.

23  Testimony of Magdalena Or-Ner (Gerta Zilber), YVA, O.3/6745.
24  Testimony of Hanna Batista, O.3/5732.
25  Testimony of Katia Tokarska, YVA, O.3/3122; testimony of Luba Wróbel, YVA, O.33/730; Altbeker Cyprys, *A Jump for Life*, p. 56.

And, indeed, compassionate individuals took in a significant number of children from the street and from institutions, even on the edge of the abyss. These people literally risked their lives to save the children, shared what little they had with them, and raised them as though they were their own. In many cases, children who were taken in by passersby were more fortunate than those who were left with families which had promised to hide them in return for payment. Their luck was entirely dependent on the home in which they found themselves, on the people who rescued them and their motives. Nothing more tellingly illustrates the horror of that period than the rescue of these children, when simple compassion and human feelings vied with evil and cruelty. The stories of these foundlings are inherently dramatic and moving, and each story merits telling in its own right. The accounts that follow are just a few that convey the atmosphere of those terrible times.

Early in the morning of October 4, 1942, Leokadia Jaromirska, who lived just outside Warsaw, left for work. As she hurried to the train, she heard children crying from the direction of the fence of the nearby convent. Investigating, she discovered two weeping little girls dressed in clothes that were too light for autumn, their cheeks swollen and their voices hoarse from crying. She immediately assumed that they were Jewish. Not wishing to miss the train, she left the girls with the owner of a nearby shop, promising her that she would decide what to do with them when she returned from work. But at work all she could think about was the girls, and at midday she returned to the shop. There she found only the older girl — the shop owner had already turned over the younger one, who was dark-complexioned, to the police. Jaromirska berated the woman for involving the police. She went over to the older girl, who was blonde and beautiful, and called to her, "Come, little doll," and the girl stretched out her hand to her and said, "Mommy." Jaromirska picked her up and carried her home. The girl's real name, as she learned after the war from her father, who survived and came to retrieve his daughter, was Shifra Junisz. A quarter of a century later, Jaromirska recalled the moment when she decided to take the girl home and raise her, despite her economic circumstances. A week later, after the girl had become accustomed to her, she decided to call her Bogushia (from Bogomila), meaning "Beloved of God," because in her perception, God had stood by her. She then began a struggle to save the girl's life, to which she devoted three full years.[26]

---

26  Leokadia Jaromirska, "Bogushia," *Yalkut Moreshet,* English Edition, vol. 3 (Winter, 2003), pp. 95–96.

One day in May 1942, when the annihilation of the Jews of Eastern Galicia was at its height, Zofia Boczkowska was on her way to town in her carriage from her estate near Busk. On the edge of the forest she saw a group of Jews who were digging pits; close by a number of amused Germans were pointing at a little girl who was running back and forth. Boczkowska was able to guess why the Jews were digging the pits. Nevertheless, she decided to take the risk and got out of the carriage to get a closer view of the situation. Approaching the site, she saw that the girl, who was about five or six, had black curly hair and large velvety black eyes and wore a red tunic, was doing a sort of dance in front of the Germans, curtsying and crossing herself. Boczkowska's heart went out to the girl immediately and she resolved to try to save her. Turning to the German police officer at the site, with whom she was acquainted, she said, as though naïvely, that she knew the girl and that her parents were Christians. Both of them knew that the girl was Jewish. Her name was Hanna Baron, and she was about five years old when her parents were murdered in an Aktion. After their death her aunt left her in the custody of a Ukrainian woman who agreed to hide her in her home. A few days later the woman decided to get rid of the girl and threw her into the river at night. The current carried Hanna to the river bank and at first light, her clothes soaking, she entered the hut of a peasant family. They fed her and handed her over to the local police station, where she was added to a group of Jews who were sent to dig their own graves.

At the killing site, Boczkowska negotiated with the German officer for the girl's release, promising him a handsome gift if he agreed. The officer said he would take her back to the police station and release her, provided she produced a certificate stating that she was a Christian. It was clear to Boczkowska that the officer was not really interested in a certificate and that to redeem the girl she would have to pay him a substantial sum. Zofia and her husband, Stanisław, had another girl at home, who had also been adopted. Agronomists by profession, they lived comfortably on the estate of Count Badeni, of which Stanisław was manager. Nevertheless, they did not have much ready cash available. They kept their meager savings — in foreign currency and jewelry — for a rainy day. The possibility of saving the Jewish girl by means of a bribe posed a dilemma for Boczkowska. Her husband was not enthusiastic at her sudden initiative when she told him she intended to use their savings to rescue Hanna. Moreover, there was no guarantee that the outcome would be as Boczkowska wished. It is not just a problem of money, he said; after all, the girl was Jewish and someone might inform on them and endanger their lives. However, his wife was determined to rescue her, whatever might happen. She went to Lvov and obtained documentation proving that the girl was the daughter of Christian parents. Then, after she thrust into the officer's hand a packet of dollars and jewelry, he handed over the girl.[27]

In 1942, Mottel and Zelda Lekach fled with their infant daughter, Marsha, from the town of Kovel, in Volhynia, into the surrounding forests. When it became clear to them that the baby girl would not be able to survive in the forest, they left her on the doorstep of a peasant family in one of the villages, in the hope that they would take her in. The baby was wrapped in a blanket to which the parents had attached a note stating that her name was Maria and that she was born out of wedlock and that her mother was unable to raise her. The inhabitants of the house took the infant to the village headman. He identified her ethnic origins by the embroidery on the blanket, but decided to keep the secret to himself and not turn her over to the authorities. Instead, he placed her in the custody of his sister, Vasilina Jarmoliuk and her husband Alexander, who lived in the town of Majdan. The couple, who were childless, willingly received the girl. The girl's parents, who continued to hide in the forest, learned who had adopted the baby and contacted them, thus they were able to see their daughter in the home of the headman. Eventually, the Germans caught the parents and sent them to a concentration camp. The Jarmoliuks raised the girl for two years as their daughter. The parents survived and after the war returned to claim their child from her benefactors, who asked for nothing in return.[28]

There were also older children, aged twelve or thirteen, who were separated from their parents during the Aktions and innocently asked Christian acquaintances for temporary refuge until the storm blew over, in the hope that after the Aktion they would be able to return to their families. Most of them were turned away and continued to roam in the area of their home, and if they were unable to find shelter they were eventually caught and murdered. However, there were also surprising manifestations of compassion. In their wanderings some of these children encountered caring people who, even though they did not know them, took them in and saved them. This was how Zofia Kozniak from the town of Brzozow survived. Zofia was twelve when she was separated from her family during an Aktion and was left on her own. Lacking an alternative, she went to her Polish teacher, who lived in a nearby village, as she knew she liked her and would probably be prepared to help her. The teacher agreed to let her stay for the night. The next day the teacher took

27 Testimonies of Zofia Boczkowska and Hanna Podoszyn, YVA, M.31/239.
28 Testimony on the rescue of Marsha Tishler-Lekach, YVA, O.31/3496.

the girl to the home of her priest and advised her to ask him for shelter. Zofia described to the priest the ordeals she had undergone. The priest's sister, Mrs. Krzywonosowa, who was present, took pity on her and took her home. She had three children of her own, but found place for Zofia as well. But the girl longed for her parents and was desperate to know what had become of them. After learning that both her parents had perished, she decided to stay with the family that had taken her in and treated her like a daughter.[29]

A similar sequence of events befell David Danieli, a boy of twelve, in the city of Rybnik, in Upper Silesia. Returning home after having been away for a time, he found the door sealed. He asked the Kapica family, which lived nearby, if they knew where his parents were, and they told him that the Jews had been deported from the city — no one knew to where. David had nowhere to go, and the Kapica family suggested that he stay with them. The families had had no connection before the war; the ties were forged only during the war in the wake of business dealings between David's mother and Martha Kapica. David accepted the Kapicas' invitation, and after breaking into his home to retrieve a few items, spent the rest of the war with them.[30]

## Life with the Rescuing Families

After a child's initial absorption in the home of his or her rescuers a new chapter, with an unknown future, began. Various factors affected the child's integration and adjustment in the new family, and no two cases were alike. Key elements were the child's age and character, and the adoptive family's attitude towards him. The location of the home and the attitude of those who were close to the child were crucial for his peace of mind. For reasons of safety, it was essential that the child stay close to home so as to avoid being seen by strangers. There was always the danger that an acquaintance might recognize him. It was preferable that the home be outside the community and away from the main road, so that passers-by were unlikely to see the new child. Usually it was easier to hide pre-school children, as children of that age were able to adjust more readily to their new surroundings and disengage from their past.

A Polish friend of Ruth Cyprys at first placed Cyprys' three-year-old daughter with relatives in the village. The cover story was that she had been

---

29 "Children Tell" (Hebrew), *Yediot Beit Lohamei Hagetaot*, vol. 21 (1959), pp. 93–94.
30 Testimony of David Danieli, OHD, (68)53.

born to a friend out of wedlock. A few months later, Ruth Cyprys visited the girl in her new home, without first identifying herself to the family as the mother of the child. She was surprised to see that her daughter had changed externally, looked like a village girl in every respect and behaved accordingly. Although not much time had passed since their separation, the girl did not recognize her. When the two of them remained alone in the courtyard, Cyprys asked her different questions to try to get her to talk. To jog her memory, she reminded her of the names of relatives, but the girl was unresponsive. Cyprys was convinced that the girl was suffering from amnesia caused by a blow to her head when the two had jumped from a train.[31] This may be an extreme case, but it reflects the rapid erosion of memory which occurred in young children because of the abrupt changes they experienced in moving from the ghetto to Christian families on the Aryan side. Indeed, erasing the experiences of the past might well have saved the girl, as otherwise she was liable to betray herself by saying something that would expose her Jewish identity.

The situation was very different for older children aged five or six and up. They were already aware of their Jewish identity and remembered their parents and families and longed for them. The sudden separation from their parents and the need to adjust to new surroundings and a new family was very difficult, especially for those who understood the circumstances. The yearning for their parents gave them no respite; they constantly awaited some signs of life from them, and when none arrived they reacted moodily, sometimes accompanied by outbursts of crying.

Vladka Meed, who visited Polish homes on the Aryan side of Warsaw where the children of her acquaintances were being hidden, describes the behavior of twin girls aged ten who lived with an elderly, kind-hearted Polish woman. They understood very well where they were and did not mention the ghetto by so much as a word. Nevertheless, one of them could not stop crying. "I want mother," she repeated incessantly. Her sister calmed her quietly. Both were distraught by the separation from their mother. They stopped eating and would not talk to anyone. They hid in corners of the house, sad and depressed among the strangers. When Vladka arrived on a visit, they snapped back to life, expecting her to bring them news and a letter from their mother. As soon as she crossed the threshold they asked, "Have you brought us anything from *over there*?" If she brought a letter from their mother with her, their joy knew no bounds. "Tell us, tell us, how does mamma look now?" they would ask.[32]

---

31 Altbeker Cyprys, pp. 143–145.
32 Meed, *On Both Sides of the Wall*, pp. 141–142.

Children whose parents had promised to join them became deeply anxious when they failed to appear. And their despondency grew when they started to comprehend, from fragments of conversations and hints from the people around them, that their parents were no longer alive.

When Alfred Mazeh was smuggled across to the Aryan side he was initially hidden in the home of a Polish family which lived near the ghetto. He was not allowed out of the house and was forbidden to go near a window. When the uprising erupted in the ghetto, he overheard the woman of the house telling one of her neighbors that the Jews were being burned alive there. After the neighbor left, he asked the woman whether it was true that the Jews were being burned. She replied that not everyone was being burned. Later, when the woman's children returned home he asked them the same question, and they told him that all the Jews had been burned and that his parents would never return. Hearing this, Alfred broke down and wept for hours, crying, "Dead, dead!"[33]

The sudden appearance of a new child in the family naturally drew attention and piqued the curiosity of neighboring children. It soon became apparent that the child was not a guest but a permanent member of the family and that since his arrival the family was buying more goods and was enjoying a higher standard of living. This fueled the envy of the neighbors, who began to suspect that the source of these goods was payment the family had received from the child's Jewish parents for hiding him in their home. To rebuff such gossip and its attendant dangers, the foster family had to invent a plausible cover story to account for the child's presence. The usual story was that the child was a newly-orphaned relative, or the fruit of forbidden love, and that they had volunteered to look after him until affairs settled down.[34] To ward off suspicion, the foster family in some cases preferred to invent a patriotic cover story for their ward, such as that his father had fallen in battle or had been captured by the enemy or arrested for subversive activity, and that they were helping the child's mother in her distress.

The Rogala family did not try to hide Martha Elbinger from the neighbors. On the contrary: to prevent malicious gossip they sent her to kindergarten, where she quickly fitted in with the other children. The neighbors were told that she was a relative and that her parents had been deported to a concentration camp. This tale gained credence among the neighbors, as they

---

33  Testimony of Alfred Mazeh, OHD, (68)1.
34  Testimony of Noa Libes, OHD, (68)13.

knew before Martha's arrival that the brother of her "aunt," Marianna Rogala, was incarcerated in Auschwitz.[35]

The complex and difficult element in the children's cover stories lay in the need for them to adjust to their assumed identity. Living for a protracted period under an assumed identity — or, more accurately, a double identity — involving a permanent contradiction between inner feelings and outer behavior, was difficult even for adults, but far more so for children who find it difficult to lie or keep a secret. Pretense runs contrary to a child's natural behavior, and he or she lacks the adult's internal safety mechanisms of alertness to situations of danger. But these lacks were counterbalanced by the survival instinct and the fear of death. It was easier to hide infants and toddlers who could not yet talk and did not understand their situation, than to fashion a borrowed identity for children of five and more who were aware of their Jewish identity and remembered their parents and their home. Nevertheless, their guardians taught them to keep their original identity a deep secret and never admit their Jewishness to anyone, no matter how friendly they might appear to be. They had to disavow their past and never so much as mention their home and their loved ones, even if they missed them terribly. Their task was to learn their new identity, cling to it unfalteringly, and act accordingly in every situation.

In most cases the move to the Aryan side entailed a change of both name and surname for the child, who had to identity himself by the new name alone. Many testimonies, from both Jews and Christians, confirm that even young children internalized the rule and did not give away their real name.[36] It was the natural naïvety of the younger children that could lead to trouble. Young children were liable to make an innocent slip of the tongue and reveal their identity by inadvertently talking about their past. A Jewish child might pass successfully as a Christian child over a lengthy period, but then might blurt out something about his past or mention a place which would divulge his Jewish origins. A suspicious police agent might ask, with feigned fondness, "What was your name before?" The child, without thinking, might innocently blurt out his real name and so reveal his Jewish identity.

Cultural or mental affinity with the adoptive family could ease a Jewish child's integration in a Christian family, but such cases were rare. Although Jews and Christians in Poland had coexisted for centuries, the differences between them were profound. They were two separate ethno-religious

---

35  Testimony of Marianna Rogala, YVA, M.31/3674.
36  Ringelblum, *Polish-Jewish Relations*, p. 145.

societies. While Jews and Christians maintained close economic ties, there was little social contact between them. In contrast to Central and Western Europe, there was little assimilation in Poland and intermarriage was rare. According to some estimates, approximately 300,000 Jews assimilated into Polish culture between the world wars — that is, no more than ten percent of the Jewish population. Assimilation was more widespread in the major cities, particularly among the more educated and affluent and among members of the liberal professions.[37] Pure "Polishness" was the exclusive characteristic of Christians, and to be a "true Pole" in effect meant being Catholic. Thus, a Jew who wished to integrate into Polish society would have had to convert. Very few Jews in Poland chose this route, which in any event was strewn with obstacles. The sociologist Aryeh Tartakower estimates that at the end of the 1920s and in the early 1930s no more than 2,000 to 2,500 Jews a year converted to Christianity. Most of them did so for economic or social reasons — to promote their own or their children's career — rather than because of a fundamental change in their religious belief.[38]

To blend into Christian society it was not enough to adopt a new identity and to have learnt one's cover story well; a deep knowledge of Christian religious customs and ritual was also necessary. Until the Second World War, Polish society was overwhelmingly religious by nature. Home, school, and church instilled in the people, from young to old, a Catholic way of life. This was emphatically Christian every day of the year, and even more so on the holy days. Christian customs were second nature to Polish children, whereas Jewish children, even those who had been raised in assimilated homes, were unfamiliar with all the abstruse elements of Christian religious practice. Some were taken by their Christian nannies to visit churches and were charmed by the pictures, the flowers, and the pungent aroma of incense,[39] but most had at best only a superficial knowledge of Catholic ritual. Some knew the dates of the holidays, but not the different prayers or when they should be recited. Inappropriate behavior by a child — such as failing genuflect to an icon before getting into bed, or showing unfamiliarity with basic customs while in church — was liable to generate immediate suspicion that he was Jewish.

At the age of ten, Hanka Grynberg, who grew up in an atheist, assimi-

---

37  Celia Stopnicka Heller, "Poles of Jewish Background — The Case of Assimilation without Integration in Interwar Poland," in Joshua A. Fishman, ed. *Studies on Polish Jewry 1919–1939* (New York: YIVO, 1974), pp. 254–255.

38  Ibid., pp. 261–263.

39  Miriam Perlberg-Shmuel, *This Girl Is Jewish!* (Hebrew) (Haifa: Shurot, 1997), p. 10.

lated Jewish home, was brought from the Bialystok Ghetto to her first Polish family. But she was at a loss when she was told to cross herself and recite the Lord's Prayer (*Ojcze nasz*), and therefore had to be moved to a different family on an isolated farm. The owner, "Aunt Zosia," who had two sons, was told that Hanka was a Polish orphan from Warsaw and she accepted her as such, without probing into her past. She treated her warmly as if she were her own daughter. Hanka joined the boys in farm work and was happy in her new home. However, the younger son, who was aged fifteen, suspected that she was Jewish and decided to test her. One day, when they were working in a field near a Jewish cemetery, he asked her whether she had been at her mother's funeral and how she had been buried. Hanka, who by chance had attended a Jewish funeral in the ghetto, replied innocently that she had been wrapped in a sheet (shrouds). The boy lashed out at her, "Then you are a Jew!" He told her that Catholics dress the deceased in clothes and bury them in a coffin. When they returned home, the boy told the family that "Hanka is a Jew and because of her we are all going to die." In an instant Hanka's world came crashing down around her.[40]

To avert such crises, the child had to be well prepared beforehand. If the move to the Aryan side was planned in advance and time allowed, an effort would be made to teach the child to cross himself and recite the basic prayers. Nina Drucker, who also came from an assimilated home, recalls that before she moved in with her Polish guardian her father helped her memorize Christian prayers, in addition to the details of her new identity. She learned them by rote, without any religious feeling.[41] However, in most cases, Jewish children learned Christian customs when they were already on the Aryan side in the home of their foster family.

If all went well and the Jewish child had become integrated into the Christian family, a new life would begin. As time went on, the child experienced many upheavals, like every child who becomes part of a foster family or is adopted. This was particularly so in the special circumstances in which Jewish children were absorbed in Christian families. Naturally, the adoptive family's attitude toward the Jewish child differed in each case and was influenced by many factors, so it would be wrong to generalize. However, there is no doubt that a child who was physically attractive, intelligent, and affable would be more likely to generate a positive attitude on the part of the new

40  Hanka Grynberg, in Wiktoria Śliwowska, ed., *The Last Eyewitnesses: Children of the Holocaust Speak (Jewish Lives)* (Evanston: Northwestern University Press, 2000), pp. 176–185.
41  Testimony of Noa Libes, OHD, (68)13.

family. Thus, if the child met the family's expectations, strong emotional ties were more likely to develop.[42]

Children who were placed in the custody of families whose motives for taking them in were humane and religious, generally felt more comfortable, even if the economic situation in the home was poor. We know from survivors' testimonies that there were some impoverished families that shared their meager resources with their ward as though he were a fully-fledged member of the family. Some rescuers, cognizant of the Jewish child's sensitivity because of his unique situation, pampered him and shielded him against their own children during quarrels, so he would not feel that he was being discriminated against.

Alexander Kelber was an infant when his parents placed him in the custody of a Polish family, the Paribeks, before fleeing into the forest. After his parents were murdered, Alexander was adopted by the Paribek family and spent the war years with them disguised as a girl. The Paribeks had three children of their own and lived modestly on the salary of the father, who was a minor state official. They treated Alexander like their own son and only after the war did he learn that he was Jewish and that they were not his biological parents. He was deeply attached to Valeria, the mother of the family, who loved him very much and constantly pampered him.[43]

It sometimes happened in such families that one of the biological children insulted the adopted child during a quarrel and reminded him of his Jewish origin. Such confrontations not only embarrassed the child but also undermined his self-confidence. An incident of this kind befell Benyamin Katz. Benyamin does not remember anything about his parents and family, but throughout his stay with the Blaszko family — the Christian family that saved him — he knew he was not their biological son. He remembers that one winter night Franciszek and Regina Blaszko removed him from the orphanage where he was living and took him to their home in a small village, where they adopted him as their son. They were a simple peasant couple, and even though they had a son of their own, a little older than Benyamin, they did not discriminate between them, nor did they make him feel that he was different because he was Jewish. On the contrary: Franciszek, the father, apparently loved him more than he did his biological son, and the boy enjoyed a good life with the family. However, in the back of his mind Benyamin felt uneasy, sensing that he was different because he was circumcised. The family's grand-

---

42 Testimony of Zofia Boczkowska, YVA, M.31/239.
43 Testimony of Alexander Kelber, YVA, O.3/1859.

mother, who lived with them, explained to him in private why he was different from the other children, though not disparagingly. Once, when he was fighting with his "brother," the latter called out to him, "You are a Jew!" Hearing this, the father hit his son viciously with his belt in the presence of the mother and berated him, "In the future you will know how to behave toward him!" This was the only time Benyamin ever heard himself referred to as a Jew in his adoptive home. Even so, the event shook his self-confidence. Years later, he described the situation in which he found himself: "I went inside, shaking with fear. I didn't know what was going to happen to me. I stood in the middle of the room and started to cry."[44]

It should be noted that those who hid children for economic reasons and viewed the act primarily as a source of income were also not a monolithic group. Some treated the children well and developed emotional ties with them, while others were indifferent or discriminatory. Vladka Meed describes the situation of one such toddler:

> The case of one-year-old Krysia Klog was simple. She had been placed with a poor Polish family in Pludy, a suburb of Warsaw. Barefoot, unkempt, unwashed, the toddler wandered through the dirty, almost empty rooms. The downtrodden, feeble Gentile landlady paid little attention to her ward, since she was hardly able to take care of her own children. She had distributed all of Krysia's belongings among her own youngsters. No matter how many dresses and shoes were bought for Krysia, she was never seen shod or in anything but rags and looked more undernourished than the other children, although the women received 2,500 zlotys each month. Nevertheless, the toddler seemed to feel at home. No matter how she was mistreated, she always reacted with a meek smile and would quietly seek a corner to hide in. Though we were aware of the child's wretched surroundings we had to keep her there — it was still safer than being in the ghetto.[45]

The adoptive family's extended relations were not always told the secret, although in some cases they were called upon to help conceal the child. For example, if the child had to be moved because neighbors suspected he was Jewish, the usual solution was to transfer him to the custody of an aunt or grandmother who lived some distance away. Nor did everyone in the extended family always view positively the fact that someone in the family was shel-

---

44 Testimony of Benyamin Katz, OHD (68)32.
45 Meed, *On Both Sides of the Wall*, p. 145.

tering a Jewish child. Eliezer Huterer was sheltered by his Ukrainian nanny, Chalkowa. When her brother, a vicious antisemite, learned of this he hounded her relentlessly, and Chalkowa had to go into hiding herself, with the boy, for fear her brother would kill the child.[46] Similarly, Leokadia Jaromirska's family was far from pleased at her decision to adopt a Jewish girl, and when she found herself in distress, she could not turn to them for help. Her sister-in-law alleged that because she had taken in a Jewish girl, there was no room for her son and the two remained at loggerheads.[47]

As we have seen, the outer circle of neighbors generally did not support the rescue of Jews and tended to be hostile. In such cases the character of the rescuer would be of crucial importance. Showing courage and defiance in the face of hardheartedness might lead to a change not only in the attitude of the neighbors but even in that of hostile local officials. Jaromirska's neighbors knew she was concealing a Jewish girl; nor could she have kept this a secret, as they saw her collect the girl from the street. The event did not escape the attention of the local police; they demanded that she hand the girl over to the Jewish community, but she refused. Some mocked her, but others helped. The village headman, whom she approached, requesting papers for the girl, agreed to register her as Jaromirska's daughter. On one occasion the local police chief summoned her for questioning about the girl, and she shook with fear at the police station. At first she denied that the girl was Jewish. Finally she admitted that she had adopted her and appealed to his conscience, asking if he had children and how he would feel if people were to pass by indifferently a child of his who had been abandoned. In the end, he promised her that the police would no longer intervene and that he would warn her of any imminent harassment. Fortunately for both her and the girl, no one denounced them. Jaromirska was a good soul and none of her neighbors held a grudge against her.[48]

A child's chances of survival might depend on the social status of the adoptive family and on the self-confidence the family displayed. Thus, mixed Polish and German families or Volksdeutsche families, were often willing to shelter a Jewish child because their status made them less fearful of being informed on by their Polish neighbors, and the German authorities were less obtrusive.

The Kapicas, who adopted David Danieli, were a mixed family of miners — Anton was a Pole, Martha a German — who followed a typical proletar-

46 Testimony of Eliezer Harari, OHD (68)22.
47 Jaromirska, "Bogushia," p. 121.
48 Ibid., pp. 97–99.

ian way of life. They attached no special importance to their national origins and were not religious. Nevertheless, they were compelled to baptize David at the priest's urging, so that he would be issued a birth certificate stating that he was their son. David attended school and joined a German youth movement. At first he was under the impression that no one in the neighborhood knew he was a Jew. Later, however, he discovered that many people had known he was Jewish but had not denounced his adoptive parents.[49]

For a child with an assumed identity to be able to lead a normal life within a foster family, it was not enough to provide his primary needs — food and a place to sleep. It was also necessary to integrate him into the family's daily life and the immediate surroundings. Younger children, up to kindergarten age, presented fewer problems, as they were still at home under close adult supervision. Not so school-age children. Only very few of the Jewish children who were sheltered by Christian families attended kindergarten or school. For safety's sake, it was preferable for a child posing as a Pole to stay close to home so that there was minimal contact with strangers. A Jewish child who attended school was in danger of having his true identity exposed, even if he had a Christian birth certificate. The custom in Polish schools was for children aged seven to twelve to take part in the first communion, a rite of passage in which the child joins the church and undertakes to make confession and partake of the Eucharist. The concern was that in the confession preceding the ceremony the child would innocently divulge to the priest the "sin" of his Jewish identity. Consequently, the guardians preferred not to send their Jewish wards to communion, and if they did they preferred that the ceremony take place in a distant church, to avert excessive probing of the past.[50]

Older children had to be kept occupied, either with studies or work. Working-class and low-income families, and peasants in the rural areas often did not send their children to school during the war, instead they began to work from an early age. This was certainly the case with children in their custody who were masquerading as Christians.

Miriam Thau was twelve when she was placed in the custody of the Danko family, her parents' neighbors in the city of Otwock, near Warsaw. The Dankos were a cohesive and cordial working-class family that worked hard during the war to earn a living. The mother of the family, Jadwiga, encountered Miriam in the market, scrounging for food. It was the autumn of 1942, and Miriam wandered about barefoot and neglected in the cold and

49 Testimony of David Danieli, OHD, (68)53.
50 Perlberg-Shmuel, *This Girl Is Jewish*, p. 37.

rain. Taking pity on her, Jadwiga brought her home, fed her, treated the sores on her legs, and suggested that she stay with them. Miriam accepted the offer and was treated like one of the family. But she was by no means a charity case. The question of whether to send her to school never arose. Everyone in the family worked hard, and so did Miriam. Despite her young age, she worked like an adult, from dawn until late at night. She looked after the Dankos' small son, cleaned the house, and helped make *bimber*, an illicit Polish home-made alcoholic drink which was one of the family's sources of income. She also became adept at smuggling the liquor to Warsaw, traveling alone on the train and carrying a few bottles of the forbidden drink. When her guardians opened a café in Warsaw, Miriam worked there as a waitress.[51]

Similarly, Hanka Grynberg, who lived with a rural family, did not attend school — not necessarily because of the family's economic situation, but because education was simply not a priority. Their children worked on the farm and so did she, taking the cows to pasture in the summer. In the winter "Aunt Zosia" wove on a loom, and taught Hanka spinning and knitting.[52]

David Danieli, who was an industrious, independent boy, understood for himself that he would have to contribute his share to the livelihood of his adoptive family. To that end he assumed responsibility for various household chores and every morning got up early to deliver newspapers before going to school. His payment as a delivery boy constituted a substantial part of the family's income. His guardians appreciated this and treated him accordingly. At meals David received the third largest portion, and the family bought him a bicycle to facilitate his paper round.[53]

In most cases, then, the question of whether the foster child would attend school did not arise. However, some children found themselves in educated families who tried to provide home schooling. In 1942, Halina Fischer, aged eight, was placed in the custody of the Tarabula family, who had three children of their own and lived in a village. After devising a cover story for Halina that she was a relative, they had her baptized, obtained a false birth certificate and raised her lovingly until the end of the war. Throughout this time she did not attend school. But the father of the family, an unemployed teacher, taught her how to read and write so that after the war she was able to enter school in a class according to her age.[54]

51   Testimony of Miriam Thau, O.3/2716.
52   Śliwowska, *The Last Eyewitnesses*, p. 182.
53   Testimony of David Danieli, OHD, (68)53.
54   Testimony of Michal Reiwitz, YVA, M.31/3255.

As we have seen, Christianity is an organic element in Polish culture; every element of life is suffused with Christian belief. Icons of Jesus and the Virgin Mary are ubiquitous, family members pray and cross themselves constantly and on Sundays they dress festively and attend church. Thus, it was essential for the Jewish child in the family to adhere to Christian rituals so as to avoid exposure. Testimonies of the children who were saved by Christian families show that most of them learned to act like Christians and that some were even baptized. Nina Drucker describes the circumstances of her baptism:

> In [her] home I absorbed the Christian atmosphere, the prayers, Christmas. I wanted security, I wanted to belong. All my close surroundings were Christian, and I wanted to be like the others, and especially because of her [Olga Zawadzka the rescuer], whom I loved so much. She was wonderful. She is the person I was closest to. She told me that she would teach me the principles of the Christian religion and that when I knew them she would baptize me. One night, when her children were asleep, she baptized me — she dripped some water on my forehead and said a few ritual words to the effect that with this she was baptizing me into the Christian religion. She did not go to the priest. Apparently she did not trust him. And even though I was young, I understood the magnitude of the occasion.[55]

Most children, and the girls in particular, adopted the Christian way of life enthusiastically. They were charmed by the church ritual and by the stories of the saints, which they took to their hearts. Sara Avinun was aged about seven when she was adopted by a childless couple, Julia and Jan Pilch. Her name at the time was Irena Yablonska. When the little girl was brought to their home from an orphanage in Kraków, the couple did not know that she was Jewish, but after she grew accustomed to them she felt she could no longer live with the lie. One day she suddenly burst into unstoppable tears and revealed to her adoptive father what she was forbidden to tell: that her name was not Irena Yablonska, that she was a Jew, and that her real name was Sara Warszawiak. "I didn't tell you the truth. I was told not to tell my name to anyone, so the Germans wouldn't know. Now I don't want that name anymore, I don't even want to be Jewish, only a Christian, like you and Julia." She told him about the ghetto in which she had lived, about her mother who had died there, and about her father and her brother who had been taken away and whose fate

---

55 Testimony of Noa Libes, OHD, (68)13.

she did not know. Jan listened quietly to her story and did not look surprised. He told her to keep the secret and never mention her Jewishness.[56]

Sara's disclosure did not change the Pilchs' attitude; they continued to care for her as though she were their own daughter. They did not baptize her, but raised her as a Christian. Forty years and more after these events, Sara recalled the experience of her path to Christianity in the home of her adoptive parents as though it had just happened:

> It was Julia who let me into the secret of Christianity, but Jan's part in it was almost as big as hers. Julia took care of the practical side; to go to mass every Sunday, to make the sign of the cross every time we passed by a church or icon, to recite the Lord's Prayer... Jan wasn't as strict with the customs and manners of the ceremony... But during the first year that I lived with them, Jan would read to me out of [the book] Lives of the Saints. When he saw how fascinated I was with the stories, he turned reading the book into a habit. I especially related to the martyrs. In their stories I found a reason for my own suffering. I discovered that suffering could have a meaning and that it had a spiritual release, one of honor. The drops of faith that trickled into my soul from Jan's stories, to which he added his own explanations, became a spouting fountain that flooded my soul. Later came the lessons of Father Achilles, a young priest from the Capuchin monastery near the school. Christianity, as conveyed to me through his soft voice, meant love, compassion, and mercifulness, and these were like a balm on my wounds.[57]

In many cases the child's baptism provided a safety net in the immediate Polish surroundings, to prevent being handed over to the Germans. Baptism usually eased the process of obtaining a Christian birth certificate for the child. Baptism also might decide the child's fate, as in the case of Hanka Grynberg. When her foster family learned she was Jewish, her custodian solicited the advice of the local priest. He instructed her to have the girl baptized and take part in first communion, so that she would be seen as a true Catholic and no one would suspect her. The woman did as the priest advised, and Hanka, who had been anxious since her secret was revealed, felt "a sudden sense of relief."[58]

---

56  Sara Avinun, *Rising from the Abyss: An Adult's Struggle with her Trauma as a Child in the Holocaust* (Hod Hasharon: Astrolog Publishing House, 2005), p. 123.

57  Ibid., pp. 123–124.

58  Śliwowska, *The Last Eyewitnesses*, pp. 183–184.

Regina Motyl was about seven when she was placed in the safekeeping of the Kaczmarek family in the city of Chelmno. The simple, God-fearing family loved her very much, and she grew attached to them. They told the neighbors that Regina was a relative, but as pious Catholics they felt it imperative to confess to their priest the truth: that the girl was Jewish. Regina's guardians did not see themselves as missionaries and had no intention of forcing Christianity on the girl. Their hope was that her parents would survive and reclaim her, so that they would not have to decide about her future. But when the time came for her to go to school they decided to baptize her in order to avoid problems when she mixed with the other children.[59]

In most cases, where the foster parents hoped to return the children to their families after the war, the act of baptism was intended to make life easier for the children; to enable them to behave naturally with their Christian friends and not be subject to discrimination. One should take special note of those noble Christian guardians, some of them deeply pious, who despite the prevailing antisemitic atmosphere, refrained from baptizing their innocent wards and from time to time would gently remind them of their origin, so as to help them preserve their identity.

In one of his sojourns on the Aryan side, Alfred Mazeh stayed with a young Polish couple who treated him well and did not mention his Jewishness. To avert suspicion, they took him with them to church every Sunday. However, they did not baptize him, as the grandmother, who lived with them, objected to it.[60]

When the uprising in the Warsaw Ghetto erupted, Martha Elbinger, looking out the window of her foster home, saw smoke rising from the ghetto. She remembers that her guardian, Marianna Rogala, took her to a corner: "Do you know where the smoke is coming from? "Yes," she replied in a whisper, "from the ghetto." "Do you know what your name is?" "Martha Brzezinska," she replied. "But what is your real name?" "Martha Elbinger." "And do you know who you are?" "Yes, I am a Jew." "Always remember your real name and always remember that you are a Jew. But never ever tell anyone."[61]

Jews who hid in the Aryan areas under an assumed identity frequently encountered the deeply-rooted Polish antisemitism. The issue of the Jews might come up in chance conversations between people in the street, on the train or around the dining table at home. The indiscriminate systematic mass

---

59  Testimony of Rivka Yisraeli, (Regina Motyl), OHD, (68)17.
60  Testimony of Alfred Mazeh, OHD, (68)1.
61  Testimony of Martha Elbinger, YVA, M.31/3674.

murder perpetrated by the Germans against Poland's Jews did not soften the hearts of those who were already prejudiced against them. On the contrary: many of them felt the Jews were getting their just desserts.[62]

A self-aware Jewish child living alone with a Christian family would have trouble coping with this attitude. Ringelblum describes one such case:

> I know an eight-year-old boy who stayed for eight months on the Aryan side without his parents. The boy was hiding with friends of his father's, who treated him like their own child. The child spoke in whispers and moved as silently as a cat, so the neighbors should not become aware of the presence of a Jewish child. He often heard the antisemitic talk of the young Poles who came to visit the landlord's daughters. He would pretend not to listen to the conversation and become engrossed in reading one of the books which he devoured in quantities. On one occasion he was present when the young visitors boasted that Hitler had taught the Poles how to deal with the Jews and that the remnant that survived the Nazi slaughter would be dealt with in the same way. The boy was choking with tears; so that no one would notice he was upset, he hid in the kitchen and there he burst out crying.[63]

Not even those who risked their lives for their Jewish wards were entirely free of this prejudice. The children often felt a certain ambivalence in their protector's attitude. On the one hand, the child was loved and the family felt a moral obligation to save him; but at the same time the child felt inferior and contemptible because of the immoral traits that he heard attributed to Jews. Regina Motyl's benefactors, though honest, compassionate and imbued with deep religious faith, were not without prejudice towards the Jews. The family, which did so much for her and put up with her capriciousness, believed that the Jews required Christian blood to bake Passover matzot. It was also here that she first heard the name Judas Iscariot as a synonym for Jewish treachery and ingratitude. It is not surprising, then, that she tried to dissociate herself from her origins. On one occasion a group of Jewish female prisoners was being marched down the street. Regina's guardian called her to the window in case her mother happened to be among them. She refused vehemently, saying, "I have no mother... I am not a Jew and I do not want to see her." Hearing this, the woman crossed herself, reprimanded the girl, and said, "That is no

---

62   Miriam Peleg (Marianska) and Mordecai Peleg, *Witnesses: Life in Occupied Kraków* (London: Routledge, 1992), pp. 9–11, 21–25, 58–59.
63   Ringelblum, *Polish-Jewish Relations*, pp. 142–143.

way to talk. You will be a good Christian, but you must not forget that you were born a Jew and that you had wonderful parents, thanks to whom we took you in."[64]

The Jewish children absorbed the antisemitic atmosphere in the street from their Polish friends, with the result that many of them became little antisemites themselves. Some custodians said nothing, viewing it as a sign that the child was well integrated into the surrounding society and believing that the antisemitism would help disguise his Jewish identity and make him safer. Others, though, scolded the child for disavowing his origins and for becoming part of the vicious atmosphere in the street.

The Schultz family were members of the impoverished Polish nobility in Eastern Galicia. During the war, the family abandoned its estates and fled to Warsaw, where they lived in a small, crowded apartment as refugees, eking out a meager subsistence from smuggling agricultural produce. But despite their plight, they did not forget their Jewish friends, the family of Attorney Winter, who in better days had served them loyally. When Winter's widow, Neta, asked them to rescue at least their little girl, seven-year-old Martha, they sent their youngest daughter, Anna, to distant Czortkow in order to bring the girl to Warsaw, where she became one of the family. Following a brief period of adjustment, she was sent to a good school, in fulfillment of her mother's wish. Martha acclimatized quickly and behaved like a Christian in every respect. The family's faithful maid, Helena Czaplinska, became Martha's nanny. Czaplinska, a pious Catholic, was uneducated and illiterate. She had known Martha's parents well, treated the girl with devotion, and risked her life to save her. During the Warsaw Ghetto uprising the children on the street were happy, because the Jews were being liquidated. Martha too was jubilant, in solidarity with the other children. Seeing this, Czaplinska called her over and hit her — the first time she had ever laid a hand on her — saying, "On the street behave like everyone, but in this house remember that Jews are good people." She reminded her that her parents were Jews and added that one day this hell would be over and she too would go back to being a Jew.[65]

---

64 Testimony of Rivka Yisraeli, OHD, (68)17.
65 Testimony of Martha Goren, YVA, M.31/4071a.

## Who were the Children's Rescuers?

Over the past two decades, sociological and psychological studies have analyzed the character and motives of those who saved Jews. Three of the leading researchers in this field — Nechama Tec, Samuel Oliner, and Eva Fogelman — starting from different approaches, reached a similar conclusion concerning the singular character of these benefactors of Jews. They noted that they were a minority in the population and constituted a special and unusual phenomenon. The reasons for their exceptional behavior lie in their past: in their formative adolescent years, their schooling, the atmosphere at home, and the influence of their surroundings.[66] Tec, whose study focused on the Polish rescuers, found that they were people of independent character who clung to their opinions consistently and did not blindly follow the mainstream. They were free of prejudices and decided on the basis of their own understanding what to believe, which views they could accept, and which social norms they had to reject as being incompatible with their beliefs. They were in fact individualists, even if they were not always aware of this.[67]

Such traits, in whole or in part, were certainly shared by all the rescuers. But those who rescued children where marked by a special sensitivity towards the helpless, and a love of humanity as such. Such feelings arose from a deep-seated humanism which they had imbibed from various sources, be they religious, secular-liberal, or on personal experience based on the credo "Do not do unto others what you yourself hate." These people gave expression to their humanity not in declarations but concretely, in their attitude towards their fellow human beings, through tenderness, affability, and day-to-day human contact. It is not surprising that women often played a decisive role in the rescue of children, because they tend to let their feelings guide their actions.[68]

Nevertheless, the more one studies testimonies concerning the rescue of children by families, the more difficult it becomes to delineate a distinct characteristic. The benefactors differed from one another both in nature and in social background. They came from all walks of life and espoused views that ranged across the entire political spectrum: they were from the aristocracy and from the middle class; workers and peasants; affluent and poor; educat-

---

66  Nechama Tec, *When Light Pierced the Darkness* (New York: Oxford University Press, 1986); Samuel P. Oliner and Pearl M. Oliner, *The Altruistic Personality: Rescuers of Jews in Nazi Europe* (New York: The Free Press, 1992); Eva Fogelman, *Conscience and Courage: Rescuers of Jews During the Holocaust* (New York: Anchor Books, 1994).

67  Tec, *When Light Pierced*, pp. 164, 188.

68  Friedman, *Roads to Extinction*, p. 414.

ed and socially committed, and uneducated and ignorant of the ways of the world; religious and secular; involved in society and alienated individualists; solitary people and those with families. Nor were their motives identical — indeed, no act of rescue was like any other. Some of them were true friends of the children's parents, whose friendship endured even those trying times, but others had no connection with the parents but helped even though they did not know them. What they all shared was a commitment to human life and compassion for the helpless.

To hide a Jewish child in one's family for a lengthy period during the Nazi occupation was not an ordinary act of altruism such as might be performed in normal times. It was, rather, a dangerous adventure of indefinite duration driven by deep commitment but with complete uncertainty with regard to the outcome, the likelihood of success, or the impact on those involved. A close scrutiny of the behavior of those who rescued children shows a certain consistency. Most of them, in addition to the direct care they gave the child, also assisted others in distress. They provided them with shelter, whether temporary or permanent, in their home, referred them to relatives and friends, and obtained documents for them. They were innately tolerant people, who were empathetic to the suffering of others. Most of them were well aware of the dangers they and their families would face should the Germans discover that they were sheltering a Jewish child. Their response, especially when compared to the behavior of most of Christian society in Poland towards Jews at the time, shows that they substantially departed from the prevailing norms and had no hesitation in swimming against the tainted currents of opportunism and antisemitism.

Most of the heroic acts of the rescue of children were carried out by women, and they naturally also bore the main burden of caring for them. Without their initiative, devotion, and readiness to risk their lives, the rescue, particularly of young children, would have been impossible. Among these women were maids and faithful nannies of affluent families who had become attached to their charges and remained loyal to their former employers. An example was Chalkowa, the aged nanny of Eliezer Huterer, who had also been his mother's nanny. During the war, this simple and solitary Ukrainian woman was left without any means of support. Nevertheless, she was determined to save her employers' only child, who was left on his own after his whole family was murdered. With him she wandered the streets of Lvov, taking shelter in the ruins of buildings and subsisting from alms.[69]

69  Testimony of Eliezer Harari, OHD, (68)22.

Some childless families took in a Jewish boy or girl in order to bring a little joy into their home. In almost all cases, they grew attached to the children and decided that if the parents did not survive they would adopt them and raise them as their own. In one case, a Jewish woman who was about to be deported to a concentration camp placed her two-year-old daughter "Krysia" in the custody of a childless mining family in the town of Wieliczka. The toddler's presence in the home stirred the wife's maternal instincts and she adopted her into the family — albeit not formally, but in the hope that the girl would remain with them always. For this reason she also refused to accept support from Żegota, the Polish organization that helped Jews who were in hiding in the Aryan areas (see Chapter 5), claiming that "Krysia is ours." The danger of death that hung over her home for sheltering a Jewish girl did not deter her; she was ready to risk everything for the joy and happiness that the little girl had brought into the house. Her husband, who used to frequent bars with his friends after work, changed his ways: after the girl's arrival he stayed home every evening. After a few months, the girl no longer remembered her real mother and referred to her adoptive parents as "Mommy" and "Daddy." Their happiness knew no bounds. On her own, the woman managed to organize documents for the girl, according to which she was the daughter of a deceased relative; she was clearly intent on adopting her if her mother did not return. When the Żegota activist Miriam Hochberg (Marianska) hinted at the situation that might arise if the girl's biological mother returned, she replied, "I shall never part with Krysia. If it turns out that I have to give her back, I will go with them, wherever they may be, even if it means leaving my husband. If there is no other way out, I shall get a job as a servant."[70]

Among the rescuers were solitary women whose lives had been filled with suffering and loneliness and were willing to risk taking in a Jewish child. For them, the struggle to save the child became the challenge and content of their life. One such story, already alluded to, was that of Leokadia Jaromirska, who took in the abandoned toddler Shifra Junisz and decided to save her and adopt her. Jaromirska led an impoverished existence, yet was imbued with a love of humanity. Before finding Shifra she had known little happiness in her life. She was born into a working-class family and endured a wretched childhood. When she was six years old her mother died and her father remarried, but he too died before she was sixteen. Her stepmother abused her and from an early age she had to support herself. Jaromirska married before the war broke out but her happiness was short-lived. She was unwell and

---

70  Peleg-Marianska, pp. 108–109.

childless when the war erupted. In 1940 she found herself alone again after her husband was arrested and deported to Auschwitz as a political prisoner. To scrape by, she took every job she could find, working as a laundress, a cleaning woman, a maid, and finally in German army storehouses, for a mere pittance. However, material want tormented her less than the mental anguish of depression and loneliness. The three years during which she cared for Shifra were fraught with ordeals. Nevertheless, the girl made her happy and aroused all her maternal instincts. Years later, Jaromirska wrote about the sudden change that occurred in her life because of Shifra and about the happiness she brought in that brutal, bleak period:

> I came home from work a little early every day… Only on Sunday could we be together the whole day. I pampered her and we played together. She began to trust me, and she began to call me "Mommy," and I called her Bogomiła [God's beloved], because God was with her and her fate was not like that of thousands of children, who were murdered in the most cruel way. I lived only with her and for her, and it was as if I had grown wings. My apathy and depression disappeared. I had nothing else to think about, except my Bogushia… When I came home from work she was so happy to see me that I had to hug and kiss her while I was still wearing my overcoat, and only then she let me take it off.[71]

There were also cases of large families that loved children and, unable to abide the distress of neglected children they encountered, took them in. An example was the Milkowski family, a well-to-do farming family from the village of Koczery, near Bialystok. Adolf and Bronislawa Milkowski and their eight children lived in a large home surrounded by a grove of fruit trees. They lacked for nothing. Before the war, Jews from neighboring towns with whom Adolf Milkowski maintained commercial ties often visited his home on business. During the war, too, in contrast to the local peasants, who turned their backs on their Jewish neighbors and cooperated with the Germans, the Milkowskis did not turn their backs on the persecuted Jews. The family made no pretense of being part of the underground, but Bronislawa left pails of soup and loaves of bread in the granary by the house at night so Jews on the run could find something to eat. One cold winter night in 1942, she heard a child crying in the garden next to the house. She ventured out into the freezing night and returned a few minutes later holding a weeping girl of about five — Sara Menshynski, from the town of Drohiczyn. Hungry and freezing, she had reached

71 Jaromirska, "Bogushia," pp. 96–97.

the garden with her last remaining strength, after having been thrown out by a village woman who had taken payment from her mother in return for agreeing to hide her. She was the last surviving member of her family. When she recovered, she wrapped her arms around Milkowska's neck and said her name was Sonia. The Milkowskis decided to let her stay, arranging a place for her in the room of their own little girls, and she quickly became part of the family. When neighbors began to take an interest in the new girl who had suddenly appeared, and to suspect she was a Jew, Milkowska sent her for a time to her sister, who lived in a remote village. After a time she brought her back but did not allow her to leave the house. The children called her "Zosia" and treated her as though she were their sister. The little ones did not know that she was a Jew, while the older children were taught to protect her and hide her whenever Germans entered the area. Sara stayed with the Milkowskis until the end of the war, and even though the couple was no longer young they did not intend to give her up unless someone from her close family arrived to claim her.

Some rescuers were deeply religious and were ready to save children from death even if this entailed mortal danger to themselves and their families. An example, as we have mentioned before, was Zofia Boczkowska, a Polish woman and a devout Catholic from Warsaw who found herself with her family in Eastern Galicia, a region populated largely by antisemitic Ukrainians who abetted the Germans in the mass murder of Jews. Boczkowska was deeply pleased when she succeeded in releasing Hanna Baron from the murderers. At home, she managed to arrange a birth certificate for her in the family name, and to avoid danger the family decided to move to Lvov. "Hanka" was an attractive, good-tempered girl, and the Boczkowskis loved her very much. Until the end of the war they lived in constant fear that someone would identify Hanna and inform on them. Hanna, for her part, was fond of Boczkowska from the very first and made her happy by agreeing to call her "Mommy." She grew up in the Boczkowskis' home until her marriage and was their daughter in every respect. Even after she married and was about to immigrate to Israel she found the separation unbearably difficult. In her diary she wrote, "I can hardly describe the longings for my parents, the separation from my mother. The greatest asset I acquired from her was a love of humanity."[72]

The question of how many children were saved by Christian families in Poland later preoccupied the Jewish public, particularly those who worked

---

72 Testimonies of Zofia Boczkowska and Hanna Podoszyn, YVA, M.31/239.

in order to return the children to the Jewish fold. The numbers that were cited ranged from hundreds, which is too low, to many thousands, which is an exaggeration. To this day there is no clear answer to the question, and probably never will be, as no detailed list of the children was ever compiled, either during the war or afterwards. The lists we have are only partial and refer mainly to those who were placed in various Jewish children's homes in Poland after the war, but do not specify where they were saved.[73] According to an early estimate conducted by the Jewish institutions in Europe, between 2,000 and 3,000 children were still living in the homes of Christian families in Poland at the end of 1945.[74] If we assume that most of the children aged twelve or younger who were rescued in Poland were hidden by families, this estimate appears reasonable.

73 Dobroszycki, *Survivors of the Holocaust in Poland*, pp. 16–18, 93–162.
74 Cable from Storch (Stockholm) to Dobkin (Jerusalem), Nov. 11, 1945, Central Zionist Archives (CZA), S26/1317.

CHAPTER THREE

# Shepherds and *Parobeks* (Farm Hands): The Village as a Refuge

## Polish Villages during the Occupation

U ntil the Second World War, Poland was largely a rural land, dotted with thousands of peasants' villages, home to more than sixty percent of the country's population.[1] Ostensibly, the villages could have been a potential place of hiding for the many Jews who fled from ghettos or escaped from concentration camps. In practice, though, this option appealed to few Jews. According to one estimate, no more than twenty-seven percent of the Jews who survived the war on Polish soil took refuge in the villages,[2] while others cite an even lower figure.[3]

Demographically, Polish Jewry was of an overwhelmingly urban character. On the eve of the war, approximately seventy-six percent of Poland's Jews resided in the towns and major cities.[4] During the German occupation, the few Jews who lived in rural regions were forced into the city ghettos. Being mainly city dwellers, the Jews were more prone to form ties with the urban rather than the rural population. So it was only natural for them when they sought refuge to turn in the first place to their neighbors in the cities. At the same time, many Jews who escaped from the ghettos or managed to jump from death trains in the countryside in desperate attempts to escape the murderous Aktions, asked villagers for shelter, but usually in vain. Many fugitive Jews perished not because the Germans hunted them down efficiently, but because a hostile rural populace spurned their pleas for help and turned them over to the Germans.

---

1   Gross, *Polish Society*, pp. 15–16.
2   Irit Czerniawski, "Polish Righteous Among the Nations" (Hebrew), *Dapim Lecheker Tkufat Hashoa*, vol. 14 (1997), pp. 348–349.
3   Tec, *When Light Pierced*, pp. 117–118, 223.
4   Heller, *Edge of Destruction*, pp. 71–72.

77

Despite the repeated claim in Polish publications that the harsh conditions of the occupation in Poland, as compared with Western Europe, prevented the Poles from doing more to rescue Jews,[5] it would be wise to avoid sweeping generalizations of the Polish population as a monolithic entity in which everyone suffered equally at the hands of the Nazis. In this respect, Poland was no different from the other occupied countries: some sectors of the population suffered more, others less. Overall, the rural regions were affected less than the urban areas. Rural Poland was a vast area lacking a modern transportation and communications infrastructure. Many of the villages were situated far from the main roads and had no electricity or telephone. Most of the German occupation forces — the army, police, and civil administration — were concentrated in and around the cities, and the villages were generally spared their direct presence. The rural population was therefore less likely to feel the boot of the occupiers than city dwellers. Moreover, the population in the countryside had long felt alienated from the Polish government — now displaced by the Germans — which had treated them with disdain or ignored them. It is not surprising, then, that the villagers did not lament the government's ouster and that some initially welcomed the invaders cordially.[6] Indeed, even later, when the occupation continued and Polish enmity toward the Germans intensified, support for the underground remained lower in the rural regions.[7]

For ideological reasons, the official historiography of communist Poland tended to highlight the suffering of rural Poland during the occupation. Postwar documentary literature portrayed the peasants and the working class as the authentic and loyal patriots of the homeland. According to this view, they assisted the Polish partisan movement and sheltered Soviet prisoners of war and Jewish fugitives who had fled to the villages, and were brutally punished for it by the Germans. The well-known Polish historian Czesław Madajczyk, who studied the effects of German terror in Poland's villages, calculated that some 20,000 men, women, and children were murdered in the pacification operations — the reprisal actions perpetrated by German forces against the villagers.[8]

5   Jerzy Turowicz, "Polish Reasons and Jewish Reasons," *Yad Vashem Studies*, vol. XIX (1988), p. 384.

6   Gross, *Polish Society*, pp. 139–140.

7   Shmuel Krakowski, *The War of the Doomed: Jewish Armed Resistance in Poland, 1942–1944* (New York: Holmes and Meier, 1984), pp. 17–19.

8   Czesław Madajczyk, *Hitlerowski terror na wsi polskiej 1939–1945* (Warsaw: Państwowe wydawnictwo naukowe, 1965), pp. 17–19.

Nevertheless, the German policy of suppression, though it certainly did not spare rural Poland, was felt there less harshly than in the cities. German economic exploitation affected all classes in Poland, but again, the situation of the city dwellers was far more acute than that of their rural counterparts. The peasant population experienced no decline in their standard of living; indeed, in the first years of the occupation they actually enjoyed a higher standard of living than before the war. True, the Germans exacted quotas of the agricultural produce (*kontingent*), and young people, like their urban peers, were sent as forced laborers to Germany. However, the villagers were released from debts to Jewish creditors, the Germans were not strict about collecting taxes, and in many cases the exorbitant prices they charged for their farm produce provided them with a higher income, enabling them to buy clothing, furniture, and household objects which were previously luxuries beyond their reach.[9]

Direct rule in the villages remained in the hands of the headmen — the *wójt* and the *soltys* — most of whom retained the posts they had held under the previous government, though there was no shortage of candidates to succeed those who fell out of favor with the new masters. In practice, the headmen were an obedient tool of the German civil administration.[10] The other representatives of the new rulers with whom the villagers came in daily contact were the German gendarmes and their henchmen, the Polish "blue police," or, in the eastern regions, the Ukrainian militiamen, who routinely patrolled the villages in order to demonstrate governmental presence. These forces were sometimes sent to the villages to execute special assignments: to ensure the collection of the farm produce quotas, to hunt down Jews who were hiding in farmyards or in the fields, or to arrest suspected underground activists or ordinary criminals. In addition, a unit of the Wehrmacht — the German armed forces — might be stationed temporarily in a village for training or for some other task. However, it is important to note that there was almost no regular presence of German forces in the villages. Police stations existed only in the cities and towns, and there was often not even a telephone connection between them and the villages under their jurisdiction.

Given the Germans' comparatively lax control in the villages and the sheer size of rural Poland, more Jews could have found refuge there if not for

9  Gross, *Polish Society*, pp. 103–105; Perec Opoczyński, *Sketches from the Warsaw Ghetto* (Hebrew) (Tel Aviv: Ghetto Fighters' House and Hakibbutz Hameuchad, 1970), p. 131.
10  Gross, *Polish Society*, pp. 141–144.

the ingrained antisemitism in most of the villages. Ringelblum described the villagers' attitude toward the Jews facing annihilation:

> The attitude of the rural population towards the Jews depended on the atmosphere that had prevailed in that region before the war. Where rabid antisemitism had prevailed, the attitude of the rural population towards Jews fleeing from the Nazi knife was not helpful. Jewish fugitives from the ghetto would be captured by the rural population and handed over to the Germans for a reward. The village guards, whose job is to fight the partisans, also play a regrettable role, specializing in hunting Jewish fugitives after "resettlement actions." The Jews' only defense against capture by the peasants lies with the armed Jewish groups which are fighting for their survival... Individual Jewish families hide in secret places contrived by peasants in barns, cellars, etc. The German authorities combat the hiding of the Jews by peasants with very severe decrees, which threaten the "red cock" (that is, by having their homes burnt down) for those who disobey, and offer rewards for catching Jews. This campaign against the Jews is linked with the German authorities' struggle against the partisans and against strangers coming to the villages. Fewer and fewer Jews find shelter in the villages. The situation was better in 1940 and 1941, when the peasants employed young Jews as farmhands and treated them humanely... Nowadays a peasant is afraid to give asylum to Jewish fugitives for fear of denunciation... The peasant is sometimes so afraid that he might give the fugitive food but not in his home nor even in the yard but at the edge of the forest. Despite all these rigors and difficulties, there are still quite a number of Jewish families concealed in huts in the villages or in specially contrived hide-outs.[11]

There were indeed peasants who took Jews into their homes and saved them, in some cases paying with their lives for their kindness. The Germans usually found out about such cases from neighbors of the rescuers. In November 1943, German gendarmes raided two homes in the village of Skwary, near Plonsk, removed five peasants and two Jews whom they were hiding, and hanged them all from trees at the edge of the village as an example to the surrounding population, who were made to watch.[12] In general, though, the attitude of most of the peasants toward the Jewish fugitives ranged from indifference to hostility. This is evident from both the testimony of survivors and

11 Ringelblum, *Polish-Jewish Relations*, pp. 203–206.
12 Testimonies on the execution of the villagers, YVA, M.31/4957

from Polish chroniclers, who note the villagers' increasingly harsh attitude toward the Jews precisely in 1942 — the period of the Aktions in which the ghettos in the provincial towns were liquidated.[13]

On November 5, 1942, S. Żeminski, a Polish teacher from the city of Łukow, happened to be in a nearby village and saw peasants buying sickles in the general store prior to a hunt for Jews. He asked them if, like Judas Iscariot, they would be paid thirty shekels for every Jew they caught. An embarrassed silence ensued. But Żeminski got his answer shortly afterward, as he passed through the forest and heard the sound of gunfire as Jews were flushed out and shot. The anti-Jewish fervor that gripped the peasants in that dark period was also documented by a Polish physician, Dr. Zygmunt Klukowski, from the city of Szczebrzeszyn in the Zamość region. The villagers behaved with exceptional brutality toward Jews who fled into the forests and villages to escape the lethal Aktions. They pursued them like beasts of prey, hunting their quarry and murdering them with their own hands or dragged them into the city and turning them over to the Germans. Like the Nazis, these peasants did not see the Jews as human beings but as animals that should be destroyed, like stray dogs and rats.[14]

## The Ways the Children Arrived in Farmers' Homes

Among the Jews who sought refuge in the villages were children, whether with parents or other relatives, or on their own. For the most part these were older children, aged twelve to fifteen, although cases are known of younger children. The difficulties they faced in finding shelter in the rural areas were more complicated than in the cities. Jewish children from the city were markedly different from peasant children. The differences went beyond mere appearances — the Jewish children usually looked more well-cared for than the village children, who grew up close to nature in primitive conditions — and extended to speech, dress, and manners. Indeed, it is difficult to conceive how alien the peasant way of life was to a Jewish child from a bourgeois urban family who suddenly found himself in a rural environment with which he was completely unfamiliar. Survival in this setting depended on adapting

13  S. Żeminski, "Kartki dziennika nauczyciela w Łukowie z okresu okupacji hitlerowskiej," *Biuletyn Żydowskiego Instytutu Historycznego (BZIH)*, vol. *27* (1958), p. 109.
14  Zygmunt Klukowski, *Dziennik z lat okupacji Zamojszczyzny 1939–1944*, (Lublin: Lubelska spoldzielnia wydawnicza, 1958), pp. 294–295, 299.

quickly to the new conditions by invoking every basic instinct, a formidable task that was beyond most children.

The usual way for a Jewish child to find refuge in a village was to be hired by a farmer as a herder or laborer — a *parobek* in the Polish term — who helped with the fieldwork and the household chores. Only older children, aged ten and up, could cope with this, and then only if they knew how to get by in that world, possessed physical stamina, and were able to work hard. Most of the children who fled to villages lived in nearby towns and came from traditional families whose parents were acquainted with the rural population through prewar commercial ties. Even though most of them were not from assimilated homes, they could speak Polish, albeit not with a local dialect. In the eastern regions, where the rural population was largely Ukrainian and Belorussian, only the children of the few families that actually lived in the villages knew those languages. But, occasionally, even children from the big cities who escaped from the ghetto reached remote villages and found a farmer willing to employ them.

The first Jewish children had appeared in the villages in 1940–1941, as the process of herding Jews into ghettos was launched. Most were from families in small towns that were forced into the newly created ghettos and could not make ends meet. To reduce the number of mouths to feed, their parents sent them to farmers with whom they had contacts, to work in exchange for food. At this stage, the mass-murder Aktions had not yet begun and German supervision over people entering and leaving the ghetto was still lax.

Bracha Lipszyc and her family were indigent fugitives when they entered the ghetto of Minsk-Mazowiecki. As the father could not provide for his large family, the children had to help by finding work. Twelve-year-old Bracha found work as a herder in a local village in exchange for food. Every weekend she returned to her family in the ghetto, bringing a bag of food which she had been given by the woman of the house.[15]

Shlomo Atzmon and his family, from the town of Sochaczew, were destitute when they arrived in the Warsaw Ghetto. In the spring of 1941, impelled by the hunger that was rife in the ghetto, he and his older brothers made their way to distant villages in search of work in return for food. Shlomo was eleven years old. He was acquainted with the village he came to: before the war he had accompanied his mother on business trips there, and the local inhabitants knew him. Fortunately, he found a peasant who was willing to

---

15  Testimony of Bracha Wisocki (Lipszyc), YVA, O.3/2777.

employ him as a herder. At the end of the harvest season he returned to his parents in the ghetto, tanned and healthy and laden with produce.[16]

Dora Brick has a similar story. When she was eleven her father sent her to do farm work in return for food, in a village adjacent to the town of Komarow. Every Sunday the farmer she worked for took her to the ghetto to visit her parents. The villagers knew she was Jewish and her employer did not try to hide the fact. However, the situation changed abruptly in the summer of 1942, when the Aktions in the nearby towns and cities intensified. One day the soltys, the village headman, came to the farmer's home and demanded that he expel the Jewish girl. His wife, who had become attached to the girl, was very sorry, and cried when they parted, but was compelled to send her away.[17]

The flight of Jews from the provincial towns and cities to the villages and forests began in earnest in 1942, during the Aktions to liquidate the ghettos. In these circumstances, the decision to flee the ghetto was almost always spontaneous, and made in an atmosphere of every person for himself. In some cases parents told their children to escape by themselves, to wherever they could, and to try to save their lives on their own. Many children left their family on their own initiative and found a place to hide for a short time, or managed to escape from the railway stations or the death trains. Afterwards, they roamed the fields and forests near the villages, seeking food and shelter, while all around them people were literally hunted down. They fled the terror of death with no thought of a specific destination. In these conditions, even adults with experience of the world could barely function rationally, and children, of course, still less. They simply followed their natural survival instincts.

In the autumn of 1942, Golda Ryba, a twelve-year-old girl, found herself wandering alone in a village near her hometown of Sokolow Podlaski. She had reached the village after the Aktion in which the ghetto was liquidated. She had been rounded up together with the rest of her family and taken to the site where the Jews were concentrated for deportation, but her mother decided that she would arrange her daughter's escape come what may. Little Golda had what was known as a "good" appearance — light hair, blue eyes — and she spoke Polish well. Her mother stuffed money into the girl's coat lining, covered her head with a kerchief to give her a peasant look, and told her to make for her aunt's place of hiding in the ghetto. At first Golda refused, fearing to

---

16  Shlomo Atzmon, *I Won the Bet* (Hebrew) (Tel Aviv: Moreshet, 1992), pp. 27–29.
17  Testimony of Dora Kislowicz, (Brick), YVA, O.3/3109.

be separated from her family, but her mother and her grandfather pushed her away. She reached her aunt's dwelling, only to find it vandalized and abandoned. At a loss, she left the ghetto and crossed to the Aryan side, with no specific destination in mind. Finally she went to the home of the family's former neighbors, a Christian family, but they would not let her even cross the threshold. With no other choice, she left the city and walked toward an area of villages. Towards evening, she lay down to sleep in a field, exhausted. When she awoke in the morning, wet from dew and shivering with cold, she encountered the owner of the field, who had known her grandfather. He agreed to let her stay for the day and work in the field in return for food. At dusk she entered the barn to sleep and found several Jewish families hiding there. No one took the slightest interest in her and they would not even share a blanket for protection against the cold. Golda slept on the bare floor and toward morning set out again. After a day of wandering, she reached another village, not far from the city from which she had fled. She knocked on the door of a peasant's home and told her story to the man who answered. It turned out that he too had known her family. He gave her food and let her stay for a few days, until the neighbors noticed her and she again had to leave.[18]

With minor variations, Golda's story is also that of other children with similar backgrounds. Their common theme is the experience of abandonment and alienation they endured in a situation of helplessness, cut off from parents and home. Ejected from their surroundings, they roamed the countryside with no clear goal, hunted like defenseless animals. Indeed, even children who had escaped from the ghetto together with their parents soon had to part from them, as a group hampered mobility, particularly if there were elderly people, small children, or infirm. A group was also less likely to find refuge and food in a village. Under these extreme conditions, families were separated: parents were lost, children left behind, brothers and sisters parted, and everyone had to fend for themselves.

Having been compelled to leave the peasant home in which she had worked, Dora Brick set out alone for the town where her family had lived. On the way, passersby told her that the ghetto no longer existed and cautioned her against falling into the hands of the Germans. She then met a Jewish girl of her age who was on her way to join her family, who had fled to a local village, and suggested that Dora accompany her. Through the night the two girls made their way to the village on foot, often losing their way, and shivering with cold and fear. Finally, before dawn they reached the village and

<hr/>

18   Testimony of Golda Ryba, YVA, O.3/2734.

found the house where the girl's family was hiding. Dora asked if she too could stay with them, but they refused. Exhausted, she lay down to sleep, and when she woke up they had gone. She continued to wander from village to village, begging for food, and at night slept under haystacks in the fields. Eventually she reached the forest and there by chance met up with her older brother, who was hiding with a group of Jews. In a state of utter despair, he told her that their whole family had been murdered and that only the two of them remained. He advised her to leave the forest and try to save herself on the Aryan side in the city, mentioning a friend of theirs who was in hiding in Zamość with Aryan papers. Dora begged him to let her stay with him, her only living relative, but he would have none of it. Abandoning her, he fled into the depths of the forest.[19]

Even in the conditions that prevailed during the flight from death, this is perhaps an extreme example of the rejection that some children encountered, particularly as it involved a blood relative. Yet it is not exceptional. The liquidation of the ghettos was a terrible ordeal for the fugitives, who sought refuge in villages, fields, and forests. In addition to the frequent Aktions in the ghettos, when the Germans rounded up and systematically murdered most of the inhabitants, they also cast a wide net to catch those who had fled into the forests and villages, organizing manhunts with the aid of the local population. These operations intensified at the end of 1942 and the beginning of 1943. Most of the fugitives were turned away by the local population and forced to hide in the open, where they were exposed to the heavy rains of autumn and the bitterly cold winter of Eastern Europe. Exhausted by the relentless hunts, battered by the harsh climate, few Jews survived in the countryside. The hardships were greatest for children who suddenly found themselves alone and forsaken, trying to survive in a brutish world they did not understand and for which nothing had prepared them. It is clear from their testimonies that this period of wandering from one village to the next confronted them with the most grueling obstacles in their ordeal. In some cases they were on their own for weeks or even months before finding shelter in a peasant home. This was the most critical period, both physically and mentally, for survival.

Shlomo Atzmon, after leaving the Warsaw Ghetto and escaping from the inhospitable and threatening city, found himself roaming the countryside between villages and trying to find farm work. He was intimately familiar with Polish winters, but the unusually cold and stormy winter of 1942–3

19  Testimony of Dora Kislowicz, YVA, O.3/3109.

would become indelibly engraved in his memory. Icy winds, dry and biting, made even breathing difficult; the peasants wrapped themselves in furs and the children stayed home from school. The entire world seemed to be in deep freeze. Shlomo scurried from village to village and from house to house, craving a warm corner. In contrast to the previous year, no one offered him shelter. Only a compassionate few allowed him in for a few hours and expected him to be gone quickly. In their eyes he saw fear mixed with hostility that seemed to burn into the very marrow of his bones. As far as these people were concerned, every Jew could die. Drifting alone between the villages, feeling forsaken by God and man, Shlomo mustered all his remaining strength to survive. He recalled that punishing winter in his memoirs:

> As I wandered I sank into the deep snow and my wet clothes froze and then thawed on my flesh, without my being able to dry them. I was seized by apathy and even cast caution to the winds. I spent the nights in haystacks situated in fields far from the farms. The method was to tear away straw and dig a hole to crawl into. I stuffed my body inside, with only my head sticking out, so I would not suffocate should the haystack collapse. The dogs sensed my presence, and their frightening barking was unavoidable. I had to find some object to defend myself against the more vicious animals. Despite the barking, I would fall asleep for a few hours out of sheer exhaustion. I was not alone. The entire community of fugitives tested the limits of human endurance.[20]

The fugitives generally wandered between villages close to their hometown, in a radius of not more than ten to fifteen kilometers, making their way on foot. Sometimes a passing farmer took pity on them and let them ride on his wagon. Automobiles were all but unknown in the rural areas, and only a few of the older children were audacious enough to board a train in order to get away from their home town, where they might be recognized and handed over to the authorities.[21] Most of them remained close to their home, and were constantly drawn to it as a moth to light, in the hope of finding a surviving relative or even Christian neighbors and acquaintances who would feed and house them. At first, some were not fully aware of the danger and made no effort to conceal their Jewish identity. In their distress they implored every passerby for help, hoping to arouse their compassion.

In that terrible winter, eleven-year-old Moshe Frank, who was com-

---

20  Atzmon, *I Won the Bet*, pp. 74–75.
21  Testimony of Alexander Sarel, YVA, O.3/5538.

pletely alone, plied the roads between the villages around his hometown of Zamość. Among the compassionate people who gave him refuge in their home was a solitary elderly woman who fed him and let him warm himself a little by her stove. Seeing his condition, she said, "Poor boy, how hungry you are, how you shiver with cold. You have no chance of escaping the clutches of the sadistic Germans. If not today, they will execute you tomorrow. Why go on suffering? Go to them and ask them to kill you, and so put an end to your torment!"[22]

Unlike the children whose parents had placed them in the custody of Christian families and provided them with a cover story and a false identity, and who learned how to behave like Christians under the tutelage of their adoptive parents, the children who fled to the villages on their own were totally unprepared for life in this completely alien environment. Few of them had Aryan papers, and if they had not previously been taught how to behave like Christians, they were instantly identifiable as Jews. Nor could they wander about for long without food and shelter. They needed someone to tutor them in the ways of village life.

Moshe Frank, no longer able to wander in the fields and villages because of the bitter cold, decided to return to Zamość. At dusk he entered the home of his Polish neighbors, the Zacharow family. Despite his ragged appearance they recognized him immediately as "the grandson of Senderowa," their friend of many years. Although knowing the danger they faced should anyone recognize the boy, they received him cordially, reassured him, cut his hair to remove the lice and dirt, let him wash, exchanged his filthy clothes for new ones, and tried to prepare him for the future. Moshe had Aryan features, but to ensure that he would not arouse suspicion by his behavior, Helena Zacharow taught him Christian prayers and gave him a crucifix to wear around his neck. The family was afraid to shelter him for a lengthy period, but taught him how to pass for a Christian. By the time he left their home, he had an assumed Christian identity, though he had no documents. He took the name of a Polish acquaintance in whose home he had hidden for a time. According to his cover story, he was from the nearby village of Mokre and had been left on his own after his parents were deported to Germany. With a child's naïvety, he did not imagine how easy it was to check the veracity of his story and uncover his true identity.[23]

22 Moshe Frank, *To Survive and Testify* (Hebrew) (Tel Aviv: Ghetto Fighters' House and Hakibbutz Hameuchad, 1993), p. 62.

23 Ibid., pp. 62–63.

The events that befell Golda Ryba, in different surroundings but under similar circumstances, recall Frank's experiences. Immediately after the liquidation of the ghetto in Sokolow Podlaski, Golda wandered among the villages in the area, telling the peasants that she was the granddaughter of a shopkeeper whose customers they had been, and asking them for food and lodging. Some of them gave her a slice of bread and let her spend the night in the barn, others set the dogs on her. Despite the many dangers she confronted, she failed to grasp that by revealing her Jewish identity to the people she met she was effectively sentencing herself to death. Naïvely, she believed that her grandfather's name would protect her. On one occasion, a farmer who allowed her into his home and gave her a little bread, asked her who she was. She told him she was Jewish and related her experiences. Surprised at her frankness and fearlessness in revealing her identity after all the Jews in the area had been murdered, he cautioned her, "If they don't kill you, our people will." The farmer gave her a Polish name, devised a cover story for her — that she was a Polish orphan from distant Posen — and provided her with a new identity. Another Polish family — acquaintances whom she used to visit before the war — taught her how to pray and gave her a prayer book and a pendant of the Holy Mother. With the little money she had, they bought her shoes and a kerchief so that she could pass for a village girl.[24]

In the spring of 1943, following the liquidation of most of the ghettos, the Germans scaled down their hunt for Jews in the countryside. The Polish expanses were largely Judenrein, and the mass murder of Jews tapered off to some extent. Although Jews in hiding continued to be exposed by informers, the hunt for fugitives stopped. The enthusiasm of the villagers with regard to fleeing Jews also abated to some degree. The majority of the Jews had already been caught, denounced, and murdered, and the rest were in hiding. Some of them found refuge with farmers or in the forests, others found various kinds of work in the towns and villages thanks to forged Aryan papers. In the summer, working hands were badly needed in the fields, along with herders and household help. More possibilities to work were now available for the Jewish children who had managed to survive the winter and possessed an assumed Christian identity.

Bone-weary after months on the road, Moshe Frank reached the village of Dębowiec, about twelve kilometers from Zamość. Using the cover story of a Christian boy, and with the experience he had gained in staying briefly with several peasant families and helping them with the household chores, he

---

24 Testimony of Golda Ryba, YVA, O.3/2734.

was finally hired by Jan Huk, a farmer. He and Anna, his wife, were poor and childless. Even though Moshe arrived during the winter, when there was no work for him, the couple took him in out of a sense of compassion, and in the hope that in the spring he would assist them with the farm work and take the cows out to pasture. They gave the weak and exhausted boy time to recover. The couple lived with Jan's widowed sister-in-law in a ramshackle one-room hut, but despite the crowded conditions they found a corner for Moshe by the stove and tried to make him feel at home. The Huks were devout Catholics who prayed regularly and attended church on Sundays and holidays. They followed a way of life of simple, modest tillers of the soil, and their humane attitude derived from their deep religious faith gleaned from the stories of the New Testament. Moshe learned the Christian prayers by heart and familiarized himself with Christian rituals. He became part of the family and was treated warmly. Jan Huk in particular was kind to him, as he, too, had been orphaned as a boy and had to work for a living from an early age.[25]

## The Life of a Jewish Parobek under an Assumed Identity

The rural folk who gave the wandering children work generally did so for purely utilitarian reasons. In most cases either their own children had already left home or were too young to help with the farm work. Young mothers with small children welcomed the opportunity to have an older girl watch over the children and help them with the housework and with the animals, enabling them to assist their husband in the fields. There were also affluent farmers with large holdings who needed temporary help, particularly during the critical harvest season, collecting potatoes, and with the everyday work in the farmyard.

The children who were hired worked hard for their living. Adjusting to village life and to the demanding farm work — even to herding animals in the pasture, which was not overly strenuous — did not come easily to Jewish children with no previous experience. Shlomo Atzmon, who was not a pampered boy — he grew up in a working-class family of artisans — and knew what hard work was before living in a village, describes the arduous period of "apprenticeship" that he endured on one of the farms. After putting him up for two days in their home, the peasant and his wife, a young couple who lived in poverty even though they worked hard, decided to let him stay on in

25  Frank, *To Survive and Testify*, pp. 67–68.

order to work as a herder in the summer. Until then, they worked him hard in fertilizing the fields. The couple hurled the manure out of the barn with pitchforks, and Shlomo's job was to load it onto the wagon. The manure was heavy and it was hard to separate the clods. The adults worked at a murderous pace, while he, an eleven-year-old boy, stood on the growing mound of manure, unable to keep up. As they worked, the man and woman taunted Shlomo for his ineptness and told him in a moralizing tone that a person had to work hard to survive. Only the intercession of the man's aged mother, who saw the boy's plight, put a stop to the couple's abusive behavior. The woman was a pious Catholic, and though she was sensitive to Shlomo's suffering, she knew he was a Jew and believed that the Jews must suffer for crucifying Jesus. "What happened to the Jews is the Redeemer's will," she would reiterate, "and no one can defy fate."[26]

Girls, too, worked hard. Irit Kuper was about twelve when she was given work by a farming family in a village near her hometown of Minsk-Mazowiecki. Her cover story could have come straight from a fairy tale. She told the family that after her mother had died her father had remarried, but the stepmother was cruel to her, made her do backbreaking work, and starved her, leaving her no choice but to escape and look for work in the villages. The young woman who hired her seemed pleasant enough. But Irit quickly discovered that the cordial exterior concealed a hard, tyrannical woman. On the day after she hired Irit, the woman woke her up early to begin a long, exhausting workday. The girl had to get up before dawn every morning and was given no respite until late in the evening. "Feed the chickens, water the cows, feed the hogs, chop the wood, wash the dishes, faster, faster, hurry up," she admonished her. Nevertheless, Irit, glad just to have the protection of a roof over her head, did not complain.[27]

Driven by force of circumstances and the will to live, the Jewish children adjusted to village life and to the onerous work that was demanded of them. In fact, they had a certain advantage over their Christian counterparts who did not show the same loyalty to their employers and did not, unlike them, slip away if they did not like the conditions, particularly in the harvest season when work was plentiful everywhere. The Jewish children longed for a little stability in their lives, having nothing to cling to outside the home of the peasant for whom they worked. Accordingly, they were industrious and loyal, so

26  Atzmon, *I Won the Bet*, pp. 64–65.
27  Irit Kuper, *At the Edge of the Forest* (Hebrew) (Tel Aviv: Hakibbutz Hamuechad, 1977), pp. 50–51.

they would not be dismissed after the harvest season. Indeed, in most cases, if no special problems arose and their true identity was not disclosed, they were allowed to remain during the off-season as well, so both sides benefited.

The peasant who employed the boy Jozef Leichter considered him industrious and loyal, and then discovered that he was a Jew. Jozef, who was from the village of Medynia Gloskowa, near the city of Lancut, eventually reached the village of Nowy-Borek, where he was hired under an assumed identity by Jan Trojanowski, a farmer. Trojanowski did not question Jozef about his origins, and the boy peacefully took the farmer's three cows out to pasture and helped with the farm work. One day, Trojanowski came home and told Jozef that an acquaintance had told him he was a Jew and that the subject was common knowledge in the surrounding villages. He demanded that Jozef tell him the name of his native village, so that he could ascertain his true identity. He also took the occasion to test Jozef about Christianity, a test Jozef passed. The headman of Jozef's village told Trojanowski that no family bearing the name the boy cited had lived there.

One evening, Trojanowski was summoned to the headman of his village to consider what should be done with Jozef. The boy waited anxiously for his return, making plans to escape that night if they decided to turn him over to the police. To his relief, the man came back and told his mother that the boy was indeed a Jew, but that nevertheless he intended to keep him, because he was a diligent worker. The headman, he said, had advised him to hide the boy. When it became known in the village that Jozef was a Jew, the local youths threatened to denounce him to the police, but Trojanowski did not back down and allowed him to stay. However, he no longer sent him to the dairy with the milk, to avoid provoking the villagers. The peasant and his mother treated Jozef well, as he was a better worker than the Polish boys they had employed previously. Impressed by his devotion, they did not abandon him but decided to let him stay, despite the danger.[28]

The case of Jozef Leichter is not, of course, representative, but it sheds a different light on the development of relations between the peasants and the Jewish parobeks. The peasants' attitude was not uniform and was influenced by numerous factors, such as their neighbors' reaction and the perceived level of risk. In the last analysis, though, personality and temperament were crucial. The testimonies show that there were rural folk whose independence of mind and high moral standards were a bulwark against the general antisemi-

---

28  Jozef Leichter, in Maria Hochberg-Marianska and Noah Gruss, eds., *The Children Accuse* (London: Vallentine, Mitchell, 1996), pp. 69–72.

tic atmosphere, and who were not deterred from continuing to shelter a child even after they found out he was a Jew, as long as he was loyal, industrious, and likable. Even if fear got the better of them and they felt compelled to remove the child from their home, they did not turn him over to the authorities and even tried to find an alternative refuge.

In the course of wandering between villages, Shlomo Atzmon was hired as a herder by the three generations of the Wozniak family who worked their farm. According to Atzmon's testimony, this family demonstrated exceptional kindness. Never before had he encountered anyone like them. When they hired him, they did not ask about his origins and believed his cover story. Atzmon, for his part, was a diligent worker, and in return was treated like one of the family. One day they learned that he was a Jew. The grandmother came out to the pasture in a panic and berated him, "Karol [his Polish name]... You fed us lies, and we ignorant farmers believed you!" Abruptly his world disintegrated and he was at a loss to know what to do. He realized that in the light of the new situation, with his Jewish identity uncovered, the family was in great danger. Disconcerted, he said, "Mrs. Wozniak, you and your family owe me nothing. I am sorry I was forced to lie to you, but I had no choice. The little goodness and rest I gained with you are due to my lie. Now I will leave you and find a place where people do not know me."

Nevertheless, the family did not evict him. The next day, the grandmother sent him to her son, who lived in a nearby town. "Stay there for a time," she said, "until the troubles end and people forget you, and then come back. We have nothing against you; we wanted to adopt a boy — his religion didn't matter to us. But there are people who are different from us, who cannot bear to see other people happy."[29]

The son received him well but would not employ him, because the secret had become known and he was afraid to lodge him in the house. However, he sent him to another village in the area, where hired hands were needed. As Atzmon walked through the village, he suddenly heard a voice, "Boy, come here!" Atzmon walked over to the house where the shout had come from. The farmer understood at once that he was a Jew, but it did not deter him. He told Atzmon frankly that he was not motivated by compassion, but simply needed a herder for the summer. "I know we are taking a risk, but we will pretend that we did not understand. Take care not to stand out, and if I am pleased with you, maybe you can to stay with us until all the troubles are over."

The man worked him hard throughout the harvest period. As the work

29  Atzmon, *I Won the Bet*, pp. 79–84.

tapered off, the farmer told him that the season was over and he was no longer needed. To underscore the point, he added, "The situation is dangerous, people are babbling, and the whole area is in an uproar." Nevertheless, he did not demand that Atzmon leave immediately, and he had a linen suit made for him as payment for his work. But one day, he said, in no uncertain terms, "Tomorrow you must leave us." And so, once more Atzmon found himself roaming the countryside, looking for work and a roof over his head.[30]

Rural life in Poland — in contrast to Western Europe — was quite primitive. At this time, the homes of the country folk were small wooden or mud huts of one or two rooms, and a kitchen with a stove for cooking. There was no running water, no electricity, and no indoor plumbing. Village families were based on a patriarchal structure, and the crowded intimacy of the household left little room for privacy. The entire family — three generations in many cases — was crammed into these small houses: the head of the household with his wife and children, the aged maternal or paternal parents, and perhaps also an unmarried brother or sister. They all slept and ate together. Some farmers co-opted the parobek to the family, giving him a place to sleep on a bench in a corner of the kitchen or on the stove, and letting him eat with the family at the same table and perhaps from the same bowls. Others, though, housed the boy in the barn or some other structure, and made him eat separately. Over time, and if a close relationship had developed between the boy and his employers, and if he was a loyal and diligent worker, they paid him in the form of used or even new clothing, and treated him well.

The farmer Jan Huk was too poor to provide Moshe Frank with clothes or shoes, but he taught him how to make brooms and household items from wood, which he could then sell in the market and use the money to buy what he needed. After he had saved up enough money in this way, the day arrived when Jan's wife, Anna Huk, went to the market in the city and bought him a pair of shoes with wooden soles, so he would not have to walk barefoot in winter. Jan Huk took a fatherly attitude toward Moshe and allowed him to attend the village school. When Moshe returned from the pasture in the morning, Jan let him off work so he could get to school on time.[31] From the information we have about the life of Jewish children in the villages, this was undoubtedly an exceptional gesture. Few farmers treated their hired hands as Huk treated Moshe Frank.[32]

30 Ibid., pp. 86–89.
31 Frank, *To Survive and Testify*, pp. 68–70.
32 Testimony of Dora Kislowicz, YVA, O.3/3109.

Shlomo Atzmon, too, was treated decently by some of the farmers he worked for, particularly by the Wozniak family, all of whose members showed him kindness. Their village was imbued by a quiet, pastoral atmosphere, and there were no Germans: one could even forget that a world war was raging. The family took him into their home and even let him sleep in the same bed as their own son, rather than in the usual quarters — a cowshed or barn. Shlomo soon became friends with the little boy and, indeed, gained the love of the whole family. They clothed him and saw to his needs, as though he were their son. Shlomo worked with all the family's members, and the imaginary freedom he suddenly experienced affected him powerfully. With the self-confidence he acquired in the Wozniaks' home, he was able to join in the company of the village boys, as though he were one of them.[33]

In general, the attitude taken by the peasants towards a stranger in their midst was a function of their character, their personal background, and the relations within the family. Various testimonies show that peasants who had themselves endured a difficult childhood — losing their parents, growing up poor, being raised by strangers — were more likely to be considerate to the parobek in their home. Jan Huk's humane treatment of Moshe Frank has already been described. Golda Ryba, too, was treated well by her employer. No longer young, he had been orphaned early and felt an obligation to be kind to the girl. On Sundays he took the animals to pasture himself, so she could spend time with girls in the village. His wife, however, was an antisemite who had felt from the beginning that the girl was Jewish. She made Golda's life miserable, giving virulent expression to her Jew-hatred. "Leprous Jew-girl, if it weren't for me, the lice would have eaten you already," she shouted at her. She exploited her mercilessly, burdening her with ceaseless work. After an arduous day in the fields, the twelve-year-old girl had to feed the animals in the yard and milk the cows. But this was not enough for the woman. She woke Golda up at night to haul buckets of leftover food to the pigs. The husband saw how she abused the girl but could not get her to change her ways. He tried to cheer the girl up, urging her to ignore his wife. Golda, for her part, had no choice but to stay with this family, where she had a roof over her head, until after liberation.[34]

Village life, though usually tranquil and offering many advantages for the Jewish children who took refuge in them under assumed names, also posed a danger of which they were not always aware. In these close-knit provincial

33   Atzmon, *I Won the Bet*, pp. 79–81.
34   Testimony of Golda Ryba, YVA, O.3/2734.

farming communities, where everyone knew everyone else, envy and enmity that often prevailed between families sometimes led to situations in which innocent children were the indirect victims. In a society in which there were no secrets and past accounts were never fully settled, children from the outside could not long remain anonymous. Sooner or later, in the intimate conditions of village life, the question of the outsider-child's identity was raised, and not necessarily by the German authorities. True, as we have seen, direct supervision by the Germans was more lax in the rural areas, but was not altogether absent. For example, the village headman was under instructions to check the documents of every newcomer who took up lodgings in the village and report to his German superiors accordingly. Not all the headmen meticulously reported on everyone who passed through the village, particularly in the case of Christian fugitives and homeless individuals who happened to stay briefly in the village. However, in cases of suspected Jews, the headmen were usually more rigorous, on the ground that if the Germans found out that Jews were hiding in the village they would mete out collective punishment. Thus, if the headman noticed a new hired hand staying with a local resident, he would demand that the stranger identify himself. If the child had no papers — as was almost always the case with the Jewish children who wandered among the villages — the employer was told to get rid of him or he would be reported to the authorities.

In April 1943, Golda Ryba was hired as a herder in the village of Niemirki Snow was still falling, but winter was nearing its end and the farmer decided to employ her, in the meantime assigning her various farm chores. After having wandered for months from one village to another, Golda believed she had at last found a true haven where she could work quietly. However, her presence immediately piqued the neighbors' curiosity. Despite her "good Aryan appearance," they suspected that she was Jewish. Her employer wanted her to stay and at first denied the allegations and tried to persuade his neighbors that the girl spoke good Polish and had nothing to do with Jews. Golda heard the whispers but pretended they did not concern her and continued to act the part of a Polish girl from Poznan. She attended church every Sunday and even made confession. One day, a neighbor who knew Poznan questioned her about her family and her home there, and concluded that her story was false. Quickly he spread the word that she was an impostor and undoubtedly a Jewess. Shortly after, her employer returned home angry one evening after a meeting of the village residents with the headman in which Golda's identity was discussed, and demanded that she admit to him that she was a Jewess. The villagers were determined to expose her true identity, he said, for fear that someone would inform on her to the Germans and the whole village would go up in flames. Golda denied the suspicions and allegations. To her good fortune, the headman died suddenly, and there the matter ended. However, the suspicion that she was a Jew hung over her throughout her stay in the village.[35]

Irit Kuper underwent a similar though more serious experience. When the farmer who employed her was told by friends that she was Jewish, he told her that he would hand her over to the Germans; and would even be rewarded. Irit begged him not to act rashly and promised to bring him a document attesting to her Christianity. She returned to her native city and in her despair asked the priest for a birth certificate, based on the names of her supposedly Christian parents. After being unable to find the name in the church records, the priest evidently understood the situation and told the girl to come back the following day. When she returned, he gave her a birth certificate in the name of a girl born out of wedlock. The peasant took the document to the village headman and came home happy and cheerful. From that moment, he no longer considered Irit to be Jewish, but an illegitimate Catholic girl.[36]

There were cases of decent headmen and priests who took pity on wandering Jewish children and tried to persuade villagers not to turn them over to the Germans. Some took a risk and turned a blind eye to documents they knew were false, or even supplied such documents themselves.

One day in 1942, Danuta Winnik and her seven-year-old son, Eugeniusz, who had been incarcerated in the Warsaw Ghetto, arrived in the village of Niezabitow, in the Lublin district, posing as Polish fugitives. Despite their "good" appearance, the local residents suspected they were Jews. However, the village priest, Father Jozef Gorajek, intervened and took the boy under his protection. He baptized him and prepared him for his first communion together with all the village children his age, signifying that he was a member of the community. The villagers protested that it was wrong for a Jewish child to have communion, but the priest silenced them and asserted that the boy was a Christian and therefore had the right to communion. It was only because the priest wielded his religious authority, at the risk of his life, that the villagers relented and allowed mother and son to remain in the village.[37]

It was easier for a girl who looked Aryan and had a good command of Polish to impersonate a Christian than it was for a boy, and by the same

35  Ibid.
36  Kuper, *At the Edge of the Forest*, pp. 88–93.
37  Testimony of Eugene Winnik, YVA, M.31/4298.

token, local residents found it more difficult to prove definitively that she was Jewish, even if she had no papers. This was the situation in cities, and certainly in rural areas. After all, not even all the homeless Christian children who roamed the countryside had birth certificates. In the case of boys, their true identity could easily be determined by seeing if they were circumcised. This was the constant fear that haunted Jewish boys in the Aryan areas and in rural districts in particular. It was difficult to hide the fact of their circumcision from the members of the household they lived with or from the village children they encountered in the pasture. Eros was not absent from the intimate way of life in the villages, and sex games among the children in the pastures were commonplace.[38]

In his memoirs Moshe Frank described the initiation rite for a new herder in the pasture, in which the veteran boys would pull down his trousers and make him lie on a teeming ant nest. Fear of this rite haunted Frank: for him it was a matter of life or death. By means of various ploys he managed to avoid being subjected to the rite, but the trauma remained with him for the rest of his life. And although he succeeded in hiding his Jewish identity from his peers in the field, he could not conceal it from the farmer and his wife. Moshe afterwards learned that they had noticed that he was circumcised and hence a Jew. They had consulted secretly with trustworthy relatives and friends about what to do. The danger they faced in sheltering a Jew generated an argument on the subject, but the Huks insisted that Moshe must under no circumstances be handed over to the Germans. They also made everyone swear to keep the matter secret and decided to go on behaving as though Moshe were a Christian.[39]

Against the background of this tranquil, pastoral village setting, it is difficult to imagine the anxiety, tension, and loneliness that marked the life of Jewish children posing as Christians. They were cut off almost completely from the outside world, and until the liberation, subsisted on rumors that they picked up from the peasants' conversations. The world seemingly closed in on them. Some of them gradually assimilated into the village community, but those who were suspected of being Jews were persecuted and lived in constant dread within their divided world, from which they saw no escape.

Golda Ryba, who was always suspected of being Jewish, described her complex relations with her village friends. As a girl, she craved peer society and made friends with local boys and girls. However, she did not always like

38  Frank, *To Survive and Testify*, pp. 71–72.
39  Ibid., p. 107.

to spend time with them, because her closest girlfriend, of all people, branded her a "leprous Jewess" when she became angry at her. Still, she notes that in time she acquired friends among the villagers, who pitied her as a poor orphan girl and protected her from her tormenters. Nothing attests more acutely to how cut off and isolated she was from events outside than the fact that she remained in the village as a herder until 1947, three full years after the liberation of Poland.[40]

We do not know how many children fled to villages and how many survived there under assumed identities as herders or farmhands. Given the harsh consequences of attempting to escape and the difficulties of integrating into village life, compounded by the hostility of most of the villagers toward Jews, there were probably not more than a few hundred.

---

40  Testimony of Golda Ryba, YVA O.3/2734.

CHAPTER FOUR

# The Street Children

J ust as some children fled to rural regions and found a haven in villages as herders or farmhands, others made their way to the Aryan side of the big cities and hid there as street children. The phenomenon of Jewish street children who struggled to survive in the midst of the urban population was most prevalent in Warsaw. It was documented by Joseph Ziemian in his book *The Cigarette Sellers of Three Crosses Square*.[1] There were Jewish street children in Kraków and Lvov as well, but they were far fewer in number.

Jewish street children first appeared on the streets of Warsaw immediately after the ghetto was sealed and the inmates' economic distress became even more acute. According to the testimony of Adolf Berman, the director of Centos, an institution that assisted children in the Warsaw Ghetto, the majority of the ghetto's approximately 100,000 children suffered from hunger and deprivation. About eighty percent of them were in urgent need of welfare aid.[2] The young poet Henryka Lazowert wrote a touching poem on the cruel fate of "The Little Smuggler," the child who smuggles food in from the Aryan side in order to save his parents from dying of starvation and is gunned down by SS guards at the gate of the ghetto.

> Past walls, past guards
> Through holes, ruins, wires, fences
> Impudent, hungry, obstinate
> I slip by, I run like a cat
> At noon, at night, at dawn
> In foul weather, a blizzard, the heat of the sun

1  Joseph Ziemian, *The Cigarette Sellers of Three Crosses Square* (Hebrew) (Tel Aviv: Moreshet and Sifriat Poalim, 1968) (English edition: London: Vallentine, Mitchell, 1970). The quotations cited are from the Hebrew edition as the English is incomplete.
2  Adolf Abraham Berman, *In the Place Where Fate Sent Me* (Hebrew) (Tel Aviv: Ghetto Fighters' House and Hakibbutz Hameuchad, 1977), p. 92; Opoczyński, *Sketches from the Warsaw Ghetto*, pp. 99–114.

A hundred times I risk my life
I risk my childish neck.

Under my arm a sack-cloth bag
On my back a torn rag
My young feet are nimble
In my heart constant fear
But all must be endured
All must be borne
So that you, ladies and gentlemen,
May have your fill of bread tomorrow.

Through walls, through holes, through bricks
At night, at dawn, by day
Daring, hungry, cunning
I move silently like a shadow
And suddenly the hand of fate
Reaches me at this game
It will be the usual trap life sets.

You mother
Don't wait for me any longer
I won't be coming back to you
My voice won't reach that far
Dust of the street will cover
The lost child's fate.
Only one grim question
The still face asks –
Mother, who will bring you bread
Tomorrow?[3]

Amazement and admiration was the response of people who encountered these solitary children trying to survive in the streets of the city, and the phenomenon was recorded by contemporary chroniclers.[4]

In the Warsaw Ghetto, where most of the food came from smuggling, children occupied a special place in the vast ring of smugglers. They searched

3 Ringelblum, *Polish-Jewish Relations*, p. 148.
4 Abraham Levin, *From the Notebook of the Teacher from Yehudiya* (Hebrew) (Tel Aviv: Ghetto Fighters' House and Hakibbutz Hameuchad, 1969), pp. 23–24, 45; Ringelblum, *Polish-Jewish Relations*, pp. 146–150.

out small breaches in the ghetto walls and with their diminutive size and agility could get through them more easily than adults.[5] The majority of the little smugglers came from families that had lost everything and were in dire economic straits, with the children replacing nonfunctioning parents as providers, or they were orphaned children who had to support themselves. The most daring of them slipped through to the Aryan side, where they were more likely to find scraps of food to keep them alive than in the starvation-wracked ghetto. Individually and in groups, the ragged beggar children roamed the streets. Sometimes compassionate people gave them a slice of bread or a worn garment, but more often they were chased off like stray dogs. In the most fortunate instances, they would by chance knock on the right door and be invited in for a hot meal and allowed to stay for the night. Most of the street children were from the city and knew its alleys and byways, and those from fugitive families familiarized themselves in the course of roving its streets. While the ghetto still existed, most of the street children brought their booty back to it. Shlomo Atzmon, who was a beggar in the city's unfamiliar streets before turning to the rural areas, describes his experiences:

I tried my luck at begging. The reactions were often scorn, curses, threats, and kicks to my fleshless bottom... My beseeching fell on deaf ears. Still, not all the Poles were wicked. Here and there the inhuman atrocities and humiliations, which were perpetrated in the full light of day, touched a human chord, and I was offered meager fare — and not necessarily from the rich. One time I went into the tram workers' restaurant. It was late afternoon. The place was warm and well-lit. The diners were smoking and drinking, and their conversation sounded a happy note. My entrance riveted their attention. Silence descended and they all fixed their gaze on me. They did not probe me or ask questions. One of the workers who was eating there took me by the hand and led me behind the counter on which the cash register stood. I waited. I was afraid he had gone to summon a policeman or a German gendarme. To my surprise, he returned with a package wrapped in a cloth and tied in a knot. He handed me the package and took me out by a side door, saying: Go, boy, and tell no one you were here.[6]

5   Israel Gutman, *The Jews of Warsaw 1939–1943, Ghetto, Underground, Revolt* (Bloomington: Indiana University Press, 1982), pp. 69–70.
6   Atzmon, *I Won the Bet*, pp. 48–49.

The onset of the transports from the ghetto was disastrous for the street children who were among the first to be sent to annihilation. The few who were on the Aryan side decided not to return to the ghetto, or if they did return they seized the first opportunity to escape back again. Some children who returned to the ghetto after scrounging for food on the Aryan side discovered that they had no one to return to: their parents had been transported to their death, their home no longer existed, there was no one to look after them, and they had no place to hide. In the meantime, they had become familiar with the streets of the city and knew there was more room to maneuver there and a better chance to hide than in the ghetto, the days of which were numbered in any case. Some children managed to contact Christian acquaintances who were prepared to hide them, and getting there became their primary task. Other street children still had relatives in the ghetto, but they were unable to shelter them and they urged the children to get back to the Aryan side.

Joseph Lev was one of the smuggler children in the Warsaw Ghetto. He grew up in Polish surroundings and was familiar with the way of life of the Christian children. After the Germans murdered his father in the ghetto, only his mother and younger sister were left, and Joseph became the sole provider for the destitute family. At the age of ten he started to smuggle food from the Aryan side into the ghetto. One evening he returned to the ghetto but found no one at home. His aunt told him that his mother and sister had been seized in an Aktion and urged him to go back to the Aryan side and not return to the ghetto. She dressed him in warm clothes, gave him five zlotys, and sent him out into the unknown. As they parted, she said, "Remember that you have an aunt."

The next day, Joseph slipped out of the ghetto to the Aryan side, but did not know where to turn. After a day of roaming the streets he reached the suburb of Praga, on the far bank of the River Vistula. At dusk he bought an ice cream at a kiosk and prepared to spend the night nearby. But he could not sleep because of the cold and his longings for his mother and sister. He felt utterly alone. He did not know how to deal with this feeling, but he knew he could not return to the ghetto, as there was nothing to return to. The next morning, he spent his last remaining money on bread. After another day of wandering he encountered a group of Polish street youths who were drinking liquor. Joseph had no papers. Before leaving the ghetto, he was told that if he were asked who he was he must not say he was from Warsaw but that he was a refugee. When the Polish youngsters asked him who he was and where he came from, Joseph told them he was Janek Sadowski, using the Polish name he had adopted, and said he was an orphan from Poznan whose parents had been killed. "So come and work with us," the boys told him, and nicknamed him "Kajtek." He quickly became part of their gang of thieves and black market operators: a fully-fledged street boy.[7]

Adina Schweiger, a young physician who worked on the Aryan side in Warsaw as a liaison for the ZOB (*Żydowska Oragnizacja Bojowa* — "Fighting Jewish Organization,") encountered the Jewish street children after the ghetto's liquidation and tried to help them. In her memoirs, she retained a fond place for these children. With deep emotion she recounts the thrill of meeting them:

> On the Aryan side, wandering children sold newspapers. This is a magnificent episode in itself — how the newspaper vendors hid their younger colleagues. I cannot offer a description, because I do not know exactly what their hiding places amid the ruins on Miodowa Street looked like — the "guardians" would not let anyone come near these havens. Yes, they said, we trust you, but you will have to do as we say. Thus, at a specified time I would arrive at an agreed heap of ruins and wait. It was always after sundown. Then, suddenly a great commotion began. Small creatures emerged from holes like so many mice. They approached me and let me pat them. The eldest of them took the money and the few sweets I had managed to buy for them, and just as they had appeared — so they disappeared, again like mice, noiselessly. I never knew where and how... My contact with the street children of Warsaw imbued me with a degree of happiness. There were moments when I forgot that I was an outsider and I would pretend that I shared in the suffering of these creatures, the victims of the war: their suffering touched the heart. These children did not know what it meant not to feel hunger, and they lived without a home and without the care of parents. I became close to them. Some of them were mature — that is, an early, cruel maturity which deprived them of their youth.[8]

It should be noted that the Jewish street children who appeared on the Aryan side during and after the ghetto's liquidation were not a mass phenomenon. Beyond the difficulties of escaping from the ghetto, few such children were capable of surviving on the city streets. Prolonged solitary self-preservation in the city under an assumed name called for a level of maturity that required

---

7    Testimony of Joseph Lev, YVA, O.3/3540.
8    Adina Schweiger-Blady, "On the Aryan Side of Warsaw" (Hebrew), *Edut*, vol. 4 (1989), pp. 43–72.

the child to see to his basic needs by finding food and a place to sleep; shelter from the weather; maintaining personal hygiene, which involved washing, doing laundry, and occasionally changing underclothing to avoid disease and ward off lice. He had to know his way around the city, be familiar with its streets and alleys, its transportation system and train stations. He needed knowledge of the way of life in the city and the capacity to fight for his life in a cruel setting of extreme alienation compounded by the dislocation of war. All this called for physical strength, intelligence, and the mental agility to deal with challenges. The street child had to be capable not only of assessing the dangers he faced at every turn, but also how to extricate himself from them. Accordingly, the average age of the street children was between twelve and fifteen, similar to that of the children who worked on farms, but older than those who were sheltered by families. In the terms of the period, they were considered youths in every respect, and sometimes more. There were also a small number of younger children, but they almost always needed the protection of the older ones. Children of ten and below usually had a short lifespan on the streets: if there was no one to place them in an orphanage or in the home of a Christian family, they were all but doomed.

The first time Joseph Ziemian, a member of the Jewish National Committee on the Aryan side, met the group of child cigarette sellers at Three Crosses Square, they seemed to him younger than they actually were. It was only after he got to know them that he discovered their true age. One boy whom he thought was about ten turned out to be thirteen, and most of them were older. Of the ten or so children in the group, only two were very young — seven and nine. The older children looked after them and protected them from harassment by Polish street children, but they were a bothersome burden. Their first request to Ziemian, after he had secured their trust, was to take the little boy and find him a safer haven. Ziemian found a Polish family who agreed to hide the boy for payment.[9]

The city's streets were hardly an empty space waiting expectantly to welcome Jewish ghetto children. The only way a lone Jewish child could survive in the streets was by becoming part of an existing gang of street children or by joining forces with another child in the same predicament and struggle for survival together. Jewish street children required traits similar to those of their Polish peers, namely an Aryan appearance, a credible cover story, good knowledge of Polish and above all fluency in the language of the streets. For the Jewish children, life in the streets did offer one advantage: they did not

---

9  Ziemian, *The Cigarette Sellers*, pp. 15–17, 24, 95–99.

have to prove that they were familiar with Christian religious customs. No one noticed or cared whether they attended church on Sunday or went for confession. The qualities they needed, rather, were agility, toughness, shame-lessness, guile, and a healthy dose of street smarts.

Life on the streets, brutal and harsh, followed the laws of natural selec-tion, and few Jewish children possessed the necessary traits to survive. The struggle for a living in conditions of a chronic shortage of basic commodities was taxing for everyone, and the will to survive validated every skill, legal or illegal. Because the street children lacked the cash to speculate in valuables, they resorted to selling cigarettes and newspapers, shining shoes, and doing occasional hauling jobs. Some of the black-marketeers employed the street children to deliver smuggled goods or sell *bimber* — the Polish home-brewed illicit liquor.

Nevertheless, many Jewish street children preferred the streets of the city with its heterogeneous population and extensive fringe population — the homeless, refugees, fugitives, beggars and prostitutes, as well as children who found themselves on the street because of family and social reasons. From this standpoint, Warsaw was unique in Poland: a true metropolis in Central Euro-pean terms, with a population of over one million. Amid this teeming mass one could disappear and remain anonymous. Thus, many Jews throughout Poland who hid in the Aryan areas under an assumed name were drawn to Warsaw. On the other hand, however, it was the capital, where the bulk of the country's political and underground activity was concentrated, and the Nazi occupation authorities exercised rigorous supervision. The streets crawled with uniformed and plainclothes police together with agents of various kinds whose mission was to keep subversive elements and black market speculators under surveillance and root out Jews in hiding. The many German soldiers who came to Warsaw on leave and frequented the places of entertainment also did nothing to put the local residents at their ease. The situation was further compounded because Warsaw was also the capital of the Polish crimi-nal underworld, whose members lacked all moral inhibitions. They had been denizens of the city in normal times as well, but during the occupation they flourished. The phenomenon of the blackmailers — the *szmalcowniki* — who specialized in identifying and denouncing Jews in hiding, was more wide-spread in Warsaw than in other cities.[10] These extortionists endangered every Jew they encountered, nor did they show any mercy to children.

10  Peleg-Marianska, *Witnesses*, pp. 148–152.

The Jewish street children operated mainly in the busy public areas — the squares, the train stations, the public parks, and at sites of leisure activity, such as cinemas, cafés, and restaurants. There they positioned themselves and offered their wares to passersby. Among their clients were German soldiers.[11] At the same time, these sites were the areas where policemen, both uniformed and undercover, were particularly vigilant in the hunt for suspected black marketeers. Little boys and girls, including Jewish street children, were often seen in cafés and trams singing popular melodies of the period, hoping for a handout from diners and passengers. Jonas Turkow, who hid on the Aryan side, describes his chance meeting with a Jewish girl, a street singer, while she was "performing" on a Warsaw commuter train:

> I sat deep in my seat: here I am, a Jew from the ghetto among merry non-Jews with no worries... Suddenly the voice of a young girl was heard in our car. The singer, who was aged about ten or twelve, was gifted with a sweet alto voice. She sang Polish patriotic songs wonderfully, and anti-Hitler songs that the Poles liked to hear. As such, she endangered her life. The Polish passengers in the car were of course delighted to hear songs against the hated occupation, and from every direction coins were thrown to the little songstress. When the light-haired young singer approached me, holding a tin bowl in which she kept the coins and bills, I struck up a conversation with her. I asked her how business was and what her parents did... A shiver ran down the girl's body and her large blue eyes misted over. "My father and mother were murdered by the accursed *Schwabs* [Germans]. I was left alone in the world. It's lucky I know how to sing," she said and gave me a forced smile... I understood she was Jewish, even though you couldn't tell by looking at her... Some time later, I asked a number of people who took smuggled goods via the Radzymin commuter train if the charming girl was still singing in her lovely alto voice for the passengers on the Warsaw-Praga-Radzymin-Marki line. The answer was extremely sad. The girl was shot to death in Radzymin. Apparently, informers told the Germans that she was Jewish.[12]

The street children were especially attracted to train stations for peddling their wares of cigarettes and newspapers. Because the stations were heated

11  Ziemian, *The Cigarette Sellers*, pp. 15–19.
12  Jonas Turkow, *The Glorious Children of the Ghetto* (Hebrew) (Tel Aviv: Eked, 1982), pp. 34–35.

they were particularly advantageous on cold winter days, when they provided shelter from the biting cold outside. The constant flow of people in the station also helped the children remain anonymous. However, because the stations were key junctions through which the Poles smuggled black-market goods and food products, they were closely supervised by the occupation authorities. Policemen were present here more than in other public places, checking papers and searching luggage. In addition, the train stations, like the streets around churches, were where the Germans would seize young people for forced labor in Germany. The searches and manhunts imperiled the Jewish street children who happened to be there at the time. Although they were not the main objects of the hunt, they might be discovered by chance during a check of papers or in a body search. The Jewish street children were well aware of the danger that lurked due to the efforts to stamp out the black market, and when they sensed that they were under police surveillance, they boarded the first available train and disappeared.[13]

Like their Polish counterparts, the Jewish street children generally circulated in groups or pairs. The company of others was very important as it provided a degree of mutual safety and helped dispel loneliness. Moreover, a group could stand up better to harassment by Polish street children, who were entirely unsympathetic to the Jews' intrusion into their territory, and hounded them and sometimes tried to steal their wares. Among the Jewish children, solidarity generally prevailed. Even if they were not working together but only met on the street, they usually recognized other Jews and exchanged information about possible sources of livelihood and places to sleep.[14] However, such idyllic relations were not always the rule. The cruel war of survival on the street sometimes generated competition for buyers and caused tension between the children, leading to the break-up of partnerships. In some cases, friends who shared the same fate and had left the ghetto together had to go their separate ways.

Avraham Blim, from Kraków, was thirteen when he and his friend Wilk made a plan to escape to the Aryan side. Avraham, an experienced smuggler, knew what to expect. He was familiar with the street children's special way of life from the period when the ghetto was still intact. At that time, he regularly traveled on the trains and smuggled in various items for his father and older brother, who lived in the ghetto. In March 1943, Avraham and Wilk escaped via the sewers from the Kraków Ghetto just before its liquidation. They based

13  Testimony of Avraham Blim, YVA, O.3/2221.
14  Ziemian, *The Cigarette Sellers*, pp. 82–91.

themselves in the train station, but had no papers of any kind. After watching Polish youths selling cigarettes in the street, they decided to try their luck in the same trade. To raise money, they had to sell the few items they had brought with them from the ghetto. With the proceeds they bought cigarettes and started to sell them to passersby. They were soon making money. But Polish youths soon began to harass them and force them to pay protection money, threatening that otherwise they would denounce them to the police. But the young Poles were not satisfied with just that. One day, when Wilk went to the "Square of the Jews" to buy a stock of cigarettes, Polish youths attacked him and took both the cigarettes and the money. He and Avraham were left penniless. In the wake of the incident they quarreled and parted. Avraham survived, but Wilk was later seized by the police and his fate is unknown. Avraham did not remain alone for long. After working for a time as a porter, helping railway passengers with their suitcases, he joined forces with a Polish youth and together they sold cigarettes on the Kraków-Warsaw train.[15]

It was advantageous for a Jewish child to join up with Polish street children. To begin with, the group provided cover, reducing suspicions of Jewish identity. Also, the partnership might open up new possibilities of making money and creating new outlets for the child's wares. Even more important, forging ties with new people meant finding safe places to stay — with friends and relatives of the new Polish friends. This was all positive as long as the Polish youths did not discover that their new comrade was a Jew.

The group that Joseph Lev joined started to suspect he was Jewish when he avoided going to the public bathhouse with them. In one of their games they pulled down his trousers, saw that he was circumcised, and decided to turn him over to the Germans. Joseph pleaded for his life but they started to drag him to the Gestapo offices. He managed to get away, jumped onto a tram, and disappeared. For a time he wandered the streets alone, until he found a job with a circus. At first he helped handle the horses. Afterwards, one of the magicians took him under his wing and trained him to be his assistant. Joseph enjoyed three good months, but one day the magician left and Joseph was again alone on the streets. Not for long, though: returning to the train station, he again joined a group of Polish youths who had a business bringing newspapers from Warsaw to the annexed territories. Joseph spent days and nights on the trains, until he was caught by the police and beaten. He lost all his money and barely survived. After being separated from the group, he again joined forces with a Polish boy. The two sang on the streets

---

15 Testimony of Avraham Blim, YVA, O.3/2221.

and with the money they earned were able to buy enough food to ward off hunger. The difference was that Joseph, unlike his Polish friend, lived in constant fear that his Jewish identity would be discovered.[16]

Polish street youths did not always denounce their Jewish comrades to the authorities. In some cases a degree of solidarity developed between them. It was not the same solidarity that existed among the Jews, but occasionally the Poles displayed tolerance and even respect for the Jews' courage and their tenacity in the face of adversity. Henryk Meller hid for a time on the Aryan side in Kraków, where he was one of the street children who sold cigarettes for a living. According to his testimony, he made enough money to allow himself to dress properly and eat well and even attend the cinema in the evening. The local Polish youths viewed him as an equal, and if they were short of stocks would shout to him, "Jew-boy, give us a Sport" (the brand of the cigarettes). They knew he was a Jew but respected him and did not inform on him.[17]

A serious problem that the Jewish street children suffered from was that they had nowhere to go in the evening to rest from the day's exertions, meet friends, eat a hot meal, wash, change clothes, and sleep. The summer nights could be spent in the ruins of destroyed buildings or in doorways or public parks. But on the long, cold, wet winter nights a warm place to sleep indoors was the dream of every Jewish street child. Those with Christian friends went to them occasionally and asked to spend the night in their home, but in most cases they were turned away.

While hiding on the Aryan side, Joseph Lev often knocked on doors and asked the occupants to give him shelter. If they identified him as a Jew they would send him packing, saying that because of him the Germans were liable to burn the house and deport the family to Germany.[18] The cigarette sellers from Three Crosses Square found shelter with "the grandmother," a poor, elderly woman who let them sleep in the loft of her wretched apartment. At first she did not ask for payment, but after learning that the children were Jews she took a small sum, a few zlotys each night.[19] Henryk Meller also found accommodation with an elderly woman. She knew he was a Jew but let him sleep in her house for twenty zlotys a night — not an excessive amount in the prevailing conditions.[20]

---

16  Testimony of Joseph Lev, YVA, O.3/3540.
17  Hochberg-Marianska and Grus, *The Children Accuse*, p. 66.
18  Testimony of Joseph Lev, YVA, O.3/3540.
19  Ziemian, *The Cigarette Sellers*, pp. 45–47, 60–63.
20  Hochberg-Marianska and Grus, *The Children Accuse*, p. 66.

To maintain personal hygiene, the Jewish street children washed in houses where they slept for payment or in public bathhouses. The cigarette sellers from Three Crosses Square went as a group to wash themselves and their clothes at the "Gigant" on Jagelonska Street, a hostel for the homeless which had a public bathhouse. To avoid being seen naked, and thus having their Jewish identity discovered, the boys adopted self-important airs and gave the guard a bribe to keep others out while they were bathing.[21]

Injury or illness posed an acute danger for the Jewish street children, as they could not get medical treatment. Among the Jewish street children in Warsaw were two sisters, Stefcia and Marysia Szurek, aged fourteen and nine, respectively. For months they roamed the streets, earning money by singing in public places and spending the nights in the homes of women they met by chance. But because of Stefcia's distinctly Jewish appearance they constantly had to find new places to sleep and often spent the night in ruined buildings. At one stage they met a Polish girl who took them to her grandmother's home, where they slept on the floor. They were able to make a fair living from their singing in the streets, enough to support them as well as the Polish girl and her grandmother. Unfortunately, Stefcia contracted typhoid fever and pneumonia. They were afraid to call a doctor, and the old woman was scared the girl would die in her home and that the authorities would discover that she had been sheltering Jews. Over the pleas of the younger sister, she insisted that the sick girl leave the apartment. Marysia took her sister to a children's hospital, where she left her by the door of the waiting room and ran off. Stefcia was examined and transferred to a hospital for infectious diseases, where she recovered. After being released from the hospital she rejoined her sister and the two resumed their street singing.[22]

This incident ended well, because the patient was a girl and the hospital staff could not know that she was Jewish. If it had been a boy he would probably not have been admitted to the hospital.

From that point of view, then, Jewish girls had an advantage over Jewish boys, particularly if they possessed an Aryan appearance: people did not inform on them, as they could not be certain of their identity. On the other hand, street life was more difficult for the girls, owing to the absence of hygienic conditions and because they were easy sexual prey for pimps and extortionists who swarmed the streets. The girls who as adults wrote memoirs

21  Ziemian, *The Cigarette Sellers*, pp. 20–21.
22  Ibid., p. 47.

or gave testimony shied away from this aspect of life in the streets, but the problem posed a constant threat. Often a "patron" would harass a girl on the street and try to impose his will on her or invite her to spend the evening with him, and she would have to defend herself by force.[23] Therefore the girls made every effort to find work with families as maids or nannies. However, such positions required Aryan papers, which were usually unobtainable.

Bracha Lipszyc found herself on the streets of Warsaw in the summer of 1943, when she was aged fourteen. Vigorous and independent, she was experienced in life on the Aryan side. She first worked in a village and then was sent to work in a steel factory outside the city of Minsk-Mazowiecki. There she became a messenger for a group of Jewish forced laborers in the plant, liaising between them and their families in the Warsaw Ghetto. To this end, she made her way to the ghetto by train, posing as a Pole. Despite her capabilities, she had a difficult time when she was forced to be on her own in the streets of Warsaw. Her only wish was to find a room to hide in and get through the night. She recalled her experience of three months as a street girl in her testimony:

> Homeless, I wandered about in places where there was movement — train stations, markets. Despite my appearance, I was always hounded. Once, when I was standing on a main street, someone came up to me, chuckling, looked me in the eyes, and left. Then he came back and looked at me again. I understood that he already knew me. My clothes were not clean and I was unkempt. When a tram went by I jumped on to it and through the window I saw that he was angry because he had lost me. That was a common experience.

In her despair, Bracha returned to Minsk-Mazowiecki and sought help from a Polish lawyer whom her aunt had known. He refused to shelter her in his home but provided her with a Christian birth certificate and referred her to a Polish family in Warsaw, which hired her as a maid.

Despite the multiple dangers and the harsh conditions of life on the streets, the children rarely hid in closed shelters. Some of them had already gone through that experience in the ghetto and preferred to live in the open air. They relied on their acting ability and on their nimble legs not to betray them when danger loomed. In one of her meetings on the Aryan side of Warsaw, Vladka Meed saw a youngster of about twelve selling newspapers on a street corner. If one of her Jewish friends had not pointed him out from a

23  Testimony of Bracha Wisocki (Lipszyc). YVA, O.3/2777.

distance as a Jew, she would never have identified him as such. He looked just like a little Polish newspaper vendor in every respect. His clothes were old and tattered, his wrinkled hat was pulled down over his ears, and he wore large, shapeless shoes: a street child of the most abject sort. His behavior, his confident declaration of his wares, and his demeanor were indistinguishable from those of his Polish peers. As she bought a paper from him she whispered that she was from the Jewish Aid Committee. He spoke like an adult, tersely and to the point. Finally, she asked him whether he wouldn't prefer to be in a hiding place, to be paid for by the committee. But he turned down the offer: a hiding place frightened him and he had no desire to be caged and to tremble at the slightest noise. He did not want to perish like his parents. He would rather remain on the street, where he was free and could make his escape when danger loomed. The street made him feel at home, he told her. Of the Jews that Meed met during this period, he was the only one who seemed to be without fear.[24]

The question of the fate of the cigarette sellers from Three Crosses Square was discussed at the time by the Jewish National Committee on the Aryan side in Warsaw. Some thought that they should be dispersed and taken in small groups to different locales, rather than concentrating in the square. Others said they should be left where they were, as their employment, appearance, and behavior concealed their origins quite well. In the end, the Committee decided not to break up the group and to leave the children where they were, in the surroundings they had chosen and adapted to, and not to alter their way of life but only to provide them with Aryan documents. Their personal details were taken down, and Batya Berman, the wife of Adolf Berman, saw to it that they received false birth and school certificates. Although these documents could not save their lives, they provided them with a little more self-confidence and allowed them to behave more freely, at least when in the company of their Polish counterparts.[25]

Not all the Jewish street children in Warsaw remained there until the liberation. Some left the city in the summer of 1944, just before the eruption of the Polish revolt or afterwards, and found shelter in villages as herders and farmhands. Others were absorbed with Polish children in institutions for the homeless run by the RGO, the Polish welfare organization, and remained there until liberation.[26]

23  Meed, *On Both Sides of the Wall*, pp. 253–254.
25  Ziemian, *The Cigarette Sellers*, pp. 23, 100–101.
26  Testimony of Avraham Blim, YVA, O.3/ 2221, testimony of Joseph Lev, YVA, O.3/3540.

The struggle for survival waged by the street children, which was the continuation of their struggle in the ghetto where they had learned how to beg and smuggle food, was extraordinary. Only the bravest among them could cope, and a mere handful of children and youths survived in this way in the big cities, particularly Warsaw, Kraków, and Lvov.[27]

---

27 Ziemian, *The Cigarette Sellers*, p. 124. Ziemian, who discovered the group of cigarette sellers and assisted them through the Jewish National Committee, lists twenty-one children from the group who survived.

CHAPTER FIVE

# The Rescue of Children by the Żegota Organization

## The Establishment of Żegota

T he systematic annihilation of Polish Jewry began in the summer of 1941, when German forces invaded the Soviet Union, and it reached its peak a year later with Operation Reinhardt. City after city was emptied of its Jewish inhabitants, who were led to slaughter as their Christian neighbors watched. Throughout this period, the Polish underground did not speak out, did not protest the mass murders, and did not call on the Polish population to assist its Jewish citizens. It is true that some Poles, among them members of the underground movement, did not remain indifferent and tried to help the condemned people. However, they did so at their own initiative, at the urging of their conscience, not in the name of the underground. All that concerned the leaders of the underground at the time was whether the Germans would turn their wrath against the Polish people in general after disposing of the Jews, and if so, how they should respond.[1]

It was not until the beginning of August 1942, at the height of the mass deportation of the Jews from the Warsaw Ghetto — when hundreds of thousands of men, women, and children were herded on to trains in the heart of the capital and sent to their death in Treblinka in the face of the indifference of the Christian population — that the first leaflet decrying Polish apathy appeared. It was issued by the Front for Reborn Poland (*Front Orodzenie Polski* — FOP), an organization of the young Catholic intelligentsia, which was a part of the general underground movement. The leaflet's author and leader of the FOP, the prominent Catholic writer Zofia Kossak-Szcucka, had no particular empathy for Judaism, nor for the Jews. Her negative opinion did not change even now — for her, the Jews remained an alien, hostile presence —

---

1  Gutman and Krakowski, *Unequal Victims*, pp. 70–71.

but her Christian conscience was stirred by the events. It was concern for Poland's moral image that prompted her to protest the Polish people's bystander attitude as hundreds of thousands of innocent people created in God's image were transported openly to their extermination, without the Poles lifting a finger to try to save them:

> This silence can be tolerated no longer. No matter what its motives are, it is abominable. Those who remain silent in the face of murder become [the] murderer's accomplices. Those who do not denounce it — condone it. We, Catholic Poles, do speak out. Our feelings toward the Jews have not changed. We still consider them as political, economic, and innate enemies of Poland... But we are not prepared to be [Pontius] Pilates. We are incapable of actively resisting German murders, we cannot help in anything, we cannot save anyone, but we do protest from the depths of our hearts, filled with compassion, indignation and dread. It is God who demands that we protest, the God who forbade killing. Christian conscience demands it... The blood of the innocent cries to the heavens for revenge. Those who do not join us in this protest are not Catholics... The forcible participation of Polish people in the bloody spectacle which is being realized on Polish soil may well engender indifference to wrong and sadism, and, above all, the dreadful conviction that the murder of fellow human beings is permissible. Those who refuse to understand this, those who would dare to link the proud free future of Poland with the abominable joy at the misfortune of one's neighbor, are therefore neither Catholics nor Poles.[2]

The publication of this protest by Polish conservative circles that were connected with the church and the army[3] shocked the Delegatura — the political leadership of the Polish underground — out of its silence. On September 17, 1942, it too issued a statement of protest through the Directorate of Civil Resistance:

> The tragic fate that befell the Polish people, decimated by the foe, is now compounded by the monstrous, planned slaughter of the Jews that has been carried on in our country for nearly a year. These mass murders are without precedent in the history of the world, and all the cruelties

2  Jan Blonski, "Polish-Catholics and Catholic-Poles: The Gospel, National Interest, Civic Solidarity, and the Destruction of the Warsaw Ghetto," *Yad Vashem Studies*, vol. XXV (1996), p. 183.
3  Prekerowa, *Konspiracyjna Rada*, p. 52.

known to man pale beside them… Unable to counteract these crimes, the Directorate of Civil Resistance protests in the name of the entire Polish nation against the atrocities perpetrated upon the Jews. All Polish political and civic groups join in this protest.[4]

With its official imprimatur behind it, this statement paved the way for the creation of an organization to assist the Jews, which was known by its code-name of Żegota. On September 27, ten days after the Delegatura statement had been issued, Kossak-Szcucka established the temporary committee of Żegota. She herself had no opportunity to work for the organization: immediately after its establishment, she was arrested by the Germans and deported to Auschwitz, where she was imprisoned until July 1944. However, after her release she resumed the underground work with all her passion, working to organize havens in convents for Jewish children.[5]

The central figures on the temporary committee were Wanda Krahelska Filipowicz, a democratic activist with roots in the Polish socialist movement that antedated the First World War, and the attorney Ignacy Barski, a conservative Catholic activist who was no friend of the Jews before the war but was moved by their calamity to find ways to rescue them, even at the risk of his life.[6] No representative from the major underground organizations joined the committee. Those who initiated the creation of Żegota represented three underground groups of relatively minor importance: the Catholic Front for Reborn Poland, the Democratic Party, and the Syndicalists. Still, this was an impressive turn of events, as these groups had never had anything to do with the Jewish public before. They represented not so much the broad strata of the Polish public, but rather a small segment of the country's elite: the enlightened and conscience-driven Warsaw intelligentsia. The tasks undertaken by the Żegota temporary committee were:

(a) To make contact with the Jewish public in order to provide financial aid.
(b) To find housing and sleeping accommodation for those fleeing the ghettos.
(c) To furnish the Jews with clothing, food, and employment.

4   Stefan Korboński, *The Polish Underground State: A Guide to the Underground, 1939–1945* (New York: Hippocrene Books, 1981), p. 125, cited at www.ucis.pitt.edu/eehistory/H200Readings/Topic4-R3.html.
5   Adolf Berman, "Jews on the Aryan Side" (Hebrew) in *Encyclopedia of the Jewish Diaspora*, Poland Series, Warsaw, vol. I (Jerusalem: Encyclopedia of the Jewish Diaspora, 1953), p. 689.
6   Ibid.

(d) To supply them with appropriate forged papers so they could pose as Aryans.

The temporary committee launched its work in and around Warsaw, with the intention of then extending the operation to other cities where Jews still remained. However, the plan was partially derailed due to a dearth of volunteers and the organization's meager resources.[7] The Delegatura, while recognizing and supporting the temporary committee, allocated only 50,000 zlotys a month for its activity[8] — merely a token amount, given the organization's many missions and the thousands of Jews who sought refuge on the Aryan side in Warsaw alone during the period of the mass transports. The temporary committee held its first meetings in October 1942, following the mass deportation from the Warsaw Ghetto. One of the subjects on its agenda was the role of Jewish representatives in the nascent organization. The Catholics maintained that the Jews should act as liaisons between the committee and the ghetto and the Jews in hiding on the Aryan side, as well as representing the interests of the general Jewish population. At the same time, they argued, the committee must be of a purely Polish character. The view of the Jewish representatives was that Żegota should represent the entire population, Poles and Jews alike, and that their representatives should enjoy full and equal rights in the organization.[9] The political significance of this was clear: to ensure the rights of the Jews and their equal status in the Polish underground movement — a radical change from the period when the Jews were seen as an inferior minority which received aid by grace, not by right. However, the combined effect of the position adopted by the Jewish representatives and the financial shortfall was that the Żegota temporary committee fell apart.

In the wake of this, an agreed alternative plan was devised, under which an expanded council with a broader public base would be formed. On December 4, 1942, a broad Council for Aid to Jews — Żegota (*Rada Pomocy Żydom — Żegota*) was duly established. Its members came from the center and leftwing parties that were subject to the authority of the London-based government-in-exile. The attorney Julian Grobelny ("Trojan,") was appointed chairman of the organization and held the post until he was arrested by the Gestapo in February 1944. Grobelny, a veteran activist in the Polish Socialist Party, the PPS (*Polska Partia Socjalistyczna*) in Łódź, had evinced special

---

7   Bartoszewski and Lewinóna, *Ten jest, z ojczyzny mojej* (Kraków: Znak, 1969), pp. 941–942.
8   Berman, "Jews on the Aryan Side," p. 689.
9   Ibid., p. 691.

sensitivity to the rescue of Jewish children from the very start of his work in Żegota.[10] His deputies were Tadeusz Rek, from the Peasant Party, and an attorney, Leon Feiner, from the Bund. Adolf Berman, from the Jewish National Committee, who until October 1942 was the coordinator in the Warsaw Ghetto of Centos, the Society for Children's Welfare, was appointed permanent secretary of the Żegota Council and did much within its framework to rescue children. Another loyal and devoted official in the organization was Irena Sendler, known by the codename "Jolanta." She joined the organization upon its establishment and was appointed head of the children's division. The Delegatura was represented by Witold Bienkowski and his deputy, Wladysław Bartoszewski, the youngest of the group, who was from the Young Catholics' Front for Reborn Poland and a member of the AK Intelligence Bureau.[11] Żegota had the status of a branch of the Delegatura but lacked the aura of other underground groups, and few Poles were willing to risk their lives working for it.[12]

Unlike the other underground groups, Żegota did not establish an independent regional network of cells, but drew on the existing structures of the organizations that joined it or on private individuals who worked with it. These activities were made possible by the connections Żegota activists had with groups in the Polish underground movement. The consequence was that Jews hiding on the Aryan side who were aided by Żegota had no idea who was behind the people who supplied them with precious forged papers or found them places to hide at reasonable prices, or where the funding for the aid originated. The Żegota Council, which ran the ramified organization, initiated special aid, requiring professional competence, for Jews who fled to the Aryan side. The key units in Żegota were those that provided false papers and found housing for those on the run, as well as the medical section, which forged ties with trustworthy doctors to whom Jews could turn for assistance without fear of being denounced to the authorities. Another important unit found shelter for Jewish children in Polish families, RGO orphanages, and convents.

The bulk of Żegota's budget came from the government-in-exile in London, through the Delegatura. From the summer of 1943, this was supplemented by funds from Jewish organizations abroad, which were transferred to Żegota by the Jewish National Committee and the Bund. In January 1943, the

10 Irena Sendlerowa, "Ci ktorzy Pomagali Żydom," *BZIH*, vol. 45/46 (1963), pp. 236–237.
11 Prekerowa, *Konspiracyjna Rada*, pp. 72–79.
12 Gutman and Krakowski, *Unequal Victims*, p. 261.

Delegatura allocated only 150,000 zlotys to Żegota, but following unrelenting pressure the budget grew consistently, reaching an average of 662,000 zlotys a month, or about $4,000 at that time. All told, Żegota received 28,750,000 zlotys from the Delegatura (approximately $215,000). In addition, from July 1943 until June 1944, Żegota received 3.2 million zlotys (about $20,000) a month from the Jewish National Committee and the Bund, but repaid this money with a certain increment at the end of 1944.[13]

This is not the place to describe the extensive activities of Żegota; this has been done by several leading activists of the organization in their memoirs, and the subject has been recorded extensively.[14] Its activities were centered in Warsaw, the heart of the underground movement in occupied Poland and the base of the major activists. Warsaw and its environs were also the preferred place of hiding for many of the Jews who had fled to the Aryan side. Of the 15,000 to 20,000 Jews who hid in and around the city in 1943–1944,[15] about 4,000 received aid from Żegota.[16] The organization also established branches in other cities throughout Poland, but in comparison to Warsaw their activity was marginal.

## How did Żegota Help Save Children?

The help Żegota was called upon to rescue children was inherently more complex than in the case of adults. The scale of the mission can be understood from the fact that of the 400,000 Jews who were incarcerated in the Warsaw Ghetto, about 100,000 were aged 15 or younger — fully a quarter of the ghetto's population.[17] The children were among the first victims when the mass deportation and annihilation of the Warsaw Ghetto's inhabitants began in the summer of 1942. At the start of the great Aktion, Centos activists

---

13  Teresa Prekerowa, "Zegota," *Encyclopedia of the Holocaust*, vol. 4, p. 1,730; Gutman and Krakowski, *Unequal Victims*, pp. 261–279.

14  Bartoszewski and Lewinóna, *Ten jest*; Prekerowa, *Konspiracyjna Rada*; Marek Arczyński and Wiesław Balcerak, *Kryptonium "Żegota"* (Warsaw: Czytelnik, 1983); Joseph Kermish, "The Activities of the Council for Aid to Jews ('Żegota') in Occupied Poland," in Yisrael Gutman and Efraim Zuroff, eds., *Rescue Attempts During the Holocaust: Proceedings of the Second Yad Vashem International Conference* (Jerusalem: Yad Vashem, 1977), pp. 367–398; Gutman and Krakowski, *Unequal Victims*.

15  Berman, "Jews on the Aryan Side," p. 686; Ringelblum, *Polish-Jewish Relations*, p. 247.

16  Berman, "Jews on the Aryan Side," p. 694.

17  Adolf Berman, *From the Days of the Underground* (Hebrew) (Tel Aviv: Hamenora, 1971), p. 204.

approached the headquarters of the Jewish police in the ghetto, hoping to spare at least the orphanages and children's homes from deportation, but in vain. They were told unequivocally that the children would receive no protection and that there would be no children left in the ghetto. The Centos leadership put forward various suggestions about how to save the children, but it quickly became apparent that none of the proposed solutions was practical, because they focused on rescue inside the ghetto.

Until then, the institutions had not considered the idea of rescuing children outside the ghetto, as there was no Polish public body willing to assist in such an effort. Without the organized aid of the Polish population, the idea of rescuing a sizable number of children was untenable. It was only when the occupants of the first children's homes began to be force-marched to the Umschlagplatz — the collection point for the death transports — that the idea was mooted to choose the most resourceful children from the children's homes, provide them with a small amount of money, and try to get them to the Aryan areas. It was a plan born out of despair and helplessness. The entire ghetto was in a panic, and it was already too late to put the plan into practice. Within a short time, most of the ghetto's institutions were liquidated, and nearly 4,000 orphans were sent to their death. The children in the Centos institutions in other ghettos near Warsaw suffered the same fate. In Otwock, the children in the Centos medical-educational institution and in a center for Jewish refugee children from Germany were murdered. In Miedzeszyn, one of the finest educational institutions, named for the Bundist leader Vladimir Medem, was destroyed and all the children, some 200, were shot in cold blood. Hundreds of devoted staff members died with the children. Most of the Centos employees — teachers, physicians, nurses, psychologists, and social workers — were sent to their deaths in the mass transports.[18]

In the conditions that existed during the Aktions, there was no practical possibility of smuggling groups of children out of the ghetto to the Aryan side in an organized manner. Żegota did not yet exist, and, as we have seen in earlier chapters, the majority of the children who reached the Aryan side during the great Aktion in the summer of 1942 were smuggled out individually at the initiative of their parents, who had some financial resources, as well as connections with Poles who assisted them, or escaped on their own and tried to survive on the streets by themselves. There were also indigent parents who fled with their children to the Aryan side and made contact with Poles who had ties with the social welfare department in the Warsaw Municipality

18  Ibid., pp. 209–217.

or with convents, and helped find places of hiding for their children. In some cases, parents had no choice but to leave their small children on the doorsteps of social welfare offices or orphanages, in the hope that they would be taken in and looked after.[19] By these means, hundreds of children were smuggled out of the ghetto.

It was at this time that the first institutional relations were established between the ghetto and the Municipal Social Welfare Department in Warsaw concerning the rescue of children. Evidently, it was a nurse, Ella Gołomb-Greenberg, from the Jewish Society for the Protection of Health (*Towarzystwo Ochrony Życia* — TOZ), a former official in the department, who contacted Christian organizations and requested that they help rescue Jewish children from the ghetto and place them in Catholic orphanages or convents. Gołomb maintained close ties with Jan Dobraczyński, the head of the Municipal Division for Homeless Children, and with the Polish social workers, Irena Sendler and Wanda Wierbowa.[20]

In the meantime, one of the first missions that the newly-founded Żegota set itself was the rescue of children. Already in its first three months of activities, children accounted for seventy percent of the more than 180 people that it dealt with. However, despite the organization's goodwill and devotion, it was severely hampered by a lack of resources. In this critical period, the Delegatura allocated only 70,000 zlotys for Żegota's rescue activity.[21] But rescuing children remained the highest priority of the organization's expanded council, established at the beginning of December 1942. Following the second mass Aktion and the first instance of armed resistance in the Warsaw Ghetto, on January 18, 1943, Żegota issued a desperate call to the Delegatura, requesting urgent large-scale financial aid to save the intelligentsia and in particular the children who still remained in the ghetto:

> For the moment, apparently because of the armed resistance demonstrated by the ghetto inhabitants, the evacuation Aktion has been halted, but the fate of the remainder of the ghetto population is sealed... Many individuals still remain in the Warsaw Ghetto, eminent people from the public, cultural, scientific, and artistic world, whom it is our obligation to rescue as quickly as possible. Several thousand children also remain there, survivors of the previous slaughters, which were perpetrated

19 Turkow, "Children of the Ghetto," p. 258.
20 Ibid.
21 Bartoszewski and Lewinóna, *Ten jest*, pp. 941–942.

brutally against children. These children, the few survivors who are still among the living, must be taken out of the ghetto and rescued. So tremendous are these missions, and so enormous the resources required, that we are compelled to turn to you, the authorized representative of the government [Delegatura], with an urgent call to allocate for this purpose the especially large sum of 500,000 zlotys at least. We request that you view our appeal as a critical matter which brooks no delay. Every day is liable to bring about the total destruction of the Warsaw Ghetto, which is engaged in an armed struggle for its life and honor.[22]

Irena Sendler had joined Żegota about two months earlier, in November 1942. Of the organization's Polish activists, no one was more closely acquainted with the plight of the ghetto's inhabitants. As a municipal social worker, she decided that she would not abandon the Jews she had assisted before they had been incarcerated in the ghetto, and continued to help them as long as she was able. After joining Żegota as a municipal employee, she utilized her connections with anyone who could help the rescue cause. One of her contacts was Alexandra Dargiel, a senior figure in the RGO, which ran several orphanages. She also found a path to the heart of Julian Grobelny, who was years older, and recruited him to the project of rescuing the children even before he was appointed chairman of the Żegota Council.[23]

The smuggling of children from the ghetto to the Aryan side began in the period of the great Aktion and its aftermath. However, getting out of the ghetto was only the first step on a lengthy and arduous road on the other side of the wall, and without someone to care for the children their prospect of survival was very limited. The testimonies indicate that most of the problems relating to the rescue of the children arose after they had managed to reach the Aryan side. The difficulties and complications intensified as the ghetto neared its end. Many children were sent back to their parents because of their "bad" appearance or for other reasons. There were families that had agreed to take in a Jewish child but changed their mind for fear of informers, and looked for ways to be rid of their ward. Children who were placed with families in return for a monthly payment found themselves in particularly dire straits if their parents had perished and there was no one to continue paying for their upkeep. At best, their guardians transferred them to an orphanage; at worst, they abandoned them to the streets.

22  Nachman Blumental and Joseph Kermish, eds., *Resistance and Revolt in the Warsaw Ghetto* (Hebrew) (Jerusalem: Yad Vashem, 1965), p. 388.
23  Sendlerowa, "Ci ktorzy Pomagali Żydom," pp. 234–237.

In a meeting of the Żegota Council held on July 10, 1943, after the liquidation of the Warsaw Ghetto, the secretary, Adolf Berman, raised the subject of the serious plight of the children who were concealed on the Aryan side. He suggested that the Council establish a special children's division to deal with the children wandering the streets or hidden in lofts and cellars. The plan was that, after locating them, the new unit would provide them with material and moral aid in cooperation with the activists of the RGO Central Welfare Council.[24] One month later, on August 16, the Żegota Council appointed a special committee for children's affairs, consisting of Irena Sendler, Izabela Kuczkowska, Leon Feiner, and Adolf Berman. Among the possible ways to assist hidden children that the committee considered were to refer them to RGO orphanages and convents, and to provide medical treatment to those who were sheltering in private homes. Irena Sendler, who was passionately involved with the issue, was appointed director of the children's division of the Żegota Council.[25]

The creation of the children's division enabled greater coordination between the personnel who dealt with the children on behalf of Żegota, thus rendering the help offered more effective and reliable. It is difficult to estimate exactly how many people were active in the children's division, as some of them helped children in the course of their regular tasks and had no idea that they were working for Żegota. The most problematic task was to find permanent and safe shelters for the children, whether in public institutions or in private homes. A child might pass through many hands before a permanent place of hiding could be found, and often had to be housed in temporary quarters in preparation for a new place of refuge. These arrangements entailed obtaining a Christian birth certificate, providing an appropriate cover story, and teaching the child basic Christian customs.

Sendler did not operate alone; she was assisted by a loyal and devoted professional staff. Most of those who worked in the children's division (nearly all of whom were women) were members of the enlightened Polish intelligentsia and were imbued with a deep sense of social commitment. Modest, dedicated, and hardly pampered in terms of their own living standards — they lived in small, crowded apartments and in some cases had young children of their own — nevertheless they made it their mission to rescue Jewish children. Apart from Sendler, the most prominent figures in the children's division were Janina Grabowska, a teacher; Jadwiga Piotrowska, a social worker

---

24  Arczyński and Balcerak, *Kryptonium "Żegota,"* pp. 227–228.
25  Prekerowa, *Konspiracyjna Rada*, p. 379; Berman, "Jews on the Aryan Side," p. 696.

who was Dobraczyński's faithful right-hand woman and also recruited her sister and her parents to help in the cause; the Ponikewski family; Zofia Wędrychowska; the Papuziński family; Izabela Kuczkowska and her mother, Kazimira Trzaskalska; Wanda Drozdowska; Stanislava Bussold, a midwife who ran a well-baby clinic and often assisted Jewish women in labor without asking for payment; Maria Kukulska; M. Felińska; A. Adamski; Alexandra Dargiel, the director of the RGO children's section; Irena Schultz, a journalist and social worker who worked with Sendler in the Warsaw Ghetto and specialized in smuggling children to the Aryan side; and several others. Some offered their own home as a temporary haven for children until a permanent place could be found — thereby endangering not only themselves but their entire family.[26]

Towards the end of 1943, according to information collected by the children's division of the Żegota Council, some 600 Jewish children were being housed in various institutions in and around Warsaw — fifty-three in municipal institutions, twenty-two in RGO institutions, and more than 500 in public and church institutions. In addition, many other children were scattered in institutions across Poland. The division's scale of activity in this period can be gauged from one of its reports, which stated that in September 1943 it dealt with fifty-eight children, of whom shelter had been found for thirty-six, while the other twenty-two cases were still being handled.[27]

The aid Żegota gave to the Polish families that took in Jewish children was not uniform and not always continuous. Each case was examined on its merits and dealt with substantively as far as was possible under circumstances in which all the traditional codes had been shattered. The amount given, which was generally determined according to the foster family's economic situation, ranged from 500 to 1,000 zlotys a month. In certain cases, payment was made in the form of goods or clothing. Families who agreed to take in children were told explicitly that the children were not being put up for adoption and would return to their parents or relatives after the war. In some cases, families initially agreed to take a child in return for payment but later decided to adopt the ward, severed their ties with Żegota, and disappeared with the child. Others refused to accept any payment at all so that after the war there would be no grounds for asking them to return the child.[28]

26  Bartoszewski and Lewinóna, *Ten jest*, p. 136.
27  Berman, "Jews on the Aryan Side," p. 696.
28  Prekerowa, *Konspiracyjna Rada*, pp. 204–205.

In the Kraków region, a childless Polish couple was given custody of two girls, one aged about eight and the other a toddler of two. The wife loved the toddler and decided to adopt her in practice, without undergoing any legal procedures. When Miriam Hochberg (Marianska), the Jewish representative of the local Żegota branch, came to the house in order to pay for taking care of the children, the woman refused to take money for the little one — "She is mine," she said — but willingly took money for the older girl.[29]

There were also guardians who at first seemed decent people, and agreed to shelter children for a specified time until a place could be found for them in an institution, but then turned the child into a hostage to extort money. One such case involved the daughter of Jonas Turkow. Irena Sendler placed the girl with a Polish family temporarily, with the intention of transferring her to a convent afterwards. But after a time, Turkow received a letter from her "guardian" stating:

> Since the day she has been with me, August 20, 1942, a total of 2,100 zlotys have been paid for her, and according to my calculations I should receive 60 zlotys a day. It follows that a substantial amount is still owed to me. Who is actually responsible for her?... Why should I keep her free of charge? I am not rich, either. On the other hand — someone who is not endangering anything is benefiting, whereas I, on whom most of the responsibility falls, receive no benefit from this. Therefore, if no one pays for her, I am not obliged to maintain her for free. I will put her out on the street, and God's will be done.

It later turned out that this "guardian" did all she could to ensure that the girl would remain with her and not be placed in a convent, and that in addition to the payment she received from Żegota she also received 500 zlotys a month from the Jewish National Committee for looking after her.[30]

Amid the cynicism and cruelty that prevailed on the Aryan side, there were also exemplary manifestations of humanity, and there were complicated, dangerous situations that were resolved by the humane, civilized touch of Żegota, as though the atrocities swirling all around did not exist. Ruth Cyprys arrived on the Aryan side of Warsaw carrying her three-year-old daughter. An affluent woman, she had managed to transfer part of her assets outside the ghetto. Unlike other Jewish women, who wandered about on the Aryan side under an assumed name, haunted by fear and waging a daily struggle for

29  Peleg-Marianska, *Witnesses*, pp. 108–109.
30  Turkow, "Children of the Ghetto," p. 263.

existence, she lived relatively comfortably and earned a living by doing various jobs in the homes of established Polish families. Drawing on her connections in the Warsaw intelligentsia, she made contact with Żegota personnel. In her memoirs, which she wrote immediately after the war, she describes being helped by the organization, although she had no idea that it was called Żegota.

Żegota offered her financial assistance, which she turned down, as she was not in need of it. She did, however, ask the organization to find a hiding place for her daughter, so that she could move about more freely. Two weeks later, she was informed that an adoptive family had been found for the girl and she could bring her to them. Cyprys arrived with her daughter at the arranged meeting place and was met by two women from the organization. They assured her that the girl would live with a cultured family in a Warsaw suburb and would take the foster family's name and be presented as their relative. The women promised to give Cyprys the family's name and address at a later date. When she thanked them for their help, they said, "Without thanks, please. This is what we do, it is our sacred duty. If you know of any other Jewish children who are in need of help, please give us their names and we promise to arrange everything."[31] After a time, Cyprys received the address of the family and went to visit her daughter. The girl's custodian was indeed a cultured woman who lived in a small villa in the prestigious Mokotow quarter. The girl herself looked very well. When Cyprys asked her if she wanted to go back to her, she replied, "No, I have a very good home here with Auntie Maria." The woman, Maria, had obtained a birth certificate for the girl issued in her family's name, according to which she was the orphaned daughter of her sister-in-law from distant Lvov, who had been killed in the war. After a few more visits, Cyprys discovered four more Jewish children and a nanny — the mother of one of the children — in the house, all of whom had different cover stories, as well as a man who was in hiding in the attic. Maria cared for the whole group efficiently and skillfully, and treated the children as though she were their true mother. The children wore clean clothes, ate good food, and even had two teachers.[32]

The kind of generous help that Cyprys received from Żegota was rare. Few Jews knew about the organization's existence — mainly those who had connections with its activists. Żegota was a small, compartmentalized organization, in which everything was done in strict secrecy and with the utmost

---

31  Altbeker Cyprys, *A Jump for Life*, pp. 149–153.
32  Ibid., pp. 161–163.

caution. The usual procedure was for a known person in the organization to provide the true name of a Jew in need of help to field activists, accompanied by an opinion about the case. The information was then checked, and only afterwards was assistance authorized.[33] Because of the degree of compartmentalization, it sometimes happened that there was no coordination between the different groups that offered assistance. The result was that some people received help throughout almost their entire period of hiding on the Aryan side, whereas others received only sporadic help.

At the end of 1942, a young couple, Leon and Alicja Guz, found themselves in a mixed Polish-Jewish group of laborers who worked in a metal plant near Minsk-Mazowiecki. Alicja was in an advanced state of pregnancy. As the due date neared, she and Leon were at their wits' end about where they could turn for help. But assistance arrived suddenly and unexpectedly. A Polish physician, Dr. Olgierd Mackiewicz, visited the factory regularly to treat sick workers. He noticed Alicja's condition but seemingly ignored her. Shortly before she was due to give birth, he gave her the address of a private maternity hospital in the city, telling her to go there when her contractions began. He said he had already arranged with the hospital's owner — who knew she was Jewish — that she would not have to pay. The lifeline that was suddenly thrown to them in their distress gave the couple new energy. When the time came, Alicja slipped out of the camp, reached the hospital, and gave birth to a daughter. It was not until after the war that the couple learned that Dr. Mackiewicz was working in the service of Żegota. In this case, the physician left the infant's future care in the hands of the parents. This occurred in December 1942 when the organization was still in its infancy, apparently not yet prepared to deal with such a complicated situation. Naturally, it was impossible for the baby to stay with the parents in the factory. Alicja sought the help of a Polish friend, Apolonia Przybojewska, who lived in Warsaw. In a plan of their joint devising, the infant was supposedly abandoned on Przybojewska's doorstep, and the next day she placed her in the Boduen children's home.[34]

Getting the infant admitted to this orphanage, which was located in the heart of Warsaw, was far from simple. The process involved an official request from the municipality's department of social welfare, and in the case of an abandoned child a police investigation of the circumstances in which the child had been acquired. Żegota personnel worked with doctors and nurses

33  Peleg-Marianska, *Witnesses*, pp. 80–93, 101–122, 129–161.
34  Leon Guz, *Targowa 64* (Warsaw: Czytelnik, 1990), pp. 135–143.

in the orphanage whom they knew could be relied on, in order to hide the Jewish origins of children they placed in the institution.[35]

The safest and hence preferred mode of rescue was to hide children with families. This was particularly critical with regard to young children who could already talk but were not yet able to keep a secret, and in the case of boys, nearly all of whom were circumcised. In these circumstances not many families were willing to assume the risks entailed in sheltering children. In the summer of 1943, after the liquidation of the ghettos, when the flight of Jews to the Aryan side was at its peak, rescuing children became even more urgent. By now, Żegota was trying to find secure places of hiding for twenty to thirty children a month. The Żegota Council discussed this mission repeatedly, but continued to be severely handicapped by the chronic shortage of funds. The Council was able to allocate only 30,000 zlotys a month for this purpose, although from the beginning of October, the Jewish organizations added another 50,000 zlotys a month for the rescue of children.[36] Sendler estimates that at this time, some 1,300 children were hidden with Polish families in Warsaw, half of them supported financially by Żegota and other organizations with which it cooperated.[37]

Another option for hiding children was to place them in Christian institutions — mainly the RGO orphanages and convents — to which Jews lacked access. According to the reports of the secretary of the Żegota Council, Marek Arczyński, in August 1943 between 700 and 1,000 children were in hiding in convents and in other institutions. The reports suggest that had more funds been available, the institutions could have taken in more children.[38]

The numerous testimonies in which the Boduen Home is mentioned indicate that many Jewish children were hidden there in 1943. The oldest and largest orphanage in Warsaw, it was established in the mid-eighteenth century by Father Gabriel Boduen, a French priest. It had a mixed staff — educators, nurses, secular nannies, and nuns. In prewar times it had been home to hundreds of Christian orphans, and the number grew during the occupation. Although the Żegota Council was not in direct contact with the orphanage, it was able to place Jewish children living under assumed names there with the help of the municipal social welfare department, with which the Council

---

35 Sendlerowa, "Ci ktorzy Pomagali Żydom," pp. 242–243.
36 Report of Żegota activity, Dec. 1942–Oct. 1943, in Bartoszewski and Lewinóna, *Ten jest*, p. 955.
37 Prekerowa, *Konspiracyjna Rada*, p. 205.
38 Gutman and Krakowski, *Unequal Victims*, p. 278.

worked. According to some estimates, between 100 and 200 Jewish children were placed in the orphanage.[39] Some stayed only briefly, before being moved to safer refuges, while others remained until the autumn of 1944, when they were evacuated, together with the other children, following the suppression of the Polish uprising.

In addition to the Boduen Home, the RGO ran a number of other orphanages in and around Warsaw, under the supervision of Alexandra Dargiel, a central Żegota activist. She referred a certain number of Jewish children to these institutions, of which the best known was a small orphanage for war orphans on the outskirts of Warsaw run by Jadwiga Strzalecka. About ten of the thirty children in this institution were Jews, as were some of the employees.[40]

Convents, both in the cities and more particularly in remote rural areas, were quite safe, including for children who did not look Aryan. Indeed, despite their economic distress, such convents were more receptive to the idea of taking in Jewish children. Their role is discussed extensively in Chapter Six. Here we will note only that, as in the secular institutions, the children entered the convents under assumed identities, and the responsible clergy needed to adopt effective means of camouflage in order not to endanger the institution's other inhabitants. The trusted liaison with the mothers superior in and around Warsaw was Jan Dobraczyński, who as head of the Municipal Division for Abandoned Children worked with the convents and sent them children who had nowhere else to go. The mothers superior knew he would avoid entangling them with the authorities, and he promised not to send them Jewish children who did not have a cover in the form of a Christian birth certificate. Dobraczyński agreed on a procedure with the convents whereby any child sent there by his department who arrived with a form bearing his signature was understood to be Jewish. He left the preparation of the documentation and the cover story to his assistants in Żegota. He himself did not know how many Jewish children had found shelter in convents through his efforts. He relied entirely on his assistants and signed the application forms they gave him without examining each case in depth. Jadwiga Piotrowska, his close aide, estimates that he signed more than 300 forms referring Jewish children to convents.[41]

---

39 Adam Slomczyński, *Dom ks. Boduena 1939–1945* (Warsaw: Panstwowy Institut Wydawniczy, 1975), pp. 116–119; Prekerowa, *Konspiracyjna Rada*, pp. 205–208.

40 Bartoszewski and Lewinóna, *Ten jest*, pp. 208–214.

41 Ewa Kurek-Lesik, "Udzial Żenskich Zgromadzeń Zakonnych w akcji ratowania dzieci żydowskich w Polsce w latach 1939–1945: część II, Źrodla i Opracowania" (hereafter Kruin-Lesik Collection), Ph.D. dissertation, Catholic University of Lublin, 1988, p. 329

How did the Żegota activists locate the children? Some were placed in their care by parents who remained in the ghetto and were later murdered, or who found refuge on the Aryan side and were unable to look after their children. In some cases, Polish families who had agreed to take in children but were afterwards fearful that they would be discovered, turned to the municipal social welfare department, where Żegota activists worked. Żegota also took the initiative in removing children from Christian families that used the children to extort money from their parents.[42]

## How Many Children were Saved by Żegota?

No confirmed data exist concerning the number of children who were rescued with Żegota's help throughout Poland. As noted, most of the organization's work was concentrated in and around Warsaw; elsewhere, its activity was quite limited due to various obstacles.[43] Accordingly, most of the statistics cited in documentation concerning the children who were rescued through Żegota, refer to the Greater Warsaw area, and they, too, are based on later estimates. In 1979, four of the leading activists from the children's division of the Żegota Council in Warsaw — Irena Sendler, Jadwiga Piotrowska, Izabela Kuczkowska, and Wanda Drozdowska-Rogowicz — gave testimony about their activity in the rescue of Jewish children. They estimate that Żegota aided approximately 2,500 children in Warsaw. About 500 were placed in convents with the help of Dobraczyński and Piotrowska; another 200 were housed in the Boduen Home with the help of Maria Krasnodębska, from the municipal social welfare department, and Stanislawa Zybert, a caregiver in the Boduen Home; approximately 500 were cared for in RGO children's institutions, which were supervised by Alexandra Dargiel; and 1,300 were placed with foster families.[44]

How many of these children survived? The historian Shymon Datner estimates their number at about 600. Irena Sendler thinks the number was higher, as some of the children were transferred by Żegota in Warsaw to institutions outside the city. To support her contention, she cites lists she was shown after the war by the Central Jewish Committee of Poland, according to which the committee located some 2,000 child survivors from Warsaw.[45]

---

42  Ibid., pp. 329–330.
43  Kermish, "Activities of the Council," pp. 375–377.
44  Prekerowa, *Konspiracyjna Rada*, pp. 215–216.
45  Ibid., p. 217.

Similarly, Jonas Turkow, who worked for the Central Jewish Committee at the time, maintains that more than 2,000 children survived on the Aryan side in Warsaw, including some from other Polish towns and cities.[46] After so many years, it is unlikely that an accurate list of the survivors can be compiled, but the estimate of approximately 600 children who were rescued in and around Warsaw with the help of Żegota seems reasonable. The others survived without the organization's aid.

After Warsaw, Kraków was the city in which Żegota was most active. There, no more than a hundred Jews were aided by the organization in its first period of activity, between April and October, 1943.[47] However, according to data supplied by Tadeusz Seweryn, a member of the Żegota Council in Kraków and its control committee, in 1944 the number of Jews receiving regular financial support from the organization was 570, and all told there were about 1,000, including those who received irregular grants in Kraków and its surroundings and in the nearby concentration camps.[48] Seweryn does not specify how many children were in this group, but there were certainly very few. In contrast to Warsaw, the Żegota branch in Kraków did not have a separate division to rescue children; they were dealt with in the same way as the adults. Miriam Hochberg (Marianska), the Jewish representative on the Żegota Council in Kraków, personally looked after the Jewish wards on the Aryan side. As part of her duties, she found shelter for children with families and institutions, including with her niece. Hochberg, who was particularly sensitive to the fate of the children in hiding, visited the foster families personally to reimburse them for the expenses they incurred in housing the children. Only a few children are mentioned in her description of her underground rescue activity in and around Kraków.[49] If this was the situation in Kraków, it stands to reason that things were no better elsewhere.

## Character of Żegota Activists who Worked to Save Children

Adolf Berman, the senior Jewish representative on the Żegota Council and its permanent secretary, wrote about the organization's activity:

46  Turkow, "Children of the Ghetto," p. 265.
47  Report of Żegota activity, Oct. 20, 1943, in Bartoszewski and Lewinóna, *Ten jest*, p. 956.
48  Ibid., p. 179.
49  Peleg-Marianska, *Witnesses*, pp. 53–56, 108–109, 131–132.

This council inscribed its name in golden letters in the annals of the activity to rescue Jews being persecuted by Hitler's murderers. For a short time, it became one of the most active and devoted organizations in the entire Polish underground. It conducted systematic and ramified activity, thanks to which thousands of Jews were spared death. It operated almost nonstop until the liberation.[50]

However, the Żegota personnel who worked to rescue children — the most formidable task of all — deserve special recognition. They were far from being a monolithic group: they came from different backgrounds, espoused diverse ideological views, and belonged to a wide spectrum of political organizations. Some of them harbored antisemitic views, which the war did not change. However, what set them apart from others and united them, in contrast to the vast numbers of bystanders in those years of anguish, was an inner moral code which constantly guided them and which would not allow them to remain indifferent in the face of the murder of innocent, helpless human beings. Many of their names are inscribed in the scroll of the Righteous among the Nations at Yad Vashem. There is no more fitting way to conclude a discussion of their activity than by providing brief portraits of some of those who risked their lives to rescue children, without asking for anything in return. The first of them is Irena Sendler.

The name of Irena Sendler, who was better known by her underground codename "Jolanta," became synonymous with the Żegota project to rescue children in Warsaw. She devoted her entire adult life to welfare work for the weak and the persecuted. She traced the wellspring of her activity and her social commitment to the atmosphere that pervaded her parents' home. She grew up in Otwock, near Warsaw, a town which had a substantial Jewish population. Her father, a doctor, espoused a socialist worldview, and most of his patients were poor Jews. She herself grew up among Jews and was familiar with their customs and way of life. Having seen at first-hand the distress and poverty of the Jewish lower classes, she was not captive to the near universal stereotype harbored by Poles, who regarded the Jews as rich and exploitative. As an employee of the municipal social welfare department in Warsaw, Sendler assisted needy Jews even before the ghetto's establishment and did not abandon them after they were incarcerated within its walls. As a municipal employee, she had an entry pass to the ghetto, ostensibly to help prevent the spread of infectious diseases. The pass enabled her to bring in clothing,

50  Berman, "Jews on the Aryan Side," p. 692.

medicines, and money on behalf of the social welfare department. Within the ghetto she maintained working ties with the staff of Centos, who aided needy children and orphans. While visiting the ghetto she wore an armband with a Star of David on it, like the inhabitants, to express her solidarity with them and so as not to draw attention to her which would distract her from her mission. In the summer of 1942, when the mass deportation of the ghetto inhabitants to Treblinka began, she reached the conclusion that it was pointless to go on bringing injections against typhoid fever into the dying ghetto; the focus had to be to smuggle out as many people as possible, and especially the children, out of the ghetto to the Aryan side and thus save their lives. She was one of the first to join Żegota when it was established in the autumn of 1942, and ardently set about rescuing children. The following summer, the Żegota Council appointed her head of the newly founded Children's Division, in which she became the driving force. Sendler also recruited her colleagues in the social welfare department for rescue work. In October 1943, she was arrested by the Gestapo for her underground activity and thrown into the notorious Pawiak Prison, where she was tortured to make her talk. When she refused to divulge information, the interrogators threatened to execute her. Fortunately, Żegota managed to obtain her release from prison by bribing a Gestapo agent. It was announced that she had been executed, and until the end of the Nazi occupation she could not appear in public, but this did not deter her from resuming her underground activity with Żegota.[51]

It was not abstract ideas that prompted Irena Sendler to come to the aid of the Jews, but simple love of humanity. This is illustrated by a less familiar story from her private life after the war. Among the many Jewish children Sendler had helped was Teresa Krener. In the summer of 1943, when Sendler met her, Krener was a solitary, homeless girl aged fourteen who was roaming the streets. Sendler arranged for her to work as a nanny for the young children of the well-known Papuzinski family, who were underground activists and aided Jews. After the war, Teresa was placed in a Jewish children's home, but was unhappy there. In her distress she fled to Sendler's home and told her that she would never go back to the home or enter another. Sendler, who was then living in a small apartment in severe economic straits, took Krener in, sent her to school, and looked after her like a mother. For two years Krener lived with Sendler, who saw to all her needs, even though the support she received from the Jewish Committee for this purpose was minimal.[52]

51  Bartoszewski and Lewinóna, *Ten jest*, pp. 131–147.
52  Testimony of Teresa Krener, YVA, O.3/2824.

Another individual who did much to rescue Jews in Warsaw was Jan Dobraczyński, who, after the war, became known as one of the leading Catholic writers in communist Poland. He had been active in the underground Armia Krajowa (Polish Home Army) during the occupation. Although not a member of the Żegota Council, he operated in its service to rescue children who managed to flee the ghetto to the Aryan side of Warsaw. The embodiment of a Catholic intellectual and Polish patriot, Dobraczyński possessed a deep social commitment inherited from his parents. His father had established the social welfare department in the Warsaw Municipality at the end of the nineteenth century and was its director for some forty years. In 1941, the son followed in his father's footsteps and began to work in the department as head of its abandoned children division.

In contrast to Sendler, Dobraczyński was no friend of the Jews. In his testimony he admits that before the war he belonged to antisemitic nationalist circles, even though there had never been any friction between his family and Jews. The Jews he knew first-hand were his classmates, who happened to be religious. Of his past relations with Jews he said, "Their religion was of no interest to me, though I found some of their religious customs peculiar." Anyone familiar with the intricacies of Polish discourse concerning Jews will discern a note of antisemitic haughtiness in this remark. Nevertheless, when the crisis came he did not hesitate to save Jewish children, though he knew he did so at the peril of his life. He first became aware of the plight of the Jewish children while helping street children in Warsaw. He discovered that ten percent of them were Jews. The ghetto was already sealed and isolated, and the children were in danger of being turned over to the Germans. Dobraczyński took advantage of his good relations with a German doctor who was seconded to the occupation authorities, whom he describes as one of the more decent in a gang of criminals. The doctor arranged for the children to be returned to the ghetto without punishment. "Who among us could have guessed that two years later that condemned them to death?" he reflected afterward.

The welfare personnel who constituted Dobraczyński's staff and knew about his close connections with mothers superior recruited him to rescue children in the summer of 1942, during the period of the mass deportation from the Warsaw Ghetto. The convent heads trusted him because of his family background and were ready to cooperate with him and take in Jewish children whom he had personally referred to them. The Jewish literature about Żegota barely mentions Dobraczyński's contribution to the rescue of children, whether because he worked behind the scenes or perhaps because of his innate antisemitism. He himself wrote little about the subject and gave all the credit to the staff in his department, who, he said, did the lion's share of the work. They were the ones who collected the children and prepared them for life with foster families or in institutions, and afterward took them there personally. The women, he said, carried out the difficult and dangerous mission boldly and with extraordinary disregard for their own safety. "My role was only to sign the applications," he summed up modestly. However, it is clear that if the Germans had discovered that any of his staff were engaged in rescuing children and had uncovered his part in the activity, he would have paid with his life. When asked about his motives for rescuing Jewish children, he replied that he had not done it to get a medal but "because there were persecuted children who were in danger of death. Because they were human beings. I would have rescued any person who was in danger of death, and certainly children, because children are close to my heart. This is what I am commanded to do by the Catholic religion."[53]

The woman who placed the applications of the Jewish children on Dobraczyński's desk for signing was his faithful assistant, Jadwiga Piotrowska, or "Jaga," as she was nicknamed. This energetic woman saved about fifty children, whom she personally transferred to Polish families and orphanages. In the testimony that she gave more than forty years after the events, she described emotionally how she carried in her arms a beautiful Jewish girl who had been smuggled out of the ghetto and took her together with her belongings by train to a convent in Chotomow. On the way, an extortionist demanded the money she was taking to the convent. Unfazed, she used the girl's charm to gain the protection of a German Luftwaffe officer who happened by. The officer freed her from the clutches of the extortionist and found her a seat in a carriage reserved for Germans only, and she and the girl reached their destination safely. On a mischievous note she added, "I traveled [with the girl] like a lady in the section that was set aside only for German soldiers on leave."

Piotrowska, like Dobraczyński, belonged to Catholic circles that were prejudiced against Jews. As an employee of the municipal social welfare department in Warsaw, she visited the ghetto and had become aware of the children's distress. In the ghetto she met with caregivers who looked after children. It was in this framework that she met the celebrated educator Janusz Korczak, who, in her Catholic eyes, was "a saint even if he was not a Christian." Piotrowska was active in smuggling children out of the ghetto to the Aryan side even before Żegota was established. In the summer of 1942, she

53  Testimony of Jan Dobraczyński, in Kurek-Lesik, "Źrodla i Opracowania," pp. 327–333.

responded to the leaflet of the writer Zofia Kossak-Szcucka, joined Żegota immediately upon its creation, and engaged in the rescue of children until the end of the war, fully aware that if she were caught she would pay with her life.

Piotrowska was a field worker. She lived with her parents in an isolated house surrounded by a garden and with two separate entrances, making it possible to slip out when danger loomed. She brought Jewish children to the house in order to prepare them for life in a permanent place of refuge. In addition to ensuring the children's legal cover, they had to be reassured, as they were very frightened and afraid of anyone in uniform. Piotrowska also recruited her sister and parents to help with the rescue work. She was proud of her part in rescuing children and of having passed the test of humanity and behaving, as she saw it, as one who is obliged to do so in such circumstances. She remembered fondly the ties of friendship she forged with her co-workers. Many of the children she transferred to convents with Dobraczyński's referral were baptized and survived the war. Both she and Dobraczyński maintained that after the war, representatives of the Jewish organizations accused them of being responsible for the conversion of the children and of severing them from their Jewish heritage. Piotrowska in particular was deeply offended by the accusation, which weighed heavily on her conscience for many years and gave her no rest. She often asked whether it would have been preferable to let the children die. "Sometimes," she said, "I pray that a wise rabbi will come and release me from this accusation."[54]

Another activist, with a different social background from the three described above, was the educator Jadwiga Strzalecka. Strzalecka, a Polish aristocrat through and through, ran a small home for war orphans near Warsaw and did not hesitate to take in Jewish children. She spoke about this to only two of her staff, but it was an open secret in the area, as the children were easily identifiable by their appearance. Strzalecka took no special precautionary measures to hide the Jewish children, treating them like all her other wards. A teacher who worked with her noted that she was one of those people who do not try to avoid problems but deal with them instead. She imbued her staff with her peace of mind and sense of humor, but when she was away — dealing with matters related to the home — they were afraid to remain alone, in case the Gestapo should pay a surprise visit. Strzalecka did not hesitate to have her eight-year-old daughter join the children of the institution, and had

54 Testimony of Jadwiga Piotrowska, ibid., pp. 333–341.

her walk hand-in-hand with a Jewish child on outings. This, she believed, was tantamount to a good-luck charm protecting the children from harm.[55]

After the suppression of the Polish uprising in Warsaw, Strzalecka and the orphans were expelled from the city, and she took them to the resort town of Poronin in the Tatra Mountains. In the autumn of 1944, Miriam Hochberg (Marianska) met her for the first time in Kraków, while searching for a refuge for Janka Hescheles, a girl who had been smuggled to the city from the Janowski concentration camp in Lvov. However, all the places of hiding that she had visited had been discovered. Strzalecka agreed without hesitation to Hochberg's request that she take in the girl. Of the period she spent in Strzalecka's orphanage, Hescheles later wrote:

> From the very first moment when I crossed the threshold of the house in Poronin and met its director, Jadwiga Strzalecka, I once again received the status of a young girl. I was again surrounded by kindness, love and care. I would like to emphasize that all the children in that house were treated the same way. There were more than fifty of us there. I was put in a room together with some slightly younger than me. These were the last months of the war. We had nothing more to do with it in our everyday existence. In the midst of beautiful mountain scenery, activities organized by our tutors, lessons and the friendliness which surrounded us, this orphanage was a fairy tale of an island.[56]

In one of her visits to the home, Hochberg-Marianska noticed a girl whose head had been shaved and bore a distinctively Jewish appearance, and was amazed to see that she was about to leave on an outing with the rest of the children. When she asked Strzalecka how she could dare send a girl like that into the street, because it was obvious at a glance that she was Jewish. "That is exactly the reason why I cannot single her out from the rest," she answered. This was what she always did: it was the guiding principle she lived by. Hochberg, who was familiar with all classes of Polish society and spent the entire war in underground activity among Poles, wrote about Strzalecka with admiration and esteem: "I never knew what her self-confidence was based on, but she radiated with something from within her... I thought then in my heart, and continue to think now that I had the privilege of meeting a person who possessed wonderful beauty, both outer and inner. To this day the image of

55  Bartoszewski and Lewinóna, *Ten jest*, pp. 208–214.
56  Peleg-Marianska, *Witnesses*, pp. 134–135.

this woman, her style and manner, and her unlimited commitment to the business of saving Jewish children has remained engraved in my memory."[57]

The activity of the Żegota activists, and particularly those who helped rescue children, provides indisputable proof that despite the harsh conditions of the occupation, far more rescue work could have been done if more people had been willing to act.

57  Ibid, pp. 133–134.

CHAPTER SIX

# The Convent Children

## The Convents in Occupied Poland

The rescue of Jewish children in convents during the Holocaust is a subject that evokes intense emotions among both Jews and Christians, as it is interwoven with the controversial question of the Church's attitude toward the Jews during that period. The Jewish collective consciousness associates the issue with the conversion of many of the children to Christianity — as if the rescuers' purpose was to stalk innocent souls and exploit the children's existential distress for conversion motives. Christians, on the other hand, consider even the hint of such a suspicion to be an expression of ingratitude on the part of people who do not sufficiently respect the fearless devotion and truly Christian conscience of priests and nuns who risked their lives in order to rescue Jews. It is a complex issue that plumbs the depths of the soul.

In this chapter we will examine the case of the children who survived the Holocaust in the convents of Poland, a country in which the Catholic Church has long possessed a special stature and exerts a powerful influence over its adherents. As in the occupied countries of Western Europe, convents in Poland were considered relatively safe havens for Jewish children. Up until the Second World War, Catholic Poland, squeezed between the mostly Orthodox Russia to the east and predominantly Lutheran Germany to the west, had a large number of monasteries and convents. Even the church establishment was not always well acquainted with all of them. According to Jerzy Kłoczowski, forty-four church orders and 350 monasteries were active in Poland on the eve of the war with a population of 6,430 monks. There were eighty-four communities of nuns who maintained 2,300 institutions in which 22,000 nuns served.[1]

---

1    Jerzy Kłoczowski, "The Religious Orders and the Jews in Nazi-Occupied Poland," *Polin, A Journal of Polish-Jewish Studies*, vol. 3 (1988), p. 238.

These figures fell sharply during the war because both the German and the Soviet authorities adopted policies that were intended to undermine the Catholic Church, which was the prime bastion of Polish nationalism. Under a policy of Germanization which was applied in the western districts of Poland — that were annexed to the Third Reich after the occupation — convents were closed and nuns were restricted from mixing freely with the population. In the eastern regions, which had been controlled by Russia until the First World War, there were far fewer Catholic monasteries or convents to begin with; in 1939–1941, the Soviet authorities closed down most of them and dispersed the monks and nuns or exiled them to Siberia.

Organized in orders and communities, the monasteries and convents in Poland filled an important social function in both education and welfare. Every holy order had its own goals, regulations, habit, tradition, and customs. In terms of status, monks and nuns are part of the Christian elite but, in contrast to priests, do not answer directly to the regular church hierarchy (which is based on the bishoprics). Every monastic order answers to its own wellspring of authority, whether in Poland, Rome, or elsewhere. Even before the war, the activities of the Polish monasteries and convents were neither coordinated by nor centralized under a specific authority. Such was the case *a fortiori* during the war, when the institutions had to fend for themselves and discharge their missions as best they could given their particular resources and personnel. This state of affairs affected the convents' decisions regarding the rescue of Jewish children.[2]

With a few exceptions, only female orders that were engaged in education and welfare participated in the rescue of Jews. Most convents of this sort administered orphanages or residential schools for girls of two distinct types. Residential convents, especially those in the big cities, were originally meant for girls from affluent homes who attended high schools (*gymnasia*) or vocational schools, paid for their room and board, and lived under the nuns' supervision. The Immaculate Order (*Niepokalanki*), for example, devoted itself chiefly to educational work; its nuns taught in primary schools and high schools and operated residences that accommodated a small number of pupils. When social needs escalated during the war, the Immaculate Sisters branched into welfare activities among additional population groups.

2   Ewa Kurek, *Your Life Is Worth Mine: How Polish Nuns Saved Hundreds of Jewish Children in German Occupied Poland* (New York: Hippocrene Books, 1997), pp. 44–49.

It was under these circumstances that Jewish girls, among others, found their way to their institutions.[3]

The orphanage convents were scattered throughout the country — in cities, suburbs, and rural areas — and intended primarily for children from the impoverished classes, homeless orphans, and foundlings from the lowest socioeconomic groups among the Christian population. Although such convents were ostensibly open to any child in need of shelter, their capacity was limited. During the war the number of orphans multiplied, and a new population group emerged: children of refugee families whose parents could not support them. Together, these groups brought the convents to full occupancy. Their standard of living, meager even in ordinary times, declined steadily during the occupation as their state subsidies ceased. Only a few such homes, which charged for their services, offered reasonable living conditions. The other convents had to make do with modest allocations from the RGO (*Rada Główna Opiekuńcza*, the Central Welfare Board), which operated with German authorization.

Among these convents, too, there were differences. Physical conditions in convents that did not lose their facilities were not too austere because they still retained their pre-war equipment, furniture, and clothing stores. In others, however, life was unbearably harsh. One example is the Convent of the Sacred Heart (*Sercanki*), in Przemyśl. This convent, established during the war with assistance from the RGO, admitted youngsters from the vicinity and from Volhynia, in eastern Poland, who had fled the Ukrainian terror. Living conditions in the convent were appalling: rampant hunger prevailed, there was no electricity, contagious diseases broke out and there was a grave shortage of medicines, and no possibility of delousing.[4] Similar conditions prevailed in the large Turkowice convent, an older institution located in the depths of a forest in the Lublin region. Its buildings were not damaged in the war, but sanitary conditions were rudimentary in the extreme. The children could rarely take a hot bath. Neither soap nor medicines were available. Children who contracted contagious illnesses were quarantined under a nun's supervision in an isolation ward, but since there was no doctor to examine the children regularly, illnesses were not always identified.[5]

Despite their geographical dispersion and differences in appearance and standard of living, internally the convents possessed several features in com-

---

3   *Kurek-Lesik Collection.*
4   *Kurek-Lesik Collection*, testimony of Miriam Klein, pp. 188–189.
5   Śliwowska, *The Last Eyewitnesses*, vol. I, p. 63.

mon, such as the regimen, living routine and educational methods. The most prominent feature of nearly every convent was its exterior wall, which isolated the institution from its immediate surroundings and acted as a buffer between its internal life and outside world. The convent interior was divided functionally: a pupils' residential wing with dormitory halls, dozens of children packed into each according to age groups; a separate, isolated wing for the nuns; and a service wing including dining hall, kitchen, storage areas, offices, halls or rooms for social activities, and, if the convent had a school of its own, classrooms. The best appointed facility in every convent was the chapel.

The more affluent convents also had a reception hall where pupils could meet with visiting relatives. Several convents on the outskirts of towns and villages had small auxiliary farms where a few chickens and pigs were raised and, if a plot of land was available, fruit or vegetables were grown. The produce from these farms was an important supplement to the RGO's scanty allocation of resources. Luxuries were altogether absent, but enough supplies were available to keep hunger at bay.

The convent staff was composed of the mother superior, who made all the important decisions, and the nuns — usually between five and fifteen in number — depending on the convent's mission and the number of its children. Each convent had its own priest, who presided over the services in the chapel and heard confession from both nuns and pupils. Some of the nuns served as teachers, and they would call on secular teachers, older pupils, or acolytes for assistance. Other nuns were responsible for administrative duties and ran the service facilities, kitchen, infirmary, and auxiliary farm. The pupils helped with the convent routine and performed various duties on a rotational basis. For farm duties that required greater skill or strength, the staff was assisted by lay workers who also lived on the premises. Before the war, about 400 convents across Poland maintained institutions for children. Some of them were closed down during the occupation and a few others were established during the war to meet urgent needs in caring for war orphans. As we have seen, as the war dragged on, the convents became full to capacity. In March 1940, for example, the remote Turkowice convent admitted children sent from Warsaw by the RGO. Afterwards it continued to take in children from the vicinity, mostly from Polish families whom the Germans had deported from the area of Zamość. In 1942, the convent housed 350 children aged six months to fifteen years.[6] Under such circumstances it was clear that

---

6   Cezary Gawryś, "Turkowice — śmierć i ocalenie," *WIĘZ*, vol. 4(342) (1987), pp. 13–14.

"charity begins at home:" the rescue of Jewish children was certainly not foremost among the convent leaders' concerns.

The convents had never formed a relationship with Jews, and their plight in the ghettos was of no concern to them. Moreover, sheltering Jewish children would place everyone in the convent in mortal danger and would also require them to share their very limited provisions.

## Saving Children in Convents: the Jewish Approach

Interestingly enough, the available Jewish sources do not attest to a flood of Jewish parents who pounded on the convent doors in an effort to save their children at any cost. Indeed, it would be difficult to imagine a starker contrast than between Polish Jewry and Catholic convents, the very embodiment of Christendom. Testimonies of nuns occasionally mention Jewish children who spent time in convents before the war, but a painstaking review of these shows that this had occurred only in exceptional cases of unwanted children, mostly born out of wedlock or to mixed couples. When the Germans established the ghettos, they ordered the convents to return such children to the Jewish community.[7]

The Jews awakened to the possibility of rescuing children by placing them in convents only at a very late stage, when the liquidation of the ghettos was well under way and all other possibilities had failed. Even then, only a few Jews were willing to save their children by entrusting them to these bastions of Christianity. According to Emanuel Ringelblum, the issue was a subject of public discussion in the Warsaw Ghetto in early December 1942, after the great deportation. It was evidently Irena Sendler, the Żegota activist, who proposed that several hundred children over the age of ten be placed in convents at a charge of 8,000 złotys per year, to be remitted in advance.[8] The plan was to record the children's whereabouts in a card file so they could be reclaimed at the end of the war.

It should be noted that despite the harsh conditions in the Warsaw Ghetto — the largest ghetto in Poland, which was already on the verge of

7  Magdalena Kaczmarzyk, *Pomoc udzielana Żydom przez Zgromadzenie Sióstr Albertynek w czasie II wojny Światowew j*, p. 1; YVA, JM/3636; Kurek, *Your Life Is Worth Mine*, pp. 50–51.
8  Ringelblum, *Polish-Jewish Relations*, pp. 150–151; Turkow, "Children of the Ghetto," pp. 259–263.

extinction — the plan was met with objections on three counts. First was the fear of proselytizing: some suspected the Catholic clergy *a priori* of wanting to exploit the Jews' agony in order to convert their children to Christianity. The second reason was material: by demanding payment in advance, it was thought the convents were looking to exploit the situation financially. Third was prestige. Until then, the Polish priesthood had done very little to rescue Jews. Now, by saving several hundred children, it might acquire a stamp of approval, proving that it had not sat idly by during the difficult times and ostensibly had spared no effort to rescue Jews in general and Jewish children specifically.[9]

Nevertheless, the plan was discussed among the ghetto's leaders and rejected in view of the profound opposition of Jewish orthodox and nationalist circles. Several affluent orthodox personalities who were asked to fund the children's upkeep opposed the plan categorically: "We will not allow our children to be handed over to convents to face spiritual destruction [*shmad*]," they said. "Let them share the fate that God has ordained for us."[10] However, not only the orthodox were opposed. Members of a circle of intellectuals who discussed the plan, including the overtly secular Ringelblum, expressed doubts because of concern for the children's future identity. Time and education, they said, would have their effect; sooner or later, notwithstanding the priests' assurances to the contrary, the children would become Christians. One participant believed that in this case they should follow the precedent of previous generations and choose martyrdom: "We must not acquiesce in the spiritual destruction of our children. The [Jewish] public must not get involved. Let us leave the decision to each individual. If more than 300,000 Jews are to be murdered in Warsaw, what is the use of saving several hundred children? Let them perish or survive together with the entire community."

Some participants, however, were aghast at this extreme view. They argued that the very future of the Jewish people was at stake, and at a time when all of European Jewry was being annihilated, every Jewish soul was precious. If a handful of Jewish children were to be transferred to the Aryan side, they maintained, a core group for a future generation of Jewry would be saved. That generation's right to life should not be negated, even if a few children would be lost to Christianity. Several people favored accepting the proposal in the conviction that the most important task was to save as many Jews as

9  Ringelblum, *Diary and Notes,* pp. 434–435.
10  Turkow, "Children of the Ghetto," pp. 258–261.

possible. Others agreed, but thought it was wrong to give the plan the official sanction of the Jewish organizations. Each family must decide for itself, they maintained.[11] In any event, the institutionalized rescue of several hundred children from the Warsaw Ghetto was no more than a potential plan and was not realized because of the many difficulties it entailed. Foremost among them was the Polish priesthood's minimal interest in the rescue of Jewish children.[12]

Jan Dobraczyński, the head of the Division for Homeless Children in the Warsaw Municipality and the man who did so much to help Żegota activists place Jewish children in convents, later said that he had learned of the discussions in the ghetto only from Ringelblum's writings. He recalled having encountered outside the ghetto a representative of the Jewish committee who had introduced himself as "Dr. Marek." Marek thanked Dobraczyński for acting to rescue Jewish children by placing them in convents and then addressed the question of their being baptized into the Church. Dobraczyński explained that this was being done for their safety. When Marek continued to press, asking about the children's disposition after the war, Dobraczyński replied that it was up to their parents or relatives to make this decision if they survived; if not, the youngsters would be raised as Catholics until they reached adulthood and would then decide for themselves. "Those are hard terms," answered Marek, adding that there was no choice but to accept them.[13]

Concurrently, the rescue of children in convents was debated in a different context and a different setting: in the Warsaw Ghetto by the leaders of the Gordonia youth movement. As a member of the movement, Sara Erlichman (Sojka) had embarked on underground activity in the capacity of a liaison officer, when she looked for a shelter for her younger sister, twelve-year-old Justynka. The leader of the movement, Eliezer Geller, suggested that Justynka be made the head of a group of little girls who would be sent to a convent in Częstochowa. The suggestion gave rise to an argument among several key movement members. The objectors claimed that even though the girls might be saved physically, their souls would be susceptible to the priests' zealous education. Here, too, the issue did not get past the talking stage, because the circumstances precluded the implementation of the plan.[14] Jewish families in other ghettos also discussed the subject.

11 Ringelblum, *Diary and Notes*, p. 435.
12 Ringelblum, *Polish-Jewish Relations*, p. 151.
13 *Kurek-Lesik Collection*, pp. 331–332.
14 Sara Erlichman-Bank, *In the Hands of the Impure* (Hebrew) (Tel Aviv: Ghetto Fighters' House and Hakibbutz Hameuchad, 1976), pp. 92–93.

Jews had good reason to distrust the intentions of the Polish clergy and to flinch from this potential path of rescue. Even secular people on the verge of extermination, hesitated to try to save their children by placing them under the protection of the crucifix. Their fears had well-founded historical roots. It is true that the Polish Church did not condone the forcible conversion of Jews, since Christianity does not permit imposing the religion on those unwilling to embrace it — but this was not the case with respect to children. In eighteenth-century Poland, many Jewish children were baptized after being abducted and similar cases were reported even in the first half of the nineteenth century.[15]

An unbearably daunting historical question for an observant Jew is whether it is permitted to save a life at the price of conversion. According to religious law, all prohibitions in the 613 obligatory Jewish commandments (*mitzvot*) are null and void when life itself is at stake. Only with respect to three commandments is death to be preferred over violation: idolatry — meaning conversion — incest, and murder. Medieval Jewish terminology actually extolled martyrs who chose suicide rather than accept Christianity. Thus, martyrdom (*kidush hashem*: literally, "Sanctification of the Name") has deep historical roots in the consciousness of European Jewry.[16]

When the eldest son of Rabbi Ezekiel Levin, chief rabbi of Lvov before the war, informed his mother that the Uniate Metropolitan, Archbishop Andrei Szeptycki, was willing to rescue him and his two younger brothers and had promised to refrain from converting them, she refused even to countenance the idea. She was convinced that by handing over her children to the priests she would be abandoning them to Christianity, and she did not believe she had the right to purchase the physical lives of children who were the offspring of rabbis at the cost of their spiritual destruction. After further entreaties, she agreed to meet with the Metropolitan, who assured her repeatedly that her children would not forget their faith and people. His promises were of no avail. Some time later, before the Aktion in the ghetto, her son returned and informed her that the head of the Studite order, Ihumen Kliment Szeptycki, the Metropolitan's brother, had promised to spare no effort to save her along with her youngest son and pleaded with her to accept this path to rescue. She refused:

15  Jacob Goldberg, *Converted Jews in the Polish Commonwealth* (Hebrew) (Jerusalem: Zalman Shazar Center, 1985), pp. 34–39.
16  Hayim Hillel Ben-Sasson, *Jewish History in the Middle Ages* (Hebrew), (Tel Aviv: Am Oved, 1958), pp. 174–184.

I will have no part of it. . . . I am not able to do what others may. The Metropolitan's promises are made in good faith, but the issue of spiritual destruction will eventually become very real. I have no doubt that you will remain loyal to Judaism and try to keep your brother Nathan Jewish. But if I place your little brother, who is still a baby, in [their] custody, who can assure me that he will not leave the Jewish fold? I abide by my decision: the boy and I will remain in the ghetto. If we are privileged to survive, all the better, and if not, we will go where your father has gone.

The little brother was shot in January 1943, in the *Kinderaktion* in the Lvov ghetto; the mother was murdered in the Janówski camp in September 1943.[17]

Rabbi David Kahane, also from Lvov, found shelter in Metropolitan Szeptycki's residence and survived. He has testified to the existence of discussions at that time about whether children should be entrusted to the convents, after due consultation with rabbis. Most of the rabbis supported the move, believing that, if the children survived, someone would remove them from the convents and return them to the fold of Judaism. Several rabbis, however, believed it was preferable for the children to die with their families and their people rather than be placed in a convent. Rabbi Kahane considered it the highest duty to save the lives of the children and demonstrated the strength of his conviction by placing his own young daughter in a convent.[18] She survived the Holocaust, as did her mother, who found refuge in a Uniate institution under Metropolitan Szeptycki.

## Path of the Children to the Convents

Very few Jews, even those who had assimilated and were fully familiar with Christian society, had direct access to convents. Those willing to place their children in such institutions had to turn to Christian mediators for assistance, or abandon their children at the convent gates in the hope that the nuns would take them in.

Max Noy, from Otwock, made the acquaintance of Sister Ludwika Małkiewicz of the Elizabethan Sisters' convent in Świder when the nun vis-

17  Yitzhak Levin, *I Immigrated [to Palestine] from Specje* (Hebrew) (Tel Aviv: Am Oved, 1947), pp. 128–129, 149–150.
18  *Kurek-Lesik Collection*, testimony of Rabbi David Kahane, pp. 344–347.

ited the furniture warehouse where he worked and asked him for a few beds for the convent. He supplied the beds, and the two struck up a friendship. In 1942, before the ghetto was liquidated, Noy contacted Sister Ludwika and asked her to rescue his young daughter. The sister took up the request with the mother superior, Gertruda Marciniak, who gave her consent. The nuns arranged a forged Christian birth certificate for the girl, and with her parents planned her staged abandonment: the mother slipped into the convent in the evening, holding the girl, and left her in a corridor. Tied around the child's neck was a small bag containing the forged birth certificate and a letter explaining that her mother could no longer support her because of her economic plight and requesting that she be admitted to the convent. The mother walked away; her daughter, left alone, burst into tears; and the nuns arrived and took her in.[19]

This complex procedure was not necessarily the general rule, but does attest to the difficulties Jewish parents faced when they wished to place their children in a convent. Thus, even though, in this case, the convent agreed to receive the girl, convoluted means had to be employed in order to place her in the custody of the nuns.

As the ghettos were liquidated, more and more children were sent to convents. They came from all strata of Jewish society, from the assimilated to the ultra-orthodox. The children reached the convents by diverse routes, but broadly speaking there were two main groups. One group consisted of children whose parents took the initiative, either through Polish welfare institutions such as Żegota or through Christian mediation. The children's upkeep was covered by payments forwarded to the convents, either by the welfare agencies or by the parents who were in hiding in Aryan areas and transmitted the money through others. In such cases, the middlemen became, in effect, the children's guardians and, posing as relatives, occasionally visited the children in the convents to give news about them to their parents in hiding. Sometimes a child's mother or a surviving relative came to visit, without disclosing their kinship to the convent staff. Only if the parents and relatives perished, leaving no one to pay, did the convents assume the expense of the children's upkeep. In any event, we do not know of a case where convents evicted children because the upkeep payments stopped.

The other group consisted of children who reached convents by chance and in ways other than through their parents' initiative. Some of them were mere infants and toddlers who were separated from their parents and left on

---

19  Ibid., testimonies of Ludwika Małkiewicz and Max Noy, pp. 36–50.

their own, and were taken in by compassionate Christians who took them to the nearest convent. In several cases, parents had placed children with Christian families in return for payment, but the supposed benefactors kept the money and then threw the children into the street. Passersby who took pity on them directed them to a convent or brought them there personally. Also among those who sought shelter in convents were older girls, aged twelve to fourteen, as well as some who had been wandering in villages and working for peasants until difficulties of subsistence and abuse by their employers prompted them to seek a refuge. Some of these children reached the convents under highly dramatic circumstances. Their experiences were indelibly engraved in their memory, particularly in the case of the older ones, and had a profound effect on their life in the convent and on the relations they formed with the nuns.[20]

Irit Kuper, having endured great suffering in her wanderings between the villages, when she was worked brutally by the farmers and treated abominably (see Chapter 3), decided to try her luck in a convent. Armed with the false birth certificate of a girl born out of wedlock, she turned to the Convent of St. Anthony run by the Gray Sisters (*Szarytki*), in Ignaców. Arriving early in the morning, she was astounded at the sight of the nun who opened the gate of the convent for her. Years later, Kuper recalled the occasion:

> She wore a dark blue wool dress and a white hat, the brim of which flopped down on both sides of her head. I could not see her face. "Madame," I said, addressing her. She raised her head and revealed the face of an angel… A broad black sash circled her waist, and on its buckle was a large wooden crucifix with a crucified Jesus in copper. "I am not a Madame," she replied. "I am a sister." "Hello to the sister," I corrected myself, "I ask to be accepted to your convent." She was not taken aback by my request. Apparently they were used to people knocking at the gates of the convent… "I do not have the authority to accept you. Come with me to the mother superior and she will decide." I followed her… "Wait here," she said, and entered a room on the left of the corridor. I heard voices from the room and then she said, "Come in" and went on her way. I stood in front of the mother superior. "Who sent you here?" she asked

20 For details as to how Jewish children reached the convents, see testimonies of Aliza Penski-Chayut, YVA, O.3/3410, and Yonah Altshuler, YVA, O.3/5568; Leah Fried-Blumenkranz, "Lilka — the Convent Girl" (Hebrew), *Edut*, vol. 10 (1994), pp. 74–76; *Kurek-Lesik Collection*, testimony of Sister Zofia Makowska, pp. 64–66, and testimony of Sister Ambilis Filipowicz, p. 119.

me. I felt frightened and I stammered. "Madame Jadwiga. She told me that it would be good for me here and that I would find shelter both in the winter and the summer, and that I would no longer be at the mercy of the farmer..." "If Madame Jadwiga wishes you to be educated in the convent, I will accept you by her grace." She took a form out of a drawer. "Your name and surname?"... "Sister," I said, "I have a certificate." She glanced at the certificate, then read it carefully, looked at me, and did not say a word. She knew the meaning of a certificate like this... Placing the certificate on her desk, she turned to me and said, "Everything is clear and understood. Go to the kitchen and Sister Zofia will show you what to do."[21]

## Did the Convents Adopt a Policy of Rescue?

Can the convents' willingness to admit Jewish children, as reflected in numerous testimonies, be considered a deliberate policy of rescue? The answer to this key question is — not necessarily. Above all, the mortal risk entailed in the rescue of Jewish children cannot be overemphasized. The nuns' vows did not require them to take such a risk, nor did any religious authority instruct the convents to undertake rescue actions. Of the many testimonies collected by Kurek-Lesik in the 1980s from nuns for her study on children who were rescued by convents, only one respondent, a mother superior, reported that she had consulted with her bishop about whether to rescue a Jewish girl — and he gave her his blessing.[22]

In occupied countries in western Europe, such as Belgium and France, the Germans left the church and its hierarchy unharmed and intact. Indeed, during the occupation the church hierarchy in those countries grew stronger after the collapse of their political leaders.[23] However, in Poland, the Germans had no qualms about directly attacking the church hierarchy, which they considered part of the national Polish elite. By destroying the church's central administration and isolating it from the outside word, they hoped to undermine the bishops' control of their flock. Polish priests who were suspected of aiding

---

21 Kuper, *At the Edge of the Forest*, pp. 115–116.

22 *Kurek-Lesik Collection,* testimony of Sister Roberta Sutkowska, pp. 88–92.

23 Mark Van Den Wijngaert, "Belgian Catholics and the Jews During the German Occupation, 1940–1944," in Dan Michman, ed., *Belgium and the Holocaust: Jews, Belgians, Germans* (Jerusalem: Yad Vashem, 1998), p. 225.

Jews faced the death penalty just as did all other Poles: their clerical garb gave them no immunity. In addition, as we have noted, the senior Polish priesthood was fundamentally hostile toward the Jews — a well-known attitude, which remained unchanged during the occupation.[24]

In contrast to western Europe, where the church hierarchy instructed the clergy to shelter fugitive Jews, especially children,[25] in Poland, the high-ranking clergy preferred to leave the matter to the discretion of each convent. Thus in most cases the decision was left in the hands of the mother superior, who acted as her conscience and the capacity of her convent dictated.[26]

Once the children were admitted, the mothers superior did their best to keep the secret to themselves, for fear someone on the convent staff would inform the Germans. In some cases they shared the secret with a few trusted nuns, mainly the children's direct caregivers, so they would know how to behave if the youngsters' true identity caused problems. Over time, though, the children's appearance or behavior often betrayed them, or they admitted their Jewishness because they could no longer endure the psychological burden of living under the pressure of convent life with a dual identity.

Some convents engaged in rescue actions on the basis of what might be described as a policy dictated by their superiors. Examples were the Uniate convents of the Studite order in Eastern Galicia, which accepted the authority of Metropolitan Andrei Szeptycki,[27] and, on a larger scale, the convents of the Franciscan Missionary Sisters of Mary. At the instructions of the order's Mother General, Ludwika Lisówna, and of the Mother Provincial of the Warsaw area, Matylda Getter, these convents gave shelter to Jews — adults and children alike. According to church data based on testimonies collected from nuns who were involved in the rescue work, thirty-five convents of the Congregation of Sisters of the Family of Mary, from the Franciscan order — five in Warsaw, three in Lvov, and the rest across Poland — rescued children.[28]

24  Heller, *Edge of Destruction*, pp. 109–114.
25  Asher Cohen, *History of the Holocaust. France* (Hebrew) (Jerusalem: Yad Vashem, 1996), pp. 327–335; Michael R. Marrus and Robert O. Paxton, *Vichy France and the Jews* (New York: Basic Books, 1981), pp. 270–279.
26  Kurek, *Your Life*, p. 49.
27  David Kahane, *Lvov Ghetto Diary* (Amherst: University of Massachusetts Press, 1990), p. 142; Levin, *Specje*, pp. 174–175.
28  Ewa Kurek-Lesik, "Conditions of Admittance and the Social Background of Jewish Children Saved by Women's Religious Orders in Poland from 1939–1945," *Polin*, vol. 3 (1988), pp. 246–247; *Kurek-Lesik Collection*, p. 296.

Like the Franciscan Sisters, the Gray Ursulines (*Urszulanki Szary*) acted on the basis of orders from above. Their rescue actions for children were coordinated by the Mother General, Pia Leśniewska, who maintained contact with Żegota activists from her headquarters in the "Gray House" in Warsaw.[29]

It may be misleading to speak of a "dictated policy" in this context, because even convents that were instructed to admit Jewish children received this message in the form of a recommendation, not an order. Since such actions endangered everyone in the convent, the ultimate decision was left to the discretion of the mother superior. She also had to take into account the convent's capacity. However, there is no doubt that an instruction from a higher authority carried much weight with the nuns, who were accustomed to obeying their superiors, particularly if they themselves were in doubt. Ultimately, this was reflected in the number of children these convents admitted. It is for good reason that the Franciscan Sisters are credited with the largest number of Jewish children saved.[30]

## Life of Jewish Children in the Convents

Outsiders tend to visualize a convent as an institution swathed in mystery and devotion that immerses visitors in a holy aura. This perception is due mainly to the convents' reluctance to reveal anything concerning their way of life to strangers. Those who enter a convent and begin to understand the living arrangements, customs, and rituals do discover moments of splendor and awe, but by and large they find a gray, bleak reality, and particularly, psychological stress. Convent life has been researched extensively, and works of fiction and nonfiction on the subject abound. Here, however, our focus is on the unique problems of Jewish children who found themselves in convents as fugitives from the certain death that threatened them outside.

To understand the experiences of these children, it is necessary to know something about the convent way of life. The convent regimen and the relationship between nuns and pupils involve elements that may seem strange to those unfamiliar with convent reality: a blend of kindness, mercy, and strictness, sometimes accompanied by eruptions of violence. The framework is a rigid hierarchical system of submissive wards subject to their superiors'

29 Kurek, *Your Life*, pp. 44–48.
30 *Kurek-Lesik Collection*, pp. 158–159.

edicts. The convent education system is entirely religion-based and traces its origins to an age-old tradition that exists throughout the Christian world.

The convents had a boarding-school character, with the children organized in learning groups by age. The sister in charge of each group, sometimes aided by older pupils, instructed her charges in the rules that govern all activities in convent life. Newly-arrived children were placed in the appropriate age group and acclimatized to a regimen of order and discipline. They were taught the rules of modesty — how to dress, undress, and bathe without exposing their bodies — and instructed to discharge their duties in unbending adherence to the convent's schedule. Discipline was strict and violators were punished. Some convents invoked humiliating corporal punishment for breaches of discipline: slapping, kneeling down for hours, and public lashings on the posterior.[31]

The convent followed a fixed, unbroken schedule, which combined devotional and lay activity. The day began with matins in the chapel and ended with vespers before bed. Between these religious services, the children engaged in study, prayer, domestic duties, and had a small amount of leisure time. The activities were interrupted by meals, before which grace was recited. The following is an example of a regular day's schedule at the orphanage in Czersk, a convent of the Sisters Servants of Mary Immaculate in Pleszew (*Służebniczki pleszewski*):

| | |
|---|---|
| 7:00 | Wake up, washing, tidying the room, exercising |
| 8:00–9:00 | Morning prayers (matins) and breakfast |
| 9:00–12:00 | Studies |
| 12:00–13:00 | Lunch, washing dishes |
| 13:00–14:00 | Rest period |
| 14:00–15:00 | Arts and crafts |
| 15:00–18:00 | Domestic duties by rotation |
| 18:00–19:00 | Supper |
| 19:00 | Evening prayers (vespers) and bed[32] |

It is the declared function of convents to turn their wards into good, devout Christians by educating them in the spirit of the Christian faith. Accordingly, apart from a few elitist residences, convents provided their pupils with no secular intellectual stimulation; formal school studies were secondary. In any

---

31 Testimony of Magdalena Orner, YVA, O.3/6745; testimony of Aliza Penski-Chayut, YVA, O.3/3410; *Kurek-Lesik Collection*, testimony of A. S., pp. 106–115.
32 Kurek-Lesik, *Your Life*, p. 71.

event, that was the situation during the war. If there was a school nearby, the children attended it. In the case of convents located in rural areas, where there was no school, the children carried out domestic duties in the convents and seasonal work for farmers in return for food. Since the religious atmosphere was the most important element of convent life, even during educational activity the children learned devotional songs and engaged in prayer and were regaled by the nuns with stories about saints, the miracles they wrought, and the life of Jesus. Worship of the Virgin Mary, which was especially intense in the Polish convents, had a profound effect on the religious beliefs of the Jewish girls.

The festivals and the preparations for them played an especially important role in convent life. In anticipation, the pupils cleaned and decorated the chapel, the nuns prepared better food, and for the festive Mass and feast the children dressed in holiday attire that was reserved for these occasions. The resplendent, highly-defined rituals that accompanied the Christian liturgy infused color into the monotonous daily life of the convent.[33]

As noted, most of the Christian children in the convents hailed from poor socioeconomic strata, including foundlings and children born out of wedlock whose parents had abandoned them, but in the convent all children were equal, irrespective of origin and social class. Their parents' background or misdeeds were not held against them, and it was not the custom to probe into the children's past. This attitude somewhat eased the plight of the Jewish children, who could not, of course, tell about their background. Irit Kuper relates that some girls in her convent in Ignac&oacute;w talked about their family and home, whereas others knew nothing about their origins. For Kuper this was a convenient state of affairs. No one in the convent asked her where she was from or the names of her parents and relatives. They accepted her as an illegitimate child, which did not bother her in the least.[34]

A Jewish child from a bourgeois home who found himself in a convent had to adjust to a new reality for which he was totally unprepared. In most cases, the convent was not his first refuge; he might have already undergone traumatic experiences involving mortal peril, loss of parents and siblings, and parting from those near and dear to him. Now left to his own devices and taken to a convent, his self-confidence, lost when his familiar world collapsed around him, was at a nadir.

---

33 Janina David, *A Touch of Earth* (New York: Orion Press, 1969), pp. 104–106; see also Shlomo Breznitz, *Memory Fields* (New York: Alfred A. Knopf, 1993), pp. 73–81.
34 Kuper, *At the Edge of the Forest*, p. 119.

Janina David, the daughter of affluent bourgeois parents, was thirteen years old — a relatively advanced age — when brought to a convent. Her guardian had prepared her for the change and found an institution that was considered prestigious. Even so, she had no idea what to expect. When told that she would have to move to a convent, Janina was gripped with fear. She knew she would have to conceal her Jewish identity and assumed this would make it hard for her to form friendships. Afraid of the unknown, she tried to imagine an optimistic picture of social life in a residence such as those in England or Russia, about which she had read. However, the Christian maid who worked devotedly in her parents' home destroyed her imaginary world in one stroke.

> "It's an orphanage you are going into," she wailed, wiping her eyes. "They will thrash you and punish you and keep you on your knees for hours. And you will go barefoot in winter and live on cabbage and potatoes. Oh, my poor child, who would have thought that it would come to that, you going into one of those places!...You'll meet there orphans and foundlings of unknown parents."[35]

Most children who were admitted to convents in an orderly, formal way arrived with forged birth certificates attesting that they had been duly baptized and were Christian. A few had been coached before the transition; they had memorized a cover story, knew what to reveal and what to conceal, and had learned to cross themselves, recite the prayers, and behave correctly in church. Those whose Christian nannies had taken them to church were familiar with basic Christian concepts. Nevertheless, most of them, however assimilated, found convent life to be utterly different.

Janina, raised in a somewhat assimilated home, had been captivated by the Christian faith since her childhood. Even in the ghetto she yearned to be a Christian, and, when taken to the Aryan side resolved to convert. However, this did not help her. Her pronounced semitic facial features, swarthy skin, and black curly hair testified to her Jewishness, and a hundred witnesses, and a certificate of baptism could not obscure this. All she knew when taken to the convent were a few Christian prayers. At morning Mass she imitated the other girls' movements and lagged behind them. Eventually she had to confess to the stunned nun in charge that, although thirteen years old, she had yet to take her first communion.[36]

---

35  David, *A Touch of Earth*, p. 24.
36  Ibid., pp. 15–16.

Miriam Klein was ten years old when, clutching a forged birth certificate in the name of an orphaned Polish girl, she was taken to the Sercanki convent in Przemyśl through the mediation of the RGO. At that time her parents were hiding with peasants in the country and paid for the girl's upkeep. Among the sixty children in the convent, thirteen were Jewish fugitives. Miriam looked Jewish, and the nuns took special care of her to keep her from being observed. The other Jewish girls were unversed in the nuances of the Catholic liturgy. To keep their mistakes from being noticed at Mass, the nuns placed them in the last row, where they genuflected and imitated their Catholic classmates standing in front of them.[37]

Some children, especially those who had previously lived with Christian families, become completely disoriented when they entered the convent and encountered black-robed nuns and submissive youngsters. After having formed a close attachment with their Christian caregivers and believing they were safe, they were abruptly torn from the homes to which they had become accustomed with no explanation, and were once again among strangers. However, once they recovered from their initial shock they began to feel that convent was bearable and, perhaps, even safer than their previous shelter.

Fredzia Student, who found refuge in the Turkowice convent, was about eight years old when the Germans captured her and her mother near the town of Hrubieszów. By then, her father and grandparents had been killed — she had lost everyone but her mother. The two roamed in fields and villages and endured the villagers' abuse until the Germans caught them and took them to detention in Hrubieszów. As they were being led away, Fredzia's mother told her to pretend not to know her and to deny being Jewish. Fredzia complied. The mother and daughter were incarcerated separately, and young Fredzia, interrogated about her mother, insisted stubbornly that she was a Polish girl and did not know "that woman." After her mother was murdered before her eyes, she was turned over to a Polish woman who treated her well. However, for reasons she did not understand, she did not stay there for long and was placed in the Turkowice convent. Years later, she described how she made her way there:

> One day, a man appeared and told me he had come to take me to a convent. The Polish woman did not want to give me up, and I did not want to leave her. I was very afraid of the convent. But the man ignored us and told the Polish woman to pack my belongings. . . I parted from her

37  Testimony of Miriam Klein, *Kurek-Lesik Collection*, p. 188–190; and in YVA, O.3/4071.

and traveled with the man to the convent. When I got off the train, I was approached by a group of children and a nun. Several of them took my bundles from me and they all walked together with us to the convent. The children looked very serious and quite sad. I was afraid to go to the convent, and I began to cry. The nun calmed me and said that all the children here have a good life where they are good Christians and pray a lot. That made me even more afraid, because I did not know how to pray. They led me into a large hall, where lots of pictures of saints were hanging. The hall was very gloomy and the children were so quiet. ... . I did not want to stay in this place and I thought how to escape. But I did not escape because I remembered that I'd have to hide in the forest all the time so they would not catch me, and I was even more afraid of that.[38]

The story of how Fredzia reached the convent and her hatred of her new home is not unusual. Almost all the Jewish children felt this way, but they also believed they had finally reached safety. In testimonies that attempt to reconstruct the experience of the first encounter with the convent, comments such as the following recur: "When I reached the convent after the nightmares I had endured, I felt a great sense of relief. I felt as if I were in Paradise. The prayers and the surroundings spoke to me. I was enamored with the quiet in the church; I felt enveloped in spiritual serenity."[39]

The quiet surroundings, the monotonous work, the sounding of bells at regular intervals, the prayers, and the nuns' singing combined to instill an atmosphere of tranquility and calm in those who had fled to convents from the commotion of the street. It was even more so with the anxiety-ridden children who had been shifted from place to place without knowing what would become of them. Now, as if hurled from a turbulent sea onto a placid island, they suddenly found themselves surrounded by quiet and seclusion. Outside, death lurked at every step; inside, behind the convent walls, life went on as if there were no war. Aliza Penski describes her first day in the convent:

I was placed with a group of children who were playing in a circle. Quickly I became re-accustomed to playing children's games. I was like a regular resident there. In the evening, after vespers, we went to bed. The room was very large and had rows of small white beds. I was given

---

38 Ephraim Dekel, *Survivors of the Sword* (Hebrew) (Tel Aviv: Ministry of Defense Publishing House, 1963), vol. I, pp. 151–156.
39 *Kurek-Lesik Collection*, testimony of Nina E., p. 60, and of Luba L., p. 194.

a bed near a little blonde girl who became my best friend. . . The supervisor of the room was a young, pretty nun named Barbara, whose bed was behind a curtain in the corner. Before I went to sleep, I was told that we all had to sleep on our backs, our arms folded over our hearts. . . . That's how I fell asleep. The next morning, I woke up before all the children. I looked around. . . and saw that everyone was sleeping quietly and calmly, meaning there was no longer anything to fear. Very slowly many heads began to rise. . . Sister Barbara stepped out from behind the curtain, fully dressed, and with a cheerful "Good morning" ordered us all to get up and wash. I took my place in the long line to wash my face and brush my teeth. We got dressed and went to a small chapel on the top floor, where I prayed fervently to Him Who sits on High, asking Him to return me quickly to my parents and my home.[40]

Aliza's idyllic account of her first day in the convent is unquestionably an accurate depiction of the sudden serenity that enveloped her in her new home after her previous anxieties. However, she and others in similar circumstances were still far from safety. Convents in Poland were exposed to brutal surprise visits whenever Gestapo agents or German police suspected that they were concealing Jews — much more than in similar institutions in occupied France or Belgium. Indeed, denunciations in convents were known to occur, although the informers were likely to be employees or outsiders, not the nuns. Janeczka Kapral, a young Jewish girl who passed for a Christian, was taken to the Nazareth Convent in Olszytyń, near Częstochowa. A sad girl, she hardly spoke with the other children, and even the nuns who cared for her knew nothing about her origins. Some time later, the Germans arrested her parents, traced her to the convent, and murdered her.[41]

One night, a car full of Gestapo men pulled up at the gate of the Ursuline convent in Siercz. They raided the dormitory, shone flashlights in the faces of the sleeping girls, and arrested two Jewish girls who were in hiding there. The girls never returned.[42] Nevertheless, the cloistered convents, separated from the surrounding population, provided relatively secure shelter for Jewish children who managed to reach them. After they made their adjustment to their new situation, the youngsters felt safer and less anxious. Under the circumstances, this subjective response should not be lightly dismissed. The

---

40 Testimony of Aliza Penski-Chayut, YVA, O.3/3410.
41 *Kurek-Lesik Collection*, testimony of Sister Rozmari Werbinska, pp. 122–123.
42 Wladyslaw Bartoszewski and Zofia Lewin, *Ten jest*, p. 811.

convent gave them a roof, enough food to fend off hunger, and a bed. However, it did not solve the problem of their Jewish identity.

Although most Jewish children reached convents under an assumed Christian identity or at least a vague identity, their Jewish identity eventually surfaced and they never managed to free themselves from it in order finally to achieve safety. The testimonies of the nuns who cared for Jewish children show that, apart from infants and toddlers, all the children who were taken in by the convents were aware of their true identity and understood its grave existential significance. Even the youngest of them, who had only a hazy knowledge of the secret of their identity, made a supreme effort to keep the truth from emerging.

The mother superior of the Franciscan Sisters' convent in Łomna, Tekla Budnowska, admitted several Jewish children who had been brought to her from Warsaw. They came with forged birth certificates, and she was told that they had been baptized. However, she knew they were Jewish and asked them to tell her their real names, so she could memorize them for when they would be looked for after the war. But her inquiries were in vain; the youngsters stuck stubbornly to the assumed names that appeared on their false birth certificates. Their mothers, Sister Budnowska explained years later, had taught them not to divulge their real names under any circumstances. In her estimation, the children were no more than three or four years old.[43]

In the convent where Irit Kuper was living, there was a girl of kindergarten age named Maryla. With blue eyes and blonde hair, she hardly looked Jewish, but her behavior at play aroused Irit's suspicions, and she took her under her wing. One day, Irit decided to get to the bottom of the mystery. She asked Maryla where she was from and whether she remembered her parents and her home. Maryla leveled her blue eyes at Irit and answered, "My mother told me not to say anything." Irit hugged her and said, "That's alright, Maryla. Never tell anyone."[44]

The older children were well aware of the dangers inherent in the exposure of their Jewish identity. They arrived at the convent haunted by the fear of being denounced and turned over to the authorities, and they did not trust anyone. This is attested to by Michał Glowiński, who reached the Turkowice convent after hiding in the countryside with his mother and having already been in two previous convents:

43 *Kurek-Lesik Collection*, testimony of Sister Tekla Budnowska, pp. 164–165.
44 Kuper, *At the Edge of the Forest*, pp. 125–126.

I was afraid of everyone and everything. However, I was not afraid of
the nuns. I knew they were rescuing me and that I would experience
nothing bad from them. Mostly I was afraid of the children of my age,
that they would denounce me. I knew that I was different, that I was a
Jew, and was therefore someone condemned to death. I learned this very
quickly. I knew I must not take my clothes off in anyone's presence, so
that no one would see "it." And in Turkowice this fear did not leave me
for one moment. Paralyzed by fear and shyness, I did not make friends
with anyone.[45]

Children who lived under assumed identities could not stand the psychological burden for very long. Inevitably, they sought out a kindred soul to
share their secret and breach the rigid barrier of isolation behind which they
lived. The Jewish girls in the Gray Ursuline convent in Milanówek learned to
trust the mother superior, Andrzeja Górska, pouring out their hearts to her
and revealing their true identity. She was profoundly moved by the children's
self-restraint and ability to keep their secret. To illustrate the prevailing situation — after the war — she explained that she had been informed of two
sisters who were living in the convent under different last names. When their
grandmother came to visit them, she described one as her granddaughter and
the other as "an acquaintance." Had they not already revealed the truth to her,
she would never have discovered it.[46]

Keeping the secret did not always help. In the crowded intimacy of convent life, it was almost impossible to conceal one's Jewish identity for long.
There was no masking the Jewish appearance of a few of the children, and
some youngsters, as we have seen, were unfamiliar with Christian customs
or, for lack of confidence, overdid their reactions and called attention to
themselves. For example, the nuns of the Servants of Jesus Convent (*Sługi
Jezusa*) in Tarnów correctly identified one of the girls as Jewish because she
prayed too loudly and crossed herself too fervently.[47] The Jewish children's
good manners, acquired at home, and their wide vocabulary also threatened
to bring them under suspicion, because these traits set them apart from the
majority of convent children, who came from the fringes of Christian society.
Sometimes, too, children revealed their secret in their sleep or while delirious
with a fever.[48]

45 Sliwowska, *The Last Eyewitnesses*, vol. I, p. 57.
46 *Kurek-Lesik Collection*, testimony of Sister Andrzeja Górska, pp. 300–301.
47 Ibid., testimony of Sister Jozefa Kolkowska, pp. 202–203.
48 Testimony of Magdalena Orner, YVA, O.3/6745.

However, most children admitted to convents soon began to integrate into their new circumstances and to feel that the mortal danger had passed. However, a new feeling quickly ensued: one of alienation and inferiority because of their Jewishness, compounded by the abusive epithets in Christian antisemitic tradition. After all, convent education was based on Christian fundamentalism which is rife with negative imagery of Jews: Jews collectively committed deicide and subjected the Son of God to torture. As such, Jews were seen as the very embodiment of evil and treachery who deserve punishment, including banishment from Christian society. The relentless contrast between the devoted care given them by the nuns in the convents and their remarks about the Jews, further exacerbated the Jewish children's guilt feelings on account of their alleged "sins."

Tamar Lubliner was about eight years old when she reached the Zagórze convent. She has nothing but praise for the nuns who cared for her but recalls that the same nuns, when teaching religion, referred ceaselessly to the Jews' contemptible nature — although they never attacked her personally for being Jewish.[49]

Obviously, in such an atmosphere, the children attempted to keep their Jewish identity secret — not only to avert denunciation to the Germans but also for the very shame of belonging to so "contemptible" a people. Relentless talk about the Jews' reprehensible traits, including derisive imitation of their behavior and manner of speech, combined with whispers behind their back, made the lives of some of the convent children unbearable. Janina David, who stood out in her convent thanks to her refined manners and high intelligence, helped tutor one of the institution's external pupils. This girl, younger than Janina, revered her and followed her everywhere. One day she approached Janina, stared straight at her, and said, "They say you are Jewish! But it can't be true! Is it?" Frightened, Janina took a deep breath and swore that she was not Jewish. "Mother will be so glad when I tell her," the girl said. Janina asked her, "And if I were Jewish, would it make difference?" The girl's eyes welled with tears, and she replied, "How can you say such a thing! You know it would — but you aren't!"[50]

Children like Janina, old enough to understand the nature of the world they were living in, looked for ways out of the mire. When they failed, they became frustrated, depressed, and lonely. Janina, for example, tried to make herself useful in the convent — notwithstanding the unspoken rule in such

49 Testimony of Tamar Lubliner, YVA, O.3/1397.
50 David, *A Touch of Earth*, p. 60.

institutions: never volunteer for anything — lest she be accused of being not only a Jew but also a lazy Jew. Thus, she offered to help with any task, be it peeling potatoes, fetching pails of water, or washing the floors, to blur the stain of her Jewishness.[51]

In such cases, the simplest way to overcome the mental hardship was to confess to a kindred soul who could listen, understand, and maybe even help. A combination of innocence and a wish to be honest with their benefactors eventually prompted some of the girls to confess their identity to nuns who had earned their trust. Janina's confessor was Sister Zofia, a nun in the classical tradition, who readied her for her first communion and escorted her to baptism. One evening, Janina suddenly began to talk to Sister Zofia about her parents' home, though until then she had not discussed it with anyone. Slowly, she began to tell her story and pour her heart out to the nun. When her account reached the stage of life in the ghetto, her voice broke. She evokes the occasion vividly in her memoirs:

> Sister Zofia turned off the lights. . . and opened the window. . . "Tell me about the ghetto," she said, leaning her head on the window frame. I scrutinized her face anxiously . . But there was no visible change of expression. I talked about our wanderings. . . of Father's illness. . . of our hunger and the beggars dying each day on the streets. Of Mother's miscarriage. . . and of the last terrible days in the cellar. And of my escape from the ghetto. . . and of Father's letters which stopped so mysteriously last autumn. The words poured out of me like blood, in an uneven flow, hot and confused. My back was covered with sweat and my hands cold and clammy, but my head was burning. When I stopped, feeling dizzy with fatigue, I was conscious only of an immense relief. The abscess had burst, the enormous burden of lies and fears which I had been carrying with me all this time was suddenly washed away. I leaned back against the wall, eyes closed . . . Sister Zofia stood motionless. . . staring into the snowy night . . . "Your father. . . must be a wonderful man. I hope I shall meet him and your mother too, soon." "You will," I promised. "I'll bring them both to meet you, when they come to look for me.". . . She smiled and, in a sudden awkward movement, patted my head. Then, embarrassed by such uncharacteristic tenderness, she looked at her watch and exclaimed in horror, "It's past midnight! Heavens! Off to bed with you, quick!" I laughed and ran upstairs, feeling as light as a feather.[52]

---

51  Ibid.
52  Ibid., pp. 94–95.

Troubled ceaselessly by the knowledge of their true identity and the secret life they had to lead as a result, the Jewish children looked for others around them who shared the same background. If there were several Jewish children in the convent, their finely tuned senses often brought them together. The nuns could not always tell Jews and non-Jews apart, but the Jewish children themselves knew. Among approximately 115 orphans in the Franciscan Sisters' convent in Łomno, twenty-two girls and one boy — according to the mother superior, Tekla Budnowska — were Jewish. Some were identifiable as such, others were not. All the girls had forged Christian birth certificates. One day, one of the older Jewish girls reported that eleven-year-old Teresa, who behaved like a Christian in every respect, was in fact Jewish. "She doesn't look like a Jew at all," the mother superior replied. But the girl insisted, and she was right. "We smell each other," she explained. Indeed, the Jewish girls felt close to each other; the younger ones would trail the older ones and help them when their turn for domestic tasks arrived.[53]

One way the Jewish girls identified each other was on the basis of exceptional behavior: clear anxiety when Jews were discussed, especially when they were maligned; exaggerated manners; or use of phrases that were common in Jewish homes. One day, as clean underwear was being handed out by a nun in the Felician convent in Kraków, a girl with the markedly Christian name of Krysia received a torn undershirt and without thinking said resentfully to her friend Nina, "Look at this torn *Leibik*" (Yiddish for undershirt). After the nun left, Nina asked her directly, "You're Jewish, aren't you?" Discomfited, Krysia at first swore that it was not true. But under pressure from Nina, who disclosed that she, too, was Jewish, Krysia confessed. From that moment the two girls became close friends. Krysia then brought a third girl, her cousin, into their secret conspiracy. Afterwards, the three of them went to the chapel to huddle together and tell one another about themselves. Three other girls in the convent were also thought to be Jewish, and Nina's threesome tried to defend them against harassment by Christian girls.[54]

Janina David's testimony provides another example of shared responsibility among Jewish children who met each other at random in a convent. A new girl, about five years old, was brought to the convent one day, and her brown hair and almond-shaped eyes made her suspect. The younger children surrounded her immediately and began to interrogate her about her name. "Is it Rivka? Sarah?" they shouted. Janina interrupted, pulled the girl toward

---

53  *Kurek-Lesik Collection*, testimony of Sister Tekla Budnowska, p. 162.
54  Ibid., testimony of Nina E., pp. 57–58.

her, and told the children, "Her name is Franka." From then on, she protected "Franka" as though she were her own little sister. But when she tried to elicit details about her past and her parents, "Franka" glared at her in silence. One night, when the girl came down with a high fever, Janina sat at her bedside and watched over her. Suddenly she sat up, looked straight at Janina, and told her clearly, "My name is Sarah." Janina, stunned, looked around to make sure no one had overheard. Then she said, "You are Franka, my little girl. Don't forget it." Afterward she pulled the blanket over the girl's head and stroked her.[55]

## Conversion of Jewish Children

One way to be rid of the burden of Jewish identity was to exchange it for a Christian identity through baptism. Some children chose this path by themselves, with the nuns' encouragement and assistance. However, many other children, especially younger ones, were baptized and thus converted without being asked and without understanding the significance of the act and its implications for their future. What the Jewish children underwent on their way to Christianity cannot be understood without some knowledge of the relevant circumstances and the prevailing atmosphere.

A convent is, above all, a proselytizing institution, in the sense that those who take the vows are expected to serve as exemplars of Christian life and attract as many people as possible to the faith. In Poland, the Franciscan Sisters, who were involved in education and the care of needy children, were especially noted for their missionary work. They were also responsible for saving many Jewish children. The statutes of the Franciscan missionary community of the Sisters of Mary (*Misjonarki Maryi*) state that, "those who care for unfortunate and abandoned children should remember that Jesus loved such children more than anyone on earth."[56] Therefore, it was only natural for nuns caring for Jewish children in the convents to strive to convert them to Christianity. The testimonies of such nuns abound with expressions of satisfaction and pride regarding prized wards who embraced Christianity and refused to return to Judaism. For example, two nuns from Lublin describe a Jewish girl who, after the war, vehemently refused to leave her convent despite the entreaties of the Jewish committee. "They offered her mountains

---

55  David, *A Touch of Earth*, pp. 87, 96–97.
56  *Kurek-Lesik Collection*, p. 62.

of gold, but Stasia defended herself courageously and insisted that she was a Christian and was resolved to remain in Poland."[57] Sister Andrzeja Górska of the Gray Ursulines testified with undisguised pride that several nuns in her order were of Jewish origin, having entered the order's convents during the war as refugees.[58] However, it would be wrong to ascribe the rescue actions of all nuns purely to missionary motives. Moreover, not all children who found shelter in convents were baptized. The reality was immeasurably more complex and not always unequivocal.

Children who reached the convent with a certificate of baptism, whether genuine or false, were rarely questioned about their background, but were simply recorded as Christians. If they lacked a certificate of baptism, as foundlings of unknown origin, they were baptized, given a Christian name, and registered as an adherent of Christianity. This procedure was identical for both children of Christian origin and for Jewish children who arrived without a baptismal certificate. If for any reason a child was not baptized immediately upon admission, this was done when he fell ill and there was concern for his life. The testimonies of many nuns who looked after Jewish children describe the baptismal procedure as being done routinely and without giving the matter much thought; from the nuns' standpoint, it was inconceivable for a child who lived in a convent, or was about to die there, to be denied the state of grace provided by baptism. Not only children without the requisite certificate were baptized; in most cases, youngsters who arrived with forged certificates also underwent the procedure.

The issue of the baptism of Jewish children arose especially as first communion approached; the sacrament marking the child's formal induction into the Christian community. This most important ritual in the life of a believing Christian is undergone by children between seven and twelve, precisely the age of most of the Jewish children in the convents. Only a Christian may take communion; those whose Christianity is in doubt must first be baptized. The ceremony is preceded by lengthy preparations, including study of the catechism and the first confession. The children are given instruction by the clergy in the deportment of devout Christians, with particular emphasis on the importance of telling only the truth in confession.

The ceremony itself, replete with pomp and ritual, is held as a public occasion in the church. The excited children, who are dressed in white, heads bedecked in floral wreathes, line up in rows, clutching lit candles. Each ap-

57  Ibid., p. 212.
58  Ibid., testimony of Sister Andrzeja Górska, pp. 301–302.

proaches the priest in turn to receive from him, for the first time, the Eucharist. It was inconceivable that a Jewish child living in a convent could avoid participation in such a ritual.

Children of this age are naturally predisposed to conform and to identify with their teachers' wishes, and certainly this was the case with Jewish children in the convents. The nuns not only served as examples of pure, faultless Christian life, but were also the people closest to them. The children, for their part, spared no effort to meet their expectations. More to the point, any attempt to evade Holy Communion might immediately reveal their true identity, with all the implications that would entail. Such behavior, beyond exposing them to denunciation to the Germans or banishment from the convent, would also cast them in a light of anti-Christ ingrates and call into question their very ability to remain in an institution that had, at risk to itself, taken them in and shared its benevolence.

It is thus not surprising that most Jewish children were anxious to take the first communion and participated wholeheartedly in the preparations. Literature on the convent children contain many accounts of their excitement, some of whom even aspired to be named as "outstanding students" in the preparations.

At Aliza Penski's convent in Brwinów, the custom was for the outstanding pupil in Christian studies to wear a long white dress to the first communion; the other girls wore short dresses. Aliza decided to compete for the long dress and labored over her catechism. In the test, administered by the priest to the whole class, Aliza answered all the questions without hesitation and recited all the prayers, as the amazed nuns looked on. She was indeed chosen to wear the prized dress. "It had been a long time since I had been so happy. I ran straight to the chapel and thanked God for His kindness," she noted in her testimony.[59]

The fact that many Jewish children arrived in convents with forged Christian birth certificates presented the nuns with an acute dilemma. To take an unbaptized child to Communion would be sacrilege — and they could not be certain that a child with an assumed identity had been baptized. Many Jewish children revealed their identity and asked to be converted as they prepared for the Communion, particularly before the first confession. Some acted out of childhood innocence and innate honesty: they did not wish to cause their benefactors to sin. Others, especially older ones who were only too aware of their status as Jews, considered this a good opportunity to rid themselves,

59  Testimony of Aliza Penski-Chayut YVA, O.3/3410.

once and for all, of the burden of their Jewishness and the suffering it caused them; after all, they were being punished for no more than their role in the collective sin of Jesus' crucifixion. Jewish children who wished to embrace Christianity were almost always baptized surreptitiously, both for their own safety — the Germans forbade the baptism of Jews and someone might denounce them — and to avoid embarrassing them before their friends. It must also be noted, however, that amid this atmosphere of extreme pressure there were also instances of Jewish children who refused to accept Christianity and were forcibly baptized.

Nina Eker arrived at the Felician convent in Kraków with a Christian birth certificate. Her guardian, a devout Catholic, had personally given her an emergency baptism using holy water only, as opposed to the conversion ceremony that requires anointment by a priest. Nina's guardian did not divulge this to the mother superior when she placed the girl in the convent. Nina's appearance and behavior dispelled any suspicion that she might be Jewish. Before she took the first communion, fearing the sacrilege she might commit, she disclosed her Jewish identity to the mother superior and asked to be baptized in full compliance with the rules. The nun, stunned, contemplated her, and said, "My good girl, daughter of the Chosen People, let us set this aside for now." The next day, the mother superior visited Nina's guardian and rebuked her for not telling her Nina was Jewish. After all, another five of the eighteen girls in the convent were also Jewish. Eventually, to be on the theologically safe side, she baptized Nina and the other five girls festively but surreptitiously. After the war, Nina reconstructed her memory of the ceremony: "When we were baptized, we were all happy. If something happened to us, we would go to Heaven."[60]

Although only fourteen years old, Janina David went to her baptism with every intention of exorcising once and for all, the Jewish identity for which she had suffered so grievously. Before entering the convent, Janina had asked her guardian to have her baptized so she would be no different from her friends. Although her father, prepared to do anything to save her life, had agreed to this, the guardian refused. He tried to dissuade her, explaining that baptism would not help her because the procedure was irrevocable and she was too young to make such a decision. Janina resolved to embrace Christianity anyway, and when she entered the convent and began to study the tenets of the faith, her wish to become a Christian became even more intense. From the outset, she was enchanted by the Christian faith and ritual.

---

60 *Kurek-Lesik Collection*, testimony of Nina E., pp. 54–61.

She loved to participate in the chapel choir and woke up before the nuns to sing in the early Mass. Janina pronounced the Latin words of the liturgy, which she did not understand, with almost sensual pleasure: "I did not feel that way about the language of the Bible, which I also did not understand, which had cost me so many tears in school." Her Jewish identity had caused her nothing but suffering, both before and after she reached the convent. Still, her appearance made her suspect as a Jewess from her first day in the convent, and all her efforts to be a good and devoted pupil were to no avail. From the standpoint of her classmates and the nuns, she was Jewish. Now, a week before Easter, the long-awaited day came. Before she stood up to receive Holy Communion, Sister Zofia, her godmother and closest confidante in the convent, led her to the edge of town, where an elderly priest secretly baptized her. After the ceremony, Sister Zofia placed a silver medallion around her neck and suddenly hugged her. In her memoirs, Janina described her feelings after this occasion:

> While she stood in the corridor I went down on my knees and confessed to all the sins my baptism had just washed away. . . Holding Sister Zofia's hand I marched through the crowded Warsaw streets breathing in the sharp spring air. . . I held my head high and chattered non-stop. Now, nobody could hurt me. I had been baptized and given absolution. My soul was spotlessly white. . . After all, I was exceptionally lucky. Most people were baptized long before they understood what it means, while I was in a position fully to appreciate the sacrament and try to live up to its demands. My head swam. I felt drunk with the spring air, with the sudden freedom of movement, freedom from fear and overwhelming joy of belonging, at last, to the Christian Church.[61]

Not everyone experienced such a spiritual epiphany when baptized. In the Convent of the Immaculate Sisters in Szymanów, one little girl in a group of children about to make their first confession before the Holy Communion burst into tears in front of the confessional. The priest could not understand why she was weeping and tried to calm her. Then she told him that when her father had moved her and her younger brother to the Aryan side of the city to save them, he had made them swear not to become Christians under any circumstances. In her isolation, this nine-year-old girl could not cope with the conflict between loyalty to her father and awareness that she was about to commit sacrilege by receiving the communion without being baptized. The

---

61   David, *A Touch of Earth*, pp. 22, 39–40, 99–101.

nuns, apprised of the secret, baptized her surreptitiously, and the other children knew nothing about it.[62]

Several Jewish girls who found shelter in the Albertine Sisters' convent in Kraków assiduously participated in worship with everyone else, aroused no suspicions, and survived. However, one of them, the daughter of a Jewish doctor from Kraków, refused to go to church, declaring openly that she was Jewish and, as such, exempt from having to recite Christian prayers. According to the testimony of the mother superior, Polish women in the convent's hostel denounced her to the Germans, who almost certainly murdered her.[63]

The baptism of Jewish children in convents is a tragic issue fraught with both religious and moral implications. From the standpoint of the nuns, it was essential for the children's own safety and, in many cases, it was done with their full consent. Nevertheless, it gives rise to a piercing moral question that cannot always be reconciled with Catholic ethics and practice. Under Catholic canon law, children are baptized only with the consent of both or, at the very least, one of the parents, and only if there is a reasonable likelihood that they will receive a Christian education.[64] In the convents, most Jewish children were obviously baptized without consultation with their parents, who in many cases were no longer alive.

Ewa Kurek-Lesik, who studied the rescue of Jewish children in convents in Poland, attempts to understand why the nuns decided to baptize the Jewish children in their care. As she explains it, the nuns took a maternal approach to the children and baptized them because Christian mothers would take such a step for their own children in a time of danger. She does not discount the nuns' underlying missionary motive, but argues that they put themselves at great risk, were willing to forfeit their lives for the children, and acted on behalf of their conscience, which was the very essence of their lives: *Imitatio Dei.*[65]

However, Kurek-Lesik also provides examples of convents in which children were not forcibly converted. Notably, too, several nuns were opposed in principle to the baptism of their Jewish wards, even when the children requested it.

---

62 Bartoszewski and Lewin, *Ten Jest,* p. 809.

63 Kaczmarzyk, "Pomoc udzielana," pp. 1–2; JM/3636, YVA.

64 Concerning Catholic practice in the matter of baptizing non-Catholic children, see Luc Dequeker, "Baptism and Conversion of Jews in Belgium, 1939–1945," in Michman, ed., *Belgium and the Holocaust,* pp. 263–264; for the principled attitude of the mother superior of the Elizabethan convent, Ludwika Małkiewicz, see *Kurek-Lesik Collection,* p. 43.

65 Kurek, *Your Life,* pp. 94–98.

The Sacred Heart Convent in Przemyśl was very poor, but its devoted nuns enveloped the concealed Jewish children in an atmosphere of serene security. As a result, the youngsters identified with the nuns, and some requested explicitly to be converted. The nuns discouraged them. Sister Liguria taught them to recite Catholic prayers and cross themselves, explaining that this was a necessary stratagem so they would not stand out from the other children, but said they should continue to follow their own faith. She told Miriam Klein, who wished ardently to convert, that faith is not a see-saw and cannot be changed at will. When you are an adult of twenty, she continued, you may convert if you still wish to. A *siddur* (Jewish prayer book) found its way to the convent, and Sister Bernarda, discovering from Miriam what it was, took it and occasionally closeted Miriam in her room and asked her to read from it. She explained, "You'll pray to the God of the Jews and we'll pray to Jesus. When we'll pray together, perhaps we'll both survive the war."[66]

In the Turkowice convent no check was made of whether all those taking communion had actually been baptized. The mother superior, Aniela Polechajło, was imbued with deep faith but was no fanatic. She was well aware that not all the children who were brought to the convent had been baptized, but did not insist that they convert. When eleven-year-old Andrzej arrived at the convent, she took him aside and told him to behave like the other children. Raised in a Jewish home, Andrzej found Catholic customs alien to him. In the convent, though, he attended Mass every week and made his confession to the priest, just like the other children. In time, he developed a serious interest in Christianity and became religiously devout. Only then did he ask the mother superior whether it was proper for him to receive the sacrament without having been baptized. She replied that it was, but that if he felt the need, the matter could be arranged formally. Not until after the liberation, in January 1945, when Andrzej turned thirteen, did the priest baptize him at his explicit request, without anyone in the convent pressing him to take the step.[67]

The fact that Jewish children, especially girls, fell under the spell of the Catholic rites is a well-known phenomenon in research on convent children. Their testimonies show that, in their psychological and physical condition and the depressing gloominess of the convent atmosphere, the children found consolation in Christian religion and ritual. The nuns' message to the Jewish children stressed that Jesus and the Virgin Mary show kindness and mercy

66  Ibid. pp. 188–199; testimony of Miriam Klein, YVA, O.3/4071.
67  Gawrys, "Turkowice — śmierć i ocalenie," pp. 22–24.

especially toward the weak and oppressed. Considering the singular plight of the Jewish children, it is self-evident as to why this message acted as a balm to their distress. Thus, Michał Głowinski describes his path to Christianity:

> In Turkowice my world changed. I suddenly became imbued with reli-
> gious fervor. To be sure, I did not know all the prayers and the songs,
> but I prayed fervently and sincerely. I truly believed. I enjoyed spending
> time in the chapel whenever it was possible… I absorbed the religious
> instruction which we received, and most of all, what the priest had to
> say… There were diverse motives to my faith in those days. First of all,
> it gave me a sense of at least modest security in a twofold sense. In the
> purely earthly dimension, I felt intuitively that in adapting myself to the
> others or even surpassing their fervor I would become more secure… It
> also can't be excluded that through devotion I wanted to earn the favor
> of the sisters… I found no common language with the children of my
> age who did not like me, and I did not become friends with anyone. I
> was very lonely… But faith undoubtedly gave me the feeling of security
> also in a different sense. I believed that God, the great protector, would
> not abandon me and would favor me.

The religious rites practiced in Turkowice, especially its aesthetic aspects, made a deep impression on Michał. The chapel was the only clean and tidy place in the institution, and he loved to listen to the choir sing, accompanied by the organ. He found the festival services profoundly moving. After the liberation, his mother arrived after much hardship and a two-year separation. The nuns gave her a warm welcome, and after she discussed the circumstances with the priest she agreed to let Michał be baptized as a gesture of gratitude for his rescue.[68]

In other convents, too, older girls felt a need, precisely on the eve of the liberation or shortly afterward, to convert and thus make a clean break with their Jewish past. In the Gray Sisters' Ursuline convent in Warsaw, six girls converted at the end of the war and were still living there in 1950.[69] According to Sister Olga Abramczuk, the Magdalene convent in Lvov rescued nine girls, and the convent's records indicate that several of them converted in August 1944, immediately following liberation.[70]

68 Sliwowska, *The Last Eyewitnesses*, vol. I, pp. 58–59, 69.
69 *Kurek-Lesik Collection*, pp. 254–255.
70 Ibid., testimony of Sister Olga Abramczuk, pp. 105–106.

It would appear, then, that those in the Jewish community who were apprehensive from the outset that the price of saving children in convents would be their conversion to Christianity were usually right. But there was no need for coercion. The youngsters' psychological condition and their total immersion in convent society made this outcome all but natural; it could not be expected that they would behave otherwise.

## Attitude of the Nuns to the Jewish Children

Although the placid atmosphere in the convent had a reassuring effect on the Jewish children, especially at the beginning, the unbending regimen, sometimes coupled with stinging insults and corporal punishment, adversely affected all the children, especially those — like most of the Jewish children — who came from middle-class bourgeois homes. For the Jewish children, there were additional hardships: loneliness because they had to keep their identity and past secret, separation from their families, and uncertainty about what the future held in store for them.

Taking refuge in the embrace of Christianity was only one of several ways that Jewish youngsters could relieve their distress, but it was effective. Much more so than Christian children, who were among their own people and faced no mortal peril, the Jewish children yearned for a kindred soul to whom they could unburden themselves and share their secret and their anguish. Naturally, they sought such souls among the nuns who were responsible for their welfare.

Most of the nuns were not professional educators noted for their pedagogical abilities. Furthermore, the convents' rigid educational system was based on hierarchy and distance between caregiver and recipient. We have very little information about the nuns, since the very purpose of convent life is to blur their personal distinctiveness and the motives that prompted them to take the vows. The little we know about them is culled from later testimonies of those who had spent part of their childhood in a convent. Clearly, though, despite their uniform exterior appearance and their common adherence to the faith, each was different from the other, just like individuals in any group of people. Each came from a particular social background, each had her own persona. Some were intelligent women with natural teaching skills and were devoted to the children. Others possessed undisguised maternal feelings that endeared them to the children, whom they smothered with affection. Still others were ignorant, prejudiced, and spiteful, and were abusive to the youngsters in their charge. As for the nuns' special attitude toward the Jewish children, once again it is necessary to avoid generalizations and discuss only cases in which the nuns knew beyond doubt that a boy or girl in their care was indeed Jewish.

It must be noted that most testimonies of convent children, written and collected years after the events, refer to the nuns in favorable, affectionate, and appreciative terms. Expressions such as "They were good to us" or "They loved me" recur frequently, sometimes singling out by name nuns with whom the children had formed especially strong bonds. Nina Eker described her relations with the nuns who looked after her: "The three nuns who cared for us were really very good and tried very hard... Sister Marcelina was a special woman. For me she was not only a mother but a friend. She cared for us and spoilt us."[71] Even those who are critical of the convents' educational methods and emphasize the bleakness of convent life, the inflexibility, and even the cruelty shown by certain nuns, sometimes behind a mask of piety, cite "good nun" who treated them well. Hana Shchori, who had lived in the Resurrection Convent in Warsaw, was generally critical of the nuns for their unbending and unfeeling attitude toward their wards, does not fail to note, "There was only one nun there who loved me very much."[72] A. S., rescued at the Magdalene Convent in Rabka, censures the nuns for hypocritical conduct but carefully avoids generalizations. She describes the mother superior, Teresa Ledochowska, as an "elegant and refined woman" and lauds Sister Julia, the convent cook, for giving her food secretly whenever she was hungry.[73]

Nevertheless, it is impossible to overlook examples of antisemitic behavior and the offensive outbursts of nuns against Jewish children in some convents. Magdalena Orner, who was sheltered in the Felician Convent in Przemyśl and remained there for many years after the war, relates that even though she was a good and diligent student and had been singled out as a candidate to become a noviate, the nuns took a different attitude toward her after she revealed her Jewish identity: their antisemitism suddenly emerged. They would sometimes beat her to the point of drawing blood for trivial breaches of discipline, such as being late for a meal. "Szymanska [her Polish family name], don't forget that you are Żydówka [a Jewess]," they would shout.[74]

---

71  Ibid., testimony of Nina E., pp. 60–61.
72  Testimony of Hana Shchori (Rosenblatt), YVA, O.3/4751.
73  *Kurek-Lesik Collection*, testimony of A.S., pp. 114–115.
74  Testimony of Magdalena Orner, YVA, O.3/5476.

When the nuns suspected that Janina David had contracted scabies, a contagious skin disease, the nurse who was supposed to treat her shouted: "We do what we can to teach you cleanliness, but what hope have we got against racial characteristics? What has been inbred from one generation to another. . . you people were always filthy and you always will be. . ."[75] This was said to a girl who had been accustomed to strict rules of hygiene at home, and in an institution that had only the most rudimentary hygienic conditions, in which a proper bath was a rarity.

But in contrast to such antisemitic manifestations, other nuns understood the singular anguish of their Jewish wards, tried to protect them and treated them with special devotion. Miriam Klein testifies that she felt safe in the convent because she knew the nuns would protect her. Sister Bernarda, her direct caregiver, was aware of her fears and gave her a key to the chapel so she could hide beneath the altar if the Germans raided the convent in search of Jews.[76]

The Abbess Josefa — Helena Witer — who headed the convents of the Uniate Studite order in Eastern Galicia, personally welcomed the Jewish children who were referred to her, distributed them among her institutions, and saw to their safety. Despite the grave risks involved, she pursued the rescue work unflaggingly, describing it as her Christian religious duty. The wife of Rabbi David Kahane, who was also sheltered in a Uniate institution, chanced to visit Mother Josefa's convent in Lvov and found her in her private bathroom looking after two neglected Jewish girls whom someone had brought to the convent after they had jumped from a train bound for the Bełżec extermination camp. Mother Josefa bathed them, deloused them, and treated the bullet wound one of them had suffered when she was shot by a German soldier. The rabbi's wife asked if she could help, but the abbess refused, saying, "I am doing my duty and I am doing it to fulfill a commandment. I want to fulfill this commandment all by myself, without any help."[77]

Yonah Altshuler was hidden in a convent in Warsaw with another Jewish girl. After the Polish uprising was suppressed, the convent was closed down and the nuns were exiled to Germany as forced laborers. The girls' caregiver, a nun about forty years old, kept them with her and did not abandon them, despite the many hardships along the way. In her place of exile she continued to care for them as if she were their mother. She took them with her to the fields

75  David, *A Touch of Earth*, p. 139.
76  *Kurek-Lesik Collection*, testimony of Miriam Klein, pp. 188–189, and YVA, O.3/4071.
77  Kahane, *Lvov Ghetto Diary*, pp. 148–150.

where she had to work at hard manual labor from sunrise to late evening, and shared with them the meager rations she received from her German peasant overseer. After the liberation, they returned with her to Poland, and before resuming her prewar life she placed them in a convent in Częstochowa. It is no wonder that Yonah, summarizing her experiences of convent life, said, "I have a sentiment for the Catholic faith and I have nothing but good things to say about the nuns."[78]

Relationships like these between nuns and Jewish children made it very difficult to remove some of the youngsters from convents after the war. Irit Kuper was brought to the convent as a little girl and discharged as a teenager. Throughout her stay, she was aware of her Jewish identity and refused to convert, despite the pressure of the mother superior. Yet she, too, could not easily bring herself to part from the mother superior and from the convent itself. Her memoirs contain an emotional account of her experiences after she refused to convert and parted from the mother superior and the convent after the liberation:

> "Sister," I said, "I can't stay here anymore. I don't like it here." She looked at me and smiled. . . "Maybe I can help you," she offered. "No, no, thanks for everything." I woke up early and left. Everyone was sleeping and I did not say goodbye to anyone. . . I hurried across the convent courtyard. I did not glance at the kitchen, where I had worked from my first day there. Tears welled up in my eyes. Why was I crying? It troubled me to leave this shelter. I loved it. Here I had found refuge from the Germans' persecutions, from the peasants' rebukes. Here I had received a bed, a sheet and a blanket, and plenty of food. I loved the holidays, the church choir, and more than that, the nuns and the mother superior. In the morning I would listen to the nuns' tender, sad tones emerging from their windows. I imbibed their tender sadness and found in it solace for my own agonized soul.[79]

Indeed, many of the convent children retained a warm spot in their hearts for the nuns who had rescued them and cared for them, as attested by the many requests Yad Vashem has received to recognize them as Righteous Among the Nations. After they reached adulthood, several of the children corresponded with the nuns for years, sent them food parcels and medicines, and visited

78  Testimony of Yonah Altshuler, YVA, O.3/5568.
79  Irit R. Kuper, *As Everything Passes* (Hebrew) (Tel Aviv: Hakibbutz Hameuchad, 1980), p. 80.

them after Poland opened its gates to tourists. A few even brought their rescuers to visit them in Israel.


## How Many Children did the Convents Save?

The subject of the convent children was one of the most sensitive issues in the relationship between the Church and the Jews during and after the Holocaust. It occupied a great deal of attention from the Jewish public immediately after the war and for years afterwards, because not all of the children returned to the Jewish fold. The convents never disclosed how many children were rescued in their institutions, and the Jewish organizations had no data that could shed light on the subject. The question remains unresolved. Although copious testimonies about children rescued in convents have accumulated over the years, no reliable record of their number exists, and probably never will.

The children reached the convents under assumed Christian identities and were registered as such in the convent records. Even if the nuns knew they were Jewish, they did not record them as such for reasons of safety, and therefore, the convent archives cannot provide statistics. No systematic compilation of testimonies subject began until the early 1970s, more than twenty-five years after the war. By that time, many of the mothers superior who might have known the numbers had died, and those who were still alive had no records to draw on.

Beginning in the 1970s, however, comprehensive research began in Poland on the activities of the Church and the convents during the Second World War.[80] Several of these studies provide partial data on Jewish children rescued in convents. According to figures cited by Teresa Frącek, for example, nuns of the Franciscan Sisters of Mary saved 750 Jews, among whom were 500 children — 420 placed in thirty-five convents and other institutions of the order, and eighty placed with families.[81] According to a study by Magdalena Kaczmarzyk, the Albertine nuns played a similar role in rescuing Jews: fifty of ninety-five Jews who found shelter in their twenty-nine convents survived the war. Kaczmarzyk does not specify how many among them were children.[82]

80  See Kloczowski, "The Religious Orders," p. 239.
81  Teresa Frącek, "Zgromadzenie Siostr Franciszkanek Rodziny Maryi w latach 1939–1945," in *Kosciół, Katolicki na ziemiach Polski,* vol. 10 (Warsaw: ATK), 1981, p. 200, cited in *Kurek-Lesik Collection,* pp. 158–159.
82  Kaczmarzyk, Pomoc udzielana, p. 1; YVA, JM/3636.

Even though the Franciscan nuns are known to have been especially active in rescuing Jews, Frącek's figures seem to be overstated. It is noteworthy that Kurek-Lesik, who studied the subject and had no interest in belittling the nuns' role in rescuing Jews, also has misgivings about this figure. She accepts it, but with the reservation that Frącek exaggerated slightly because she did not, for example, examine the possibility that children who spent time in two convents were counted twice among those rescued.[83] According to Kurek-Lesik, 189 convents took part in rescuing children in Poland within its 1939 frontiers, of which 173 were in the area of the Generalgouvernement, including sixty-four in Warsaw and the vicinity.

In her doctoral dissertation for the Catholic University in Lublin, subsequently published in book form, Kurek-Lesik estimates that no fewer than 1,200 Jewish children were rescued in convents.[84] Elsewhere, Jerzy Kłoczowski describes the difficulties that the lack of authentic documents poses for researchers, but states in his summary that several thousand children and several hundred adults were rescued by the religious orders.[85] According to Kurek-Lesik's estimates, also based on later testimonies, three-fourths of all Polish convent orphanages and residential institutions took part in the rescue of Jewish children.[86]

The implication of these figures, if they are correct, would be that the convents rescued about one-fourth of the 5,000 Jewish children who survived the war in Poland — an untenable number according to both Jewish sources[87] and to the many testimonies from the convents that Kurek-Lesik appended to her dissertation. In most convents only a few children were rescued, in some cases only one. Accordingly, several convents deserve special mention for rescuing a relatively large number of Jewish children. For example, the Turkowice convent saved about thirty children;[88] thirteen girls survived in the Sacred Heart Convent in Przemyśl;[89] and the Franciscan Sisters' convent in Łomno rescued more than twenty.[90] Also noteworthy were the seven Stu-

---

83  Kurek, *Your Life*, p. 235.
84  Ibid., p. 102–103.
85  Kloczowski, "The Religious Orders," p. 243.
86  Kurek, *Your Life*, p. 105.
87  Dobroszycki, *Survivors of the Holocaust*, pp. 14–18.
88  Testimony of Irena Sendler, YVA, M.31/4394.
89  Testimony of Miriam Klein; *Kurek-Lesik Collection*, testimony of Liguria Grenda, pp. 184–186.
90  *Kurek-Lesik Collection*, testimony of Mother Superior Tekla Budnowska, p. 162.

dite convents of the Uniate Church in Eastern Galicia, where an estimated 150 Jews, many of them children, were rescued.[91]

In the absence of reliable sources on the number of Jewish children rescued in convents in Poland, the subject is likely to remain in the realm of conjecture.[92] In the view of this author, the number is in the hundreds, not the thousands.

Similarly nebulous is the number of convent children who did not return to Judaism. As we have stated, some of these children were toddlers or infants who knew nothing about their origins. Since most convents were not equipped to admit and care for children so young, they tried to be rid of them at the first opportunity, and after baptizing them, placed them with adoptive Christian families. According to data provided by the Franciscan Sisters, eighty such children survived after having been placed with families, but their fate remains unknown. Several nuns testified that Jewish children had been placed for adoption after lengthy stays in convents.[93] In one case, a Jewish girl was adopted by the family of a German officer. The story began when an anonymous woman placed a lovely little Jewish girl named Zosia in the nursery of the Albertine nuns in Tarnów. At first the woman visited the toddler pretending to be her mother, but soon disappeared. A German officer who visited the nursery took a liking to the girl. One day he arrived with his wife, and after he convinced the nun in charge to surrender her, the couple took the girl back to Germany.[94]

A study of the convent testimonies concerning the adoption procedures used shows that not only were the records haphazard and that the nuns did not check to see if the children had parents or other relatives, but all trace of the children was deliberately obscured. The nuns kept the names of the adoptive parents secret. After the war, when the children's parents or relatives arrived to retrieve them, there were nuns who refused to reveal the identity of the adoptive parents. On several occasion, government agencies and the courts had to intervene in order to force nuns and adoptive parents to return children to their families.[95]

91  Levin, *I Immigrated from Specje*, pp. 174–175.
92  Zygmunt Zielinski, "Activities of Catholic Orders on Behalf of Jews in Nazi-Occupied Poland," in Otto Dov Kulka, ed., *Judaism and Christianity under the Impact of National Socialism* (Jerusalem: Zalman Shazar Center, 1987), p. 391.
93  Regarding one such case, in which the Albertine Sisters in Tarnopol placed a Jewish infant with a Christian adoptive family, see Kaczmarzyk, Pomoc udzielana, p. 16; also YVA, JM/3636.
94  Ibid., p. 13.
95  Ibid., pp. 5–6.

The story of the convent children who did not return to the Jewish fold is complicated and painful and beyond the purview of this study. Suffice it to note that the difficulties that arose in this regard in Poland were no different from those in other European countries. The main difficulty was that, in the absence of parents or other relatives, the convents were unwilling to return children to Jewish institutions and refused to recognize them as the youngsters' guardians *in loco parentis*.

CHAPTER SEVEN

# The Problem of the Children after Liberation

## Situation of the Survivors after Liberation

The liberation of Poland took about a year. In January 1944, Soviet forces crossed the old, pre-1939 eastern border, and by the end of the following January had reached the Oder River, which would become the western border of the new Poland. As the German troops retreated in the face of the advancing Soviet army, the full scale of the Jewish catastrophe throughout Poland became increasingly known. Regions which only a few years earlier had been bustling centers of Jewish life were now utterly bereft of a Jewish community. Jews no longer resided in their old homes in any town or city in Poland. The first survivors emerged from their places of hiding at the beginning of 1944, when the cities in the eastern provinces began to be liberated. There were appallingly few. Of approximately a quarter of a million Jews who had lived in the Volhynia region before the Nazi occupation, only about 3,500 survived, less than two percent.[1] The Soviet forces' summer offensive, which liberated White Russia, eastern Galicia and substantial sections of central Poland, also resulted in a trickle of survivors. Here, too, the numbers were pitifully small. For example, of the 620,000 Jews who lived in eastern Galicia in the summer of 1941, just before the German conquest, no more than 10,000 to 15,000 are estimated to have survived, again about two percent.[2]

Threadbare and harried, the survivors drifted like ghosts through the streets of the cities and towns and by their former homes, now occupied by their Christian neighbors, searching for any relatives or acquaintances who may have survived, and endeavoring to reclaim at least something of their plundered property, but in vain. Those who had taken over the properties were surprised to discover that there were still Jews alive in Poland, and they

1   Shmuel Spector, *The Holocaust of Volhynian Jews 1941–1944* (Jerusalem: Yad Vashem, 1990), pp. 157–158.
2   *Pinkas Hakehillot — Encyclopedia of Jewish Communities, Poland* (Hebrew) (Jerusalem: Yad Vashem, 1980), vol. II, Eastern Galicia, pp. 17, 29.

had no intention of returning the booty. Nazi rule had been eradicated and Poland was liberated, but the old antisemitism remained and actually become more acute in the aftermath of the war. Many of the local population, Ukrainians and Poles alike, had learned from the Germans how cheap Jewish life was and that Jews could be killed with impunity. Following liberation, the traditional antisemitism was compounded by material cupidity. Those who had laid their hands on Jewish assets during the occupation now feared for the fate of their plunder, apprehensive that they would be required to return it to the former owners. Accordingly, the local population harassed and threatened the survivors if they so much as dared to approach their homes and try to claim their property.[3] Physically and mentally, the survivors were in a sorry state; many were sick and injured, and needed urgent medical treatment after years in which their health had been completely neglected. They were destitute — they had no warm clothing, no footwear, no roof over their heads, no bed on which to rest. Sometimes, if they were lucky enough to encounter Jewish soldiers or officers from the liberating forces, they received a little help in the form of food and items of clothing. But apart from that, no one came to help them. The Christian surroundings broadcast hostility and alienation. Even devout Christians, who only a short time before had assisted Jews during the Nazi occupation, and rescued them at risk to their own lives, were now afraid to come to their aid, fearing their neighbors' wrath for having dared to rescue them in the first place. The local authorities simply ignored the survivors as though they did not exist.[4]

In western Europe, the Jewish survivors were aided by welfare agencies — UNRRA (United Nations Relief and Rehabilitation Administration) and the American Joint Distribution Committee (JDC) — immediately upon their liberation, but help was slow in reaching remote Poland, now under Soviet hegemony. Aid from the JDC was delayed for almost a year after the liberation.[5] The survivors had no recourse but to rely on themselves. Indeed,

3 Hanna Shlomi, "The First Stages of Organizing the Jews in Poland at the End of World War II" (Hebrew) *Gal-Ed*, vol. 2 (1975), pp. 299–301; for a description of the situation on the ground, see Jonas Turkow, *After Liberation* (Yiddish) (Buenos Aires: Association of Polish Jews in Argentina, 1959), pp. 23–33; David Kahane, *After the Flood* (Hebrew) (Jerusalem: Mossad Harav Kook, 1981), p. 18.

4 Michal Szulkin, "Sprawozdanie z działalnoscie Referatu dla Spraw Pomocy Ludności Zydowskiej przy Polskiego Komitetu Wyzwolenia Narodowego," *BZIH*, vol. 3 (79) (1971), pp. 75–77.

5 Joseph Litwak, "The JDC Contribution to the Rehabilitation of the Jewish Survivors in Poland 1944–1949," in Benjamin Pinkus (ed), *Eastern-European Jewry from Holocaust to Redemption, 1944–1948* (Hebrew) (Sde Boker: Ben-Gurion Research Center, 1987), pp. 336–340.

spontaneous organizing by communities of survivors began immediately after the liberation of the eastern provinces of Poland. This involved mutual assistance, searching for relatives, fencing off mass graves — and also looking for ways to leave Poland, which had become one vast Jewish cemetery.[6] However, it was only within sovereign Poland, west of the Bug River, that these organizations became institutionalized. Initially, this took the form of local committees being affiliated with the Central Committee of Jews in Poland, which was established in Lublin in November 1944 and was recognized by the Polish government.[7]

On August 8, 1944, two weeks after the liberation of the city of Lublin, which functioned as the temporary headquarters of the Polish government until the liberation of Warsaw, there were some 300 Jews in the city — only fifteen of them local residents. Soon more survivors began arriving, and by the end of the month there were some 1,200 survivors in Lublin, of whom 200 were children. Their condition was desperate. As the Central Committee of Jews started to become organized, the municipal authorities restored the Y.L. Peretz Cultural Center to it, which was to become the Committee's headquarters and a place of gathering for refugees, where they were given small amounts of money and food. However, this help was not enough to meet even their most basic needs. Only about 200 of the survivors managed to find accommodation in the city on their own. The others milled around, utterly destitute, at the Jewish Committee building, at the headquarters of the Red Cross, and in other parts of the city.[8] The local committees that were established in other liberated cities at first focused solely on the need to find the survivors a place to stay and a hot meal every day, but their activities gradually expanded in the light of the ever-mounting needs and problems.

6   Yehuda Bauer, *Flight and Rescue: Brichah* (New York: Random House, 1970), pp. 3–5; Kahane, *After the Flood*, pp. 11–14; Eliezer Lidowski, *The Spark has not been Extinguished* (Hebrew) (Tel Aviv: The Partisans and Ghetto Fighters' Organization in Israel, 1987, pp. 141–161.

7   Shlomi, "The First Stages," pp. 299–313; David Engel, *Between Liberation and Flight: Holocaust Survivors in Poland and the Struggle for Leadership, 1944–1946* (Hebrew) (Tel Aviv: Am Oved, 1996), pp. 54–58.

8   Szulkin, "Sprawozdanie z działalnosci," pp. 76–77.

## Concern for Orphans

One of the most acute problems that emerged in Poland immediately after the liberation was that of the child survivors, many of whom had been orphaned and had no one to look after them. The problem was particularly serious in the Soviet-annexed eastern provinces, where there was no official Jewish committee or other Jewish organization trying to reclaim children who had been left in the care of Christian families. The older children, who were aware of their Jewish identity, took the initiative in looking for relatives in their near surroundings; when they failed to find them, they had no choice but to turn to the orphanages established by the Soviet authorities in the big cities, in the hope that someone would eventually take them out of the institution. In the orphanages they made every effort to forge ties with other Jewish children.

Sonja Altman, from the town of Werba, in the Volhynia district, had survived the war under an assumed name in a village where she lived with a Christian family who employed her as a herder. Liberated in the summer of 1944 at the age of thirteen, she returned to Werba to look for possible survivors from her family. Finding none, she entered an orphanage in a nearby city, where she suffered from antisemitic harassment, which only strengthened her Jewish consciousness. She knew she had relatives in England, but had no idea how to get away from the orphanage and join them. Six months later, she returned to Werba, where she encountered a Jewish family she knew. She left Poland together with them and reached a displaced persons camp in Germany, with the aim of joining her family in Britain.[9]

In contemporary terms, Sonja was a big girl, a young woman. Independent and resourceful, she had acquired experience of life during her struggle to survive, and was able to fend for herself even when she found herself alone after liberation. She was fortunate to encounter a Jewish family that was ready to help get her to the west. Nor was that family's attitude toward Sonja exceptional among the Jewish survivors in Poland. Few in number and surrounded by a hostile environment, the survivors drew close to one another and forged bonds of mutual aid. They sought one another out, and if they heard of Jewish children who were still living with Christian families they tried to remove them from the adoptive families. Despite their own distress and homelessness, they made every effort to return solitary children to the Jewish fold. In Rowno, a city in the Volhynia district, the survivors banded together into an unofficial community. One of their first initiatives was to remove from Chris-

9   Testimony of Sonja Altman, YVA, O.3/4057.

tian families Jewish children who had no one else to look after them. Similarly, they removed from the municipal orphanage a group of Jewish children
who were being abused by Christians. The children were placed with survivor
families who took them under their wing until they reached Poland in its new
boundaries.[10] In adopting the lone orphans, the survivors followed the ancient Jewish tenet that Jewish captives should not be left in the hands of Gentiles. It was apparently at this time that the notion of "ransoming children"
(*pidyon yeladim*) was born, based on the concept of "ransoming prisoners"
(*pidyon shvuyim*), one of the supreme precepts of Judaism.[11]

A truly formidable problem was the fate of the infants and toddlers who
had been placed in the custody of Christian families and had no idea they
were Jewish. Rabbi David Kahane, who survived the war in Lvov, learned after
his liberation that the infant daughter of his friends, Rabbi Halberstam and
his wife, who was born in the midst of the war on the Aryan side in Lvov, had
been placed with a childless Polish family for safekeeping. The parents had
perished and Kahane decided to attempt to remove the girl from the Christian family. When he arrived at their home and asked to be given custody
of the girl, they vehemently denied that she was adopted and insisted that
she was their biological daughter. After being convinced that the toddler was
indeed Rabbi Halberstam's daughter, Kahane sought the help of the police in
restoring the girl to a Jewish home, but in vain. The local police chief refused
to intervene and told him that under Soviet law it was not necessarily the
woman who bore the child who was considered the mother, but the woman
who had raised him. Since the biological mother was no longer alive in this
case, he added, what purpose would be served by taking the girl away from
her adoptive parents? Kahane decided not to let the matter rest, and as long
as he was in Lvov he continued to keep an eye on the family. After a time, in
the wake of the mass repatriation in 1946 — in which Polish citizens who had
become refugees during the war returned to their homeland — the family left
Lvov for Poland, taking the girl with them, and all trace of them vanished.[12]

From the outset, the efforts to remove surviving Jewish children from
Christian families and orphanages proved more difficult in the eastern provinces of Poland, which were annexed to the Soviet Union, than in Poland
proper. If no relatives or family friends had survived who knew of the children's whereabouts, there was virtually no way to locate them. The majority

10  Lidowski, *The Spark*, pp. 154–156.
11  Kahane, *After the Flood*, p. 15.
12  Ibid., pp. 15–16.

of the survivors in these regions seized the first opportunity after liberation to leave the Soviet-controlled areas for sovereign Poland and then try to emigrate to the west. As the Soviet regime consolidated its power in the east and the remaining Jewish survivors left, there was no one to deal with the issue of the children. An example is the fate of the toddler son of the Klonicki family from Buczacz. His parents had left him with a Polish woman in a village, and after they were murdered the woman turned him over to Ukrainian nuns and all trace of him vanished. After the war, when his relatives in Palestine and the United States learned about it, they made considerable efforts to locate him in the area which was then behind the Iron Curtain. The search lasted for many years. Finally, in 1962, aided by a local resident, they managed to trace him. But it was too late: the toddler was now a young man aged twenty and as far as he was concerned, he was a Ukrainian in every respect, and had no wish to return to the Jewish fold.[13]

Even though most of the children had spent only two or three years in Christian society before the liberation, bringing them back into the Jewish community turned out to be a complex and far from self-evident process. This was true not only for the very young children, who knew nothing about their origins, but equally for children of twelve or thirteen or even older, who were aware of their Jewish identity and of their extraordinary situation, from which it seemed only natural that they would try to extricate themselves. Some of them abandoned their places of hiding immediately after liberation and joined the survivor communities. However, many children were afraid to shed their assumed identity and leave the security of the Christian home or convent in which they had been rescued. They remained not because they felt particularly good there or because their rescuers prevented them from leaving, but because they saw no other alternative. Their testimonies show that they had longed for liberation and awaited the day impatiently, but that its actual arrival left them bewildered. After the fighting had passed by them and the liberating forces entered, they understood that a very dramatic event had occurred, but could not quite fathom what the liberation meant for them personally. Their instinctive first reaction was to wait and see what would develop.

Alex Czuban, from Lvov, was fourteen when he and his twelve-year-old sister Aviva fled from the site where both their parents had just been murdered. Searching for work with farmers in nearby villages, they were compelled to part. Aviva was taken in by a convent in Przemyśl, and her brother lost track

---

13　Aryeh Klonicki, *The Diary of Adam's Father*, pp. 83, 87–95, 108–109.

of her. Alex found work in a *plebania* (presbytery) with an antisemitic priest who did not suspect that he was Jewish. What he overheard the priest say about the Jews did not enamor him to either Christianity or the Polish nation. At the time of his liberation by the Soviet army in the summer of 1944, he was fifteen years old and mature for his age, because of his life experiences. Even so, he was utterly incapable of evaluating the new situation and had no idea what he should do, so he just continued with his work routine. He then heard rumors — which in his eyes seemed very likely — that the Russians too were killing Jews. One day, on a visit to the nearby city, he was surprised to learn that the Russian soldiers were not abusing the Jewish survivors in the streets. Only then did he decide to return to his hometown of Lvov. On the way, he stopped in Przemyśl and chanced to meet his sister walking in the street with a nun. It was their first meeting in almost a year, a period during which neither knew what had become of the other. It was a peculiar reunion between the orphaned brother and sister. To Alex's disappointment, Aviva was not happy to see him: she was evidently afraid that because of him she would be identified as a Jewess. He asked her to go with him but she refused, declaring that she now believed in Jesus and did not want to be Jewish.

In Lvov, Alex joined a municipal orphanage where other parentless Jewish survivors like him were living. He soon became an accepted member of the group and began to attend school. For some reason, he gave no thought to the fate of his sister, who had remained in the convent. About six months later, a Polish acquaintance told him he had met his sister in Przemyśl, but when he asked her whether she intended to join her brother she had immediately ended the conversation. Her behavior seemed odd, the acquaintance said. It was only then that Alex decided to go to Przemyśl and remove his sister from the convent, whatever the consequences might be. After an eventful journey, he met his sister in the convent and tried to persuade her to join him, playing on her family feelings and reminding her that they were the last survivors of the family. Imploring her to go with him, he promised her that she would be able to attend church freely. However, his arguments fell on deaf ears. Only after he threatened that if she did not agree to leave the convent of her own free will, he would disclose the fact that she was a Jewess and remove her by force with the aid of the police did she agree to go to Lvov with him.[14]

Bizarre as this story may seem, it was not unusual at the time. The two adolescents, both sentient beings, had suffered grievously, and their world had collapsed in ruins when they lost their parents. In their struggle for sur-

14  Testimony of Alexander Sarel (Czuban), YVA, O.3/5538.

vival, they made prodigious efforts to find something to cling to so as to ensure their sheer existence — food to eat and a roof over their heads. When they succeeded in finding what they craved for — he with a farmer in a village, she in a convent — they clung to it as long as they could see no better alternative for the future, however difficult the conditions might be. Some outside influence was essential to help them muster their inner forces anew and break away from their surroundings. Alex's encounter with the liberating Soviet army did not convince him that he was truly free or that his life was no longer in danger. Until he actually saw Jews walking freely in the street he was not able to fathom the full meaning of liberation. Aviva, after enduring many ordeals as she wandered between the homes of acquaintances and farmers who turned her away, had finally found a modicum of tranquility within a convent, even though it meant disavowing her Jewish identity. She was ready to forgo everything, including her ties with her brother, her only remaining relative, if she would just be left alone. Both of them knew that all their family had perished and that there was no home to return to. There is probably no more poignant example than this encounter between sister and brother who found themselves unable to draw together again, to illustrate the anguish and torment that were the lot of the survivors who had lost everything and were cut off irrevocably from their home.

The liberation and the process of returning to Jewish society is also recounted by Moshe Frank, then a boy of twelve and a cow herder in a village not far from his native city of Zamość:

> The Russian front approached us in the summer of 1944. We heard artillery fire, and occasionally planes appeared in the sky and bombed the retreating German convoys… I ran to the roads to see the debacle for myself. Intensely glad at their defeat, I watched with eyes burning with a desire for revenge. The roads were flooded with Germans… Within a day or two rumors spread that Russian troops had been seen in the area. It was hard to believe. I went to the square and saw three Russian soldiers on horseback surrounded by many farmers… Afterward, convoys of dust-covered soldiers rolled into the square. Suddenly I heard Russian songs… My joy knew no bounds… The war had moved away from us to the west. We thought that the liberation from the German yoke would bring us salvation. However, it quickly became clear that what had been lost could not be restored. During the Nazi occupation there had been some vague ray of hope that those who would survive the horrific war could look forward to a certain reward for all they had suffered

when it was all over. Yet nothing was happening. All that remained was bereavement, emptiness, and deep grief. By then I already believed in Jesus and in Christianity. Partly out of inertia, partly for lack of an alternative, I remained in the village. I tried to continue with life's routine. I found it psychologically difficult to reveal my true identity, and the truth is that I saw no point or purpose in doing so. On a visit to the market in Zamość to sell wooden objects I had made… I was approached by a group of people who wanted to buy apples from me. They spoke a language that sounded familiar; immediately I realized that it was Yiddish. I introduced myself and they at once invited me to their home, which was in the Old City, not far from the market.[15]

Moshe's testimony reveals an intriguing phenomenon. Even though he had been born and grew up in Zamość, he did not try to return to his parents' home after the liberation. Perhaps he was still apprehensive that he might be identified there before he had decided whether or not to return to Jewish society. He stayed on with the farmer in the village and went on herding the cows as though nothing had happened. In Zamość, where he went occasionally to sell his wares, he visited survivor families, who embraced him warmly and gave him clothing. However, he still showed no inclination to leave the village and join them. He remained in the village for more than a year after liberation. Toward the end of 1945, his uncle — his mother's brother — returned to Zamość from Russia, and after learning that Moshe was alive tracked him down and tried to persuade him to leave the village and join him. Moshe refused to accept that the man was really his uncle and ran away from him: he did not want to go back to being a Jew. Finally, the uncle was able to dissuade him from returning to the village with the promise that he would let him study whatever he wished — Moshe longed to go to school but this was impossible in the village.[16]

Moshe, though well aware of his Jewish identity, had become a typical Polish village youth. Even though he forged ties with Jewish survivors after the liberation, he was unable to break away from his new Christian life and was fearful of returning to Jewish society, from which he had been cut off two years earlier. Restored to the Jewish fold almost by coercion, he remained there less because of his relations with his uncle and more because of the prospect of a better life than the one to which a village herdsman could pos-

15 Moshe Frank, *To Survive and Testify*, pp. 74–75, 77–79.
16 Ibid., p. 81.

sibly aspire. Ultimately, it was the yearning for knowledge that brought him back to Judaism.

Not all the children who had been separated from their families and immersed in Christian society chanced to meet Jews who could help them return to Jewish society after the liberation. A major point is that after the war hardly any of the survivors, including those who had returned from the Soviet Union, went back to the towns from where they had been uprooted. For reasons of safety, most of the survivors preferred the big cities, where there were better economic opportunities. After the war, Jews rarely visited the hundreds of towns and villages scattered across Poland, and those who did so stayed for only a short time out of fear of possible harm. Although there were few survivors of Polish Jewry who were unaffected by the turbulent events of the postwar period, it was still possible for a solitary Jewish child, in a remote village or provincial town, to conclude that no Jews remained in Poland and thus see no reason to disclose his true identity. A case in point is Golda Ryba.

Like Alex and Moshe, she knew she was Jewish. The difference was that while they were orphans, she knew her father had immigrated to Argentina before the war, although she had no idea how to find him. And like them, she too was disoriented by the liberation and did not know to whom to turn. Thus out of sheer inertia, she remained with her village employers for more than two years after liberation. Throughout this period, she tried to think how to extricate herself from the trap in which she was caught. She suffered periods of depression. What she feared most was leaving the village and facing the unknown. In 1947, she was 16, the age at which the village youngsters started to attend high school in the city, and she wanted to do so as well. In her distress, she appealed to the mayor of her native city, Sokolow Podlaski, presenting herself as an orphan wishing to attend school, but without informing him that she was Jewish or revealing her surname. With the mayor's help, she was able to work and attend school in the city. For two years, Golda wandered the streets of the city where she was born without meeting a solitary Jew. She passed by her family's destroyed home and her grandfather's store, now taken over by Poles. She saw their former maid walking about wrapped in the family's furs. It was not until some years later, after she had become a registered nurse and was on night shift in a Warsaw hospital, that she struck up a conversation with a Jewish woman patient and admitted to her and her husband that she too was Jewish. The couple helped her locate her father in Argentina.[17]

---

17 Testimony of Golda Ryba, YVA, O.3/2734.

Children begging for alms, Warsaw Ghetto
Yad Vashem Photo Archives

Young cigarette sellers
in a Warsaw street
Yad Vashem Photo Archives

Members of a Jewish children's gang, Warsaw
Yad Vashem Photo Archives

Newspaper seller, Nowy Sącz Ghetto
Yad Vashem Photo Archives

Young smugglers, Warsaw Ghetto
Yad Vashem Photo Archives

Deportation of children to their deaths, Łódź Ghetto
Yad Vashem Photo Archives

ewish child with her Christian guardian, Vilna — the Aryan side
United States Holocaust Memorial Museum Photo Archives

Janina Nebel with Leokadia Nawroc[...]
her Christian guardian
United States Holocaust Memorial Museum
Photo Archives

Janina Nebel preparing for her first Communion
United States Holocaust Memorial Museum Photo Archives

Children celebrating their first Communion at the convent of the Felician Sisters in Wawer; among them are several Jewish children with a false Christian identity
United States Holocaust Memorial Museum Photo Archives

# Children saved on the Aryan side — after liberation

Children's home in Otwock; the younger children with their caregiver, Franciszka Oliwa
Yad Vashem Photo Archives

Children's home in Zakopane; the older children with their caregiver, Lena Küchler-Silberman (center)
Nahum Bogner, Private Collection

# The first children redeemed by the Koordynacja

Pola Miller, Stefcia Zenfman, Halina Feldenstein
Nahum Bogner, Private Collection

Marcel Landsberger
Nahum Bogner, Private Collection

Izio Miller
Nahum Bogner, Private Collection

Koordynacja children together with
their caregiver
Yad Vashem Photo Archives

Koordynacja children's home: education
toward self-help
Yad Vashem Photo Archives

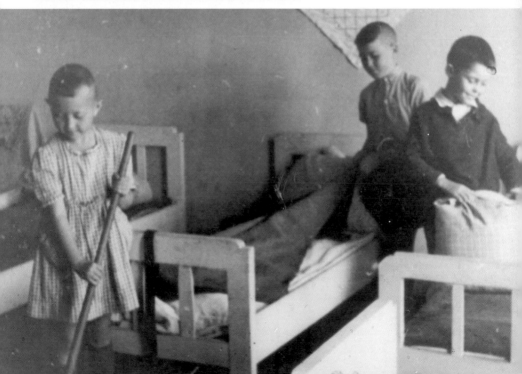

Koordynacja children's home, Łódź. The older children
Yad Vashem Photo Archives

The caregiver, Chasia Bielicka, with two of her wards
Efraim Dekel, *Remnants from the Sword: Rescuing Children During the Holocaust and After*
(Tel Aviv: Ministry of Defense, 1963)

Hanukah celebrations at the Koordynacja children's home, Łódź
United States Holocaust Memorial Museum Photo Archives

Hashomer Hatza'ir children's kibbutz
Yad Vashem Photo Archives

Yeshayahu Drucker (in uniform) with fellow educators at the Zabrze children's home
Yad Vashem Photo Archives

Visiting time at the children's home, Zabrze
Yad Vashem Photo Archives

The Directors of the Koordynacja. Front row: Aryeh Sarid (center) on his right Sara Neshamit and left Hela Leneman; Center row (r to l): Ovadia Peled, Chaim Bzora, (unidentified) Pinhas Krivos, Leibel Koriski; Top row (r to l): P. Zeidenberg, Menachem Kunda, Kleinberg
Yad Vashem Photo Archives

The educator, Lena Küchler-Silberman, who established the children's home in Zakopane and linked her fate with the children for many years
Lena Küchler-Silberman, *We Accuse: Children's Accounts from the Holocaust* (Tel Aviv: Sifriyat Hapoalim, 1969)

The educator, Chasia Bielicka, who accompanied the first Koordynacja children to Eretz Israel
Efraim Dekel, *Remnants from the Sword: Rescuing Children During the Holocaust and After* (Tel Aviv: Ministry of Defense, 1963)

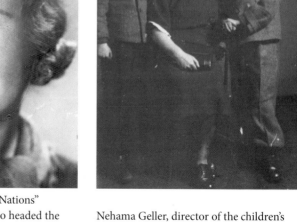

The "Righteous Among the Nations" Irena Sendler ("Jolanta") who headed the Children's Department of Żegota
Yad Vashem Photo Archives

Nehama Geller, director of the children's home in Zabrze
Yad Vashem Photo Archives

The Dror children's kibbutz in Bytom before its emigration to Eretz Israel
Yad Vashem Photo Archives

Exodus from Poland, 1946. Departure parade before emigration to Eretz Israel

Yad Vashem Photo Archives

IV. NÁSTUPIŠTĚ

Exodus from Poland via Czechoslovakia, 1946: children on the "Bricha" illegal immigration route to Palesti

Efraim Dekel, *Remnants from the Sword: Rescuing Children During the Holocaust and After* (Tel Aviv: Ministry of Defense, 1963)

This is admittedly an extreme case of the quandaries faced by an adolescent child in Poland after the liberation, but it also raises questions. Golda's story exemplifies the vast loneliness of Jewish children who were torn from their families and swallowed up in Christian surroundings. Their isolation became even more acute after the liberation if there was no one left to find them. In the chaos then prevailing in the Jewish centers in Poland, removing the children from Christian homes and convents was only the first phase of the operation. Someone had to care for them, find them a place to live and provide food and clothing. These were among the urgent missions undertaken by the newly-organized Jewish committees.

## Establishment of the Children's Homes

In July 1944, a few days after the liberation of Lublin, homeless Jewish children clad only in rags began to appear in the city's streets. During the day they worked as peddlers to earn a few zlotys, and at night they joined the adults at the headquarters of the Red Cross or in the former Peretz Cultural Center.[18] The abandoned children constituted a serious problem and demanded an urgent solution from the coalescing community of Jewish survivors in the city. One of the first tasks undertaken by the city's newly-formed Jewish committee was to establish a hostel for seventy-five orphans. The first problem was to find suitable accommodations. The Lublin municipality was prepared to allocate only one apartment consisting of two rooms and a kitchen. About 50 children moved in at the end of November, but these were temporary lodgings, until a larger place could be found. The Jewish committees in Przemyśl, Bialystok, and Otwock made efforts to find similar solutions for the homeless children in their locales.[19]

The Lublin children's home, which opened at the end of 1944, was the first of its kind. In 1945, the Central Jewish Committee established eleven similar homes. In August 1945, the children's home in Lublin was transferred to a more suitable venue, Pietrolesie, in Lower Silesia. Other children's homes were established in Otwock, Helenówek, near Łodź, Chorzów, Bielsko, Zatrzebie, Częstochowa, Kraków, Przemyśl, Szczyrk, Rabka, and Zakopane. The last two, which also served as recuperation centers for sick children, operated

18  Anna Walk-Natanblut, *Ci co przeżyli,* p. 6, YVA, JM/2619.
19  Szulkin, "Sprawozdanie z działalnosci," pp. 78–79, 83–84.

only briefly.[20] Immediately after the children's home in Rabka was opened, in the summer of 1945, it was attacked three times in close succession by Polish nationalists. There was no choice but to close it down and disperse the children among the other homes. Most of them were moved to the Zakopane house, which was established at the same time. However, it, too, proved short-lived. In the light of the antisemitic atmosphere and the unstable security situation in the area, the home's director, Lena Kuchler, saw no future for the children in Poland. In March 1946, with the aid of the Va'ad haHatzalah (Rescue Committee of the Orthodox Rabbis in America) she managed to smuggle out most of the orphans who were under her care to France. The Zakopane children's home was then permanently shut down.[21]

In summer, 1945, of the approximately 5,000 children who were registered with the Jewish Committees throughout Poland, about 1,000 were admitted to the twelve children's homes. Some 600 of them were orphans, about 300 had one parent, and only 100 still had both parents living.[22]

The story of the establishment of the children's homes in Poland and what they managed to accomplish in their few years of operation, is a poetic pedagogical triumph and deserves separate treatment. Nothing illustrates this better than the sheer vitality, public responsibility, and moral concern of the remnants of Polish Jewry after the Holocaust. These qualities shone forth in the group of people — most of whom remain anonymous — who established the homes and cared for the orphans devotedly and lovingly. Indeed, most of the caregivers were themselves solitary survivors who had lost their families. However, their personal distress did not prevent them from responding to the plight of the homeless orphans and assuming the onerous task of looking after them. In some sense, the children's homes replaced the homes both they and the wards in their charge had lost.[23]

The first homes were not established by fiat from above, but were a natural outgrowth of the organic process in which renewed communal life began to revive among Poland's surviving Jews. This is exemplified by the children's homes that were established in two different regions of the country: in Otwock, outside devastated Warsaw, and in the resort town of Zakopane in the Tatra Mountains. Both institutions were established at the initiative of young

20  Turkow, After Liberation, pp. 60–62.
21  Lena Kuchler-Silberman, My 100 Children (New York: Souvenir Press, 1961), pp. 221–284.
22  Sprawozdanie wydzial opieki nad dzieckiem C.K.Ż. w P. na rok 1946, AŻIH
23  On the founding of the orphanages in Lublin, Otwock and Zkopane see: Walk-Natanblut, Ci co przeżyli; YVA, JM/2619, Franciszka Oliwa, Dom ocalonych dzieci w Otwocku, YVA, M.49; and, Kuchler-Silberman, My 100 Children.

women on their own, Franciszka Oliwa and Lena Kuchler. They differed considerably in professional training and social background, but were driven by the same dictate of conscience, which made them unable to ignore the plight of homeless children. Establishing homes for the children, looking after them, and furthering their education also helped them escape their own solitude in that anguished period and became the great experience of their lives.

Franciszka Oliwa had survived in the town of Kielce by means of Aryan papers. In January 1945, immediately after the liberation, she arrived in Otwock to seek out possible survivors from her family. On the street, she encountered a group of tattered, starving children who had attached themselves to a Russian soldier. It was a shocking yet touching sight. When the soldier saw she was looking at the children, he told her to look after them, because they were Jewish. When she replied that she herself did not have a home, he took them to an abandoned apartment which had no windows, no running water, no heating, and no furniture. Thus, abruptly, Oliwa found that she bore sole responsibility for about ten orphans. The next day, several more children joined the group. She had no food to give them and no place for them to sleep. She presented her problem to the commander of a nearby Soviet field hospital. Colonel Dr. Obuchowsky, whom she later discovered was himself Jewish, did not remain indifferent. The fate of the children moved him deeply and he set about helping to the best of his ability. From the hospital's stocks he provided her with mattresses and blankets, and had the broken windows in the apartment repaired. He had no children's clothing but gave her hospital gowns. Thus was the children's home in Otwock founded.

It was not until March 1945 that the Central Jewish Committee, which was then organizing in a Warsaw suburb, took responsibility for the improvised hostel in Otwock and appointed as its director Luba Blum-Bielicka, the widow of the Bund leader, Abrasha Blum. Oliwa stayed on and worked together with her as the homeroom teacher of the intermediate class. Luba Blum became the institution's driving spirit. Thanks to her initiative, and with the devoted help of the teachers and staff, together with material aid from the JDC (which arrived after the war ended), the Otwock institution became a warm, thriving home for its orphaned children.[24]

Lena Kuchler had been liberated in the summer of 1944 in the remote village where she had found sanctuary under an assumed Polish identity. She was in no hurry to return to her home in Wieliczka, near Kraków. Upon returning to Kraków at the end of the war, she tried to envision her future.

---

24 Oliwa, *Dom ocalonych*, YVA, M.49.

At first, she thought she would pursue a scientific career at the Jagiellonian University in the city, where she had completed a Ph.D. thesis in psychology before the war. However, she was unable to muster the peace of mind called for by academic life. She knew that a local Jewish committee had organized at 38, Długa Street and that it was the center of activity for many survivors. She had avoided visiting the site, but one day she felt drawn there and met a group of neglected child survivors, and her destiny became entwined with theirs for years to come. She described the circumstances of that first encounter with the children's plight in her book *My 100 Children*:

> I went from the Market Square to Długa Street...Up until now I had always avoided passing that way. And I knew why...I had refrained from passing that house because I did not have the strength to witness once again the sickening uproar of Jewish suffering concentrated between those walls. But now something had changed inside me and I went that way... suddenly I heard among the commotion and noise, the sound of a child crying... I immediately pushed my way inside and saw children crying...I made my way upstairs into a corridor. It was dark, the air was stale and fetid. I didn't know where to go. From behind a door I heard the sound of children crying and shouting. I opened the door and stood in the doorway. In a large and dim room in a corner close to the window a woman stood with a large ladle beside a soup cauldron. Around her children with small bowls were pushing near her with outstretched hands: "More, more — I didn't get enough!"[25]

The children that Lena Kuchler met that spring day in 1945 were in urgent need of physical and psychological rehabilitation. This was not possible in the conditions that existed in the Jewish Committee center, as its directors understood only too well. After obtaining the necessary funds, the Committee rented two health resorts at spas, one in Rabka and the other in Zakopane, and moved the children to them.[26] Lena Kuchler undertook the task of establishing the children's home in Zakopane. Plunging into the work with typical tenacity and passion, she founded a hostel for about a hundred orphans, from kindergarten age to sixteen, some of them healthy, others suffering from various diseases, among them children with tuberculosis, for whom the home also functioned as a sanatorium.

25  Kuchler-Silberman, *My 100 Children*, pp. 95–103.
26  Ibid., pp. 139–141.

Who were the children in the network of orphanages established by the Central Jewish Committee, and how did they find their way there? The first group in the first children's home in Lublin numbered about fifteen who had miraculously survived the Majdanek death camp, and another twenty-five or so adolescents, aged 16 to 18, who had arrived from the forests, different places of hiding, and villages.[27] The ages of the first group of children who came to the headquarters of the Jewish Committee headquarters in Daługa Street were similar. Miriam Hochberg (Marianska), who moved from her underground work with Żegota immediately after the city's liberation to join the nascent Jewish Committee, and was appointed head of the Childcare Division, describes the arrival of the first children:

> As it happened, the first groups of Jewish children arrived from Auschwitz. Without our having expected it, a handful of children survived there. They had been taken to Auschwitz in the last transports, which as is known were not put into the crematoria immediately. The children survived by chance, apparently because they were intended for future "racial" experiments. Their parents had been murdered some time earlier, and they remained alive... They knew Dr. Mengele well and realized that their life and death were in his hands. They related that whenever he visited their hut, they made an effort to smile at him. In this way they hoped to save themselves from death. They also knew very well all the tricks of camouflage and concealment... Despite the atrocities they had undergone, they were very receptive to psychological treatment. They acclimatized to the new conditions very quickly and regained their mental acumen. They were capable of telling about their ordeals without batting an eyelash...
>
> After being liberated, the children transferred the doctrine of life they had learned to their new existence. They knew how to demand what was coming to them. Within a few weeks they felt at home and wanted to go to the cinema, to the park, asked for books — and, most important, they knew exactly where they belonged, they had no religious complexes. They had suffered in the camp because they were Jewish, and now they wanted to enjoy a happy life... I do not know what their concept of God was, but they liked the holidays and Sabbath eve, the festive table and the holiday foods...
>
> After a few weeks, children in possession of Aryan papers began

---

27  Walk-Natanblut, *Ci co przeżyli*, p. 16, YVA, JM/2619

arriving at our home... I want to say something about the children who came alone, or whose Christian guardians brought them. Only older children came unaccompanied. The same instincts that helped them survive the war, now whispered to them to go and look for their people. Thus, girls arrived — village herders — and children of ten, twelve, or older who had been farm workers... They understood the mind of the Polish farmer as though they were trained psychologists... but they were frightened — precisely now, after the war had ended although they were unable to articulate the fear that existed in their subconscious. In general, they were children who had developed well beyond their age, excelling in maturity and cleverness. They remembered their date of birth, the names of their family members, the addresses of their relatives in Poland and abroad. All these children were waiting for their parents. In this, they did not use their common sense but seized at hope without any concrete foundation. When they discovered that they were waiting in vain, they did not fall apart. All of them, without exception, wanted to study in order to achieve a certain goal in life. For them, the concept of freedom was related to wealth and the possibility of traveling all over the world.[28]

The plight of these children would become one of the most critical and daunting problems facing the Jewish institutions in Poland and elsewhere. The initial solutions were makeshift at best, but as Jewish public life in Poland became increasingly organized, the children's situation improved. They were the first beneficiaries of the aid from Jewish organizations which began to arrive from western countries. Suffice it to note that in 1946, fully 13.6 percent of the JDC's entire aid budget for Poland was earmarked for the approximately 2,800 orphans who were living in thirty-two children's homes scattered across Poland.[29] One of the most acute problems that awaited a solution was the future of the children who had survived under an assumed identity and still remained in Christian homes or institutions.

As we have seen, some of the orphaned children who had survived under an assumed identity reached the children's homes by themselves; others had arrived with relatives or acquaintances. At the same time, non-Jews be-

28 Miriam Hochberg (Marianska) (Peleg), "I looked after survivor children" (Hebrew), *Yediot Yad Vashem*, vol. 8–9 (1956), p. 12.
29 AJDC Activities in Poland, Summary for 1946, Givat Joint Archives (GJA), (Jerusalem), 12B/C-61.034; Yehuda Bauer, *Out of the Ashes: The Impact of American Jews on Post-Holocaust European Jewry* (New York: Pergamon Press, 1989), p. 118.

gan bringing to the Jewish committees small children whose parents had left them in their custody for safekeeping. As no one from the child's family had appeared to claim him after the war, the foster family usually decided to turn the child over to a Jewish organization, not least because of the substantial economic burden entailed in continuing to look after him.

At the end of the war, one village woman who declined to identify herself appeared at the headquarters of the Jewish committee in Kraków and informed Miriam Hochberg (Marianska) that she had been concealing two Jewish children, a boy and a girl, in her loft. Even her husband did not know of their presence, she said. She wanted to hand them over to Hochberg, but because of the antisemitic atmosphere in her village, she did not want it known that she had rescued them. Thus, one night, when the woman's husband was away, personnel from the Jewish committee came to her house and took the children away. In another case, also in Kraków, a Polish refugee family from Lvov handed over to the Jewish committee a Jewish girl aged about five whom they had sheltered. She had been placed in their custody by a stranger, and no one had come to claim her after the war. As they were indigent refugees, they decided that it would be in the girl's best interest if they returned her to a Jewish organization, even though they loved her very much and she was attached to them. They asked for nothing in return for rescuing her, but the committee nevertheless recompensed them with food and clothing, though not with money.[30]

The first rescuers who brought children to the Jewish committees did not ask for payment. Later, though, some families asked to be reimbursed for their expenses and for the risk they had run in hiding the child. Rumors soon spread that the Jews were receiving aid and goods of all kinds from America. It was not long before some rescuers began to view their wards as a means of improving their economic condition and to demand payment from the Jewish committee or from the child's relatives. Commerce in rescued children spread in Poland, as described by Jewish officials who encountered the phenomenon.

One day a village woman arrived with a large box at the headquarters of the Central Jewish Committee in Warsaw. She said neighbors had told her that Jewish children were being bought by the committee, and she had one for sale. She then opened the box, revealing, to the horrified astonishment of everyone present, a boy aged about three with deformed limbs. Seeing the

---

30  Testimony Miriam Hochberg (Marianska) (Peleg), OHD, (68)24.

stunned reaction, she explained that she had been compelled to keep the boy
hidden for fear that neighbors would inform on her, but would take him out
to feed him. The committee ransomed the child from her and hospitalized
him.[31]

A flagrant case of extortion occurred in the children's home in Otwock,
where, as in Kraków, non-Jewish rescuers had been bringing children without asking for payment. One day, a Polish woman arrived with a weeping girl
of about five who did not want to part from the woman. She received payment before handing the girl over. The next day, she returned, created a fuss,
and demanded, "Take the money and give me back the girl." In the ensuing
fracas, she snatched the girl but did not return the money.[32]

Documentation from the period and later testimonies show that at least
until the end of 1945, the official Jewish committees did not take the initiative
in trying to remove unclaimed children from Christian custody. The problem
was not lost on the members of the Central Jewish Committee who dealt
with the children. According to a report from October 1944 of the nascent
Central Jewish Committee in Lublin, a committee member discovered Jewish
orphans in farmers' homes while visiting local villages. The report makes no
recommendation as to what to do with the children, apart from a notation,
"They are being well looked after."[33] Generally, in the first year after liberation,
parents who had survived reclaimed their children from the Christian rescuers; or, if the parents had perished, relatives and friends did so. Those who
could afford it ransomed the children. Others, lacking resources and confronted with the rescuers' recalcitrance, sometimes resorted to force, assisted
by police and Jewish security personnel.[34] Occasionally, parents with influence on the local committee or in the Central Jewish Committee received
financial aid to ransom their child, but this was not common.

After liberation, Jonas Turkow located his daughter in the home of
a Christian woman who had hidden her. She demanded 10,000 zlotys for
returning the girl and refused to hand her over until the ransom was paid.
Turkow, who was a member of the Central Jewish Committee, received the
money from a special fund the Committee had established for this purpose.
After returning the girl, the woman tried to extort more money from him,
seeking medical treatment for her own daughter, among other requests. The

31 Turkow, *After Liberation*, pp. 64–65.
32 Oliwa, *Dom ocalonych*, pp. 6–7, YVA, M.49.
33 Szulkin, "Sprawozdanie z działalnoscie," pp. 83–84.
34 Turkow, *After Liberation*, pp. 57–58; testimony of Rivka Lustigman, YVA, O.3/4152.

Central Committee agreed to underwrite all the girl's medical expenses, including a stay in a sanatorium. The woman, though, demanded a cash payment, and at this the Committee balked.[35]

From the outset, removing children from Christian families and institutions which were not eager to hand them over to Jewish representatives constituted a painful and complex problem. The local Jewish committees were acutely aware of this, as they received requests for financial aid from parents and relatives to reclaim children, and from rescuers who were still looking after children and wanted reimbursement for the expenses they incurred. The committees were concerned about possible blackmail. On June 9, 1945, the Central Jewish Committee discussed the subject of the children who were still in non-Jewish hands. The head of the committee's Childcare Division, the Bund activist Shlomo Hirschenhorn, urged that action be taken to return the children to the Jewish fold. Everyone agreed that the children's rightful place was in Jewish society. No one in the Central Committee objected to this approach on ideological grounds — not even the communists, who advocated the Jews' full integration in Polish society.[36]

In this period the Central Jewish Committee was still operating on the basis of an ideological compromise among its constituent public bodies: the Communists, the Bund, and the Zionist Movements. With regard to the children's education, even the most ardent communists were sensitive to the Jewish dimension. The educational platform, which was decided on by the Central Jewish Committee on July 5, 1945, still bore the imprint of the ideological compromise that can be seen in its two main sections. Article Two stated, "The children shall be imbued with a positive attitude toward resurgent democratic Poland," and Article Three added, "They shall also be imbued with national respect and love for the Jewish language, literature, and history, and their ties with the Jewish people around the world shall be cultivated, particularly with its democratic elements who are fighting for the national and social liberation of the Jewish masses." On October 19, the Central Jewish Committee decided on a secular educational orientation in the children's homes; however, if the children or their parents should request lessons in religion, the Central Committee would bring in external teachers for this purpose. The language of instruction would be Yiddish, although the possibility of learning

---

35  Turkow, *After Liberation*, pp. 242–244.
36  Engel, *Between Liberation and Flight*, p. 118.

Hebrew also existed. Another decision was that the weekly day of rest would be the Jewish Sabbath (Saturday).[37]

According to Jonas Turkow, in its first year of existence, the Central Jewish Committee paid 157,500 zlotys to Polish families to regain Jewish children whom they had hidden.[38] This is only a fraction of the amount that was spent later to ransom the children, but it is evidence that the children were not ignored, either knowingly or by negligence, contrary to later allegations by Zionist officials who had been engaged in ransom activity.[39] At the same time, it was probably generally understood that the manifold needs being dealt with by the Central Jewish Committee, by comparison with its available resources, ruled out the ransoming of children. At that time, the Committee had its hands full trying to cope with the many hundreds of orphans who were already living in the children's homes and had not yet integrated, even as others had to be turned away due to insufficient space and a shortage of basic necessities — bedding, clothing, footwear, and food. Some of the orphans, who lived with relatives because there was no room for them in the children's homes, also received material support from the Jewish committees. The soaring outlays for the children's homes forced even the rejection of a proposal by Hirschenhorn to expand his staff in order to collect data about children who were still in non-Jewish hands. What was lacking was not a desire to ransom the children, but the necessary funds to accomplish this, as well as a change of priorities so as to place the problem of the children first on the list. The Central Jewish Committee believed that every attempt to ransom Jewish children would entail a high price and feared that it would not be able to raise the funds.[40] Sporadic attempts by activists in the field to remove Jewish children from Christian institutions with the backing and aid of the local Jewish committee were not always successful.

When Miriam Hochberg (Marianska) learned that some of the occupants in a Polish orphanage near Rabka were Jewish children who had been moved there during the war from the Boduen Home in Warsaw, she took upon herself the task of removing them from the institution. Furnished with the required official documents, she presented herself to the orphanage

---

37 Helena Datner Spiewak, "Institucje opieki nad dzieckiem I szkoly powszechne Centralnego Komitetu Żydow Polskich w latach 1945–1946," *BŻIH* vol. 3/19, (1981), pp. 42–43.

38 Turkow, *After Liberation*, p. 58.

39 Arye Sarid, in *Mission to Diaspora 1945–1948* (Hebrew) (Tel Aviv: Yad Tabenkin and Ghetto Fighters' House, 1989), p. 83; Zerah Warhaftig, *Refugee and Survivor: Rescue Efforts during the Holocaust* (Jerusalem: Yad Vashem 1998), p. 332.

40 Engel, *Between Liberation and Flight*, p. 118.

director as a representative of the Central Jewish Committee and said she had come to take the Jewish children. The director confirmed that there were several young Jewish children in the orphanage but said he did not know who they were. He invited her to see the children, but despite their evidently Jewish appearance she could not be certain which of them were Jews; they had been born during the war and so the boys had not been circumcised. However, irrespective of their ethnic identity, the director said he would not hand them over to another institution but only to their parents or relatives, after they identified them by certain signs. Hochberg returned to Kraków empty-handed and with the knowledge that there was no way she would be able to remove the children from the orphanage by conventional means, while the use of force was out of the question.[41]

Lena Kuchler encountered a similar situation in Zakopane, although it had a happier ending. When she learned that there were Jewish children in the St. Bobola Convent near the city, she decided to remove them from the institution and take them to the children's home. At the convent, she introduced herself to the mother superior as the director of the Jewish children's home and a representative of the Central Jewish Committee. At first the mother superior declined to hand over the children on the grounds that they had already been baptized and were therefore no longer Jews. She also put forward a formal reason, namely that the children were from Warsaw and could not be handed over without authorization from the municipal authorities of that city. Kuchler did not give up. Drawing on her personal connections with a senior official in the Warsaw social welfare department, she obtained the necessary authorization. Confronted with the document, the mother superior relented, albeit with unconcealed unwillingness, and handed over the five Jewish children who had been living in the convent. As a gesture of gratitude for their rescue, Kuchler donated 10,000 zlotys to the convent, together with items of food she had brought with her.[42]

The unstable security situation in Poland immediately after the war, when the new regime was not yet stabilized, combined with the country's poor transportation facilities, compounded the difficulty of locating Jewish children who had been swallowed up in Christian society. Some of the children had moved locations during the period when they were hidden, and after the war their relatives or family friends could not always find them. In some cases, even if they found the child and reclaimed him, they could not

---

41  Testimony of Miriam Hochberg (Marianska) (Peleg), OHD, (68)24.
42  Kuchler-Silberman, *My 100 Children*, pp. 246–262.

204 • *At the Mercy of Strangers*

always look after him properly because they themselves still lacked resources. In some cases, relatives or friends took in the rescued child for a time but then placed him in an orphanage, either because the economic burden was too great or because they could not provide a suitable educational framework. Others considered adopting the rescued child but then found that his presence was detrimental to the rehabilitation of the family, and sought out an institution that would be willing to take him. Ironically, in some cases this resulted in a child being removed from the warm Christian family which had rescued him and cared for him lovingly, and being placed in an orphanage which in some cases was not even Jewish.

Ten-year-old Joseph Sliwa was sheltered by a Polish foster family on the outskirts of Warsaw. The family received payment from the boy's mother, who was hiding elsewhere. After the Polish uprising in Warsaw in late 1944, contact with the mother was lost — Joseph never saw her again — and the payments stopped. Nevertheless, Joseph's benefactors continued to look after him at their expense and treated him lovingly. After liberation, the boy's uncle, who was a soldier in the Polish army, arrived and took him. Joseph was pleased at the thought that he would be living with a relative. However, it transpired that the uncle did not yet have a home of his own and saw no other choice than to place his nephew in a convent. There he began to follow the usual path of a Jewish child in such an institution, even as other children in the same situation were already leaving them. It was not until a few months later, when his relatives had managed to get settled, that they moved him to a Jewish children's home.[43] This extreme but not unique case exemplifies the fate of the Jewish children who were left in the hands of strangers. As noted, some non-Jewish families continued to look after the children in their custody when no one claimed them, rather than placing them in a Jewish orphanage, and they received material aid from the Jewish committees.[44]

At the beginning of 1946, in the wake of repeated requests to the Central Jewish Committee from parents and relatives in Poland and elsewhere to search for lost children and help reclaim children from their non-Jewish guardians, a special unit was created in the Childcare Division for this purpose. The new unit followed the usual bureaucratic methods of exploiting ties with government ministries and other official institutions, such as the Polish Red Cross, the social welfare department in the Warsaw municipality, and the

---

43  Testimony of Joseph Sliwa, OHD, (68) 42.
44  Sara Neshamit, "Coordinating Child Rescue in Liberated Poland" (Hebrew), *Dapim Le-heker Hashoa ve'Hamered*, vol. 2 (1952), p. 118, Testimony of Arye Sarid, 0HD (68)10.

convents, as well as exploiting the medium of the press and radio. However, the results of all this activity in 1946 — a critical year in terms of being able to locate children and claim them from the guardians — were quite modest. All told, forty-five children were located and reclaimed: five from convents, twenty-five from families (twenty of whom were ransomed), and fifteen in Polish children's homes. The unit was unable to locate 203 children whose relatives had turned to the Committee for assistance. Its point of departure was that some of the children were not prepared to identify themselves and were denying their Jewish origins, either due to fear or because they preferred to remain with the Christian families that had sheltered them during the war.[45]

Considerable financial resources were needed to remove these children from their rescuers and restore them to Jewish society. In addition, an organizational structure had to be established which could act with determination, in some cases using unconventional methods not necessarily consistent with the strict letter of the law. However, neither the Central Jewish Committee nor the local Jewish committees were capable of this. Miriam Hochberg (Marianska), who devoted herself unsparingly to the problem of orphan children on behalf of the Kraków Jewish Committee, admitted as much. In her testimony, she describes the Polish women who came to her so as to return rescued children, either openly or covertly, but also those who refused to return them but asked for — and received — material aid to go on looking after them.

In one case, a childless Polish woman who had rescued a four-year-old Jewish boy who came into her custody by chance had become attached to him and refused to return him, asked the Jewish committee for money to look after him, which she received. After she returned a number of times, Hochberg remarked to her that it was morally wrong to ask for money to look after the child: if she claimed the child was hers, she should provide for him, and if not, she should hand him over to the Jewish committee.[46]

Because of the working methods of the Central Jewish Committee's department for locating children, it was unable to reclaim children from their rescuers if the latter refused to hand them over. In these circumstances, this effectively meant giving up on the children, forsaking the desire to restore them to the Jewish people, and abandoning hope of finding their relatives, whether in Poland or in the west. The committee officials faced a formidable

45  *Sprawozdanie wydzial opieki nad dzieckiem CKŻ w P na rok 1946*, AŻIH. Probably the five children listed as having been in convents were those whom Lena Kuchler removed from the St. Bobola Convent (note 42, above).
46  Testimony of Miriam Hochberg (Marianska), Peleg, OHD, (68)24.

national, moral, and even legal dilemma. The question was whether, in the absence of parents or other relatives, the Jewish committees had the right to become the children's guardians. No one on the committees, which were statutory bodies, believed that they had the right to attempt to extract children by force if rescuers refused to part with them. "We cannot take the boy from you by force, because we do not know who he belongs to," Hochberg told the Polish woman who refused to hand over her Jewish ward, and she continued to give her material support on behalf of the Jewish committee. As far as she knew, the child remained with the woman.[47]

The Jewish committees thus took in and looked after children who had no other source of support, whether they were brought by their non-Jewish rescuers or by private individuals who had removed them from the rescuers. However, the committees themselves made no serious effort to reclaim children who remained in the rescuers' hands. Their approach was fundamentally legalistic: they did not think they possessed the authority to claim guardianship of the children in the name of the Jewish people. To change this state of affairs, a different approach was needed, together with large-scale financial support from Jewish organizations in the west. That new approach took shape at the beginning of 1946, in the form of the first emissaries to Poland from Palestine and America.

47  Ibid.

CHAPTER EIGHT

# Holocaust Orphans and the National Agenda

## First Information in the West on the Fate of Child Survivors

The first concrete eyewitness information about the scale of the Holocaust and its consequences was provided by Jewish soldiers in the Allied forces who took part in the liberation of Europe. Survivors in former Jewish communities told the soldiers of their experiences under the Nazi occupation. The soldiers, in turn, passed on the survivors' descriptions in letters to their families and to Jewish organizations. The two organizations that systematically monitored developments in the Jewish world — the Jewish Agency for Palestine, based in Jerusalem, and the World Jewish Congress, headquartered in the United States — were the main recipients of the information from Europe.

One of the most painful problems encountered by the Jewish soldiers in liberated Europe was the assimilation into local communities and conversion to Christianity of some survivors. Soldiers from the Yishuv — the pre-state Jewish community of Palestine — serving in the British Army first encountered this phenomenon in Italy. These were Jews who had been rescued by Christian institutions and had converted with the help of the clergy, whether by persuasion or opportunism, under the influence of their rescuers. Some had married their non-Jewish rescuer and had converted to Christianity. The soldiers were particularly concerned that hundreds of Jewish children who had survived in convents and Christian families would be lost to the Jewish people.[1]

The fact that some survivors had opted for assimilation only heightened the grief of the Jewish soldiers over the catastrophe that had befallen the Jewish people. They blamed not only the Germans but also the Christian neighbors of the Jews for having been mere bystanders. It was intolerable to them that the few surviving children would remain with their Christian rescuers.

---

1   Yoav Gelber, *Jewish Palestinian Volunteers in the British Army during the Second World War*, Vol. III. *The Standard Bearers* (Hebrew) (Jerusalem: Yad Yitzhak Ben Zvi, 1983), pp. 282–283.

The soldiers believed that the entire Jewish world would have to mobilize to deal with this problem. In autumn 1944, a Jewish soldier serving in the Polish Army in Normandy was shocked to discover that Jews in the liberated areas were resuming their normal life without making an attempt to restore the Jewish orphans in Christian institutions to the Jewish fold. Having no local authority to turn to, he wrote to the Jewish Agency in Jerusalem (in Hebrew), urging that it undertake the mission:

> After my arrival on the Continent, as we liberated one place after another, I began to organize searches for Jews. To our great regret, the situation in Normandy was very gloomy. We went through Normandy along the coast as far as the Belgian border without finding even one Jew. Happily, the situation changed after we crossed the Belgian border. In Brussels, Antwerp, Ghent, and many other places we found Jews, who were among the surviving remnant who had managed to hide from deportation to Poland. You have undoubtedly received detailed reports about their condition and their life. But one question, which in my opinion is the most important and cries out to the heavens for a solution, is that of the children. About 2,500 Jewish children whose parents were transported to the extermination camps in Poland are now under the custodianship of Catholic clergy in various institutions in Belgium and awaiting redemption.
>
> It is urgently necessary to collect all the children and organize children's homes, teachers, provisions, etc., for them. The Jewish public in Belgium and its institutions is completely unable to cope with the task. Factionalism, disputes, shortages, and the poverty of the Jews here make it impossible to move the issue forward... There are also assimilationist elements here who are interfering, claiming that if we remove the children from the institutions they will cease to be Belgians... I am now in Holland, and here, too, the question of rescuing children exists. In areas that have already been liberated from Nazi rule many abandoned Jewish children whose parents were transported to Poland are living under the protection of Christian ladies... The precept of ransoming prisoners confronts you, redeeming the souls of the children of Israel from assimilation and degeneration. Will you not fulfill this mission? It is not for me to make proposals. My aim is to awaken your conscience to this question and leave the implementation to you, and may God be with you in the endeavor.[2]

2   Shaltiel to Dobkin, December 24, 1944, CZA, S26/1317.

This letter contains no details about the condition of the children and very little about their rescuers, though the writer suspects that they harbor missionary tendencies, hence the urgent need to remove the children from their custody. We should take note of two synonymous terms that the writer invokes in this connection in the Hebrew original: "rescue" (*hatzalah*) and "ransom" or "redemption" (*pidyon*). In his view, Jewish orphans who were still living with their Christian benefactors were *tinokot shenishbu* — "captive infants," meaning children raised among Gentiles and therefore unfamiliar with the Jewish world. Their parents, or persons acting for their parents, had placed them in the custody of the Gentiles in order to save their lives. According to the writer of the letter, just because these non-Jews had risked their lives to save the children and continued to look after them in place of their murdered parents even after liberation, did not imply they had a right to keep the children. Their rescue will not be complete, he believed, until they are restored to their Jewish roots, and it is the duty and obligation of Jewish institutions everywhere to redeem the children from the Gentiles.

The writer, an anonymous soldier, did not purport to represent any organization, but his letter reflects a view that was widely held by Jewish institutions, religious and secular alike: namely that the physical rescue of the children in Christian custody must be complemented by their redemption and return to the Jewish people. This pair of terms — "rescue" and "redemption" — would constantly be invoked by the various Jewish bodies that worked for the children's return. The guiding principle was that everything should be done to return them to their origins; legal means were to be preferred, but if necessary they would have to be circumvented without hesitation.

In western Europe, as in Poland, Jewish soldiers were active in removing children from the custody of non-Jewish rescuers. Soldiers from Palestine scoured convents in Italy, located children whose existence had not previously been known, and accompanied relatives or representatives of the Jewish aid organizations who negotiated for the children's release. They did not hesitate to exert pressure on nuns who were reluctant to part with Jewish orphans. In Belgium and Holland, soldiers in the Jewish Brigade of the British Army helped remove children from convents and Christian families and transfer them to the newly-established Jewish orphanages.[3]

3   Gelber, *The Standard Bearers*, pp. 283–284, 477.

## Diplomatic Attempts to Return Children held by Christians

Even as the war raged, reports had reached the west that Catholic clergy in the occupied countries were exploiting the distress of the Jews sheltering in convents and trying to persuade them to accept Christianity; in the case of children, this practice was routine and indiscriminate. Already at that time, efforts were being made to combat the conversions by diplomatic means. The Jewish Agency, the Chief Rabbinate of Palestine, and the World Jewish Congress sought the intercession of Pope Pius XII, requesting that he issue a clear and unequivocal statement to the Catholic priesthood against pressuring survivors to convert — but the Vatican did not respond. Toward the end of the war, the Chief Rabbi of Palestine, Isaac Halevy Herzog, sought an audience with the Pope in order to discuss the issues arising from the rescue of Jews by Christians, but in vain.[4] Only at the end of the war did the Pope agree to receive secular Jewish officials and hear what they had to say. The first such representative to be received by the Pope, in April 1945, was Moshe Shertok (Sharett), the head of the Jewish Agency's Political Department. The central issue that Shertok raised in the audience was the return of the Jewish children who were in Christian custody.

> According to our reports, five million Jews perished in Europe in the war. We are a people with a good memory and we do not forget, just as we will not forget the kindnesses either. Now we must insist on getting back the rescued children. I understand well the convents' viewpoint, but for us it is not just a question of the children's rescue as human beings, but also their rescue as Jews. It is essential that they return to the bosom of Judaism and to the guardianship of the Jewish people. We hope to bring them all to Eretz Israel and make it possible for them to lead a full Jewish life.

The Pope replied politely, "Yes, I understand," though without promising to take any action. Shertok emerged from the meeting disappointed. Reporting to the Jewish Agency Executive, he said, "I saw that he had not met me in order to hold an honest conversation. He was there only to demonstrate good will, and his reply was no more than an expression of just that. The only thing that came out of the conversation is that I can say that I saw the Pope and told

---

4    Chaim Barlas, *Rescue during the Holocaust* (Hebrew) (Tel Aviv: Ghetto Fighters' House and Hakibbutz Hameuchad, 1975) , p. 168; Yuval Frenkel, "The Activity of Monsignor Angelo Roncalli," (Hebrew) *Yalkut Moreshet*, vol. 59 (1995), p. 121.

him that we are asking to get our children back from the convents. He did not express any opposition."[5]

On September 21, 1945, some four months after the end of the war, the Pope granted an audience to the secretary of the World Jewish Congress, Aryeh Kubovy, who also raised the issue of the Jewish children:

> We have no statistics about the children who were killed but we think their numbers reaches at least a million… The Church has saved a number of our children; a few, very few compared to the numbers who were murdered, but to us they are many. We should like to have them returned to the Jewish community… But we have met with difficulties in certain cases in France, Belgium and Holland. Our feeling is that the Jewish community has certain duties toward these children which it alone can fulfill. Now that their parents are no longer alive these children are broken souls. We believe that only we are able to provide them with the necessary psychological climate to restore them to health and to a normal conception of life.[6]

The Pope listened politely to Kubovy, just as he had to Shertok, and asked him to submit a memorandum on the subject. Nothing came of this meeting either.

Despite the Pope's evasiveness, representatives of religious Jewry persisted in their efforts. In September 1945, the apostolic nuncio to the Middle East, Msgr. Hughes, visited Jerusalem and was interviewed by the newspaper *Hatzofeh*, the organ of the religious Zionist movement. Asked about the fate of the Jewish children in the convents, he replied that the Catholic Church had sought to give them a temporary haven and that many had already returned to their relatives. Everything was being done to place them in the hands of faithful guardians — families or institutions — he said.[7]

The reality, though, was different. The senior church hierarchy failed to issue an instruction that Christian institutions should return Jewish children. At the beginning of 1946, Rabbi Herzog undertook a personal diplomatic journey to Europe in order to deal with the issue. In the course of his "rescue mission," as it was called at the time, he tried to persuade senior church

5 Barlas, *Rescue during the Holocaust*, p. 169; Minutes of Jewish Agency Executive meeting, April 22, 1945, CZA, 44.
6 Arye L. Kubovy, "The Silence of Pope XII and the Beginning of the 'Jewish Document,'" *Yad Vashem Studies* VI, (1967), pp. 21–22.
7 "Church not out to adopt Jewish children," (Hebrew) *Hatzofeh*, September 13, 1945.

officials and political leaders to agree to restore the children to the Jewish community. Rabbi Herzog faced two major problems in his mission: first, obtaining lists of children who were living in Christian institutions or with non-Jewish families, and second, establishing a statutory Jewish body that would act as the children's legal guardian.[8]

After numerous refusals and evasions, Pius XII finally agreed to grant Rabbi Herzog a private audience, Herzog launched his mission at this meeting with the Pope on March 10, 1946, at the Vatican. He first raised the issue of the return of the Jewish children. "With all the gratitude that the Jewish people feel towards those who rescued the children," he told the Pope, "we cannot, under any circumstances, be able to accept their continued stay [where they are], as this would imply their complete severance from their religious origins." The rabbi asked the Pope to issue a pastoral letter to the clergy on the subject, wherein they would be instructed to reveal the whereabouts of known Jewish children, and act to restore them to Jewish hands. The Pope made no reply, requesting only a detailed memorandum. Two days later, when Herzog delivered the memorandum to the Vatican secretariat, the papal response was made known to him orally. The possibility of issuing a pastoral letter would be considered, he was told. At the same time, Herzog was assured that if he learned of children residing in Catholic institutions and encountered difficulties in removing them, he could apply directly for the intercession of the Vatican. This would be forthcoming on condition that the rabbi himself would visit each location and investigate each case himself. He was also given permission in his encounters with clergy to quote what the Pope had told him.[9]

This was another evasive response, couched, typically, in the diplomatic language favored by the pontiff. The pastoral letter that Rabbi Herzog had requested because its intended recipients, the clergy and heads of monasteries and convents, were the most knowledgeable regarding the whereabouts of the children, was not sent. Moreover, the Vatican's promise to help restore to the Jewish fold the children still in church institutions was cynical, as it stipulated an impossible condition, namely that Rabbi Herzog personally investigate each case before requesting the intercession of the Holy See. The Pope also chose to ignore the issue of Jewish children who were in the custody of Christian families.

8  Yitzhak Goldshlag, ed. *Rescue Mission* (Hebrew) (Jerusalem: YVA-1463, 1947), p. 23.
9  Minutes of National Council Executive meeting, October 3, 1946, CZA, J1/7264; Goldshlag, *Rescue Mission*, pp. 14–16.

After his visit to Italy, Herzog visited other countries where Jewish children were known to be in the custody of non-Jews, raising the issue with government officials and local church leaders. He put forward two main requests: firstly, for legislation to be enacted obliging all institutions and individuals who had orphan children in their custody to provide a list of their names to the government, noting the children's religious affiliation; and secondly, to recognize the established Jewish organizations or the special institutions that would be established to deal with the problem. These would be statutory bodies authorized to act as legal guardians of the Jewish children, and would be empowered to request any institution or individual to transfer such children to their custody.[10]

In France, Herzog met with representatives of the Jewish institutions that were dealing with the issue of the children. He consulted with the president of the French Jewish Communities Organization (*Consistoire*), Judge Leon Meiss, concerning proposed legislation relating to the subject. The judge told him that he would work for the passage of a law for the registration of the children. However, he added, French constitutional law would probably not authorize legislation by which the French Jewish community would be appointed the recognized legal guardian of all Jewish war orphans.

In a meeting with President Félix Gouin of France, Herzog received his promise to support a law to register the children, but no steps were taken to enact such legislation. With regard to the return of Jewish orphans, Herzog met with Father Pierre Chaillet, who had done a great deal to rescue Jewish children during the war and now headed the French government commission, COSOR, which had assumed responsibility for all the country's war orphans. Even though he was a Jesuit, Father Chaillet was known to be strongly opposed to converting Jewish children. In his new post, he was ready to help remove the Jewish orphans from Christian custody and place them in Jewish institutions under the supervision of the French Jewish committee, an orthodox body, on condition that it undertake to relieve the government of the burden of the children's upkeep.[11]

Rabbi Herzog also held a talk on the subject of the children with an old acquaintance, Msgr. Angelo Roncalli, who was then the apostolic nuncio to France and would later become Pope John XXIII, succeeding Pius XII. During the war, when he was apostolic nuncio in Turkey, he did all he could within his power to help rescue Jews. In their meeting, Roncalli suggested how it

10  Goldshlag, *Rescue Mission*, p. 23.
11  Ibid., p. 25.

would be best to approach the Church hierarchy on the sensitive problem of the Jewish children. Roncalli, who opposed attempts by the Church to turn the Jewish people's catastrophe to its advantage, promised Herzog his help in locating the children. At the same time, he explained that calling openly on the Catholic clergy in France to help locate Jewish orphans would not be efficacious. Roncalli preferred to act behind the scenes and promised to raise the issue at a forthcoming meeting of French bishops. He told Herzog that he would request that each bishop declare that it was the religious duty of every Catholic to return the children to their Jewish heritage, and that attempting to convert them would be a sin.[12]

In Belgium, where quite a number of Jewish children had been rescued by church institutions and Christian families, Rabbi Herzog met with the minister of justice concerning legislation to register the children. As with the president of France, the minister promised to help, but nothing came of it. Herzog also met with the head of the Catholic Church in Belgium, Cardinal Van Roey, who heard him out and told him that he was ready to help in the spirit of the Vatican's undertakings. He said he would try to exert his influence to remove the Jewish children from Christian custody, but added that he did not know where such children were to be found and he was not able to launch a search for them. "It is necessary for the rabbi to provide me with the names of the children," he said.[13] This was consistent with the Vatican's policy on the subject.

In the Netherlands, the government rejected outright Rabbi Herzog's request for the Jewish orphans to be returned to the Jewish community. The issue was under the authority of the War Orphans Committee, a Dutch government body, whose policy from the outset was that no Jewish orphans would be returned without proof that their parents were orthodox Jews. Herzog engaged the Dutch prime minister in a trenchant conversation on the subject of "Who is a Jew," but the differences between them remained unbridgeable. In a meeting with the cardinal of the Netherlands, Herzog asked his interlocutor, "If the Catholic community in the Netherlands had suffered a calamity as catastrophic as this, and its orphans were in Protestant hands, would you not go to great lengths to restore them to the Catholic community?" To which the cardinal replied, "In theory I agree with you, but I will not be able to take practical action without consulting my colleagues." Rabbi Herzog received a similar reply from the Protestant bishop.[14] The Dutch leadership gave Herzog

12 Ibid., pp. 26–27.
13 Minutes of National Council Executive meeting, October 3, 1946, CZA, J1/7264.
14 Goldshlag, *Rescue Mission*, pp. 37–39.

a polite welcome and expressed its sympathy for the Jewish people, but he left the country empty-handed.

In communist eastern Europe the situation in regard to the Jewish orphans was even more complex than in the west. Rabbi Herzog chose to focus his efforts on Poland, where the pogrom perpetrated in Kielce on July 4, 1946, had left the remnant of the Jewish community badly shaken and deeply concerned for its physical safety. In addition to his efforts to restore to the Jewish fold the children still in Christian custody, Herzog also sought to remove from Poland those orphans who were already living in a Jewish environment and settle them in surroundings where they would receive a Jewish education. Before leaving for Poland, he met with the prime minister of France, Georges Bidauly, who provided him with 1,000 entry permits to France, of the 5,000 that had been promised by President Gouin for Jewish refugees from Poland.[15]

Rabbi Herzog arrived in Poland at the beginning of August 1946 and, accompanied by Rabbi David Kahane, the chief rabbinical chaplain of the Polish army and chief rabbi of the Jewish community, met with the Polish prime minister, Edvard Osubka-Morawski, and his assistants for Jewish affairs. Herzog's requests were primarily political in character, notably to allow the departure of Jews from the country and to ensure their safety. Only in passing did he mention the subject of a law for the registration of orphan children still in Christian custody. In any event, such legislation would have been of dubious practical value, given the unstable situation in Poland at the time. The reply he received was that such matters were not within the purview of a socialist government. It was intimated that the leadership was well aware that Jewish children in Poland were being redeemed by the Committee of Religious Communities and by the Zionist Federation, and that in the government's view this was an internal Jewish matter.[16]

Rabbi Herzog had decided in advance not to meet with the head of the Catholic Church in Poland, Cardinal August Hlond, whose antisemitic outlook was common knowledge before the war. The Holocaust had ostensibly given him second thoughts, and he told representatives of the Committee of Religious Communities that objective reasons for antisemitism in liberated Poland no longer existed and that attacks on Jews saddened him.[17] However, his reaction to the Kielce pogrom revealed his true face. In a statement to the international press after the atrocity, he alleged that the positive attitude

15  Ibid., pp. 56–57.
16  Ibid., p. 60; Kahane, *After the Flood*, p. 78.
17  Kahane, *After the Flood*, pp. 60–61.

toward the Jews had now changed because they had seized senior state posts and were trying to impose a regime that was repellent to the majority of Poles.[18] This was tantamount to pouring oil on the fire of antisemitism, and in the circumstances it was highly improbable that Cardinal Hlond would help the Jewish community regain its missing children.

Rabbi Herzog's major activity in Poland on behalf of the children was to organize a train that took some 500 children and yeshiva students to France, using the entry permits he had been given. Most of the children were orphans. Some had been removed from Christian custody, others repatriated from the Soviet Union. Herzog also left in Poland a sum of money he had brought from Palestine in order to ransom children from non-Jews.[19] Returning home, he summed up his mission on a note of disappointment, stating, "The activity to rescue the children of Israel not only has not ended, but has been implemented only to a limited degree."[20]

The failure of Rabbi Herzog's rescue mission was probably caused by his decision to employ personal diplomacy in the form of direct negotiations with political leaders and senior church figures, in which his only weapon lay in an appeal to their Christian conscience. The government and religious leaders with whom he met viewed him as a religious-spiritual leader who spoke for only part of the Jewish public, namely orthodox Jewry. As an outsider wielding no political power, it was clearly out of the question that he would be able to induce sovereign states to pass legislation compelling non-Jewish citizens who had rescued Jewish children and become attached to them to hand them over to the Jewish community. Further complicating the situation were the differences among the survivors themselves; there was no common cause in which the leaders of the religious communities represented all of the country's Jewish citizens. Moreover, in some countries, such as Belgium, influential Jews refused to cooperate with Rabbi Herzog, viewing his efforts with regard to the children as intervention in their internal affairs which would only stir up antisemitism and cause harm.[21] Akiva Levinsky, a senior emissary of Youth Aliyah in Europe, who was familiar with the many problems entailed in removing Jewish children from non-Jewish rescuers, argued correctly that instead of political activity at a senior government level, it was preferable to engage in quiet, individual actions involving direct ne-

18 Gutman, *The Jews in Poland*, p. 147.
19 Goldshlag, *Rescue Mission*, pp. 56–57, 61, 81.
20 Ibid., p. 100.
21 Minutes of National Council Executive meeting, October 3, 1946, CZA, J1/7264.

gotiations with those involved, drawing on the assistance of the lower-level bureaucracy.[22]

But Herzog was undeterred. Following his failed attempt to persuade the Netherlands to return the Jewish orphans to the Jewish community, he consulted with the rabbinate of Great Britain. It was decided to raise the issue at the United Nations, in the name of the British, American, and Palestinian rabbinates.[23] Learning about the idea, the New York office of the World Jewish Congress (WJC) began to examine its feasibility, and asked the Rescue Committee of the Jewish Agency in Jerusalem how many children remained in Christian custody across Europe. The plan was to ask the United Nations' Economic and Social Council to call on the European governments to enact legislation which would transfer the Jewish children to a Jewish environment.[24] WJC officials in Europe were skeptical about the efficacy of such a move. In an opinion to his colleagues in New York, the distinguished British Jewish historian, Prof. Cecil Roth, wrote:

> I have discussed at length with my colleagues of the European Secretariat your suggestion... The unanimous opinion was that such an international action would be rather a superfluous effort, and I want to point out the following objections: 1. In most of the countries where the problem has been of particular interest, the matter has been settled by national legislation in a more or less satisfactory way. 2. There are still some countries where we can suppose Jewish children can be found in non-Jewish surroundings, the number of those children being, however, absolutely unknown. We do not, however, think that in order to achieve legislative measures in those few countries we should bring the problem to the Economic and Social Council where at least 50 governments would be absolutely uninterested in the whole question, but where with regard to the religious connection of this problem we could meet with serious opposition. It seems to us much easier to take up the matter with the governments of those countries where the problem is supposed to still exist.[25]

In the wake of this opinion the WJC abandoned the plan to turn to the United Nations, but the initiative did not die. In 1948, the Commission on the

---

22  A. Levinsky to G. Landauer, July 27, 1947, CZA, S75/1907.
23  Minutes of National Council Executive meeting, October 3, 1946, CZA, J1/7264.
24  K. Stein to Y. Gruenbaum, July 21, 1947, and September 12, 1947, CZA, S26/1317.
25  C. Roth to K. Stein, October 17, 1947, CZA, C2/427.

218 • *At the Mercy of Strangers*

Status of Jewish War Orphans in Europe was established in London under the leadership of Rabbi Yishai Greenfeld. Consisting of representatives of religious Jewry in Britain — Agudat Israel and Hamizrahi — the Commission monitored the developments relating to the return of Jewish children in western Europe, particularly in France, Belgium, and the Netherlands.[26] No attempt was made to investigate the situation in eastern Europe, including Poland, probably because the communist regimes there had already begun to restrict activity by Jews and cut them off from Jewish organizations in the Free World.

At the beginning of 1949, the Commission again took up Rabbi Herzog's initiative and asked the United Nations Commission on Human Rights to amend Article 16 of the Declaration of the Rights of the Child, according to which parents of underage children are entitled to determine the religion the children will follow and orphans will receive religious instruction based on their parents' presumed wishes. By this means, it was believed, religious Jewish bodies would be entitled to take custody of the Jewish children who were still in Christian hands. The representative of the Philippines agreed to put the draft amendment to the body for a vote, but it was rejected overwhelmingly by 18-4, with the opposition led by the United States, China, Great Britain, and the Soviet Union. The four countries that supported the amendment were France, Guatemala, Iran, and the Philippines.[27]

Lobbying government officials for the return of the Jewish orphans was essentially a naïve effort, based on the assumption that the Holocaust had awoken the conscience of Christendom, which in a gesture of atonement for its bystander role would return the children still in non-Jewish custody. Governments, though, are driven not by conscience but by interests. No government was willing to act against the wishes of the majority of its citizens in order to placate the Jews, still less to enact legislation on a subject that was perceived as trivial and inconsequential: that of the religion in which several hundred orphans of Jewish origin would be raised. Just as these governments were unwilling to bring about the return of property which had been plundered by Christians from their rightful Jewish neighbors, they were also not prepared to flaunt the wishes of their citizens in order to ensure that Jewish orphans would be restored to the Jewish fold.

---

26 Minutes of a meeting of the Commission on the Status of Jewish War Orphans in Europe, January 16, 1949, CZA, C2/378.
27 Ibid., meeting of July 11, 1949.

## A Plan for the Emigration of Orphans from Poland to Sweden — and its Failure

As noted, the first reports about the child survivors had reached the Yishuv at the end of 1944, as Europe was being liberated. One such report, which reached the head of the Jewish Agency's Aliyah (immigration) Department, Eliyahu Dobkin, claimed that in France alone about 10,000 children had survived.[28] Few authenticated reports reached the Jewish institutions in the west from eastern Europe. With the war still raging, it was difficult to verify even the reports arriving from liberated areas of western Europe, with which communications had already been restored, still less from parts of remote Poland, liberated by Soviet forces but still cut off from the west. Moreover, at this stage there was little the Yishuv could do for the survivors.

Nevertheless, some officials in Palestine were already considering how to cope with the problem of the Jewish orphans which would arise in Europe after the war. As the first reports on the issue arrived, Mordechai Shatner, a member of Kibbutz Ein Harod, drew up a memorandum suggesting possible ways to deal with the problem. When the war broke out, Shatner was a Youth Aliyah emissary in London, in charge of the organization's European operations. He returned to Palestine in the middle of the war to be appointed to the National Council Executive. Having been involved in extricating Jewish youth from Germany on the eve of the war, he was familiar with rescue work. Based on the incoming fragmentary reports, he concluded that tens of thousands of Jewish orphans would remain in Europe after the war and would have to be looked after. This would involve immediate basic needs — food, clothing, housing, health care — but also their future. Shatner viewed this as a national challenge, in which the weight of responsibility devolved primarily on the Zionist movement and the Yishuv. In regard to the orphans who would remain in non-Jewish custody, he wrote:

> I believe that great efforts will also be needed to search for and locate the orphans and remove them from their Christian environment (convents, Christian families, etc.) and place them in exclusively Jewish custody. This operation will undoubtedly encounter many difficulties on the part of the convents and Christian families that housed the children, and possibly some of the children themselves will not willingly agree to be placed in a Jewish educational institution. However, these difficulties must not

28  M. Shatner to Mapai Central Committee, draft of memorandum on immigration of orphans to Eretz Israel, October 10.1944, Shatner family archive.

deter us from rescuing every Jewish child for the Jewish people. Orphan camps must be established in every country and be solely under *Jewish* authority [emphasis in the original]... Virtually all of these children have to be brought to Eretz Israel. Only in Eretz Israel will they be able to grow, after years of suffering and distress, and achieve mental equilibrium; only in Eretz Israel will they have a human and Jewish future. By creating the Youth Aliyah project, the Zionist movement has proved its ability to deal with this. This project, which is unique in content and scale in the world, will find its natural continuation in caring for and absorbing the tens of thousands of orphans from the Diaspora. The Jewish community in Eretz Israel, particularly the land-settlement movement [referring mainly to the kibbutzim], has demonstrated its ability to educate youth and replace the family they lost in the Diaspora. In the accomplishment of this task — caring for the Jewish orphans in Europe and bringing them to Eretz Israel — the efforts of all the Jewish public bodies must be concentrated, led by the Jewish Agency, the JDC, Hadassah, the Jewish communities in Britain, America, South Africa, and so forth. If the Jewish communities in Europe revive, they, too, must be made part of the effort... It is to be hoped that the JDC and the other Jewish bodies will lend a hand to this program... We must endeavor to obtain the maximum assistance from the international aid organizations (the Red Cross, UNRRA). Although we may hope that some governments will support us, it is possible that the governments of France and Holland will not be pleased at the removal of children from their countries. This will require an information effort and [other] activity on our part... Bringing the orphans to Eretz Israel can save for the Jewish people the remnant of our national strength in Europe and educate a generation of builders of the homeland... The Jewish Agency, together with the whole Yishuv, must therefore embark on the necessary actions at once, namely: (a) Preparing places of schooling for the children in Eretz Israel. (b) Negotiating with the JDC and other Jewish bodies regarding the cooperation proposed above. (c) Negotiating with international and intergovernmental organizations. (d) Preparing staff for this mission and sending them abroad. (e) Transferring Youth Aliyah headquarters from London to one of the countries on the continent and charging it with the task of concentrating training and immigration. (f) Mobilizing resources for this goal.[29]

29 Shatner, Memorandum on Absorption of the Holocaust Orphans in the Yishuv, October 18, 1944, Haganah Archives, 114/25. The addressee was probably the Mapai Central Committee.

Like the anonymous soldier on the Normandy front, Shatner, too, from his perspective in Palestine, saw the orphans as a national asset who belonged to the Jewish people and for whose sake it was necessary to muster all available forces and act uncompromisingly to restore the children to the Jewish people. In his eyes, these children were the last remnant of European Jewry, and the best way to rehabilitate them was to bring them to Palestine and integrate them into the land-settlement movement where they would become builders of the homeland, with the Yishuv replacing the family that had perished. The most suitable body to execute this mission, Shatner believed, was Youth Aliyah, an organization which had already proved itself by absorbing Jewish youth from Germany, thus saving them from death in the Holocaust. To underwrite this vast new project, the major Jewish organizations abroad must be mobilized.

It is not clear whether any of the decision-makers in the Yishuv's national institutions seriously contemplated Shatner's ideas, with all they entailed. In any event, on November 27, 1944, six weeks after Shatner had written his memorandum, Eliyahu Dobkin asked Henrietta Szold, the head of Youth Aliyah, to prepare urgently a detailed plan to absorb 20,000 children and adolescents in the organization's educational institutions, half of which were located in kibbutzim. He also requested that a long-term plan for the absorption of 100,000 children be prepared.[30] Georg Landauer, then a dominant figure in Youth Aliyah, said that he doubted whether the organization could cope with a project on that scale, even if the funding could be found.[31] In his view, the numbers cited by Dobkin were simply political propaganda, aimed at obtaining immigration certificates from the British authorities. Dobkin did not deny that this was his goal, "because the only weapon that can be effective against the White Paper" (a British government document concerning policy in Palestine) "is the ability to absorb new immigrants." He added, however, "The major task is to link the fate of the orphans of Israel with that of the Land of Israel."[32] On December 10, 1944, the Executive Committee of Youth Aliyah discussed the first memorandum submitted by the organization's director, Hans Beith, concerning the future integration program. His guiding

---

30  Shlomo Bar-Gil, *Youth Aliyah: Policy and Activity in the Absorption* and *Rehabilitation of Holocaust Survivors 1945–1955* (Hebrew), Ph.D. dissertation, Hebrew University of Jerusalem, 1995, p. 149.

31  Ibid.

32  Minutes of the executive meeting of Youth Aliyah, December 10, 1944, CZA, S75/1371.

principle was "the commitment of Youth Aliyah to be the primary reserve movement for the land-settlement movement in Eretz Israel."[33]

The initial discussions by the Youth Aliyah leadership about the fate of the child survivors and their absorption in Palestine bore a theoretical character. The approach was similar to that of Shatner in his memorandum, but with one basic difference: Dobkin and the senior personnel of Youth Aliyah considered the future of the children only from their arrival in Palestine, and concentrated on the technical details of fundraising and housing in the country, whereas Shatner foresaw the difficulties involved in removing the children from the custody of their non-Jewish rescuers. He believed that it would be necessary to seek out the children and fight for their removal, as their guardians would not easily relinquish them and the children themselves would not always be willing to return to Jewish society. Although Shatner recommended enlisting the help of international bodies and talking to the governments concerned, he appears to have held out little hope that that would help. His conclusion was that there would be no choice but to restore the children to their nation even against their will. On this point, he was nothing short of prophetic. Apart from him, no one in the Yishuv seems to have considered this aspect of the problem. However, it would not be long before others, in widely different places, would address the issue and try to devise means to solve it.

At the end of the war in Europe, the WJC in the United States established a Children's Committee, which convened for the first time on July 11, 1945, in the presence of the leader of American Zionism, Rabbi Stephen Wise, to discuss the fate of the Holocaust orphans. The secretary of the WJC, Aryeh Tartakower, who chaired the meeting, opened with several practical proposals on the subject, in the following order:

1. Removing the children from Christian homes, institutions, and convents.
2. Ensuring assistance for solitary children.
3. Establishing children's homes with the help of the WJC or maintaining the children in the existing institutions of OZE (Jewish Health Society), WIZO (Women's International Zionist Organization), and others.
4. Assisting in moving the children from Europe to Palestine, the United States, and elsewhere.

33 Bar-Gil, *Youth Aliyah*, p. 150.

These costly proposals were beyond the means of the WJC, and moreover, the Children's Committee was an advisory rather than an executive body. To underwrite the project, Tartakower suggested a grandiose worldwide program under which United States Jewry would adopt 10,000 child survivors by donating funds for their upkeep in Europe.[34] The most urgent concrete problem, Tartakower believed, was to remove about 700 children from non-Jewish homes in France and place them in Jewish institutions. He saw this as only a modest beginning for a broader operation to be carried out in western and southern Europe — in France, Belgium, Netherlands, Italy, and Greece.[35]

The problem of the child survivors in Poland went unmentioned in the meeting of the Children's Committee. Indeed, probably none of its members had any idea of its scale and complexity, as no regular connections with the Jewish institutions in Poland had yet been established, even though the war was over and Poland had been liberated more than six months before. It was not until late 1945 that initial reports about the problem of the children in Christian custody in Poland reached the Jewish Agency in Jerusalem and the London office of the WJC.

On November 4, 1945, Dobkin, in Jerusalem, received a cable from Hillel Storch, the representative of the WJC and the Jewish Agency in Sweden, stating that according to information in his possession, between 2,000 and 3,000 Jewish children were living in Christian homes in Poland, not out of compassion but as a means for the foster family to secure an income. The Polish legation in Stockholm had informed him that the government was willing to help remove the children from their guardians, even by force. The legation was also ready to issue transit permits to two Jewish representatives, enabling them to move back and forth freely between Poland and Sweden. Storch immediately began negotiating with the Swedish government to enable the temporary absorption of these children in Sweden. He was told that Sweden would be ready to take in 1,000 children if Jewish institutions would pay for their upkeep. The outlay would come to $25,000 a month and twice that amount in the first three months in order to purchase clothing for the children and meet the costs involved in moving them from Poland to Sweden. Storch wanted to know whether he could count on the assistance of the Jewish institutions for this project.[36]

---

34  Minutes of meeting of the Committee for Children of the World Jewish Congress, July 11, 1945, YVA, M.20/22.

35  Ibid.

36  Storch to Dobkin, November 4, 1945, CZA, S26/1317.

Dobkin, who was apparently taken aback by the cable, particularly its financial implications, immediately referred the matter to the London offices of the Jewish Agency and the WJC and to the Central Fund of British Jewry. Their assessment was that the project's enormous cost was probably beyond the reach of the Jewish institutions. The budget was estimated at 100,000 pounds sterling for just one year, a vast amount at the time, and this even before the children had reached their final destination — and no one yet knew where that might be. After all, the British were not waiting to hand out immigration certificates into Palestine. The whole project looked like wishful thinking. It was also unclear from Storch's cable whether he had been in touch with the Central Jewish Committee in Warsaw before entering into talks with the Swedish government. The problem was that in the circumstances prevailing at the time, a plan of this kind could not be implemented without the cooperation of the Central Jewish Committee. Shalom Adler Rudel, who was the Jewish Agency's liaison officer with the WJC in London, was doubtful that the Central Jewish Committee in Warsaw would agree to allow the children to be taken out of Poland, given the small number who had survived. Nevertheless, it was decided not to abandon the plan outright, in order to gain time and try to interest other Jewish bodies, such as the Jewish community of Stockholm and the JDC, in the project. Storch was asked whether the Jewish community of Stockholm had agreed to the plan, whether he had informed the JDC, and how much money he had available.[37]

Industrious and devoted, Storch decided to maintain pressure on the Swedish government to agree to allow 1,000 children from Poland into Sweden, against a declaration that their final goal was Palestine. In the meantime, the government of Finland announced that it was willing to take in fifty children and 200 adults.[38] Storch was joined in his efforts by two WJC emissaries, Louis Segal and Shmuel Margoshes, who had stopped in Sweden on their way from the United States to Poland and met with the Swedish prime minister to explain the problem of the children in Poland. The prime minister was sympathetic and referred the two emissaries to the chief secretary of the Ministry for Social Affairs, within whose purview the subject fell. But that conversation produced only an expression of sympathy and was unaccompanied by a concrete promise to take action. The emissaries, though, construed the official's words of sympathy as a positive decision, and Margoshes immediately cabled New York to that effect. Two days after the cable was made public in New

37  Adler Rudel to Easterman, November 9, 1945, CZA, C2/602.
38  Moshe Yishai to Aliyah Department, Jerusalem, January 25, 1946, CZA, S26/1248.

York, the government of Sweden received a cable of thanks from Rabbi Wise for its humanitarian approach to the rescue of Jewish children. The Swedish Ministry of Social Affairs thereupon issued an official denial that Stockholm had agreed to allow the children to pass through Sweden and that the entire matter still required clarification.[39]

Segal and Margoshes arrived in Poland in January 1946, with only the promise of the Finnish government to admit fifty Jewish children from Poland. Nevertheless, they decided to broach the question of removing the orphans from Poland to the Central Jewish Committee in Warsaw. The subject was discussed by the Committee's presidium on January 29, 1946, in the presence of the visitors from the United States and Meyerson and Blaugrund, representatives of the Jewish communities of Sweden and Finland. As expected, the Communist members of the presidium objected to the children's removal from Poland. The chairman, Marek Bitter, claimed that moving the children to new surroundings for an interim period would be detrimental to them. However, in order not to embarrass the important guests, whose material support the Central Jewish Committee sought, their proposal was not rejected outright. Instead, they were told that this was a matter of principle which had to be considered by an inter-party committee.[40]

At the beginning of March 1946, Zerach Warhaftig arrived in Poland as an emissary of Hamizrahi, the religious Zionist movement, and of the WJC. He too tried to implement a plan to move 1,000 children from Poland to Sweden, even though he was skeptical about the ability of the small Swedish Jewish community to absorb them. After consulting with Rabbi Kahane, Warhaftig again raised the matter before the Central Jewish Committee, this time proposing that permits be granted to 800 children from the children's homes of the Central Committee and 200 others at the instructions of the Chief Religious Council.[41] Like the two emissaries who had preceded him, he was told, "Children belonging to the Polish Jewish community were not to be taken out of Poland. Their future lies in Poland."[42]

The plan to send 1,000 orphans from Poland to Sweden continued to be tossed around like a dead weight in Jewish institutions for a few more months. Its origins lay in a vague promise by the Polish legation in Stock-

---

39  Hanan Berkowitz to Dobkin, July 25, 1946, Haganah Archives, 24.85-25/50.
40  Minutes of meeting of Central Jewish Committee of Poland, January 29, 1946, YVA, P.20/6.
41  Z. Warhaftig note, March 10, 1946, ibid.
42  Warhaftig, *Refugee and Survivor,* p. 340.

holm that Warsaw would assist in the removal of the Jewish children who remained in non-Jewish families, and it continued with an attempt to remove from Poland at least the few orphans who were already in Jewish institutions. The initiators of the plan, the Jewish institutions in the West, did not realize how convoluted and complex the problem was and went ahead without consulting other Jewish bodies besides the Central Jewish Committee. In order to remove the children from Poland, and particularly those still in non-Jewish custody, external initiative and support, primarily of a financial character, was required, which could have been provided by the Jewish institutions overseas. However, none of this was practicable without the cooperation of the local Jewish groups, who were familiar with the conditions firsthand.

On July 24, 1946, the secretary of the Swedish Ministry for Social Affairs informed the Jewish representatives that in the wake of recent events in Palestine (The "Black Sabbath" — when the British authorities arrested Yishuv leaders — and the blowing-up by the Etzel of a wing of the King David Hotel in Jerusalem that housed British administrative offices and the military headquarters), he was inclined to recommend that the cabinet reject their request to transfer 1,000 Jewish children from Poland to Sweden, as he doubted that they would receive immigration certificates to Palestine from the British in the foreseeable future.[43] This spelled the end of the plan. Still, the attempts to implement it made clear two important points about the future of the child survivors from Poland. In the first place, the Polish government regarded as self-evident the affiliation of the Jewish children who remained in the custody of Christian families with the Jewish nation; and secondly, that the Polish government was not opposed to the children leaving Poland.

At the same time that the Jewish Agency and the WJC were informed of the failure of the project to transfer children from Poland to Sweden, a different and more efficient operation was already operating intensively in Poland. Under its aegis, children were ransomed from non-Jews and thousands of children and adolescents were taken out of the country.

43 Hanan Berkowitz to Dobkin, July 25, 1946, Haganah Archives, 24.85-25/50.

CHAPTER NINE

# "The Zionist Koordynacja for the Redemption of Jewish Children"

## Children's Kibbutzim

After the Holocaust and from the beginning of survivor activities in Poland, the *She'erit Hapletah* ("surviving remnant") — was organized largely along party lines. In this context, the Zionist youth movements were revived and a large number of "kibbutzim" were established on Polish soil. The first such kibbutz was established jointly by the Dror and Hashomer Hatza'ir movements in March 1945 at 38, Poznanska Street in Warsaw, amid the ruins of the city. The founding members were a group of orphaned youngsters who had grown up in the ghettos, concentration camps, and forests. Before the war, their leaders — Michael Litvak, Tuvia Bożekovski, Yisrael Shklar, and Bronka Klibanska — were members of the *Aktiva*, the activists of the movements.[1] Other movements followed in their wake, and kibbutzim, which young people organized collectively, sprang up in the few remaining Jewish concentrations across Poland. In theory, the new kibbutzim were based on the old prewar *hahshara* ("training") collectives, which provided preparation for agricultural labor in Eretz Israel. In practice, the new kibbutzim were different both in their human component and in their atmosphere. Thus Yohanan Cohen, from the Noar Hatzioni movement, who had immigrated to Palestine from Poland in 1937 and returned to his native land in October 1945 as an emissary of the *Mossad le'Aliyah Bet* — the clandestine organization responsible for the illegal immigration of Jews to Palestine — was overwhelmed by the new reality he found in the kibbutzim, only eight years after he himself had been part of the prewar Zionist youth movement experience:

---

1   Stefan Grayek, *The Struggle: Polish Jews 1945–1949* (Hebrew) (Tel Aviv: Am Oved, 1989), p. 18.

227

I found that all my conceptions about "movements," "hahshara kib-butzim," and so forth were anachronisms bearing no relation to reality. I was still in the conceptual world of the day before yesterday, of my youthful memories… I thought in ideological, pedagogical, aesthetic terms. In my mind's eye I saw one more youth movement, which taught noble ideals: human and Jewish. I thought of kibbutzim that prepare young pioneers for a life of labor and defense. I found a different reality. I will not exaggerate or distort the situation if I say that the kibbutz in Poland at that time was a kind of orphanage. It was a substitute for home and family, and in it Holocaust orphans were gathered… The kibbut-zim were the first place of support for youngsters who were witness to the degeneration and demoralization that emerged during the war. The young people, alone and hurt, found in the kibbutz a belief in the future. They found an atmosphere of family warmth, the absence of which they had felt painfully.[2]

The positive atmosphere in these kibbutzim was created by the survivors of the old Aktiva, who had established them and were their leaders. They suc-ceeded in imbuing the youngsters with the feeling that despite all the horrors they had experienced, life was still worth living and there was no reason for them to feel inferior because they were Jews — on the contrary, they should take pride in belonging to the Jewish people. The kibbutz offered them a clear goal: to rehabilitate their lives by immigrating to Eretz Israel by any possible means and joining the builders of the homeland in the farming settlements. From the outset, life in the Polish kibbutzim was governed by their inherently transient existence. Everyone was ready and poised to embark on *Bricha* — the underground exodus of Jews from eastern Europe to the DP (displaced persons) camps in western Europe — and *Ha'apala*, illegal immigration to Palestine under the nose of the British. Accordingly, the Polish kibbutzim were not so much preparatory collectives as they were immigration groups or "kibbutzim in the making," in the contemporary term. The group's cohesion was achieved not through the lofty abstract ideals with which their leaders tried to imbue them, but by the shared, almost palpable feeling of a com-mon destiny and goal, which welded them into an impassioned community that knew what it wanted. Indeed, it was this sense of purpose that made the kibbutzim a magnet for the young and the reason for the rapid spread of the

2   Yohanan Cohen, *Operation "Bricha," Poland 1945–1946* (Hebrew) (Tel Aviv: Zmora Bitan, 1995), p. 198.

concept. Suffice it to note that at the beginning of August 1945, only about four months after the establishment of the first Polish kibbutz, there were already more than seventeen such groups of young people aged sixteen to twenty-one, and many more would soon come into being.[3]

In their effort to win over the hearts of the young generation, the pioneer movements also sought to establish kibbutzim for children aged twelve to fifteen, the classic age for joining a youth movement. The problem was to find both the necessary financial resources and educators who could address the needs of this age group. But as is often the case in emergencies, improvisation combined with enthusiasm and dedication found a way. Concurrent with the establishment of the first kibbutzim for older youths, members of the *Aktiva* began to train a cadre of new leaders from among the young people who had just joined the movements. The framework was short: improvised ideological seminars beginning as early as the summer of 1945. The first Dror-Hashomer Hatza'ir kibbutz based in Warsaw produced the initial group of *madrichim* (group leaders) for children, among them Utta Wargon-Grayek, Natka Gold, Dorka Bram-Sternberg, Leah Rosenblum-Tzur, Zalman Ackerman, Dziunia Karo-Weinberg, Lonia Goldstein, Mordechai Goldhecht, and others.[4] They were joined by former members of the movements from before the war, some of whom had survived in Poland, the others arriving from the Soviet Union in the first waves of repatriation. They included Nesia Orlowicz-Reznik, Chasia Bornstein-Bielicka, Mordechai Binczuk (Bahat), and others. The years of separation from their compatriots had made them nostalgic for the movement, and they threw themselves into its activities, as if in atonement for having remained alive.[5]

Activities for the younger children underwent a revolutionary change, with the elimination of the classic prewar stage of education in a *ken* (literally "nest") in favor of direct transition to a "children's kibbutz." This new creation in the immediate post-Holocaust period was unexampled in the history of the Zionist youth movements. In the normal course of events before the war, the children would have lived at home and attended school, and devoted only a small part of their leisure time to the youth movement, consisting of games and educational activity in the local ken or branch. These activities were in

---

3   Itzhak Zukerman, *The Polish Exodus and the Reconstruction of the Pioneer Movement* (Hebrew) (Tel Aviv: Ghetto Fighters' House and Hakibbutz Hameuchad, 1988), p. 20.
4   Grayek, *The Struggle*, p. 18.
5   Nesia Orlovich-Reznik, "Shomeri Children's home," in Dror Levy, ed., *Book of Hashomer Hatzair* vol. II (Hebrew) (Merhavia: Sifriat Poalim, 1961), pp. 311–312.

addition to the concrete, prosaic areas of life. The children's organic environment was the parental home, and the youth movements tried to undermine their parents' bourgeois way of life. After the war, most of the surviving children had no parental home to rebel against. They needed a home in the most basic sense of the term and someone to care for them. These were the tasks undertaken by the resurgent youth movements. Thus the children's kibbutz in many ways mirrored the kibbutz for the older group. Fusing an orphanage and a movement ken, it actually resembled — without anyone having planned it — the children's homes which existed in the kibbutzim in Palestine as part of the collective education system. In Poland, however, the children's kibbutz was a temporary home, the purpose of which was to prepare them for immigration to Palestine.[6] In short order the children's kibbutzim became an educational stream competing with the children's institutions run by the Central Jewish Committee.

As noted, in 1945 the Central Jewish Committee had established a network of children's homes throughout Poland in which considerable resources were invested, though only a fraction of the child survivors — less than twenty percent of the total — entered them, nearly all of them orphans, including the very young and some who were sick. As the wave of repatriation gathered momentum, the Central Jewish Committee established another fifty-four day schools for the returning children in order to facilitate their parents' efforts to find work in their new places of residence. All these institutions, which were attended by about 3,800 children,[7] were dominated by Jewish communists and by the Bund. The educational line they advocated, albeit not declaratively, advocated assimilation into Polish culture and society. The dominant language in these institutions was Polish, and Jewish subjects, such as the festivals and the study of Hebrew, were increasingly ignored on various pretexts. After the children had recovered somewhat from the traumas of the war, an effort was made to integrate them into the Polish state education system so they would grow up to be loyal citizens of the new Poland.

In contrast, the children's kibbutzim, despite the small teaching staff, sought to impart to the youngsters something of the new Hebrew culture and the atmosphere of Eretz Israel. The Zionist movements were also determined from the outset to remove the children from Poland by any means, legal or illegal, with the aim of getting them to Palestine. As a result, many children joined them. The composition of the children in the first children's kibbutzim

6 Zalman Livneh and Yeshayahu Weiner, "Movement on Ruins," ibid., pp. 290–291.
7 *Sprawozdanie wydzial opieki nad dzieckiem C.K.Ż. w P. na rok 1946*, AŻIH (CKŻ WO).

was identical to that in the Central Jewish Committee institutions. Most of them were orphans who had been collected by older youths after surviving in villages, with non-Jewish families, and in the forests. Some were the siblings or other relatives of the older youths but were not suited to their kibbutzim.[8] When the refugees from the Soviet Union began to stream back to Poland, activists from the youth movements met them at the train stations and tried to persuade the parents to place their children in the kibbutzim, promising to get them out of Poland via the *Bricha*.[9] Many of the parents, who had not yet decided about their future when they handed over the children, eventually followed their children to Palestine.[10]

By the end of 1945, eight children's kibbutzim had been established — two each by Dror and Hashomer Hatza'ir, and four by Hanoar Hatzioni — though each housed only a few dozen children. However, they multiplied rapidly as the repatriates from the Soviet Union arrived in growing numbers, and reached a peak in the summer of 1946, when about fifty such kibbutzim existed across Poland, with 3,300 children ready for the move to Palestine.[11] Recruitment of children was competitive, and each movement boasted about the large numbers who had joined its ranks. The movements also had no compunction about sending activists to the Central Jewish Committee children's homes in order to lure away the children there by various stratagems and promises.[12]

Amid all this feverish activity, the orphans who remained with non-Jewish families and in convents and who were under twelve — some of whom did not even know they were Jewish — were forgotten. As we saw, this complex problem, which was common knowledge, still awaited a solution. Occasional attempts made by older members of the movements to remove the children from villages and convents met with little success.[13] This difficult mission was beyond the capabilities of the youth movements. They had neither the means nor the tools to search for individual children who were scat-

8 Orlovich-Reznik, "Shomeri Children's home," pp. 312–313.
9 Sara Shner-Neshamit, *I Did Not Find Rest* (Hebrew) (Tel Aviv: Ghetto Fighters' House and Hakibbutz Hameuchad, 1986), p. 190.
10 Zalman Avigdori, "Letters from Mission to Poland," in *Mission to the Diaspora 1945-1948* (Hebrew) (Tel Aviv: Yad Tabenkin and Ghetto Fighters' House, 1989), p. 99.
11 Cohen, *Operation "Bricha,"* Appendix V, pp. 464–465.
12 Uri Yanai, in *Mission to the Diaspora*, p. 67.
13 Testimony of Chasia Bornstein-Bielicka, OHD, (68)26; Leibel Koriski, "The Zionist Koordynacja for the Rescue of the Children in Poland 1946–1949" (Hebrew) *Gal-Ed*, vol. 7–8 (1985), p. 253.

tered across Poland in private homes or church institutions. Nor were they capable of looking after such young children, some of whom were sick and all of whom required specialized treatment and appropriate care.[14]

The problem was compounded by the arrival of orphans with the returning refugees from the Soviet Union. After their parents had perished, they had been placed in mixed orphanages, Russian or Polish, which were established in the Soviet Union by the Union of Polish Patriots (*Związek Patriotów Polskich* — ZPP). Now, upon their return to Poland, the Central Jewish Committee tried to place them in its institutions. Some of them arrived with Jewish guardians, who in the encounter at the train stations were susceptible to persuasion that the best place for them was in the children's kibbutzim.[15] However, not all the arriving orphans were in the care of guardians, and thus were liable to be placed in Polish orphanages from which it would be then difficult to remove them.[16] The solution that was eventually found for all the orphans, both those who were still living with their non-Jewish rescuers in Poland and the new arrivals from the mixed orphanages in the Soviet Union, was to create an organization especially for this purpose: "The Zionist *Koordynacja* [Coordination Committee] for the Redemption of Jewish Children" — known simply as the Koordynacja.

## Establishment of the Koordynacja

Arye Sarid (Leibele Goldberg), at the time a member of Kibbutz Yagur and one of the first emissaries of Eretz Israel to reach Poland, toward the end of 1945, was instrumental in establishing the Koordynacja. Sarid was sent by the Mapai faction in the Kibbutz Hameuchad movement to work with the Dror kibbutzim. He had no concrete information about the situation of the survivors in Poland. Like many in the Yishuv, he had high regard for Yitzhak (Antek) Zuckerman and Zivia Lubetkin — among the leaders of the fighters in the Warsaw Ghetto who, despite everything they had been through, rehabilitated the movement after the war. Sarid aspired to follow in their footsteps. In Italy, while on his way to Poland, he met Zuckerman, and the two considered how Sarid could best integrate into Dror's educational activity.[17] Nothing

14  Shner-Neshamit, *I Did Not Find Rest*, p. 190.
15  Arye Sarid, in *Mission to the Diaspora*, p. 91.
16  Testimony of Chasia Bornstein-Bielicka, OHD, (68)26.
17  Sarid, in *Mission to the Diaspora,* pp. 78–79.

was said about the orphan children, a subject in which Sarid took little interest. Like all the Yishuv emissaries to Poland, he visited the area where he had grown up to see if any of his family or friends had survived, and encountered the phenomenon of the hidden Jews who had immersed themselves in Polish society and refused to admit their true identity.[18] These assimilation attempts by some survivors were particularly painful and offensive to representatives of Jewish national life in Eretz Israel.

During a visit to Central Jewish Committee headquarters in Kraków, Sarid met a Polish women who had arrived with a boy she had rescued in order to receive the monthly allocation for his support. Intrigued, Sarid asked the woman how much longer she wanted to keep the child in her custody. From her reply, Sarid gathered that he was an orphan and that she planned to raise him as her son and not surrender him to a Jewish organization. When the boy grows up, she told him, he can decide on his path in life. Sarid asked the Central Jewish Committee officials whether they intended to remove children from Christian guardians and place them in Jewish orphanages. He was told that there was no money for such an operation.[19] Sarid, for whom this was a new problem, rejected this approach. Years later he said, "Coming from Eretz Israel, it was self-evident to me that a Jewish child who was raised among Gentiles had to be returned to the Jewish people after the war. I found the phenomenon of children who remained with Gentiles who asked for support from Jews repugnant, both morally and emotionally. It was alien to my mindset."[20]

It then suddenly struck him that action had to be taken. From the Central Jewish Committee he received the addresses of such Jewish children. One address was that of a Polish woman who had two Jewish children in her custody, a boy and a girl. For 3,000 zlotys she agreed to hand over the girl.[21]

It was not only in Kraków that Gentile women looking after Jewish children received financial support from the Central Jewish Committee. In some cases the children themselves solicited Jewish institutions for assistance for their Christian guardians. In Warsaw, Sarid met a brother and sister of about ten and thirteen, respectively, who were going to the JDC office to seek aid for their Polish "aunt." Sarid asked them if they were Jews. They replied that they were, that their parents had been killed, and that they were now

18  Ibid., pp. 76–77.
19  Ibid., p. 83.
20  Testimony of Arye Sarid, OHD, (68)10.
21  Sarid, in *Mission to the Diaspora*, p. 83.

234 • *At the Mercy of Strangers*

living with the Polish family that had sheltered them and they now wanted to help the "aunt" who had rescued them because she was poor. They told Sarid, in reply to his question, that they would be willing to go to Palestine. Sarid suggested that they bring their "aunt" so that she could formally return them to the Jews, and then they could go to Palestine.[22] In February 1946, the two children, Izio and Pola Miller, came to the hostel of the Poalei Zion party in Warsaw with their Polish guardian. Sara Neshamit, who conducted the negotiations, gave the woman 15,000 zlotys for the two children.[23] The Polish woman did not haggle. Clearly discomfited, she apologized for taking money in return for the children; it was only because she was so poor, she said, adding that she hoped the children would be well looked after.[24]

The next day, the two visitors from the United States mentioned before arrived at the hostel: Louis Segal, the secretary of the *Natzional Arbeiter Farband*, a Labor Zionist organization, and Shmuel Margoshes, the editor of the Yiddish daily *Der Tog*, who were on a mission for the World Jewish Congress. Sarid introduced Pola and Izio Miller to them and proposed the creation of a project to recover such children. The two Americans informed New York about the new initiative and requested funds urgently. The money was forwarded at once. However, the leaders of the WJC were apparently unaware of the tangled political relations existing among the remnants of Polish Jewry, or of the struggle being waged between the Zionists on the one hand and the communists and the Bund on the other for the children's souls. Thus, of the $5,000 that was transferred to the emissaries in Poland, $3,000 was earmarked for the Central Jewish Committee and only $2,000 for the new project of the Zionist Labor movement.[25] However, Segal, a Zionist, who knew that the communists on the Central Jewish Committee had no intention of allowing the orphans' removal from Poland, ensured that the redemption project remained in Zionist hands and gave all the money to Sarid.[26]

After the recovery of the first children, the initiative began to gather momentum. Apparently motivated by rumors that the Central Jewish Committee would pay a substantial sum for Jewish children, their Gentile guardians

22  Ibid., p. 84.
23  Neshamit, "Coordinating Child Rescue," p. 118.
24  Sarid, in *Mission to the Diaspora*, pp. 84–85. According to Sarid, the woman received 60,000 zlotys; I favor Neshamit's testimony because of its proximity to the event and owing to various inaccuracies in Sarid's testimonies on this subject,
25  Aryeh Tartakower (New York) to Abraham Silverstein (Geneva), February 14, 1946, YVA, M.20/22.
26  Sarid, in *Mission to the Diaspora*, p. 85.

began to bring them to the organization's Warsaw headquarters. There they were met by Joseph Bodniew, who was affiliated with the pioneer movements, and he referred them to the party's Poalei Zion hostel.[27] Within a short time twenty-eight children were ransomed and sent to the Dror children's kibbutz in Bytom. Besides Pola and Izio Miller, the first children in this group included Halina Feldenstein, Stefcia Zenfman, and Marcel Landsberger. Segal and Margoshes visited the children in Bytom and took an interest in the new project. At the same time, they explained to the initiators that effective publicity was essential in order to raise money in the United States. They also insisted that the project be removed from Dror and become a coordinated enterprise of all the Zionist organizations in Poland.[28]

To this end, wearisome negotiations began among the Zionist movements. Everyone was enthusiastic, but formulating the platform turned out to be a thorny problem. All agreed that the operation should be entrusted to the youth movements, which had already absorbed hundreds of youths aged over twelve in their local kibbutzim. It was also clear that institutions would have to be established specifically to absorb the ransomed children in order to guide them back to Jewish society and prepare them for immigration to Palestine. However, competition among the movements made it difficult to reach agreement on the educational track for the ransomed children. The problem was compounded by the arrival of the repatriates from the Soviet Union. These thousands of children and adolescents, who had been in mixed institutions and cut off from Jewish education, were the equivalent of a blank slate, and became the main reserve of the resurgent youth movements in Poland.

In the light of the developing situation, the Zionist youth movements decided to expand the base of the new organization. Thus, in addition to the children recovered from their non-Jewish guardians, the movements would also take custody of the repatriate orphans, who had no one to look after them even if one of the parents had survived. Following a series of meetings, the representatives of the movements — Dror, Hashomer Hatza'ir, Noar Borochov, Gordonia, Ha'ihud (General Zionists), Hanoar Hatzioni, Akiva, and WIZO — agreed to establish the joint organization to be called "The Zionist Koordynacja for the Redemption of Jewish Children," to be headed by a directorate.[29]

27 Shner-Neshamit, *I Did Not Find Rest*, p. 191.
28 Neshamit, "Coordinating Child Rescue," p. 120; and see also testimony of Bornstein-Bielicka., OHD, (68)26.
29 Neshamit, "Coordinating Child Rescue," p. 120.

"Koordynacja" was essentially a technical term which was used in Poland by the Zionist groups for ad hoc organizing. In contrast, "redemption" (*geula*) or "redeemed" (*geulim*) were charged terms invoked with regard to the children who were recovered from their non-Jewish rescuers. It should be emphasized that the majority of these children had been placed in the custody of non-Jews by their parents, who were unable to protect them. As we have seen, many of the children became emotionally attached to their benefactors, who had risked their lives for them, had given them their love, and looked after them devotedly. Accordingly, it is an affront to them to use the term "redemption" or "rescue" for the act of recovery. The notion of "rescue," is particularly offensive. It was in widespread use among the emissaries from Eretz Israel, who had been far removed from the events; it did not embody the full complexity of the situation, while the emissaries did not always understand what the survivors and their guardians had gone through. But these terms reflected the feelings of the people who were determined to restore the children to their roots. Their attitude derived primarily from the reactions they encountered when trying to remove the children from their rescuers, whether these were due to emotional bonds and religious wellsprings or to material calculations. The founders of the Koordynacja were well aware of the sensitive nature of this terminology and invoked it primarily for internal purposes. Outwardly they preferred neutral language. Thus the official name of the new organization was *Koordynacja dla spraw dzieci i młodzieży w Polsce* ("Coordination Committee for Children and Youth in Poland.")[30]

The Koordynacja directorate was headquartered in Łódź, the major Jewish center in Poland after the war. Some of its members — representatives of the organization's founding movements — worked full-time at specific tasks, while the others, the public's representatives, took part in meetings concerning issues of principle. The directorate's powers and procedures were not set down in written form, but the members divided the tasks among themselves and assumed specific responsibilities.[31] The central figure of the directorate was Leibel Koriski from Hashomer Hatza'ir, who was responsible for organization and finances. He was the manager of the Koordynacja throughout most of its existence, from March 1946 until his immigration to Palestine in April 1948. His successor was Pinhas Krivos, from the Borochov youth movement, who directed the project until it closed down in the summer of 1949. The other members of the directorate were Sara Neshamit, from Dror

---

30  This is the name that appears in the organization's official statements and letters.
31  Testimonies of Leibel Koriski, OHD, (68)15b, Pesach Zeidman, OHD, (68)41.

(education); Mela Mandelbaum, the delegate from Gordonia (the children's homes in Łódź); the delegates from Ihud, Hanoar Hatzioni, and Akiva were Menachem Kunda (education and finances), Moshe Unger, Ovadia Peled, and Chaim Bzora (secretariat); and representing WIZO were Elitsia Keil and Bella Paszpiorka (supervision of children's homes).

In addition to the local people, the directorate always included a representative from Palestine, in charge of liaising with the Jewish institutions in Eretz Israel.[32] The first of these was Aryeh Sarid, the founder of the Koordynacja and its moving spirit. Even after concluding his work in Poland, in September 1946, and moving on to Germany, he continued to stay in touch with the Koordynacja, which was the apple of his eye. It was Sarid who raised most of the funds to recover the children. Yohanan Cohen, who was then in Poland as an emissary of the Mossad le'Aliyah Bet (the organization for "illegal" immigration), recalled the impression Sarid made: "A chunky fellow whose whole appearance suggested roughness, a pair of alert eyes, a dry style of speech — it seemed we were dealing with a party *politruk*. But that impression faded quickly. It turned out that behind the exterior appearance is a volcano of inexhaustible energy fired by love of Israel... Leibele (Aryeh) loved his party, yes, but he loved the people of Israel more, and especially the children of Israel who had survived the Holocaust."[33]

The two emissaries who succeeded him in the post were also from Hakibbutz Hameuchad: Abraham Berenson, from Kibbutz Dafna, and Shaike Zhukovsky, from Kibbutz Glil Yam.[34] Another emissary, who, although not an official member of the Koordynacja directorate, exerted considerable influence on its work, was Shaike Weiner from Kibbutz Ein Hashofet, which belonged to the left-wing Kibbutz Ha'artzi movement of Hashomer Hatza'ir. It should be noted that even though the members of the directorate were appointed on a party basis, as was customary in the Zionist movement, the appointees were chosen and assigned tasks commensurate with their age, qualifications, and emotional approach to the project. Most of them were in their thirties or older, and had a great deal of experience in public activity.

Leibel Koriski, born in Vilna, was thirty-three when he started to work for the Koordynacja. As a boy he had attended a school of the Jewish network *Tarbut* ("Culture") and afterwards had joined Hashomer Hatza'ir. Before the war he was the head of the Printers' Union in Vilna. He spent the war years

---

32  Koriski, "The Zionist Koordynacja," p. 254.
33  Cohen, *Operation "Bricha,"* pp. 236–237.
34  Koriski, "The Zionist Koordynacja," p. 254.

deep inside the Soviet Union and served in the Soviet army. In Poland, which he reached after the war on his way to Palestine, Shaike Weiner recruited him for the movement. After all he had gone through, Koriski had no interest in party activity, but when he was entrusted with the task of restoring children to the Jewish fold he undertook the task willingly, extending his stay in Poland for two years and devoting himself to the mission wholeheartedly. Explaining his motives, he said:

> My family and my wife, with our daughter who was born in the meantime who had remained in Vilna, did not survive. I had no information about their fate, no trace remained of them... The proposal to redeem the children who remained with Gentiles in convents and villages, and restore them to the Jewish fold, captivated me... I was also captivated because I too had had a daughter, one I never knew and never saw, who was born in the ghetto... Maybe I will find someone, maybe my wife before she was taken to her death, who gave the girl to someone to look after, as had happened in similar cases... If I have to be in Łódź for a time anyway, let me do work that will be to my liking and will allow me to help with something essential for the nation.[35]

Another key activist of the Koordynacja from its founding until the end of 1947 was Sara Neshamit (Dusznicka), who helped formulate the special educational curriculum for the children. Lithuanian-born, Neshamit was also a graduate of a Tarbut school and a local high school and was an educational psychology student at the University of Kovno before the war. A member of Dror since her youth, she joined the partisans in the war. After the liberation she returned to Kovno and taught in an orphanage. In December 1945 she arrived in Poland on the way to Palestine. In Łodz she met Aryeh Sarid, who told her about his plan to recover children who were still in Christian keeping. They found a common language, and when Sarid invited her to join the new project she agreed to stay in Poland for the time being and work with him.[36]

The goals of the Koordynacja were set forth in written form and later published in its one-time publication, *Farn Yiddishn Kind* ("For the Jewish Child,") which appeared in November 1946. Its goals were:

1. To recover children from non-Jewish hands.

---

35 Testimony of Leibel Koriski, OHD, (68)15a.
36 Shner-Neshamit, *I Did Not Find Rest*, p. 189.

2. To establish children's kibbutzim for the age group aged three to thirteen.
3. To absorb in these kibbutzim, ransomed children, orphans, and repatriated children whose parents had placed them in the organization's care until their immigration to Palestine.
4. To give the children a pioneer-oriented education.

The purpose for which the Koordynacja was established was aptly summed up in the headline of its programmatic editorial: *Alle Yiddishe kinder musen tzurikkumen tzum folk!* ("All Jewish children must return to their nation"). The publication, which appeared at the height of the organization's activity, contained articles surveying its various activities and the children's special problems. It also listed the names of the 216 children who were then in Koordynacja institutions.[37]

Following internal disagreements between the Ihud organization and the Eretz Israel Ha'ovedet (land-settlement) movements, it was decided that the Koordynacja educational institutions would have a pioneer orientation, similar to the children's kibbutzim. Concretely, this meant a fully cooperative way of life and educating the children from an early age to self-sufficiency and work; that the educators' approach to the children would be that of an older person to a younger friend; and that the language of instruction would be Hebrew.[38]

Even though the Koordynacja was supposed to be an apolitical body operating on the basis of a broad consensus, in the competitive atmosphere then prevailing between the youth movements, it was difficult to neutralize the political interests of the movements represented on the directorate. One area in which politics did not play a part was the effort to recover the children. Here, the activists set their party interests aside and worked, as Sarid said, "for the sake of heaven," driven by personal integrity and national responsibility. This approach was primarily due to the personality of Leibel Koriski, who guided Koordynacja activity during most of its existence.[39] The sensitive subject of the children's recovery overrode transitory party disputes, and the activists set their priorities accordingly. Many problems which occurred during the work were solved by mutual understanding. Thus, for example, the directorate reached general agreement without dissension on the order in which

37 *Farn Yiddishn Kind* (Yiddish), November 1946, CZA, 5612.
38 Neshamit, "Coordinating Child Rescue," p. 121.
39 Sarid, in *Mission to the Diaspora*, p. 86.

children aged thirteen and above who came under the care of the Koordynacja would be transferred to each movement.[40]

Pointedly absent from the Koordynacja were the religious groups, particularly Hamizrahi and Bnei Akiva, which were integral elements of the Zionist movement and whose leaders were members of all its institutions. It is not clear from the surviving documentation whether the religious movements were involved in the discussions on the creation of the Koordynacja. A report from Aryeh Sarid to his headquarters in Palestine regarding the start of the project noted, "Although the Agudah [Agudat Israel] and Hamizrahi are working on this a little, the fact is that hundreds of children still remain with Gentiles."[41] This brief comment would indicate that at the time the Koordynacja was established, the religious movements were already trying to recover children on their own. Sara Neshamit, wrote later, "The religious [groups] left this framework and undertook separate activity."[42]

In fact, the religious groups in Poland, Zionist and non-Zionist alike, which were organized in the Committee of Religious Communities founded by Rabbi David Kahane, began at this time to recover children through Yeshayahu Drucker, who had served as a military chaplain even though he was not an ordained rabbi. In later years, Kahane accused the Jewish Agency of not having allowed Drucker to take part in the work of the Koordynacja. Much of his anger was aimed at Yitzhak Gruenbaum, a member of the Jewish Agency Executive, who had headed the Rescue Committee of the Yishuv and helped finance the recovery of the children. Kahane wrote in his memoirs, "We offered cooperation, but apart from vague promises we received nothing from them. I believe that the leaders of the Koordynacja, and above all Yitzhak Gruenbaum, who was then in Poland, would not tolerate a religious children's home within its framework."[43]

But this is not accurate. Yitzhak Gruenbaum had nothing to do with the creation of the Koordynacja and was not involved in its activity until the summer of 1947. The Koordynacja was placed under his authority, in his capacity as head of the Jewish Agency's Rescue Committee, only after his second visit to Poland, in September 1947. In fact, he tried to bring Hamizrahi into the body, with a promise of full educational autonomy for the children's

---

40 Testimony of Leibel Koriski. OHD, (68)15b.
41 Aryeh Sarid (Leibel Goldberg), "Emissaries' Letters," in *Mapai Central Committee Bulletin* (Hebrew), 182 (April 7, 1946), Haganah Archives, 44.8-19.
42 Neshamit, "Coordinating Child Rescue," p. 120.
43 Kahane, *After the Flood*, p. 54.

home of the Committee of Religious Communities in Zabrze, where the children rescued by Drucker were housed.[44] According to Drucker's testimony, he did not meet Aryeh Sarid when he was in Poland. He maintains that the Mizrahi movement was not represented on the Koordynacja following the rejection of its request to give the recovered children a religious education.[45] This is apparently the real reason that the religious groups did not join the Koordynacja and chose to work alone.

To set up its new educational system, which lacked a logistical infrastructure, the Koordynacja needed funding from the start. The Christian families had to be paid for having looked after the children during the war, and special hostels had to be established for the younger children, many of whom were neglected and sick and required medical care and special food, and all of whom were in dire need of clothing and footwear. Poland, itself devastated and hungry, could not supply the large-scale financing that the project required. The natural place to turn to was the Jewry of the free world, and particularly the JDC, which supported all the Jewish institutions in Poland irrespective of their political affiliation. The founders of the Koordynacja had hoped to find an attentive ear in David Guzik, the JDC's veteran local director, who administered its activity in Poland during the war and immediately afterward, and cooperated with Yitzhak Zuckerman and the pioneer movement. However, in March 1946, when the Koordynacja was established, Guzik was killed in a plane crash. His successor, William Bein, an American, was not inclined to cooperate with the fledgling Koordynacja and was in no hurry to respond to its requests. To bypass him, the Koordynacja leaders tried to exert pressure on his superiors in Paris through the WJC. Concretely, they asked the JDC for a budget of $140,000 for the first three months in order to rescue children and set up homes for them. "It is a matter of our national honor and the honor of the martyrs who perished that these children should find their place in children's homes, in which they will be educated in the spirit of loyalty to the Jewish people's loyalty and devotion to the Land of Israel," they wrote in a memorandum to the WJC.[46] With a view to the multiple needs of the entire survivor population in Poland, they requested a large sum. The result was that the JDC's director in Europe, Joseph Schwartz, agreed to underwrite the

44 Minutes of meetings on continued activity of the Koordynacja, Łódź, September 27,1947 — October 2, 1947, CZA, S26/1424.
45 Testimony of Yeshayahu Drucker, OHD, (68)28a.
46 Koordynacja Committee to World Jewish Congress (undated, though its content would indicate that it was written in April-May 1946), CZA, S26/317.

upkeep of the children's homes of both the Koordynacja and the Central Jew-ish Committee, but declined to allocate funds to ransom children.[47]

Care for the children was a major item of the JDC budget in postwar Poland. From 1945–1948, the organization earmarked between eighteen and twenty-three percent of its total budget for Poland for the maintenance of the children's homes and assistance to families that adopted children.[48] The JDC was aware of the problem of the children who remained in non-Jewish cus-tody. A unit established by the JDC to search for missing relatives in Poland contained a special section for the location of such children. At the beginning of 1947, the JDC provided direct assistance to remove some sixty children from non-Jewish custody.[49] Internal JDC correspondence expresses high re-gard for the activity of the Koordynacja and its crucial role. Having undertak-en to finance the upkeep of the children's homes, the JDC displayed great gen-erosity. Suffice it to note that from March 1946 to August 1947, it transferred about 35.5 million zlotys to the Koordynacja for the upkeep of more than 1,000 children in its institutions and for their removal from Poland.[50] How-ever, the JDC did not take part directly in the Koordynacja efforts to recover Jewish children. The Koordynacja records cite only minuscule amounts that were received from the JDC for this purpose.[51] Such as there were, they were exceptional cases, in which parents and relatives from the United States and South Africa provided the children's names and locations and requested the JDC to remove them on their behalf from the hands of their Christian rescu-ers. In these cases the JDC worked through an agent who paid the necessary ransom and ensured that the children were transferred to their parents.[52]

The JDC's reluctance to become directly involved in recovering children was probably due to the methods adopted by the Koordynacja, which often slid into a gray legal area. The JDC, a Jewish American organization with an international reputation, enjoyed special status in postwar Poland. The com-munist government in Warsaw viewed it positively, not only because it was a significant economic factor that injected much-needed foreign currency into the country's empty coffers, but also because such an approach could obtain legitimacy for the Polish government in the eyes of the west. The JDC tradi-tionally stayed within the bounds of the law in the sovereign states in which

47 Sarid, in *Mission to the Diaspora*, p. 92.
48 AJDC Poland, Annual Reports 1946–1947, GJA/125B/126A.(Jerusalem).
49 Report of AJDC Poland, first quarter 1947, GJA/12B/C-61.034.
50 Financial Report of the Koordynacja (Poland), March 1946–August 1947, CZA, S26/1424.
51 Ibid.
52 Testimony of Leibel Koriski. OHD, (68)15b.

it was permitted to operate. Nevertheless, after the war it frequently departed from this policy, for example by providing generous financing for the Bricha and Ha'apala clandestine immigration organizations.[53] However, on the ultra-sensitive issue of removing Jewish children from Christian custody in a Catholic country in which the majority opposed the communist government and perceived the Jews as its principal agents, the JDC adopted a highly cautious approach, making do with financing the children's upkeep and their removal from the country — nevertheless, in itself a substantial amount.

In the absence of any other institution capable of paying for the ransom of the children, the task of raising the needed funds fell to the Koordynacja itself. Arye Sarid threw himself into the mission with characteristic fervor, firing off letters to the Jewish Agency and the Actions Committee of the Histadrut (General Federation of Labor in the Yishuv,) in which he urged them to establish a fund to redeem the children. "Love of Israel is splendid," he wrote, "but there is no one to carry out the deed of redeeming survivors… Lose no time in establishing the great project of redemption and implement the ransom of the little prisoners before it is too late!"[54]

In March 1946, Lova Levite, a Kibbutz Hameuchad emissary, arrived in Poland with $14,000, which Eliahu Dobkin had sent on behalf of the Jewish Agency.[55] Sarid also stayed in touch with the Americans Louis Segal and Shmuel Margoshes, who had donated the initial ransom funds, and through them he obtained $20,000 from the aid fund of the Natzional Arbeiter Farband. He also raised money from other bodies in the United States, such as the Hadassah Women's Organization, the American Federation for Polish Jews led by Joseph Tenenbaum, and from affluent Jews in Poland itself.[56] In 1946 Sarid raised more than $40,000 to ransom children.[57] Although this was not much in terms of free world currency, on the prevailing Polish black market it converted into twenty million zlotys, a substantial sum in a period when the average per capita monthly subsistence budget was 3,000–4,000 zlotys.[58]

---

53  Yehuda Bauer, "Joint," in *Encyclopedia of the Holocaust*, vol. II, p. 250, (Hebrew edition).

54  Sarid, "Emissaries' Letters" *Mapai Bulletin* (April 4, 1946), Haganah Archives, 44.8-19.

55  Sarid, in *Mission to the Diaspora*, p. 92. Sarid cites an amount of $15,000, whereas the Koordynacja financial report states that only $14,000 was received from the Jewish Agency from March 1946 to August 1947; see note 50, above.

56  Testimony of Leibel Koriski.OHD, (68)15a.

57  Financial Report of the Koordynacja (Poland), March 1946–August 1947.

58  Moshe Yishay (Stockholm) to Aliyah Department (Jerusalem), January 25, 1946, CZA S26/1248.

ח ש ב ו ן    ה כ נ ס ה

קו|או|3׳.

פון אנמאנג פון אונדזער טעטיקים,פון 3.1946 ביז 8.1947    S26/1474

| ראשט | פון וועמען | | סטנג'ים | | חובים |
|---|---|---|---|---|---|
| 1 | 2 | | תכנסה 3 | תוצאה 4 | תכנסת (אי1 סויוגטער) 5 |
| צאר 1986 | | | | | |
| 4.1946 | ח׳ סיגאל – דורך אריח .1 | 8.000 | | | |
| 9.1946 | „        „        „ | 10.000 | 18.000 | | |
| 4.-8.1946 | ח׳ י .ו , אגגל | | 2.000 | | |
| 4.1946 | ח׳ א י . מענענבוים | | 14.000 | | |
| | ר7נשאינט | | 2.000 | | |
| 6. " | ח׳ בלקמא–אי ה׳ פאר דאס מידעלע קאנדעל. | | 500 | | |
| 12. " | אלטח–מרוי׳ עשטטי,קאנגרעם | | 450 | | |
| | מתנות פאר קאנדער אין בריח | | 3.750 | | |
| | | | 34 | | |
| 8.-8.1946 | פינאנסירונג : םט׳ פון | | | 23.300 | 8.940.2 |
| 6.-81. " | דישאינט–או׳סתאלמבונולן | | | | 6.550.0 |
| | קינדער–היי ער . | | | | 3.300.0 |
| | אויף גאולח–ילדים „ | | | | |
| 1947 | | | | | |
| 1.-8.1947 | אריח ._ 1.פאר קאארדינאצ ,באהארי –עם׳ פון | | | 14.335 | 10.498.0 |
| 2. " | רושאינט–או׳סתאלמבונו | | | 950 | |
| 11.-8. " | קינדער–הי ער . | | | | 5.150.0 |
| | אויף גאולח–ילדים „ | | | | 1.000.0 |
| | צוזאמען | 40.703 | 38.585 | | 35.438.2 |
| | סאלדא םט׳או׳םם.9.1947. | | 2.118 | | |
| | | 40.703 | 40.703 | | |

חשבונות

(אין מיליאנער זלאטעס)   פון 3.1946 ביז 8.1947   S26/144

| 10 | 9 | 8 | 7 | 6 | 5 | 4 | 3 | 2 | 1 |
|---|---|---|---|---|---|---|---|---|---|
| צוזאמען הוצאות | אין ה"ן קברים עליה | מעשר־ סערטעם | א"נ־ שטענאל בורסט | יין אפ | צוזאמען אנדערע | אנדערע חזצאות | אמ?פאו אמ?טר | פינ?דר צו־צל | ראמ? חוני |
| | | | | | | | | | 1946 |
| 2,355,9 | - | 173,0 | 576,0 | 787,5 | 819,4 | 182,9 | 636,8 | 46 | 3.-4. |
| 2,165,5 | - | 186,0 | 532,0 | 832,5 | 605,0 | 184,5 | 420,5 | 26 | 5. |
| 2,536,4 | 706,6 | 180,0 | 299,2 | 803,0 | 547,6 | 186,1 | 361,5 | 44 | 6. |
| 1,413,0 | - | 162,0 | 182,0 | 780,0 | 289,0 | 107,0 | 182,0 | 46 | 7. |
| 2,182,6 | 723,6 | 181,0 | - | 683,5 | 594,5 | 123,0 | 471,5 | 18 | 8. |
| 2,397,2 | - | 183,0 | 113,5 | 849,8 | 1,250,9 | 221,4 | 1,029,5 | 22 | 9. |
| 1,738,4 | - | 192,5 | 89,0 | 878,8 | 578,1 | 108,6 | 469,5 | 14 | 10. |
| 1,563,6 | - | 190,4 | - | 717,0 | 646,2 | 211,2 | 435,0 | 9 | 11. |
| 1,937,8 | 283,0 | 143,0 | - | 896,0 | 615,8 | 130,8 | 485,0 | 14 | 12. |
| | | | | | | | | | 1947 |
| 2,657,1 | - | 158,0 | 18,0 | 574,0 | 1,907,1 | 283,6 | 1,623,5 | 17 | 1. |
| 2,313,0 | 189,0 | 121,0 | - | 449,0 | 1,554,0 | 189,0 | 1,365,0 | 14 | 2. |
| 2,283,8 | - | 183,0 | - | 641,0 | 1,459,8 | 274,8 | 1,185,0 | 9 | 3. |
| 2,293,9 | - | 175,0 | - | 529,0 | 1,589,9 | 194,9 | 1,395,0 | 10 | 4. |
| 2,335,3 | - | 165,0 | - | 674,0 | 1,496,3 | 286,3 | 1,210,0 | 10 | 5. |
| 2,097,6 | - | 164,7 | - | 622,0 | 1,310,9 | 325,9 | 985,0 | 4 | 6. |
| 1,484,1 | - | 172,0 | - | 517,0 | 795,1 | 185,1 | 610,0 | 3 | 7. |
| 1,703,0 | - | 163,0 | - | 636,0 | 905,0 | 250,0 | 655,0 | 8 | 8. |
| | | | | | | | | | צו־ |
| 35,438,2 | 1,902,2 | 2,892,6 | 1,809,7 | 11,669,1 | 16,964,6 | 3,445,1 | 13,519,5 | 509 | זאמען |

אויפקלערונגען צו די באזונדערטע רובריקן לויט די לויפנדע נומערן:

1. די סומע געלט, וועלכע אין באצאלט געווארן די קריסטלעכע אפיסטורופסים פארן אויס-האלטן די ידישע קינדער אין דער צײם פון אקופאצ?יע.
4. הוצאות בײם ארומפארן אין 'אלע עקן פון לאנד בדי אויסמזומזוכן און אויסצוסליין די ידישע קינדער פון קריסטן. דיעטעם בײם פארן און ברענגען די קינדער. שכירות פאר די פארנדע.
6. אויסמאהלטונג פון די קינדער־הייזער אין באשעדיונג;באקלידונג;בילדונג;סערדיצין, שכירות דעם דערציערישן און מעכנישן פארסאנאל, פארמאנסן, דיזה־געלט, באהיצונג, א"א (אין 1946 האבן מיר נאהאם 4 קינדער־הייזער א"ו לדרוש און 2 אין נידערשלעזיען, פון 1947 האבן מיר 2 קינדער־הייזער א"ז לדרוש. צוזאמען דינען זיך אין דובכשניטלעכן אונדזרטרע חיזער ב" 300 1. אויסנעלייטן און פון דער רעאאבראציע פון ר"פ.)
7. אינגעקויפטער אינוענטאר פארן מעבעל, באסנקהאנם, קיך־הערשסאאמא.
8. אויסגאבן פון דער צענטראלע, פון צענטראלן מאלאוין און אנדערע אדמינ?סטראס?וע פאר די קינדער, שכירות פארן פערסאנאל פון צענטראלע און משערי.
9. הוצאות פון עליה פאר די קינדער. אויסגאבן אויפן וועג פון בילן קין באוואריען אדער פראנקרייד. פון דער "ברי" האבן מיר קיינע געלטסער אויף דעם צוועק נים באקומען.

The first children were ransomed as soon as the initial funds became available and even before an appropriate infrastructure for their absorption had been established. The initial successes exceeded all expectations. Within less than two months after the creation of the Koordynacja, about seventy children were restored to the Jewish fold.[59] The first two children's homes were established in Łódź, one for children aged seven to thirteen, the other for toddlers and kindergarten children of six and under. These two hostels were earmarked mainly for children who had survived in Poland. Two other large children's homes were established in Pietrolesie and in Biały-Kamień, in Lower Silesia. Most of the children in them had arrived from the Soviet Union in the repatriation wave, while the others were survivors from Poland.[60]

The increasing numbers of children that arrived in Koordynacja hostels posed challenges for which the organization's leaders were ill-prepared, both organizationally and in terms of personnel. To help cope, the Koordynacja sought aid from the regional bodies of the Zionist parties throughout Poland in locating the children and establishing relief institutions.[61] They hoped to be able to recruit educational staff from among the youth movements. However, the parties were preoccupied with their own affairs and the orphans were not their first priority, while the youth movements, which were themselves suffering from a shortage of qualified *madrichim* (youth leaders) and were busy absorbing thousands of repatriated youngsters from the Soviet Union, were little inclined to supply personnel to the Koordynacja.[62] The exception was Hashomer Hatza'ir, which sent Chasia Bielicka, a veteran prewar movement activist, who had established the first children's homes in Łódź for older children. Her successor, after she left for Palestine with the first group of children, was Mordechai Binchuk (Bahat), an educator and veteran movement member who had also returned from the Soviet Union.[63] The other directors and many of the educational staff were recruited from non-movement sources. Appointed director of the second children's home in Łódź, which served the younger, most at-risk children, was Hela Leneman, who devoted herself to them and held the position for a long period. The director of the

---

59 Koordynacja Committee to Zionist District Committees (Poland), April 12, 1946, Haganah Archives, 24.58.

60 Koriski, "The Zionist Koordynacja," p. 260.

61 Koordynacja Committee to Zionist District Committees (Poland), April 12, 1946, Haganah Archives, 24.58.

62 Neshamit, "Coordinating Child Rescue," p. 121.

63 Testimony of Chasia Bornstein-Bielicka; OHD, (68)26 testimony of Mordechai Bahat, OHD (68)20.

Pietrolesie and Biały-Kamień facilities were Ashkenazi and Abraham Halperin, respectively.[64] They were assisted by veteran teachers who had returned from the Soviet Union, among them Abraham Czarny, Masha Kaplinska, Dvora Haberberg, and younger teachers who were graduates of the Tarbut school network.[65] The two children's homes in Łódź operated until the summer of 1949, when the Koordynacja terminated its operations, while the two facilities in Silesia existed very briefly, until the end of the large-scale repatriation waves and the mass exodus from Poland at the end of 1946.

The educational needs of the young children under the care of the Koordynacja differed from those of the older children in the youth movements' kibbutzim. Many of them were physically neglected, sick, and traumatized, and needed the care of educators with an understanding of child psychology and of devoted caregivers, of whom there were few among the survivors in Poland. Moreover, even when such individuals were found, the instability and constant movement of the Jews in Poland at the time made it impossible to extract from them a solid commitment to the children. The gravity of the situation is illustrated by the fact that a full year after the establishment of the children's homes, no experienced professional kindergarten teacher had yet been engaged for the Łódź facility.[66]

Having encountered the problem of a shortage of teachers from the outset, the Koordynacja leaders tried to deal with the issue themselves. Concurrent with the establishment of the first children's homes, Sara Neshamit recruited about twenty youth movement members for a seminar designed to train them to work with the children. In practice, this was an emergency course of about three weeks, from the end of March until April 18, 1946, to prepare the first educational team that would work with the youngest children.[67] The group heard lectures in early-childhood psychology, preventive medicine, and kindergarten teaching methods, and was taught children's songs in Hebrew. There were also enrichment talks on Jewish history and the land-settlement movement in Eretz Israel, subjects with which some in the group were unfamiliar.[68]

64  Koriski, "The Zionist Koordynacja," p. 260.
65  Aryeh Levy Sarid, *Ruin and Deliverance,* vol. II (Hebrew) (Tel Aviv: Moreshet, 1997), p. 410.
66  Baruch Kaplinsky, report from Koordynacja Children's Home, April 1, 1947, CZA, S75/1760.
67  Koordynacja Committee, invitation to reception marking conclusion of seminar course, April 17, 1946, Haganah Archives, 24.58.
68  *Farn Yiddishn Kind,* November 1946, CZA, 5612 ; Neshamit, "Coordinating Child Rescue," pp. 121–122.

## The Activities of Yeshayahu Drucker

As we have seen, the religious Jewish groups had begun to ransom children even before the establishment of the Koordynacja. The initiator of this activity, Rabbi David Kahane, the Chief Jewish Chaplain of the Polish Army, was also appointed by the Polish government at the end of the war to head the Committee of Religious Communities. One of the missions this body undertook as part of its effort to renew religious life among the survivors in Poland was to recover children who remained under the care of non-Jews. Rabbi Kahane assigned the task to Yeshayahu Drucker.[69]

Drucker was born in 1914 in the town of Jordanów, near Kraków, grew up in a religious-Zionist home and was a member of the Mizrahi movement. After attending Hebrew school he trained himself to teach subjects related to Judaism. A refugee during the war in the Soviet Union, he joined the Polish People's Army, which was under Soviet command. In his unit he stood out for his activity to keep the Jewish embers burning among his coreligionists, organizing prayers on holy days and conducting a Passover *seder*. After the war, Rabbi Kahane, who had heard about Drucker's army activity, appointed him a field chaplain with the rank of captain, even though he was not an ordained rabbi. In fact, Drucker was about to be discharged from the army and had no special wish to handle rabbinical affairs. However, when Kahane placed him in charge of the task of recovering children he decided to stay in the army.[70] Drucker was acquainted with the plight of the Holocaust survivors in Poland, but knew nothing about the problem of the children who remained in non-Jewish hands until he started to deal with the issue.

In their distress, the survivors turned to every Jewish institution for help, including the Committee of Religious Communities, which was not affiliated with the Central Jewish Committee. The Jewish chaplaincy, under Rabbi Kahane, had a natural affinity with the Committee of Religious Communities, and as its members, uniformed and bearing officers' ranks, seemed to represent state authority, Jews solicited their help. One day a Jew arrived at the headquarters of the Jewish Chaplaincy in Warsaw and asked Drucker to help him obtain custody of a relative, a boy who was living with a Polish family. Not knowing what procedure to follow in such cases, Drucker accompanied the man, and after a few visits with the rescuers was able to persuade them to relinquish the child to his care. No special problems arose in this instance,

69  Kahane, *After the Flood*, pp. 47–52.
70  Testimony of Yeshayahu Drucker, YVA, O.3/3249.

because the relative wanted the boy and also reimbursed the guardian family for looking after him.[71]

Initially, Drucker only assisted relatives who had encountered problems in trying to regain children from their non-Jewish rescuers. However, when reports began to arrive about children living in Christian families in villages and provincial towns whom no one was evidently looking for, he made it his mission to recover them. Drucker thus became the redeemer of children on behalf of religious Jewry. The Committee of Religious Communities did not want these children, who had grown up in a Christian atmosphere, to be placed in the children's homes of the Central Jewish Committee, where they would receive a secular education. Accordingly, in the summer of 1945, the Committee of Religious Communities established two homes where the children would be given a traditional religious education — one in Zabrze, near Katowice in Upper Silesia, and the other in Gęszcze Puste, in Lower Silesia. The latter was intended mainly for children repatriated from the Soviet Union and was in operation for only a year and a half. The facility in Zabrze became the home for the children whom Drucker ransomed and operated for three years, until 1949, becoming the symbol of religious Jewry's "children's ransom" project in Poland.[72]

In contrast to the Koordynacja, which was an inter-movement Zionist organization and operated through a professional administrative apparatus under an executive body, Drucker operated alone, aided only by the Jewish Army Chaplaincy and the Committee of Religious Communities. He was not only an emissary of his movement but represented the whole religious establishment, both Zionist and non-Zionist. Effectively, Drucker was an unofficial one-man mission who represented three different religious bodies — the Jewish Chaplaincy, the Committee of Religious Communities, and Mizrahi — which engaged in overlapping activity.[73] Organizationally, too, it was Drucker's personal project. Like the Koordynacja, Drucker's activity was also funded from diverse sources abroad — not directly, but through the Committee of Religious Communities.

The Mizrahi movement had not joined the Koordynacja upon its creation, so until the end of 1947, Drucker could not draw on funds from the Rescue Committee which the Jewish Agency sent for the recovery of children. This does not mean that the Rescue Committee ignored Drucker's separate

---

71  Ibid.
72  Kahane, *After the Flood*, p. 51.
73  Testimony of Yeshayahu Drucker, YVA, O.3/3249.

project and did not transfer money to him.[74] In the summer of 1946, when
Rabbi Herzog embarked on his European mission to recover children, the
Rescue Committee placed at his disposal 10,000 Palestine pounds ($40,000).
Of this, Herzog left more than 4,000 pounds in Poland, half for the Koordynacja and half "for the ransom of 300 children and their upkeep in special
children's homes" — that is, for the religious sector.[75] It is not clear from the
surviving reports whether all the money Rabbi Herzog earmarked for the
ransom project was intended for Drucker's project, but Drucker was the recipient of $5,000 of the amount that Herzog left in Poland.[76] As with the Koor-
dynacja, Drucker's project also suffered from a cash shortfall, particularly
when large amounts were needed immediately. However, it was not money
that was an obstacle to Drucker's activity. In his testimony he repeatedly emphasized, "I cannot complain that I was short of money, or that we did not
remove children because of a lack of money."[77]

Until the beginning of 1947, the Koordynacja financed the recovery of
children from the funds that Sarid raised through his party connections with
Louis Segal in the United States and with Eliahu Dobkin in Palestine. After
Sarid left Poland and began to work in Germany, the Koordynacja funds
dwindled until no money was left for the ransom project. On April 2, 1947,
the Koordynacja made a direct appeal to the Jewish Agency in Jerusalem,
reporting on its achievements in reclaiming children and on the disposal of
the funds it had received from the organization, and requesting continued
financial support.[78] Concurrently, Drucker's financial resources also ran out.
He asked for help from the executive of the Mizrahi movement in Palestine,
which forwarded the request to Yitzhak Gruenbaum, the head of the Rescue
Committee. In his letter, Drucker described the situation in which he found
himself:

> The work grows more and more difficult each day. Many children remain
> in Christian hands and in convents, and I am constantly receiving new
> addresses. I am working on my own... The money for this purpose has
> almost run out, and I do not see that anyone in our wide world takes an
> interest in this problem. Apparently the Jews in the world have accepted

74 Testimony of Yeshayahu Drucker, OHD. (68)28a.
75 Office of Chief Rabbi of Palestine to Rescue Committee, April 20, 1947, CZA, S26/1266.
76 Drucker, Report on Activities to Redeem Children by Committee of Communities,
Poland, September 12, 1947, CZA, S26/1424.
77 Testimony of Yeshayahu Drucker, OHD. (68)28a.
78 Koordynacja Committee to Jewish Agency, April 2, 1947, CZA, S75/1760.

the fact that many Jewish children will remain with Christians, and here in Poland there is hardly a village without a Jewish boy or girl living with Christians. Redemption becomes more difficult with each passing day. True, relatively speaking, the cost of a child is about fifty thousand gulden (zlotys), which is a small amount here, but unfortunately I no longer have any money and I do not know how to manage the work — if no aid is forthcoming, we will be forced to terminate the project.[79]

The natural recipient of requests for financial aid to reclaim the children was the Jewish Agency's Rescue Committee in Jerusalem. Its director, Yitzhak Gruenbaum, a prominent leader of Polish Jewry before the war, took a special interest in the remnants of the community. Yet, the requests for aid that piled up on his desk beginning in April 1947 show that for a full year — from the time the Koordynacja and Yeshayahu Drucker started to recover children — not only was Gruenbaum unaware of their activities, but he did not know about the existence of the Koordynacja, even though the effort to recover the children who were in Christian hands was close to his heart. Gruenbaum's first visit to Poland after the war took place from February 24 to March 6, 1947. He met with representatives of the survivors, but for unknown reasons no one from the Koordynacja met him. However, he did meet with Mendel Kossower and his sister, Emilia, who were central activists in the Ihud movement of the General Zionists, Gruenbaum's party. The subject of recovering the children came up in conversation, and he left a sum of money with them for that purpose. What is puzzling is that the Ihud leaders on the Koordynacja directorate did not bother to report to Gruenbaum about the organization's work and did not transfer to the directorate the money he left with them for recovering children.[80]

Following appeals for help from groups trying to recover children, the Rescue Committee in Jerusalem became involved, allocating 5,000 Palestine pounds ($20,000) in May 1947 to reclaim children throughout Europe. Concurrently, Chaim Barlas, a member of the Rescue Committee and a close aide to Gruenbaum, was assigned to find out what was being done with regard to the issue of the children in Poland and in western Europe.[81] Barlas did not visit Poland but after visiting several countries in western Europe and speak-

---

79  World Mizrahi Center to Y. Gruenbaum, May 21, 1947, CZA, S26/1317.
80  Y. Gruenbaum to Koordynacja, July 21, 1947, CZA, S26/1601; Koordynacja Committee to Y. Gruenbaum, August 14, 1947, CZA, S26/1424.
81  Concerning the Rescue Committee, May 4, 1947, CZA, S26/1410.

ing to the relevant officials, he forwarded his impressions and conclusions to Gruenbaum:

> ... I set about clarifying the issue of recovering the children in the spirit of our conversation. Regrettably, I found considerable confusion in this matter. All the institutions have a part in this, and there is no method or review of the activity... I reached the conclusion that only an institution that deals optimally and naturally with children's affairs can coordinate this operation. I refer to Youth Aliyah. But clearly there has to be a special supervisory committee for Youth Aliyah, on which will be represented all the institutions that can be taken into consideration regarding the recovery of the children. Otherwise there is no possibility of review... My request from you is: (a) to approve my approach regarding the recovery of the children by Youth Aliyah in order to centralize this activity; (b) to place at my disposal 10,000 Palestine pounds in order to launch the activity in the [various] countries.[82]

Barlas was perspicacious in his analysis that too many groups were involved in the sensitive matter of recovering children. However, the solution he proposed — transferring responsibility to Youth Aliyah — was impractical in the light of the many educational tasks already undertaken by that organization, with which it was already finding it difficult to cope due to a shortage of personnel and funds. Moreover, only local residents could regain the children, not advice and actions suggested by the Yishuv leaders in Palestine. Given the prevailing political atmosphere, particularly the competition among the youth movements for the hearts and minds of the young generation, the only recourse was to improve coordination between the bodies engaged in the mission by means of a joint supervised budget which would prevent competition in the "children's market," which only drove up the price. This was the path Gruenbaum chose after studying the subject.[83]

On September 22, 1947, Gruenbaum arrived in Poland for a second visit, this one lasting three weeks. Among other actions, he combined the Koordynacja with Drucker's project and subordinated both to the Rescue Committee in Jerusalem. On September 27, Gruenbaum told a preliminary meeting with the Koordynacja directorate that from his point of view, the Koordynacja was now operating on behalf of the Rescue Committee and henceforth should engage only in the actual redemption of children and place its children's homes

---

82  Barlas to Gruenbaum, June 5, 1947, CZA, S26/1317.
83  Gruenbaum to Koordynacja, July 21, 1947, CZA, S26/1601.

under the aegis of Youth Aliyah. He also insisted that the project of recovering children must be united with the efforts of the Mizrahi movement — that is, with Drucker — and demanded that the money which had been given to Emilia Kossower, the Ihud official, be returned to the Koordynacja. As for the continued efforts to recover children, Gruenbaum promised that the Rescue Committee would make available to the Koordynacja a monthly budget of 3,000 Palestine pounds ($12,000) and that the Koordynacja would no longer have to engage in fundraising. It was decided to meet with representatives of Hamizrahi at the earliest opportunity to discuss how to unite the activity of redeeming the children.[84]

A few days later, as Gruenbaum had suggested, the Koordynacja directorate met with three representatives of Hamizrahi: Yehuda Bialer, Yeshayahu Drucker, and Yisrael Goniadzki. The Mizrahi officials raised the question of education and declared that their condition for unifying the projects was to leave the management of the children's homes as it was. The Koordynacja accepted this condition, and it was decided that cooperation between the bodies would take the following form: Two permanent representatives from Hamizrahi, Drucker and a second person, would join the directorate of the Koordynacja; the children to be recovered by Drucker would be placed in the Mizrahi children's home in Zabrze; the Koordynacja would only coordinate the operation to redeem the children, in order to eliminate competition; and requests for financial aid would be submitted jointly by the two bodies to the Rescue Committee.[85]

In practice, the situation remained unchanged, apart from the official decision to cooperate in recovering the children in order to avert competition. Gruenbaum, who did not take part in this meeting, accepted the new arrangement and added his signature to it on behalf of the Jewish Agency. On October 29, 1947, the presidium of the Rescue Committee in Jerusalem endorsed the agreement and decided, in accordance with Gruenbaum's promise, to allocate 9,000 Palestine pounds ($36,000) to the Koordynacja for the last three months of 1947. The directorate of the Koordynacja was also requested to co-opt a representative of the ultra-Orthodox Agudat Israel movement and reach an agreement similar to the one signed with Hamizrahi.[86]

---

84  Minutes of meeting of Koordynacja directorate with Y. Gruenbaum, September 27, 1947, CZA, S26/1424.
85  Minutes of Koordyncja directorate meeting with Mizrahi representatives, October 2, 1947, ibid.
86  Gruenbaum to Koordynacja, November 3, 1947, ibid.

Toward the end of 1947, the recovery of the children in Europe in general and in Poland in particular became the Rescue Committee's leading priority. Of the approximately 21,000 Palestine pounds which the Rescue Committee had at its disposal in October 1947, 12,000 pounds were allocated for the rest of the year to recover children — 9,000 pounds to the Koordynacja in Poland, as promised, and 3,000 pounds for the rest of Europe. In the same period the Rescue Committee allocated only 4,000 pounds to the refugees interned by the British authorities in Cyprus and those who had sailed on the immigrant ship "Exodus" and had been turned back to Europe. Thus, in the last quarter of 1947, seventy-five percent of the Rescue Committee's funds were earmarked for the recovery of children.[87]

In December 1947, with the eruption of the Israeli War of Independence, priorities changed and it became difficult to transfer money to Poland. Nevertheless, recovering the children remained a high priority. Of the Rescue Committee's budget of 40,000 Palestine pounds for January-May 1948, 3,000 pounds a month was allocated for the children's project — a total of 15,000 pounds, or thirty-seven percent of the budget. Of this amount, the Koordynacja received 2,000 pounds a month.[88] The subordination of the Koordynacja to the Rescue Committee in Jerusalem assured it regular funding, and thus resuscitated the children's project — but only temporarily. Despite the organization's experience and the many addresses in its possession, the number of children being recovered dwindled constantly to no more than an average of ten a month.[89] This was in marked contrast to the previous year, 1946, when the Koordynacja recovered about sixty percent of the children on its list.

In addition to the Koordynacja and Drucker, other groups and individuals of religious Jewry were also active in the effort to recover children, but on a much smaller scale. According to a report of the Kraków religious community for 1945–1946, the community undertook to search for and reclaim Jewish children from non-Jews and ransomed fourteen children for 140,000 zlotys during this period.[90] The report does not make it clear whether it was Drucker or members of the local community who recovered the children.

---

87  Rescue Committee to Financial Department of Jewish Agency November 3, 1947, CZA, S26/1410.

88  Shefer to Gruenbaum, March 2, 1948, ibid.; [Rescue Committee] to Jewish National Fund head office, March 10, 1948, ibid.

89  Koordynacja presidium to Rescue Committee, August 10, 1947, CZA, S26/1317; Koriski to Rescue Committee, December 8, 1947, CZA, S26/1424.

90  Report on religious congregation activity in Kraków, 1946–1948, YVA, P.20/33,

In addition to the JDC, one of the first individuals who came to the aid of the religious communities in liberated Poland was Rabbi Solomon Schonfeld — the head of the Religious Emergency Council established during the war by the Chief Rabbi of the British Empire, Rabbi Joseph Hertz. Rabbi Schonfeld arrived in Poland as early as November 1945, bringing food, clothing, medicines and a truck for the religious congregations. He returned to Poland twice more, in March and December of 1946, bringing more aid in the form of goods and money on behalf of the Rescue Committee of the Orthodox Rabbis of the United States. During his visit in March, Schonfeld was a guest of the children's home in Zabrze. He was favorably impressed by the treatment the children were evidently receiving, and assured Drucker that he could turn to him whenever he was in need of money. In the two visits he also took with him back to Britain some 250 children and youths using visas he had obtained from the British embassy in Warsaw. Among the first 100 children whom he brought to Britain, in March 1946, in order to place them with foster families, was a group of orphans from the Zabrze facility.[91]

The Zionist Koordynacja looked askance at the transfer of the children to Britain, just when it was waging a struggle to get them to Palestine.[92] Among the children Schonfeld brought to Britain were some from the Torah veAvodah and Mizrahi movements, whose leaders were also displeased at the move, out of concern for the children's Zionist future. Accordingly, they requested the Mizrahi movement in Britain to integrate the children into its ranks:

After much labor we were able to found a children's home for the children whom we recovered from the Christians... And now, because they are leaving us and going with Rabbi Schonfeld to Britain, we very much request that you accept the children to *Bachad* [Association of Religious Pioneers] and see to it that they receive the appropriate education from you, until they will be privileged to go up to the Land of Israel and gather under the banner of Hapoel Hamizrahi. We are attaching a list of 22 children who were educated by us, but a regiment of 104 children is leaving with Rabbi Schonfeld... We hope you will appreciate the enormity of the responsibility you bear and that our children will find a family environment and a sensitive heart among you. You should know that

91  Solomon Schonfeld, *Message to Jewry* (London: Jewish Secondary Schools Movement, (undated), pp. 138–139, 156–160; testimony of Yeshayahu Drucker, YVA, O.3/3249.
92  Testimony of Yeshayahu Drucker, OHD (68)28b.

we are entrusting you with our finest youngsters, whom we succeeded in rescuing from assimilation and from spiritual and moral perdition.[93]

On February 14, 1946, Zerach Warhaftig, a leading member of the Mizrahi movement in prewar Poland and later Israel's minister of religious affairs, arrived in Poland to join the WJC delegation led by Segal and Margoshes. Warhaftig devoted most of his five-week stay to the Mizrahi movement and the religious communities. Just as Segal and Margoshes had allocated $5,000 from the WJC budget for the Koordynacja, Warhaftig earmarked $1,500 from the same source for the Mizrahi children's homes. This, though, was just a preliminary payment. According to Warhaftig, during his mission to Poland he injected tens of thousands of dollars into the Mizrahi and Torah veAvodah movements as well as the Committee of Religious Communities. The source of the funds was the Mizrahi movement in the United States, the Rescue Committee of the Orthodox Rabbis, the American Federation for Polish Jews, and the WJC. Part of the money was earmarked for the recovery of children and for the upkeep of the Zabrze facility.[94]

Another religious group that tried to reclaim Jewish children was the Child Rescue Committee, established by the Rescue Committee of the Orthodox Rabbis in America and directed by Recha Sternbuch, who was based in Switzerland. Sternbuch worked through Sara Lederman, an ultra-orthodox repatriate to Poland from the Soviet Union who devoted herself to the children. From Sternbuch, Lederman received addresses of children, money, and passports with which to transfer the children she reclaimed to Czechoslovakia. In Bytom, Lower Silesia, Lederman established a children's home in which children could stay before leaving Poland. She did not start to recover children until the end of 1946, and did not manage to do much before she was arrested by the police and sentenced to a prison term for smuggling children out of Poland. According to her testimony, she collected a few dozen children before her arrest and was able to get twenty-five of them into Czechoslovakia. However, a close perusal of her testimony shows that only a few of the children were reclaimed from non-Jews; the majority were removed from the children's homes of the Central Jewish Committee.[95]

93  Central Committee of Mizrahi Poland to Mizrahi Britain, March 13, 1947, YVA, P.20/6.
94  Warhaftig, *Refugee and Survivor*, pp. 334–336.
95  Testimony of Sara Lederman, OHD, (68)50.

CHAPTER TEN

# Redeeming the Children

## Removal of Children from Christian Families

By the beginning of 1946, when the Koordynacja and Yeshayahu Drucker had began their projects to restore Jewish children to their heritage, most of the children who had been in non-Jewish hands were either back with their families or in the newly-established children's homes. Other rescuers continued to hold on to the children for a variety of reasons. Some of the Christian families had no idea where the child had come from or who his parents were, and when no one came to claim him did not turn him out but waited to see whether someone would eventually arrive. Moreover, not every resident of a small Polish provincial town or village who was looking after a Jewish child knew about the Jewish committees and the children's homes. In addition, it was very difficult to locate children who had moved together with their rescuers to different regions of the country when its borders were redrawn following the war.

There were families that had reached agreements with the child's parents about his future should they not survive. These were usually verbal agreements, made without witnesses under extreme pressure, and were impossible to verify. Often they would involve the promise of material and other remuneration to the rescuers in return for sheltering the child, including the right to adopt him and inherit his family's assets. In such cases, rescuers had no incentive to hand the child over to a Jewish institution.[1] In other cases, the rescuing family had been given addresses of the child's relatives abroad, in order to send him to them should the parents not survive. The rescuers in these cases preferred to negotiate directly with the foreign relatives, hoping to receive both a remuneration in foreign currency and the assets of the child's parents.[2]

---

1   Testimony of Avraham Gvirztman, OHD, (68)34.
2   Koriski, "The Zionist Koordynacja," pp. 256–257.

There were also lonely families and solitary women who endured harrowing ordeals with the child they were sheltering and developed deep bonds of parental love. They would have been prepared to return the child, but under the circumstances, with both parents presumed dead, they believed it was their natural right to adopt him. They were unwilling to hand the child over to anyone else, least of all to an orphanage. As for convents, the Jewish children in their care had been baptized and the nuns and priests no longer considered them Jewish, and accordingly had no intention of handing them over to Jewish hands.

Information about children still remaining in the custody of their rescuers reached the Koordynacja and Drucker from diverse sources. For example, the local Jewish committees knew the location of children because it was providing material aid to rescuers so they could continue to look after their orphaned wards. The communist and Bund representatives on the local committees and on the Central Jewish Committee refused to cooperate with the Koordynacja in ransoming children, but the Zionist representatives worked openly with the Koordynacja and provided the addresses of Poles who still had Jewish children in their custody. Thus Joseph Rotenberg, from the Poalei Zion Left party and a member of the Łódź Jewish Committee, regularly supplied such information to Pinhas Krivos, his party colleague on the Koordynacja directorate.[3] Similarly, Joseph Bodniew, from the Central Jewish Committee in Warsaw, referred every Pole who came to him with a Jewish child to the Koordynacja or to the Dror movement.[4] The testimony of Miriam Hochberg (Marianska), who headed the children's department of the Kraków Jewish Committee, describes the sort of information about children in non-Jewish custody that was given to the Koordynacja by local Jewish committees and the cooperation between them:

> I did not belong to any party, neither to the Zionists nor to the communists. In general, I was against collecting the children and sending them straight to DP camps in Germany while they were still sick and worn out… I was in favor of letting them stay in Poland for a time and recover their strength… At the same time, I already saw the antisemitism and the attitude of the Communist Party, and I knew that these children had no future in Poland. I wanted them to get to Eretz Israel. So when the Koordynacja asked me to sign a document to the effect that relatives

3   Testimony of Pinhas Krivos, OHD, (68)45.
4   Shner-Neshamit, *I Did Not Find Rest*, p. 191.

had come to take a child who was in the care of the Jewish committee, I signed wholeheartedly even if I knew they were not relatives. There were many instances of this kind... The committee did not have rescuers or a mechanism like the Koordynacja, who were able to monitor events and sent people to all kinds of places to remove children. Politically, this was not to the liking of the Jewish leaders who were on the Jewish committee at the time. However, there were also Zionists on the directorate of the Kraków committee, and if any of them came into possession of an address he certainly made it available to the Koordynacja.[5]

Drucker and the Koordynacja also received information from survivors who, while searching for their relatives, had happened by chance to discover the location or other details of children who remained in the custody of non-Jews. Similarly, Koordynacja personnel who were looking for a particular child whose location they knew sometimes came across information about the whereabouts of other children.[6] Relatives abroad who discovered the location of a member of their family living with a Christian family, but who were unable themselves to get to Poland, tried to reclaim the child through the services of the Koordynacja, which they had contacted through the Jewish Agency or the JDC.

Centralizing the information about the children's location was a prior condition for finding them, but the main difficulty lay in removing them from the families and convents. The problem was particularly acute in the remote towns and villages, which were accessible only by irregular public transport in journeys sometimes lasting days. Moreover, for a Jew to visit such places was a mortal risk, further heightened if he sought to remove a child from a family, which involved an infringement of privacy and a probe of financial and property affairs. The project required fieldworkers who could locate and identify the children and then conduct the negotiations for their return. An excellent command of Polish was essential, as well as familiarity with the local mentality and ways of life at different levels of society. Another prerequisite was an exterior appearance and demeanor capable of inspiring confidence and winning the child's trust, so he would be willing to part from the family of which he was now a member and leave with a stranger. The negotiations with the rescuers demanded sensitivity and affability, but also a certain aggressiveness and the ability to rebuff attempts at extortion.

5  Testimony of Miriam Hochberg (Marianska), Peleg, OHD, (68)24.
6  Koriski, "The Zionist Koordynacja," p. 254.

In different periods, the Koordynacja dispatched at least nine people in order to gain custody of children from their rescuers: Devora Fleischer-Zilber, Akiva Gershter, Moshe Yankovski, Yaakov Gissis, Yosef Birger, Grynszpan, Yehuda Bernstein, A. Shayniuk-Slucki, and Sonia Margalit-Kaminsky.[7] There were others, too, each with a distinct personal background and style of work. What they had in common was they were older and rich in life experience.

The most famous of the nine was Devora Fleischer, known as "Marysia." Even though she was already in her fifties, she was the first to be recruited for the mission. Her husband and only child were murdered in the Holocaust, and she survived on the Aryan side thanks to her Polish appearance. After the war, she wandered across Poland searching for survivors from her family. Arye Sarid met her by chance and was impressed by her appearance — she was tall and striking — and by her command of Polish. She willingly accepted his suggestion to work for the Koordynacja in rescuing children. Fleischer knew Polish society well and was familiar with the Christian way of life. She was usually assigned the more difficult cases in remote locations. Fleischer viewed the children's redemption as a challenge. She was not deterred by obstacles and dangers, traveling alone by train and in wagons. During six months of work, until her departure for Palestine in November 1946, she ransomed twenty-four children.[8]

Akiva Gershter and Moshe Yankovski were in the prime of life and also had an Aryan appearance. Yankovski had spent the war with Polish partisans and had himself adopted one of the orphan children. Grynszpan and Birger joined the project after their discharge from the Polish army as officers. They wore their uniform with officer's insignia when negotiating with rescuers, as did Drucker, in order to impress their interlocutors and create the impression that they were acting on behalf of the authorities. This usually facilitated the negotiations. Yaakov Gissis was a teacher who also had a military background.[9]

Because no two cases were alike, there was no standard approach in regard to the children. Structurally, though, two principal stages existed in each ransom project: locating and identifying the child, which was generally the easier part; and the negotiations, which tended to be complex and prolonged. After information was received about a child's whereabouts, a Koordynacja

7   Ibid., p. 256.
8   Testimony of Devora Fleischer-Zilber, OHD, (68)27.
9   Testimony of Leibel Koriski, OHD, (68)15b.

operative visited the family in order to identify the Jewish ward and learn what he could about the family, so that he could try and assess the conditions under which they would release the child. In their testimonies, the Poles did not distinguish between the different Jewish organizations, seeing all the emissaries as representatives of the "Jewish Committee." This played into the hands of the Koordynacja with its lack of official status: its emissaries did nothing to dispel the impression that they were official representatives of the Jewish Committee and were acting on behalf of the child's family.[10]

It was rare for a child to be handed over on a first visit; the terms had to be negotiated. In some cases the negotiations dragged on for weeks, even months, requiring repeated visits, tough bargaining over the amount of payment, and correspondence with the child's relatives abroad to obtain a power-of-attorney for his removal. Much depended on the rescuers' character, their motives for sheltering the child and their attitude toward him, and not least, their economic situation.

Some rescuers were individuals of noble spirit and conscience, and were concerned solely for the child's welfare. When it became clear to them that the child's family had perished and that he would be better off in a Jewish institution that was ready to take responsibility for him and treat him well, they released him willingly. Indeed, there were families who brought the child to the Koordynacja on their own and did not even expect to be reimbursed for their expenses. In such cases, the Koordynacja usually offered them a modest sum of a few thousand zlotys as a token of appreciation. The Koordynacja's task was facilitated greatly if the rescuing family had no desire to adopt the child and if no material interests had motivated the act of rescue. At the same time, it should be remembered that many of the rescuers were in dire financial straits in the aftermath of the war, so that when the Koordynacja offered them a handsome sum for having looked after the child they accepted it and returned the child without raising any problems. Some felt awkward about haggling over payment and took whatever they were offered without complaints or objections. In any event, the payment did not even begin to cover the cost of the food and clothing that the child had received, let alone the risk the family had undertaken. Such kindheartedness could not be calculated in monetary terms.[11]

In some cases, the child's relatives abroad created obstacles to his removal from the rescuing family, albeit unintentionally, by working through

---

10  Testimony of Leibel Koriski, OHD, (68)15a.
11  Ibid.; Shner-Neshamit, *I Did Not Find Rest*, p. 200.

two parallel channels. While utilizing the services of the Koordynacja, they also established a direct connection with the rescuers, sending them food packages and clothing to ensure continued contact with the child. Consequently, the rescuers had no incentive to part with the child, as this would terminate the material support from his family. Some families wanted to leave communist Poland, and declared that they would only send the child to his relatives abroad if they were allowed to go with him.[12] The activity of relatives often hampered the Koordynacja operatives in their negotiations, when rescuers asserted that they would hand over the child only to the relatives and in so doing, raised the ransom price, using the child to extort more money.

In 1942, Leopold Strauss placed his five-year-old daughter in the custody of a Polish family in a village near Zamość, and she survived the war. When her uncle in Palestine learned where she was, he contacted the Koordynacja, which began negotiations with the family. The head of the Polish family treated the girl like a gold-mine. He informed the uncle that the girl's father had given him a document designating him as the exclusive mediator with regard to his daughter.[13] He demanded that the Koordynacja pay him two million zlotys for rescuing the girl and looking after her.[14] This amount, equivalent to about $5,000, was a veritable fortune at the time in Poland. Following lengthy and wearying negotiations, the Koordynacja finally succeeded in ransoming the girl, probably paying less than the original price demanded. There were other cases where sums in excess of 1,000 dollars were paid.[15]

In regard to payment, every case was unique and both sides tried to get the better of the bargaining process. Koordynacja reports show that at the beginning of 1946 the rescuers accepted quite modest payments.[16] Afterwards, higher ransoms were demanded, the negotiations became longer and tougher, and the amounts paid soared. Suffice it to note that in April 1946, the Koordynacja, then at the outset of its activity, paid 636,500 zlotys to ransom forty-six children, or about 14,000 zlotys per child, the equivalent of less than $35 each at the prevailing black-market rate, whereas a year later, in April 1947, the organization paid 1,395,000 zlotys to redeem ten children, almost 140,000 zlotys per child, a tenfold increase.[17]

12  Koriski, "The Zionist Koordynacja," p. 257.
13  See correspondence between Daniel Strauss and Yitzhak Gruenbaum, July 29, 1947; Gruenbaum to Mendel Kosover, August 4, 1947, CZA, S26/1317.
14  Koordynacja Committee to Rescue Committee in Jerusalem, June 23, 1947, ibid.
15  Ibid.
16  Koordynacja Committee to Jewish Agency in Jerusalem, April 2, 1947, CZA, S75/1760.
17  Koordynacja Financial Report, March 1946–August 1947, CZA, S26/1426.

The Koordynacja made every effort, based on the ability of its emissaries, to locate and gain custody of every Jewish child who remained in non-Jewish hands. Failure was not due to money. In addition to the unclaimed orphans, Drucker and the Koordynacja ransomed children who had parents or other relatives. With regard to the participation of the children's families in covering the expenses, it is undeniable that in some cases public funds were exploited. There was more than one case of an uncle who knew that his nephew had survived and was living with a Christian family, but who nevertheless left Poland without claiming the child, even though he had the necessary means — and then asked the Koordynacja to intervene. Some affluent parents asked the Koordynacja to redeem their child but did not contribute their share of the costs. They then left the child in a Koordynacja home and went about their business, taking custody of the child only when he arrived in Palestine.[18]

Some wealthy families in Palestine and in the United States used their connections with the JDC and the Jewish Agency to pressure the Koordynacja to gain custody of their relatives from the rescuers, even though this entailed high ransom payments. In such cases, the Koordynacja asked for at least partial reimbursement, but rarely received it. In September 1946, the Koordynacja received a request from a Jerusalem physician to reclaim his niece from a Polish woman. The process took some six months and involved a payment of 300 Palestine pounds ($1,200). Afterward, it was explained to the uncle that there were still many orphans to be redeemed, and he was asked to make a donation to help offset the expenses that were incurred in ransoming his niece.[19] According to the organization's financial report, only one relative from Palestine reimbursed it, in the amount of $450, for ransoming a relative — and it was not the Jerusalem physician.[20]

Removing a child from a rescuers' home, irrespective of the economic circumstances, severing him abruptly and irrevocably from those who had care for him, inflicted the pain of uprooting on both the child and his benefactors. Emotions ran particularly high in the case of sensitive people who had raised the child devotedly amid the warmth of a loving family. Children who had become attached to their rescuers were like members of the family — in some cases the only family they knew. Some benefactors could

18  Testimonies: Leibel Koriski, OHD, (68)15b, Arye Sarid, OHD, (68)10.
19  B.Kaplinsky, report from Poland, October 25, 1947; CZA, S75/1760, Koordynacja Committee to Dr. K., Jerusalem, March 4, 1947, CZA, S26/1601.
20  Koordynacja Financial Report, March 1946–August 1947, CZA, S26/1424.

not bring themselves to hand the child over to strangers, not knowing what would become of him. But the child, too, suffered a wrenching experience on leaving his adoptive rescuers, his sole support and protection in the face of a hostile world. Every such parting was fraught with emotion on the part of all those involved.

The child would become deeply anxious when he suddenly realized that a stranger had entered his world and was taking an interest in him with the intention of removing him from his home and from those who were now his family. The anxiety was heightened when negotiations on his future began. In most cases, the negotiations were conducted between a Koordynacja operative and the rescuers, but the child was present and was a witness to the unfolding developments. At some point it would dawn on him that from being one of the family, he had become a bargaining card. This bewildering turn of events was deeply destabilizing for the child. The memoirs and testimonies of Koordynacja operatives and the former children show that the events, which often led to bitter tears, remained etched in their hearts as a traumatic experience. With the experience still vivid in her memory, Sara Neshamit described the negotiations she conducted in her Warsaw apartment for the return of Pola and Izio Miller, the first two children of the Koordynacja:

> On the sofa in our room, on the fifth floor of a busy Warsaw street, sit two children — a boy of 9 and his sister, who is 13. Next to them is a woman of middle age. She is their "aunt" — the Christian woman in whose home they found shelter during the war. She is pleased: she did a good deed and also received a sum of money that will partially cover the expenses she incurred in the children's upkeep. To pay for the actual act of rescuing the children — that no one can do! The children are worried. The boy's lips quiver with pent-up tears — "Am I a lamb that you are about to sell me?" The Christian woman conducted the financial negotiations in the presence of the children, and they understood that they were going to be turned over to strangers and that their "aunt" was receiving money for them. With their suspicious eyes they scan those present, trying to attach themselves to the "aunt." Their eyes are filled with tears and they are afraid of the new future that awaits them — What is your name? — Olek. — No, Madame, his name is Izio, the Polish woman says in correction — my name is Olek, I don't want Izio, please, I don't want Izio! The name Izio (Yitzhak) is frightening. It evokes memories of horrors, albeit quite vague: of a father lying in a pool of his blood, on the floor of their home, of a mother who left, though no one knows where, leaving them

to the grace of God. It recalls days of wandering without shelter, when they were required to forget mommy-daddy as well as their names. The children "forgot" and in the end found shelter. Why is it necessary to remind them all over again?[21]

It was less complicated to remove children up to the age of seven than older children. After everything was agreed upon and the financial arrangements concluded, a young child could be diverted by means of a toy, a sweet, or a new item of clothing, and the emissary could leave with him. However, older children were not so easily distracted. It was preferable to talk to them first in order to obtain their trust, explain where they were going, and assure them that life there would be good for them. This was a formidable task, requiring time and powers of persuasion — and with no guarantee of success. An attempt to counter the child's will was liable to foment resistance and generate a scene leading to a hostile reaction by the rescuers. A cautious approach toward both the child and his benefactors was crucial, but time did not always permit this.

Devora Fleischer's search for survivor children brought her to Lublin in order to remove an older girl from the home of a police officer. During the war, the girl had wandered in the forests and encountered Jews in hiding, but they would not let her join their group. She survived by working as a shepherd for local farmers. Afterward, she found her way to the home of the police officer and was hired as a nanny for the family's little boy. Her new employers treated her well, gave her clothes, and sent her to school. After the war, her aunt arrived to claim her, but the girl refused to go with her. When Fleischer tried to persuade her to enter a children's home, she lashed back that the Jews had abandoned her in the forest, whereas the Poles had saved her, so she had no desire to return to the Jews. Fleischer eventually managed to bring her to the children's home run by Chasia Bielicka in Łódź, but she had a very difficult time integrating there.[22]

Decades later, the former children who were parted from their rescuers — their proxy parents — still recalled the event as traumatic. Binyamin Katz, who was rescued by a farming family who treated him like a son, remembered that one day an elderly man suddenly turned up in the house and looked at him, but said nothing. Long afterward he learned that the man was the Koordynacja operative, Akiva Gershter. A few days later, his adop-

---

21  *Farn Yiddishn Kind*, November, 1946, CZA, 5612.
22  Testimony of Devora Fleischer-Zilber, OHD, (68)27c.

tive mother took him to the organization's office in Łódź, where a group of people asked him questions. However, he did not understand what was going on. Soon, packages of food and sweets began to arrive at the farmers' home, presumably to induce the rescuers to return the boy. Some time later, his adoptive mother took him to Łódź again, and this time left him in a children's home. Katz never discovered how he was located, who had arranged his removal from his adoptive home, or how much was paid for him.[23]

Negotiations did not always go as easily as they had in the case of Binyamin Katz, nor did the child's actual removal always proceed smoothly. The Koordynacja emissaries, determined to reclaim the survivor children for the Jewish people at all costs, often resorted to rough methods incompatible with the principles of good education. In some cases the child was removed deceitfully, with false promises. The process took a deep emotional toll both on the child and on the removal operatives and they felt his anguish. In her testimony, Devora Fleischer recalled the agonizing experience of her first effort to redeem a child — a little girl who was the ward of a poor peasant woman near Lublin. After the negotiations had been concluded, the woman suddenly informed Fleischer that the girl was refusing to go with her and would leave only with her mother. Fleischer, who had presented herself as the girl's aunt, took the girl, who was trembling and crying, to the home of acquaintances. Neither of them slept at all that night:

> I thought that maybe it was wrong for me to take her from the Polish family — after all, she had grown accustomed to them and they are the closest people to her. She felt good in their home. True, she didn't have enough to eat, but it was her home and roof. I was afraid of that... I told myself that if I was going to be so sentimental I would never reclaim a child. It will be the same in every case. Every child will want to remain where he is living. The child does not know me and will not want to go with me. It is impossible like that... After I bought the girl a dress and shoes, she said she wants to go back with the "aunt"...[24]

Fleischer was not always able to induce a recalcitrant child to leave. In one case, a nine-year-old Jewish girl who was living with a Baptist farming family in a village near Chelm refused to leave with her. The head of the house told Fleischer bluntly that he would not allow her to be taken if she did not agree to leave of her own free will. He refused to discuss payment: money, he said,

23 Testimony of Binyamin Katz, OHD, (68)32
24 Testimony of Devora Fleischer-Zilber, OHD, (68)27c.

had not been his motive for rescuing her. Unable to persuade the girl or the farmer, Fleischer left; the girl remained with the family.[25]

Perhaps the most difficult cases involved childless rescuers who had become attached to the child and wished to adopt him. Some of them moved to a new location when they realized they had been discovered and were liable to come under pressure to release the child. Others waged a stubborn struggle, not only against Koordynacja emissaries but even against parents who had survived.

The father of "Bogushia" — Shifra Junisz — whom he had abandoned outside Warsaw and who was taken in and sheltered by Leokadia Jaromirska (see Chapter Two), survived a concentration camp in Germany. After the war, he returned to Poland and managed to track down his daughter. Jaromirska, who had endured severe want and mortal danger with the girl, had psychologically adopted her as her own daughter, and had come to love her like a mother. She was wholly unprepared for the possibility that either of the girl's parents would survive and show up to claim her. One day, though, a stranger came to her apartment and, after looking long and hard at the girl, identified her as his daughter. He told Jaromirska where and why he had abandoned her and what she had been wearing at the time. It was clear to Jaromirska that the man was the girl's father. From that moment the two were locked in a struggle for the girl's soul. Jaromirska said later that if her husband, Bolek, had not returned just then from a concentration camp as a shattered wreck needing her support, she would have fled with the girl and no one would have found them. In the meantime, the father began to pay frequent visits and bring Shifra toys, sweets, and clothes. Seeing the desperate plight of Jaromirska and her husband, he gave them a little money to buy food. Jaromirska consulted a lawyer, but to no avail, because under the law the father was the girl's legal guardian. The moment of decision loomed. Twenty years later, she recalled her emotional distress in a letter to the husband of her "Bogushia," who was by then a mother herself:

> I imagined to myself how the problem would be solved — that he [the father] would stay with us meanwhile, then he would get married and that Bogushia would stay with me and he would visit her from time to time. But it turned out differently. He simply told me that he was taking her from me. There was a very big scene. I told him that I wouldn't give her up… I couldn't imagine my life without her… He saw my sor-

25  Testimony of Devora Fleischer-Zilber, OHD, 68)27c,d.

row, claimed that it was his right; that the law was on his side… Junisz [the girl's father] suggested that I go away with them. If not for Bolek I wouldn't have thought twice. But how could I leave such a man? For five years he had dreamt about being with me again, for me he wanted to live… I was the most broken-hearted person in the world. I would go to the church and tell the Holy Mother of all my suffering and ask her how to find a way out of this visious circle.[26]

Finally Jaromirska demanded money, knowing that he had none and believing that she could thus delay returning the girl for at least a year. To her astonishment, the father gave her 75,000 zlotys — which he had received from the Koordynacja in Łódź — to cover her expenses in looking after his daughter. He then took the girl and left without telling Jaromirska their destination. "I parted with her. I went with Bolek without seeing where I was walking. For a long time I heard her voice, filled with despair. I can still hear it. Thus we parted forever. I returned to Wrocław a different person."[27]

The Koordynacja tried to be fair and pay the rescuers at least part of what they had spent on the child, but was absolutely determined to take the children away and brooked no compromise. An orphaned child survivor was a national asset and had to be restored to his Jewish roots at any price and by all possible means. However, success was by no means guaranteed. In some cases, after payment was made and the child taken away, the rescuers came to the children's home and took him back by fraudulent means, albeit with his cooperation.[28]

To prevent this, the Koordynacja insisted that the rescuers sign a formal contract declaring that they had no further financial claims and would not try to reclaim the child. The document listed the child's personal details, described the circumstances under which he had reached the rescuers, and included a declaration that they were returning him of their own volition to his parents or to Koordynacja representatives. They affirmed that they had been reimbursed for their expenses in maintaining the child and that they had no further claims from the institution or the individual now taking custody of the child. The following contract, for example, was signed by the Bombas family:

26  Leokadia Jaromirska, "Bogushia," pp. 120–121, 125–126.
27  Ibid., pp. 125–126, 128; *Farn Yiddishn Kind*, CZA, 5612.
28  Testimony of Leibel Koriski, OHD, (68)15a.

We received Krzysztof Chodźba from his mother with the aim of rescuing him as a Jew from the German murderers and returning him
at the first opportunity to his parents or to any Jewish person dealing
with survivor children. We confirm that the name Krzysztof Chodźba is
false and that his real [family] name is Pilpel. We are returning him of
our own goodwill and without coercion, in order to fulfill his parents'
wishes, and are transferring him to the care of a representative of the
Koordynacja Committee in Łódź to continue his education through the
Koordynacja. For the expenses we incurred during six years of educating and looking after the boy, we are receiving 250,000 zlotys and have
no further claims in this matter.[29]

The wording of this dry, businesslike contract, ostensibly describing how the
mother placed the child in his rescuers' custody and declaring their postwar
commitment, conceals the human drama that forced the biological parents
to place the child in a family of strangers, what the latter underwent, and
how the child was removed from their custody. In this case, the late date
of the child's transfer to the Koordynacja — two years after the end of the
war — and the high amount that was paid, indicate that the rescuers did not
release him easily.

The boy in question was born in 1941, at the height of the war, in a
town in Eastern Galicia. The exact circumstances under which he reached the
Bombas family — a Polish working-class family — are not clear. Apparently
his mother left him for safekeeping with a Polish woman who was not a local
resident. The woman rented a room in the Bombas home but after a time disappeared, abandoning the boy. Roman and Rozalia Bombas, who had daughters, decided to keep the boy, even though they knew he was Jewish and were
well aware of the risks their decision entailed. They obtained a Christian birth
certificate for him and he spent the war years with them as though he were
their son. Years later, he retained only vague, fragmented memories of the
war period. He did not know how he had come to live with the Bombas family or what their motives were for sheltering him. He did remember, though,
that Rozalia and her daughters looked after him devotedly and lovingly, and
protected him. After the war, the Bombas family moved to western Poland,
taking the baby with them. How the Koordynacja discovered his whereabouts
remains a mystery, but he remembered that when he was about six years old,
a man came to the house, introduced himself as his uncle, and told the family

---

29  Bombas family file, YVA, M.31/3550.

that the boy's parents had perished and that he had come to take him. The family refused to hand him over. Rozalia Bombas said she had rescued him for humanitarian reasons at risk to her life and that he was now hers. A few weeks later, Koordynacja emissaries, accompanied by security men, arrived and told the family that if they did not hand over the boy willingly they would take him by force. Forty years later, in his recommendation to Yad Vashem to recognize the Bombas family as "Righteous among the Nations," he wrote:

> To this day, I cannot forget the scenes of the lengthy negotiations concerning my removal from the Bombas family, and the protracted attempts to persuade, and perhaps to tempt, the mother of the family to forgo me and hand me over to the people who had come to claim me. I can still see vividly the scattering of the money on the bed and the way the whole family cried when they had to let me go. I would not consider the fact that they accepted money — 250,000 zlotys — a reason to accuse the Bombas family of having rescued me out of greed. The circumstances — the hardships and the poverty — are definitely a mitigating factor which helps one understand their motives... I am convinced that in granting this recognition we are showing humane and Jewish graciousness and gratefulness to people who in a dark time displayed more than a spark of humanity and civilized values, despite the difficulties and the horrors of the war.[30]

As we have seen, in their determination to restore the child survivors to the Jewish people, the Koordynacja operatives and Drucker did not hesitate to resort to deception or even force. If the rescuers increased the ransom price during the negotiations in an apparent attempt at extortion, the Koordynacja operatives threatened to take the child away from them against their will. In practice, this was an empty threat, and besides, it was undesirable to involve the police. Under the law, authority for determining guardianship lay with the courts, not with the police. Nevertheless, the Koordynacja and Drucker often brought in the police — after paying them off — to remove children by force. This was usually done when the child's relatives wanted to help reclaim him. In the town of Tykocin, near Bialystok, a Catholic family which had rescued two children refused to hand them over to their relatives. Seeing no other alternative, the Koordynacja bribed Polish police officers, who removed the children from the family by guile and transferred them to the children's home in Łódź.[31]

---

30  Ibid.
31  Testimony of Arye Sarid, OHD, (68)10b.

The many testimonies concerning the removal of children from non-Jewish rescuers show that most were returned willingly following negotiations. The use of strong-arm tactics, as occurred in not a few cases, was seen as a demonstration of ingratitude toward the rescuers. Deception and force were resorted to mainly in villages, when agreement on the amount of payment could not be reached. These methods were avoided in the cities, where they were liable to have serious repercussions and jeopardize the entire project. Large segments of the Christian population still believed the ancient blood libels against the Jews. The use of deception or force to remove a child from his Christian rescuers often left a lasting negative impression.

On January 29, 1947, a Koordynacja representative traveled to a village in the Szczecin area in order to take custody of two brothers, aged fourteen and seventeen, from the peasant family that had rescued them. The operative located the youngsters but they escaped from him. He caught them with the aid of a local policeman. The brothers told him how their rescuers had hidden and protected them from the Germans and had been tortured for refusing to cooperate. After the war, the brothers had worked on local farms in order to help their impoverished rescuers. After hearing their story, the Koordynacja emissary paid the family 100,000 zlotys for looking after the two brothers. He also paid a "finder's fee" to the Polish woman who had supplied the information about the boys' whereabouts, and he rewarded the police chief for his assistance. However, it was clear to him that the boys would escape back to their rescuers from the children's home in Łódź, which is what they eventually did.[32] It took some time to bring them back, and they were then sent to Germany en route to Palestine.[33] Drucker, who was involved in several abductions of children from their non-Jewish rescuers, explained the underlying motivations, adding that he regretted that such behavior was necessary:[34]

> It is hard to say that the abductions of children were appropriate, because, after all, the people who rescued them had taken care of them and risked their lives. But we did not delve into the moral problem: the shock of the Holocaust was so powerful that we thought saving one soul for the Jewish people was a tremendous achievement. Looking back at

32 Report on the Cyngiser brothers affair, February 23, 1947, Beit Lohamei Hagetaot Archives (BLHA), BL/790.
33 Neshamit, "Coordinating Child Rescue," pp. 143–144.
34 Testimony of Yeshayahu Drucker, YVA; O.3/3249, for a description of Sara Gold's abduction from the home of her rescuers at the initiative of a family acquaintance and in coordination with Drucker, see YVA, M.31/4028.

this from the perspective of time, I don't know if it was really so essential, if such drastic measures were necessary. I don't know if there was sufficient justification to entitle us to act.[35]


## Legal Proceedings

Relatives frequently had to turn to the courts to force rescuers to hand over their young wards, though this was usually as a last resort after all other means had failed. The court proceedings, which revolved around the right of legal guardianship, pitted the rescuers — a family or an individual who had risked their lives for the child and become attached to him — against a relative whom the child usually did not know and with whom he had no desire to live. The judges based their decision on the child's welfare and wishes. Given the tragic circumstances, the trials were highly emotional for all concerned. In some cases, though, the rescuers' argument that they had become emotionally attached to the child masked a clear economic interest: an attempt to gain control of the assets of the child's family by becoming his legal guardian. With all these elements playing a part, some of the trials were quite lengthy.

Avraham Gvirtzman, from Tel Aviv, fought a stubborn court battle for more than three years against a Pole in remote Częstochowa in order to gain custody of his niece, whom the man had raised for more than seven years, from 1942 until the end of 1949. In the background was the property of the girl's family. The negotiations for her return began through correspondence. The rescuer occasionally added new demands and finally stipulated impossible terms. In 1949, Gewircman, armed with an adoption order issued by an Israeli court, went to Częstochowa and with the aid of Drucker and the newly-established Israeli embassy in Warsaw, set in motion complex legal proceedings. After a lengthy ordeal he was finally granted custody of the girl, but not before he transferred ownership of the family's property in Poland to the rescuer, in addition to a large cash payment as compensation for his expenses in looking after the girl. According to Gvirtzman, reclaiming the girl cost about $5,000, a substantial amount at the time for a private individual.[36]

Although this was an extreme case, it reflects the tribulations of reclaiming Jewish children through the courts. A study of the historical documentation and testimonies suggests that the judges much preferred the sides to

---

35  Testimony of Yeshayahu Drucker, OHD, (68)28c.
36  Testimony of Avraham Gvirtzman, OHD, (68)34.

reach an out-of-court settlement. That the Polish courts did not adopt a uniform attitude in these cases is shown by the fact that different judgments were handed down depending on place and circumstances. According to the testimony of the attorney Bernard Kongis-Karski, who helped Yeshayahu Drucker obtain legal guardianship for relatives of Jewish children, in consideration of the tragic circumstances, courts in Warsaw tended to accede to the requests from Jews, granting custody to both genuine and fictitious relatives without examining their papers. In the provinces, however, the courts more often than not ruled in favor of the local residents. The religious factor also played a part. After the war, the old law stipulating that a legal guardian had to be of the same religion as his ward was repealed, thus rendering immaterial the argument that the child had been baptized and was therefore a Christian. In practice, though, this change was of little relevance. Despite the regime change in Poland, many judges were still devout Catholics and were inclined to take into account the child's certificate of baptism, though without citing this in their decision.[37]

As a rule, the Koordynacja tried to avoid going to court, not wishing to aggravate even further the already strained relations with the rescuers. Moreover, because the organization was not formally recognized, its representatives could not appear before the court. In any event, an institution inevitably occupied an inferior position by comparison to a family or a woman who had risked their lives in rescuing a child and had cared for him devotedly. Another problem was that court cases dragged on without anyone being able to predict the outcome. In most cases, the judges' decision was based on their perception of the child's welfare and wishes. Despite these drawbacks, the Koordynacja was involved in a number of court cases, aided by official Jewish committees.[38]

During the occupation, a Jewish woman and her infant son, Shmuel Rozenkrantz, found shelter in the home of a solitary Polish woman, Maria Krzywdzik, in Lublin. Following the mother's murder by the Germans, the woman had the child baptized, gave him her family name, and effectively adopted him. After the war the Koordynacja located the boy and set out to remove him from the woman's custody. Two court hearings dealt with the case, beginning in February 1947. Both courts ruled against the Koordynacja, which was represented by a representative of the Lublin District Jewish Committee. A study of the judgments shows that what tipped the scales

37  Testimony of Bernard Kongis-Karski, OHD, (68)49.
38  Testimony of Leibel Koriski, OHD, (68)15a.

was neither the child's Jewish origins nor the circumstances of his baptism and adoption, but his best interests as perceived by the court. Character witnesses — neighbors and friends of the woman — told the court that she was a decent, sensitive person and was a good mother. The boy, now aged eight, asked what he preferred, replied that he wanted to stay with "mommy." Justice, the court ruled, demanded that the boy remain with the adoptive woman and be considered her son, and this did not conflict with the public interest.[39] This outcome demonstrates the weakness of a Koordynacja legal argument in court based solely on a child's Jewish origins. As noted, the judges took into account the child's welfare, as they perceived it, with the result that even a child's relatives were not always granted custody.

In Minsk-Mazowiecki, a childless Polish couple rescued a Jewish girl aged about five. Her uncle, a young man, located her after the war, and because he was still serving in the Polish army asked Devora Fleischer to reclaim her. However, the family refused to hand her over. With Koordynacja support, the case went to court. The judgment was in favor of the girl's rescuers, who were declared her legal guardians for having looked after her and because their home was now her home. As for the soldier-uncle, the court noted that he did not have a home of his own and concluded that he would not be able to give her proper care.[40]

Despite these failures, the Koordynacja continued to be involved behind the scenes in similar court cases. Usually it was a child's relatives who initiated the appeal to the court, with the Koordynacja helping to defray the costs. In some cases, the organization also had someone pose as a relative of the child. As noted, the courts did not adopt a uniform approach in these cases, and with a properly prepared argument, it was often possible to regain the child from his rescuers, even if they had adopted him in practice.

In 1942, a Jewish couple Avraham and Ester Fuchsberg in Drohobycz, Eastern Galicia, placed their infant daughter, Lifsha, in the custody of a Polish couple, Władyslaw and Helena Grzegorczyk. After the parents perished, the Grzegorczyks baptized the girl and adopted her, and after the war moved with her from the Soviet area to Poland. The girl's aunt located her and demanded her return, but the family refused. With Koordynacja backing, the case was heard in two judicial instances. Witnesses described the circumstances in which the girl's parents left her with the Polish couple. One witness

39  Judgment of Lublin district court (in Polish) in the matter of the boy Shmuel Rosenkrantz, June 11, 1947, BLHA, Z/6BL/798.
40  Testimony of Devora Fleischer-Zilber, OHD, (68)27e.

claimed to have heard the girl's father say, "Take the girl and do with her what you want." On October 13, 1948, in the second instance, the district court in Klodzko ruled in the aunt's favor, declaring her the girl's legal guardian. The court took into consideration the special circumstances in which the girl was placed in the custody of the Polish family, and annulled the adoption carried out when the girl was still in hiding with the family. The court noted that the girl had not been handed over for adoption but to be sheltered, and that her father had taken this step when his life was in danger and in the hope of reclaiming her later. The judge found it unlikely that the girl's father had told the rescuers that they could do with his daughter as they wished. A child is not an object to be given as a gift, the court asserted. In handing down such judgments, the court usually obliged the relatives to reimburse the rescuers for their expenses in looking after the child. In this case, however, the court acted harshly with the rescuers and did not grant them financial compensation for the six years during which they looked after the girl.[41]

Among the documentation we have concerning the Koordynacja's involvement in custody battles there is the case of the Zając sisters, who were sheltered in a convent in Tarnów. The two girls were aged between ten and twelve and seven and eight respectively. The Koordynacja sought the transfer of the girls to a Jewish institution. After their parents were murdered, the Tarnów municipality, which thought they were Polish orphans, placed them in an orphanage run by the *Slugi Jezusa* order (Servants of Jesus) in the city. The Koordynacja discovered the girls' whereabouts, but the nuns refused to relinquish them. Having no other recourse, the Koordynacja sought a court order for their removal from the orphanage. In this case it was not a family that tried to adopt Jewish children but a Catholic institution which had converted the girls to Christianity and in which the living conditions were inferior to those in the Jewish children's homes. Here, too, the case was heard in two judicial instances.

The Koordynacja was represented in court by officials of the Kraków Jewish Committee. They argued that from both a Christian and a moral point of view the girls should be moved to a Jewish children's home. To begin with, they were of Jewish origin; second, the conditions in the children's homes were better than those in the convent; and, finally, in the children's home they would receive an education and acquire a profession before being united with their relatives abroad. The Koordynacja agreed to pay the convent 60,000 zlotys for its expenses in taking care of the girls. The mayor of Tarnów told the

---

41 Judgment (in Polish) in the matter of Lifsha Fuchsberg, October 13, 1948, BLHA, ibid.

court that he supported the request of the Jewish representatives. It would be to the girls' benefit, he said, and would also make available two places in the convent for needy Polish orphans. Nevertheless, the court ruled in favor of the convent. The judge noted that the girls had elected to stay in the convent of their own free will and that he had reached his decision after hearing their testimony about their lives and the circumstances of their rescue. His impression, he said, was that their mental development was sufficient to allow them to choose the institution in which they wished to be educated. On November 12, 1946, the Tarnów district court let the decision of the lower court stand.[42]

## Removal of Children from the Convents

The Koordynacja's failure in the Tarnów case is an example of the difficulties encountered by Jewish institutions when they appealed to the courts to reclaim Jewish children from convents. The problems in such cases were different from those involving families.

Parting from nuns did not subject children to the same degree of emotional distress as from families: interpersonal relations in convents were less intimate; nor did the convents expect material remuneration. Despite their poverty and hardship, they never sought financial compensation for their expenses in looking after rescued children. Some convents agreed to accept a personal gift from parents who had arrived to claim their child, as a token of gratitude.[43] They were also willing to accept a donation in the form of cash or goods from a Jewish institution as a gesture of thanks for rescuing children or adults.[44] However, in contrast to families, negotiating a ransom payment with the convents was out of the question, as this would have amounted to trafficking in children, a violation of the sisters' moral precepts. Indeed, it was not pecuniary motives that spurred convents to rescue Jewish children but a humanitarian approach stemming from their missionary avocation; hence their desire that the children remain practicing Christians.

Parents seeking to reclaim a child from a convent rarely encountered obstacles. The nuns' only expectation was that the child would continue to be

---

42  Judgment of Tarnów district court (in Polish) in the matter of the Zając sisters, November 12, 1946, BLHA, ibid.

43  See Kaczmarzyk, *Pomoc udzielana*, pp. 17–18, YVA, JM/6363, for the case of a Jewish mother who gave the sisters leather for shoes as a token of gratitude for rescuing her son.

44  Testimony of Sister Charitas Soczek, *Kurek-Lesik Collection*, p. 177.

raised as a Christian. However, their attitude was radically different with regard to orphans whose whole family had perished, and particularly the older children among them, who had accepted Christianity by conscious decision. The nuns clung tenaciously to these children and saw no reason why Jewish institutions had a greater claim on them. As evidence of this is the readiness of the Tarnów convent to embark upon a legal battle with the Jewish establishment over the souls of the two little orphan girls.

Drucker and the Koordynacja were at a loss in the struggle to reclaim Jewish orphans from convents. Neither the local Jewish committees nor the Central Jewish Committee knew how many children had been rescued by convents in Poland, or in which ones. The convents were scattered throughout the country and outsiders had no access to them. Making contact with nuns and priests to obtain information about their Jewish wards was highly problematic, and the convents also placed obstacles in the way of strangers wishing to communicate directly with the children.[45]

According to Ewa Kurek, after the war Żegota activists had lists of Jewish children whom the organization had placed in the custody of convents, but these were only partial and did not indicate how many had survived or where. Approaches were made to bishops, but they were not involved in the convents' rescue operations and were unable to provide information. Kurek maintains that in her interviews with nuns who were involved in rescuing children, she never encountered a case in which a convent prevented a Jewish child from leaving with someone who was ready to look after him. At the same time, she notes, a convent would not hand over a child to a Jew as such, without knowing his identity and where he intended to take the child. They adopted the same attitude toward Polish, Ukrainian, and Roma (gypsy) children. In their view, national identity alone was no guarantee of ability to provide properly for a child and give him security.[46]

This assertion will be disputed by those who are aware of the ease with which convents gave Jewish children to Christian families for adoption, as reflected in nuns' testimonies. However, the Church in postwar Poland did not follow a deliberate policy against giving custody of Jewish children who had survived in convents to Jews. The senior clergy, who had not taken part in their rescue, were similarly not involved in their return. The behavior and judgment of the mothers superior continued to derive from their missionary- driven religious faith. Certainly they did not volunteer to restore the

45  Koriski, "The Zionist Koordynacja," p. 257.
46  Kurek-Lesik, *Your Life*, pp. 118, 237–238.

children to Jewish hands, and therefore did not initiate a dialogue with Jewish institutions. Nor did they inform the Jewish committees which children had survived and where, so that relatives could claim them.

There is only one known instance in which nuns handed over rescued children to a Jewish children's home. After the liberation, Sister Eugenia Wąsowska, from the small and poor Convent of the Sacred Heart, in Przemyśl, Galicia, transferred the thirteen children whom the institution had rescued to a Jewish children's home through the district Jewish committee.[47] This convent was also unusual in that it did not baptize the Jewish children, objecting to this practice on principle. Only one of the older girls declined to enter the Jewish children's home, maintaining that she owed her allegiance to her rescuers. She moved to a different Christian institution and a few years later converted to Christianity.[48]

This case is a rare exception. After the war, when the convents had to vacate the children they had sheltered, they preferred to place the Jewish children in Polish orphanages. This was the case, for example, with the Servants of Jesus convent in Czersk, near Warsaw, which rescued a number of children from the city. Some of them were afterward claimed by their parents, but the orphans were sent to a Polish orphanage, where they remained until they completed school and began to lead an independent life.[49]

In testimony given forty years after the events, Jan Dobraczyński, who helped the Żegota activists in Warsaw place children in convents, maintained that after the war the Jews were no longer interested in these children, because they had been baptized. He added that when he learned, after the war, that the JDC had brought food and clothing to Warsaw for Jewish children, he urged that they not overlook the Jewish children who were still in Polish orphanages and in convents, and received an astonishing reply: "You said once that the children who hid in convents would remain Christians if their parents did not reclaim them? So take them for yourselves. They are not our children."[50] Similar testimony was given by Jadwiga Piotrowska, who had personally placed dozens of Jewish children with Christian families and in convents. After the war, she related, in a meeting she and Dobraczyński had with

---

47  Confirmation of District Jewish Committee, Przemyśl, to Eugenia Wąsowska concerning thirteen children she returned, March 25, 1950; the confirmation was apparently given to her after she renounced her vows, YVA M.31/1929.

48  Testimony of S. Ligoria Grenda, *Kurik-Lesik Collection*, p. 185.

49  Testimony of Sister Maria Ruminska, ibid., pp. 207–208.

50  Testimony of Jan Dobraczyński, ibid., p. 333.

representatives of the Warsaw Jewish Committee, she gave the committee a partial list of children who had survived. She describes the encounter:

> We did not expect thanks, but we also did not think we would stand accused. In the conversation we were told that we had committed a crime: We had stolen hundreds of children from the Jews, converted them to Christianity, and uprooted them from Jewish culture. It was further said that we were worse than the Germans. The Germans took only the body, we had stolen the soul. Our arguments that we had fought for the children's lives were rejected simplistically: It would have been better if these children had not lived, rather than what happened.[51]

We have no testimony from the Jewish side, either contemporary or later, about such a meeting, which could confirm or refute this account. It is certainly possible that the meeting took place as the two people had testified. However, it is unlikely that such extreme language was resorted to. It simply does not stand to reason that anyone from the Jewish establishment in Poland at the time — whether communist, Bundist, Zionist, or religious — would have been willing, in the light of the almost total annihilation of the country's Jewish children, to forgo the few children who remained in convents only because they had been baptized. According to halakha — Jewish religious law — a Jew remains a Jew even if baptized. This is certainly the case with regard to children who were converted in an emergency situation without understanding the implications for their future. That these children were meaningful for Jewry is attested to by the many efforts made immediately after the war and years later by Jewish organizations — both religious and secular, in Poland and elsewhere — to restore them to their roots.

At the same time, Dobraczyński's testimony merits careful study, as it reinforces the testimonies about the convents' refusal to transfer the children to Jewish hands. Dobraczyński notes that he asked the JDC to assist the Jewish children living in convents. The obvious question is why he did not propose transferring them to Jewish custody, thereby easing the conditions in the convents and creating room for needy Polish orphans. Moreover, according to his testimony, it was the nuns who directed him to the JDC office.[52] As for what he and Piotrowska imply about the Jews' ingratitude toward the Christian rescuers, the contemporary documentation indicates the opposite. The reports of the JDC mission in Poland concerning the range of aid opera-

---

51 Testimony of Jadwiga Piotrowska, ibid., pp. 349–351.
52 Kurek-Lesik, *Your Life*, p. 114.

tions that organization carried out in the first years after the war indicate that particular sensitivity was shown towards needy Poles who had helped rescue Jews during the war, especially toward institutions and convents that sheltered children. The 1947 JDC report states in this connection:

> During the occupation a number of non-Jews rendered important services to Jews and in many instances endangered their own lives through the saving of Jewish persons. Some of these non-Jews are now in great financial and economic distress. For this reason an ad-hoc committee under the supervision of the Central Committee with the participation of a JDC representative, was set up, which received in the course of the year 930 applications for aid... Another phase of assistance to non-Jews, which is considered by the ministers as very important, is the distribution by the JDC of food supplies to non-Jewish children's homes, and to convents which harbored Jewish children during the occupation. The Ministry of Social Welfare submits every month a list of children's institutions in need of special aid. During the year under review 61 such institutions, housing about 5,500 non-Jewish children received a total of 25,747 kgs. of food supplies. Seven other non-Jewish organizations received 4,800 kgs. of food supplies.[53]

This is confirmed in later testimony taken by Kurek-Lesik from a nun whose convent received generous material aid from the JDC in gratitude for rescuing Jewish children and returning them to Jewish organizations.[54]

Locating the children in the convents posed a difficulty in which the Koordynacja and Drucker had no advantage over private individuals — if anything, the reverse was the case. The convents were tolerant toward parents and other relatives who were searching for the children, but not toward strangers who claimed to represent an institution they had never heard of and whose authority was not clear. Such cases generated immediate suspicion. Owing to the convents' secretive nature, the Koordynacja had scant information about the Jewish children who remained in them. Of 270 children who had been located but not yet reclaimed and whose personal details appear in the Koordynacja lists for 1947, only thirty-six resided in convents and other Christian institutions. Not all their names were known or clear.[55] For the most

53  AJDC Poland, Annual Report 1947, GJA, 125/B/126/A.
54  Testimony of Sister Charitas Soczek. *Kurek-Lesik Collection*, p. 177.
55  For a partial list of Christian families and institutions in which Jewish orphans resided, see CZA, S26/1424.

part, the Koordynacja received its information about convent children from parents and relatives who, while conducting their own searches, discovered the existence of other unclaimed Jewish children.

In cases where a confrontation with a convent was unavoidable, the outcome was usually more satisfactory when relatives were involved rather than representatives of the Jewish organizations. In contrast to private individuals, Koordynacja personnel were bound by the rules of conventional courtesy in a convent; as public emissaries, they were obliged to behave cautiously and cordially — and, as a result, often ineffectually. The Koordynacja representative had to persuade the Jewish child in a convent — who did not know him — that it would be to his benefit to leave the institution which he now regarded as his home, and join the Jewish community. This was a major obstacle to removing Jewish children from convents. The little ones knew nothing of their Jewish identity — at best, it was nothing but a hazy memory — and in any event they would not leave without the sisters' consent. Older children were aware of their Jewish identity but spurned it because it was the root of all their sufferings. Its very mention aroused fear and loathing. In addition, some of them were by now devout Catholics and, as such, refused to leave the convent.

Gerta Zilber, who was sheltered in the Felician convent in Przemyśl, was twelve when the war ended. She was the only surviving member of her family. After the war, a new and lengthy phase began in her convent life, as she relates:

> I entered the regime of the Christian religion. The Jews learned that I was still in the convent and sent someone to get me out. I didn't want to hear about it — I was afraid of the Jews. A young man arrived who pretended to be my relative in order to get me to leave the convent. I would not receive him. I told the nuns that he was not my relative. I could have got up and left, but I did not. I stayed in the convent for ten years. I became a Christian. I prayed and I liked it. I underwent the baptismal ceremony in the church. At the same time, I did not want to forget my father. I worried about what had happened to him.[56]

Gerta's story (her name was changed to Magdalena in the convent) is not an unusual one among the convent children. In 1946, Anna Shonert-Likierman, a woman in her forties, lay dying in a Łódź hospital. Before her death she

56 Testimony of Magdalena Or-Ner (Gerta Zilber), YVA, O.3/6745.

asked for someone from the Koordynacja to visit her in order to dictate her last will:

> I am physically ill but sound of mind. In 1942, at my husband's advice, I and my daughter, Irena, who was ten, were baptized as Christians for the sake of our safety. Afterward I placed her in a Catholic orphanage in a convent in Miedzyrzec Podlaski. Please give this letter to the mother superior and take the girl into your custody and educate her in the spirit of Judaism. This is my last wish before dying.[57]

She signed the will in the presence of the duty nurse and died a few weeks later. In the meantime, the Koordynacja secured the necessary papers to remove the girl from the convent. The organization's representatives visited the convent twice, but Irena, who was now aged fourteen, refused to abide by her mother's testament. Her mother was very dear to her, she said, but she could not do as she had asked. She knew she was Jewish, but had found a better and more beautiful religion, thanks to which she had been spared death. Nothing the Koordynacja representatives said could make her change her mind: she remained in the convent. At the end of 1946 the Jewish emissaries still hoped they would be able to carry out the mother's last request, but it was not to be.

The reactions of these two girls, Gerta and Irena, who in the terms of the time were considered mature despite their young age, make it perfectly clear that they knew they were Jewish but nevertheless consciously decided not to return to Judaism. Their decision stemmed from the Christian education they had received and from their fear for the fate of the Jews, as they knew it from their own brutal experience. At least one of them, Gerta Zilber, had a change of heart when she reached adulthood and returned to Judaism, but others did not. As for the younger children who had been converted to Christianity, if no relatives could be found, or family acquaintances who knew enough about the family to pose as relatives and claim them, there was little the Koordynacja could do, as in this respect the organization acted mainly to assist relatives. On their own, Drucker and the Koordynacja removed very few children from convents.

Drucker, who represented the religious establishment, found it untenable that Jewish girls should remain in convents and become practicing Christians. He made great efforts in this regard, spurred by urgent requests from well-known religious families in Palestine and in America. They pressed

---

57  *Farn Yiddishn Kind*, CZA, 5612.

him to obtain custody of girls who had been sheltered in convents and reunite them with their relatives.[58] However, he encountered the same difficulties as the Koordynacja. In most cases these were older girls with a mind of their own. The convents did not prevent them from leaving, and allowed Drucker to try to persuade them, but the girls refused. Zerach Warhaftig, who accompanied Drucker to one convent in Kraków, describes their failed meeting with three Jewish girls there. The oldest of them, who was probably aged about fourteen, spoke on behalf of all three. She told the two emissaries in no uncertain terms that that they had no desire to leave the convent: "When we were hounded like beasts, you did not come to rescue us. We were saved by this convent, and now we will not leave our rescuers. We refuse to join you. Nevertheless, after some time Drucker did succeed in removing the three from the convent.[59] No reliable data exist about how many girls Drucker removed from convents: in his testimonies he describes his personal involvement in the cases of five girls, four of whom were older than fourteen, the other under ten.[60] Other convent girls probably also passed through the Zabrze children's home.

The Turkowice convent rescued about thirty children, although when Devora Fleischer arrived there, in June 1946, only eight remained, the others apparently having been claimed by parents or relatives. Fleischer, who was on a mission for a woman who asked her to remove a relative of hers, a young girl, from the institution, took the opportunity to find out whether other Jewish children remained in the convent. At first the mother superior was suspicious. Only after Fleischer told her frankly that she represented a Jewish organization that was seeking to reclaim rescued Jewish children did the mother superior engage her in a dialogue about the children's future. She gave Fleischer custody of three young children from the group of eight, including the girl she was looking for. As for the others, she told Fleischer, they were now fully-fledged Christians and would stay in the convent. On another occasion, when Fleischer tried to gain custody of a girl from a convent near Lubicz, the mother superior rejected her request outright. Only after the priest intervened was she able to meet with the girl, but in vain: the girl refused to accompany her.[61]

As noted, parents or relatives who located their child in a convent and could furnish proof of their identity rarely encountered problems. The pro-

58  Testimony of Yeshayahu Drucker, YVA, O.3/3249.
59  Warhaftig, *Refugee and Survivor*, p. 330–331.
60  Testimony of Yeshayahu Drucker, YV, O.3/3249.
61  Testimony of Devora Fleischer-Zilber, OHD, (68)27e,f.

cess is described in the testimony of a nun belonging to the Albertine order. A convent in Drohobycz rescued a Jewish boy but did not know who his parents were. They baptized him and gave him a Polish name. After liberation, a Polish officer accompanied by a woman arrived at the convent in search of the boy. The officer, who was the boy's father, waited outside while the woman, who introduced herself as the boy's aunt, went in and identified him on the basis of a photograph. The couple thanked the nuns for rescuing the child and he was transferred to the custody of the relatives without any problems. Later, chance offered the father an opportunity to repay the convent for its act of mercy. During the postwar repatriation process, the nuns moved to Wrocław, in western Poland, but could not find a suitable place for their institution. They were referred to an official in the municipality, who turned out to be the boy's father, and he found them an apartment immediately.[62]

Not all the stories of the convent children had happy endings. Many Jewish children reached convents as foundlings whose identity no one had checked, and the nuns placed them for adoption with Christian families, deliberately obfuscating their background. After the war, relatives had to pressure the nuns to make them divulge the children's location. In Kraków, a woman anonymously brought a sick Jewish toddler to a convent, saying he was a foundling. He was baptized, regained his health, and was given over to a Polish family for adoption. After the war, his older brothers arrived at the convent and demanded that he be handed over to them. At first the nuns refused to divulge his location. Finally, though, the mother superior was compelled to provide the information, and the boy was removed from his adoptive family following legal proceedings.[63]

There were also difficulties of a different kind. Two Jewish sisters found shelter in the Albertine convent in Wolomin and were baptized. The younger sister was placed with a Polish family for adoption; the elder, who was sick, remained in the convent. After the war, her brother arrived to claim her, but she refused to accompany him. He obtained the necessary document from the authorities and removed her from the convent against her will. A similar episode occurred in a Tarnów convent, which had sheltered a little Jewish boy. After the war, four Jewish men came to the convent bearing an order signed by the mayor for the boy's release to their custody. Informed by the nuns that people had come to take him away, the boy hid in the church and finally had to be removed by force.[64]

62 Kaczmarzyk , *Pomoc udzielana*, pp. 19–20.
63 Ibid., pp. 5–6.
64 Ibid., pp. 12–13, 22.

The testimonies of those who had endured the ordeal of the war as children and of nuns who were involved, make it clear that the convents viewed the children as Christians in every respect and therefore did not encourage them, no matter how young, to leave and rejoin their families. In cases when they did return a Jewish child to his family, they informed them that he had been baptized. If the child was old enough, they expected him to continue practicing the Christian faith, and if he did not yet understand, they enjoined the parents to give him a Christian education. This message was sometimes conveyed implicitly and in some cases stated outright.

After the liberation, Aliza Penski's mother arrived at the convent to claim her nine-year-old daughter (see Chapter Six). Before leaving, she went to the mother superior to thank her for her kindness. The mother superior blessed mother and daughter warmly and said to the girl: "You are leaving here as Krysia [her Christian name]. Be a good girl and remember to pray to Jesus."[65] When Janina David left the convent where she had been sheltered (see Chapter Six), accompanied by a Christian guardian, the mother superior kissed her and Janina promised her solemnly that she would never forsake the Christian religion. Then the other sisters took leave of her. They each embraced her and each in her way made her promise that she would adhere to Christianity.[66]

After the liberation, Alicja Guz located her little daughter in an orphanage run by nuns in Nowy-Targ (see Chapter Five). The sister in charge agreed to return her if her mother would undertake to raise her as a Catholic, because she had been baptized. Hearing this, Alicja became distraught and threatened to enlist the help of the authorities. Only then was her daughter returned to her. The next day, Guz went back to placate the nuns and thank them for looking after her daughter. She gave them a small amount of money as a token of gratitude for their act of mercy.[67]

The many testimonies in our possession show clearly that in the majority of cases it was parents or other relatives or Christian guardians who removed rescued children from convents in Poland, not the Koordynacja or Drucker. The episode of the Jewish convent children is harsh, convoluted, and painful. The nuns' noble acts were tarnished by their attempt to convert the children to Christianity by means of baptism and then by the obstacles they created after the war to prevent their return to the Jewish community. The

---

65  Testimony of Aliza Penski-Chayut. YVA, O.3/3410.
66  David, *A Touch of Earth*, p. 164.
67  Guz, *Targowa 64*, p. 240.

286 • At the Mercy of Strangers

difficulties of removing Jewish children from convents were common to all the countries that had been occupied by the Nazis, and Communist Poland was no exception. The knowledge that some of them had assimilated into Christian society in the wake of the Catholic education they had received, left those who tried to recover the children for Judaism with a sour feeling of loss. Some Koordynacja activists claimed that dozens and perhaps hundreds of Jewish children remained in convents in Poland and could not be restored to the Jewish fold.[68]

The postwar period saw a reduction in the scale of the educational and care-giving activity of the convents in Poland. Convent orphanages transferred many of their wards to state-run secular institutions. Jewish children, too, were part of this transition stage, which was crucial for their future. Those who were not removed from the convents and the Polish orphanages by the end of the 1940s, or were not part of a Jewish framework — the children's homes of the Central Jewish Committee or the children's kibbutzim run by the Zionist movements — had little prospect of rejoining the Jewish community. In the end, they assimilated into Christian society.

## Dealing with Special Problems

The Koordynacja's official mandate was to deal with the children who remained in non-Jewish hands and with the orphans who were repatriated from the Soviet Union. In the nature of things, though, unanticipated dilemmas also arose, involving children of mixed marriages, unwanted children, and older girls who had formed a relationship with a Christian man while hiding on the Aryan side but now wanted to return to the Jewish community. In the absence of any other body willing to address these problems, the individuals involved turned to the Koordynacja and to Drucker for help. In cases of children of mixed marriages, it was usually the mother who sought help from the Koordynacja, which did not initiate action in these instances. Some of the children had been born before the war, others during its course. In some cases, non-Jewish mothers decided, for reasons that were not always fully clear, to turn the child over to the Jewish organizations in the wake of the Jewish father's death.

---

68 Neshamit, "Coordinating Child Rescue," p. 129; testimony of Leibel Koriski, OHD, (68)15b.

Anastasia's Jewish husband perished in the war, leaving her to care for their two boys, born in 1935 and 1943. After the war she brought them to the Koordynacja and said that their father's last wish was for them to be raised as Jews, and that she wanted to fulfill his testament. The youngsters were placed in a children's home run by the organization. Their mother visited them frequently, but they longed for her constantly. Finally she decided to reclaim the younger son; the older brother went to Palestine with the rest of his group.[69] In October 1947, the Koordynacja received a letter from a fifteen-year-old boy whose mother was Polish and his father Jewish, requesting to enter a children's home. He explained that he felt Jewish and wanted to remain a Jew, and promised to do everything the teachers said.[70] It is not clear whether he wrote the letter at his own initiative or with the encouragement of one of the parents or a relative. These were not isolated instances.

A particularly difficult situation was faced by Jewish women and girls who had become unwillingly involved with non-Jewish men while hiding on the Aryan side and after the war found it difficult to end the relationship.[71] The already complicated problem was further compounded if the couple had children. Drucker dealt with several such cases. The requests for help originated with the women or their relatives. Druker's role was to help them hide from their husband until they could leave Poland.[72] A special section was established in the Zabrze institution for children of Jewish mothers who had a non-Jewish partner who had hidden them during the occupation. Some of the couples were legally married, but in the postwar circumstances the wife decided to leave and return to the Jewish fold, often due to the husband's antisemitism or under pressure from Jewish relatives.[73]

A few Jewish girls who had been rescued by convents decided, as a gesture of gratitude and in identification with the sisters, to take the vows. The testimonies indicate that there were only a handful of such cases.[74] For the girl's family, if she had one, this was a tragedy. Deeply grieved, the family

69 Neshamit, "Coordinating Child Rescue," pp. 145–146.
70 Gabriel Moshanski to Koordynacja Committee, October 12, 1947, BLHA, Z6/BL/798.
71 Neshamit, "Coordinating Child Rescue," pp. 125–126.
72 Testimony of Yeshayahu Drucker, YVA., O.3/3249.
73 Excerpts from a letter from the director of the childrens' house. Zabrze, February 1948, YVA, O.33/1376.
74 Stela Zylbersztajn, *A Gdyby to Bylo Wasze Dziecko?* (Łódź: Oficyna Biblofilow, 1994), p. 105. Zylbersztajn converted to Christianity after the war and became a nun before reverting to Judaism. In 1968, before emigrating from Poland to Israel, she met another three nuns of Jewish origin. For another case, see the testimony of Sister Irena Szczepanska in *Kurik-Lesik Collection*, pp. 294–295.

viewed the decision as a betrayal and a desecration of the memory of the family members who had perished. One girl who intended to take the vows had relatives in Australia. They learned about her intention and tried to dissuade her, but unsuccessfully. They then turned to the Koordynacja for assistance. The girl's uncle, who felt that his world had crumbled about him, asked the organization to take every possible measure to remove the girl from the convent. After receiving a report from the Koordynacja about her situation, he wrote:

> I am in receipt of your letter of 5 September [1947]. I am very grateful to you for your devoted work on behalf of my niece. I delayed a few days before writing to you because I was waiting for a letter and photographs from her and hoped to be able to give you good news about her... We hoped the letter would bring us glad tidings, that she would inform us she had changed her mind, because we write her letters filled with love and call her our daughter. Finally a very sad letter arrived, with photographs. She writes us that she has found great happiness and that she has already gone through the two-year test period and passed the examinations, and is now going to marry Jesus. She is already wearing the black clothes of sadness... One's heart could burst at the sight of these photographs — that a Jewish girl could reach such a gloomy situation. I understand that now it is far more difficult to remove her. It is no use talking to her: she will not leave of her own volition. We are perhaps the first to experience a tragedy like the sad case of my niece.[75]

The uncle implored the Koordynacja to persist in its efforts, promising to pay all expenses. But it was to no avail: the girl remained in the convent.[76]

### Final Stages in the Redemption of the Children

The year 1946 was an extraordinarily turbulent period for the Jewish remnant in postwar Poland. It began with the return of tens of thousands of refugees from the depths of the Soviet Union within the framework of repatriation and continued with the panic-stricken flight of the vast majority of the remaining Jewish population from Poland to the DP camps in Germany in the wake of the Kielce pogrom of July 4, 1946. It was also the peak year in the redemption

75  I. Kurz to Koordynacja, September 28, 1947, BLHA, Z6/BL/798.
76  Neshamit, "Coordinating Child Rescue," p. 126.

of the children, which took place in the shadow of these events. From March 1946 to August 1947, the Koordynacja took custody of 309 children, and another thousand or so arrived in the repatriation from the Soviet Union. They were housed in the children's homes, but only briefly. Most of them, along with those in the children's kibbutzim, were removed from Poland in 1946 by the Bricha organization and lodged in DP camps in Germany or temporary children's homes in France.[77]

At the end of 1946, as the waves of repatriation ebbed and the survivors streamed out of Poland, three children's homes — two belonging to the Koordynacja and one run by the religious communities in Silesia — were shut down because they were no longer needed. There remained only two small Koordynacja homes in Łódź and the home run by the Committee of Religious Communities in Zabrze. In 1947, the Koordynacja had the addresses of some 270 children who still remained in Christian families and institutions across Poland, though this number was not definitive.[78] The passage of time worked against the ransoming of these children, not least because of the increasingly exorbitant payments demanded by the rescuers. If at the outset, rescuers would accept a ransom of 30,000 to 60,000 zlotys per child, the amount later soared to 200,000 to 400,000 zlotys, and some demanded half a million zlotys ($1,000) or more.[79]

In 1948, the Polish authorities intensified their supervision of Zionist activity in the country and began to interfere with the work of the Koordynacja. In March, the Polish security service (UB) arrested Leibel Koriski, the central figure in the Koordynacja directorate, questioned him about his efforts to remove children from Poland, and threatened to shut down the organization's children's homes. After his release he immigrated to Israel and was succeeded by Pinhas Krivos.[80] The Koordynacja remained in existence for more than a year after these events, until the summer of 1949, but its activity gradually declined. The efforts to ransom children faltered, not for lack of money, but because most of the organization's activists had already left for Israel. The final blow to the Koordynacja was the takeover of the Central Jewish Committee by the communist faction. In March 1949, the UB arrested Krivos, and it was only after the vigorous intervention of Adolf Berman, the

---

77  Koordynacja Financial Report for March 1946 — November 1947, CZA, S26/1424.
78  Partial list of Christian families and institutions, CZA, S26/1424.
79  Koordynacja Committee to Rescue Committee in Jerusalem, June 23, 1947, CZA, S26/1317.
80  Koriski, "The Zionist Coordination," pp. 260–261.

leader of the Poalei Zion Left party, who had good connections in the Polish government, that Krivos was released and allowed to leave the country.[81] In June 1949, the police raided the Koordynacja headquarters, confiscated documents, and seized the apartment in which the offices were located.[82] At the same time, the last thirty children in the organization's care — who were in the Łódź children's home — were transferred to homes of the Central Jewish Committee.

This marked the end of the Koordynacja's project to redeem Jewish children in Poland. On July 9, 1949, the director of the JDC in Poland, William Bein, reported to his organization's European headquarters in Paris: "The Zionist Coordination for Children in Łódź, which was occupied in recovering children from Gentile families, was closed by the authorities. Through this action, an organization which did not have an official status but which performed a remarkable task and which was instrumental in recovering under trying circumstances a few hundred children, came to an end."[83] Shortly thereafter, the children's home of the Committee of Religious Communities in Zabrze was also closed down and the last of its children brought to Israel.[84]

The project undertaken by the Koordynacja and Drucker was terminated prematurely. At its conclusion, some Jewish children still remained in the custody of non-Jews, though their number is difficult to estimate. As noted, it was not a shortage of funds that prevented their restoration to the Jewish community but the new political conditions prevailing in Poland, as manifested in the government's tough anti-Jewish Stalinist political line. The result was the liquidation of Zionist activity in Poland and the severance of the remnants of Polish Jewry from the Jewish world.

According to the reports of the Koordynacja directorate to the Rescue Committee in Jerusalem and the records remaining in Koriski's possession, in the period from March 1946 to April 1948, the Koordynacja reclaimed some 355 children from non-Jewish hands: from families, convents, and Polish orphanages.[85] No documentation exists after this date. Part of the Koordynacja archive was destroyed, part was confiscated by the Polish authorities when they shut down the organization's offices, and part was lost on the way to Israel.[86] Arye Sarid estimates that the Koordynacja redeemed more than

81  Testimony of Pinhas Krivos, OHD, (68)45.
82  Koriski, "The Zionist Koordynacja," p. 261.
83  W. Bein to JDC Paris, Current Matters, July 9, 1949, GJA, 12B/C-61.034.
84  Testimony of Yeshayahu Drucker, OHD, (68)28b
85  Koriski, "The Zionist Koordynacja," p. 260.
86  Neshamit, "Coordinating Child Rescue," p. 116.

400 children.[87] This is a reasonable estimate, as the Koordynacja project continued for more than a year after Koriski's departure.

We have no authenticated data about how many children Drucker redeemed in his three years of activity. In the absence of documentation, various people who dealt with the Holocaust orphans in Poland issued estimates of their own. These figures are of dubious credibility, and some are patently exaggerated and tendentious. Already at the time, the different bodies that dealt with the survivor children in Poland were inclined to "round off the numbers upward," in order to magnify their activities or to obtain more funds from Jewish institutions. Later, these numbers found their way unhesitatingly into the memoirs literature. The following example is from the book by Zerach Warhaftig, who was involved in ransoming children in Poland: "A total of 2,500 children were rescued from Christian families and convents in Poland. This includes 1,000 released by the religious circles, about 1,000 by the central and local Jewish committees, and some 500 by the Zionist Koordynacja… The true reason for the success of the religious elements in this campaign was their unsurpassed commitment and readiness for self-sacrifice — not surplus funds."[88]

One of the sources for these estimates is the series of testimonies given by Yeshayahu Drucker in 1968 and 1971. In one case, Drucker cited a sweeping number: "All told, we rescued some 2,000 to 3,000 children apart from the children who came from Soviet Union."[89] Elsewhere, he said, "I estimate that the number of Holocaust orphans whom we removed [from Polish custody] is at most 1,000."[90] He seems to be referring to the total number of children redeemed by him and by the Koordynacja. He does not say how many of them he himself recovered for Judaism, but estimates that between 600 and 700 children passed through the Zabrze institution — not all of whom were ransomed children.[91] Among them, as in the children's homes of the Koordynacja, were children who had been placed in the home by their parents or other relatives so they would be taken to Palestine, as well as some who were sent to a home for reasons of personal convenience by a single surviving parent who had remarried.[92]

87  Arye Sarid, in *Mission to the Diaspora*, p. 93.
88  Warhaftig, *Refugee and Survivor*, pp. 332, 334.
89  Testimony of Yeshayahu Drucker, YVA, O.3/3249.
90  Testimony of Yeshayahu Drucker, OHD, (68)28c.
91  Testimony of Yeshayahu Drucker, YVA, O.3/3249.
92  Testimony of Yeshayahu Drucker, OHD, (68)28c.

In contrast to these estimates, there are two statistics from the period that can shed light on the scale of Drucker's project. In a report by the Youth Aliyah emissary to Poland, Baruch Kaplinsky, about the Zabrze children's home, which he visited in February 1947, he wrote: "I found 21 children there, almost all of them ransomed... This home was founded in November 1945. Since then, 140 children have been educated in it. Seventy of them are in France, in Rabbi Herzog's institution and in the Hamizrahi kibbutz. Twelve went to England with the aid of Rabbi Schonfeld. A few dozen left the home and went with their parents to various countries."[93] On September 22, 1947, Drucker reported to the Rescue Committee in Jerusalem that between August 1946 and September 1947, he ransomed fifty-five children with the $5,000 he received from Rabbi Herzog.[94]

It follows from these figures that fewer children were ransomed by Drucker and housed in the Zabrze facility than he cited in later testimonies, a conclusion reinforced by the fact that 1946 was the peak year in this project for both Drucker and the Koordynacja. In that year of the great exodus from Poland, most of the ransomed children were also taken out of the country. Although Drucker continued to ransom children and the Zabrze home remained in existence for almost two more years, by the end of 1947 it had already passed its peak of activity — as was also the case with the Koordynacja. Given the fact that Drucker worked alone, the ransom of fifty-five children in one year is an extremely impressive achievement. At the same time, it is unlikely that he ransomed more than a hundred children in all.

In the light of the above data, it would appear that of several thousand children who were saved by non-Jews, the Koordynacja and Drucker between them ransomed no more than six hundred. The others were returned by their rescuers voluntarily or claimed from them by parents and other relatives. And, as noted, many of the older children, who already possessed full Jewish awareness, returned to the Jewish fold by themselves.

It must also be emphasized that the hundreds of children collected by the Koordynacja and Drucker were the difficult cases. They were mainly very young children who knew nothing about their origins or whose Jewish identity was hazy at best. Many of them were unclaimed orphans who

93  B. Kaplinsky, Report on Visit to Children's Homes in Poland, February 10, 1947, CZA, S75/1760.
94  Yeshayahu Drucker, Report on Activity to Redeem Children Conducted by Committee of Congregations in Poland, September 22, 1947, CZA, S26/1424. A list of the children's names is appended to the report.

could not have returned to their roots on their own. Only those who can fully appreciate the circumstances under which the children were rescued and of the unflagging devotion of those who searched for them in countless remote places — in villages, provincial towns, and convents — can properly appreciate their activity. The conclusion of the war did not bring tranquility to the remnant of Polish Jewry, and the window of opportunity to redeem the children who remained in non-Jewish custody closed quickly. It was a tumultuous period. Even as the survivors were trying to rehabilitate themselves and restore a measure of stability to their lives, they were again forced to abandon everything and resume their wandering. In this lies the cardinal reason that the project of restoring the children to the Jewish fold was not completed.

The ransom project undertaken by the Koordynacja and Drucker in Poland was unexampled elsewhere in Europe. Despite its modest scale, which quantitatively may not be impressive, this was one of the most crucial national projects of the last vestiges of Polish Jewry, in addition to the rehabilitation of the Zionist youth movements and the creation of the Bricha organization. Those who bore the burden of the project were involved in one of the most complex and sensitive humanitarian dilemmas of the time. Did they believe in what they were doing? The answer must be affirmative — otherwise they could not have done what they did. At the time, they viewed their effort as a national mission, even though some of them admitted that they frequently wept when they removed a child from his adoptive rescuers in order to place him in an orphanage. Their testimonies show that together with their pride at having restored the children to their roots, their very success disturbed them deeply. In later years, some of them felt a need to explain their motives and describe the qualms and doubts that gnawed at them. Arye Sarid, the founder of the Koordynacja, wrote:

> There are those who ask me whether it would not have been better to leave the children with their adoptive families and not shatter their tranquility, particularly if coercion was used… And there are some who ask whether I have no pangs of conscience for thrusting these children into a fate of suffering, calamities, and new experiences. The truth is, I admit, that such thoughts did cross my mind. Especially in the complex cases of redeeming children who were lovingly cared for by a Christian family. But at that very moment I lacerated myself for such bursts of weakness. In the final analysis, we are fulfilling the last request of their parents: to leave them descendants. We are ensuring that their child will remain Jewish and not become one of those who attack and murder

Jews. An individual's biological attachment to the Jewish people does not call for an apology. In any event, among the qualms that accompanied the redemption project and which we had to overcome, were those noted above.[95]

Sara Neshamit expressed similar thoughts:

> Sometimes we had serious qualms about whether we had the right to remove a child from the home of his adoptive parents and thrust him into a psychological crisis. It was hard to be a witness to the tears shed by children when they parted with their Christian adopters, in whose home they had been so warmly treated. It was also hard to be a witness to the tears in the eyes of the adoptive mother when she handed over the child she had nurtured. Frequently we were apprehensive about the wrong that we were doing both to the children and to their "parents"... However, the national motive was the decisive factor. We had lost too many Jews, so it was our obligation to restore to our people everyone who survived.[96]

It was in fact Yeshayahu Drucker — who was on a mission for religious Jewry and personally ransomed more children than anyone else — who was heedful of the children's distress. For years afterward he followed their development and their integration difficulties in the Jewish society to which he brought them, and he of all people was left with mixed feelings, to the point of casting doubt on the necessity of the ransom project:

> As this operation ends, I have mixed feelings. We carried out an operation for the good of the nation. We rescued children. And especially after the Holocaust. But for the children themselves, this return to the Jewish fold fomented in many of them a psychological crisis from which I fear they have not recovered to this day... If we consider the matter from the viewpoint of the individual himself, was it worth all the effort? The boy had no idea he was a Jew, and the very knowledge that he was only humiliated him... Had we left him, perhaps he would not have undergone the whole crisis he went through after returning to the fold of Judaism... After all, the child had found his place and his home in a particular family, and the family sometimes loved him more and sometimes less, but he had people to whom he could turn and say "daddy," "mommy"... But

95 Sarid, in *Mission to the Diaspora*, p. 88.
96 Shner-Neshamit, *I Did Not Find Rest*, p. 204.

we came along and removed him and made him a child of the general public... I have often heard these children say: I want to be someone's already; I don't want to be everyone's. From this point of view, we need to think carefully about whether we acted for the good of the children themselves.[97]

---

97 Testimony of Yeshayahu Drucker, YVA, O.3/3249.

CHAPTER ELEVEN

# Back to the Bosom of their People

## The Return to Jewish Identity

T he children's removal from their non-Jewish rescuers was only the first step on the long road to their rehabilitation. The difficulties that arose as they were wrenched from their Christian surroundings foreshadowed the problems they would encounter in trying to recover their Jewish identity. This was, however, a concern that none of those involved in the redemption work seems to have taken into consideration. The folly of their belief that the task would end when the child was reunited with his family or placed in a Jewish children's home soon became apparent. The children were viewed as a national asset, so no effort was spared in trying to bring them fully back into the Jewish fold. The question of how this was to be done in practice arose acutely at the reintegration stage, when it became obvious that the majority of the children did not wish to return to a Jewish way of life or resume their Jewish identity. Parents, relatives, and educators were suddenly faced with a complex web of psychological and educational problems that no one had contemplated. Only now, on the brink of the children's reintroduction into Jewish society, did it become clear that their ordeals in the war since being cut off from their parents meant that a painful and taxing process still lay ahead before they could reconnect psychologically with their origins within the framework of their radically different surroundings.

In most cases, the children had been cut off from a Jewish environment for three to five years. This period, it now became clear, was a long and fateful one in their young lives and had left a powerful, possibly indelible imprint. Compounding the harsh experience of being cut off from their family, most of whose members were murdered, and being left at the mercy of strangers, they had lived in a Christian atmosphere and acquired new habits and concepts. Inevitably, their attitude toward Judaism was profoundly affected, but so too were their relations with the adult world as a whole and particularly with those who had given them refuge. The incontrovertible fact was that after achieving a modicum of stability and peace of mind under the protection of their rescuers, the return to the Jewish fold was yet another shattering experience in their young lives, undermining whatever self-confidence they had acquired. Suddenly they found themselves back in the same Jewish world from which they had barely managed to escape and because of which they had suffered so cruelly. Yet another adjustment to new and unfamiliar conditions was forced upon them. The return to Jewish society frightened and bewildered the children, rendering integration little short of traumatic, and the new caregivers possessed no magic formula to ease the process.

An attempt at understanding what these children went through on their way back to the Jewish world must begin with what they knew and felt at the time of liberation. Their lives were no longer in danger, but they found themselves at a turning point into the unknown. The youngest among them, who were unaware of their true identity or their situation, were malleable. In contrast, those who were eight years old or more at the end of the war and were aware of their Jewish identity, understood that changes were under way and felt troubled and anxious about the future.

Sara Avinun was nine when the war ended (see Chapter Two). She recalls being happy in her adoptive family's home during the first year after the liberation. One day, however, Julia Pilch, her adoptive mother, took her to the headquarters of the Jewish committee in Kraków, where she informed the officials of the girl's existence, related the story of her rescue, and registered her under her true identity. The event shook and bewildered Sara, and left her feeling deeply anxious.

> A strong stench of human sweat mixed with the acrid breath of dozens of people hit us as we entered the dark corridor... People moved through the long passage, occasionally going inside, coming out and then going in again, bumping into each other, an aimless wandering, as if they didn't really know where it was they wanted to go to. Sometimes a door opened and then slammed shut, somebody peeked inside and immediately went out, confused, befuddled, in despair. People sat there, on long benches along the walls, between one locked door and another, half awake, half dozing, waiting for something but not sure what... I think that that most of them were old, but maybe they only looked old. I knew that I must have looked the same only a year and a half before when Julia took me from the orphanage. And how different I was now. Even now everyone said that I looked much older than nine. Did I be-

long to these people? Did I want to belong to them? Their whole appearance screamed of wretched misery, their clothes, their faces, and their incomprehensible speech in which I heard mostly questions. Most of them spoke Yiddish, and that language reminded me of something that I didn't want to remember. Why were we here? What did we have in common with these people? Julia looked so different with her erect stature, her blond hair, her made-up face and her energetic step.[1]

This unexpected encounter with survivors, the need to confess to the official across the table that the name Irena Yablonska, with which she introduced herself, was fictitious and that her real name was Sara Warszawiak, and the testimony taken from her about what befell her family in the war left her feeling fearful about the future. What most troubled Sara was the possibility that one of her relatives should suddenly appear and want to take her away. How would she be able to choose between him or her and her Christian benefactors?

Most of the children whose parents had placed them in the custody of Christian families or in convents waited expectantly for them to return and claim them, but few were fortunate enough to experience this. Yet, even for those whose parents returned, rejoining the family was a difficult process, owing to the deep rift that had formed between children and parents in the war period. The majority of the survivor children had lost one or both parents, and had no one to expect if neither parent had survived and there were no other close relatives to claim them. These children preferred to remain where they were, in a place where they felt secure and fairly tranquil. Having effectively erased their past in the course of the brutal battle for survival, they had no wish to relive it by returning to Jewish society. Their personal experiences, combined with the antisemitism they often absorbed from their rescuers and the surrounding Christian environment, taught them that the catastrophes they had suffered were due to their Jewish origin. Self-preservation therefore dictated keeping their distance from Jews and denying their true identity.

Sara's grandfather, grandmother, and her aunt and uncles had survived as refugees in the Soviet Union. Returning to Poland after the war, they located Sara and were determined to remove her from the custody of the family that had rescued her. One of her uncles, who was still a soldier, placed her in the

---

1   Sara Avinun, *Rising from the Abyss: An Adult's Struggle with Her Trauma as a Child in the Holocaust* (Hod Hasharon: Astrolog, 2005), p. 151.

religious children's home in Zabrze. Again she found herself in an orphanage filled with children scurrying about, but this time the caregivers were not nuns but men and women speaking Yiddish. Again her little braids, which had just begun to grow, were cut off. "Now we will wash your hair. With short hair it will be easier to keep your hair clean of lice," one of the women told her.[2] Within in a few days she seized the first opportunity to escape back to her adoptive family, determined to convert to Christianity and put her Jewish past behind her for good.[3] Her relatives did not give up, and waged a four-year struggle, going to court repeatedly, in order to gain legal custody of Sara.[4] Finally, they abducted her to her grandfather's home and then to Israel.[5] These traumatic events, coming together with the turbulent period of adolescence, shook the degree of self-confidence Sara had acquired in her rescuers' home and caused her profound doubts about her identity and her future.

> I asked myself, Who am I really? Who should I be? Sara? Irena? Marysia? What was more important, the identity that I was born with or what I felt now? And who were my real parents? Those who gave birth to me and were now gone, or those in whose house I lived — who took care of me, looked after me, educated me? Whom did I belong to? Or maybe I didn't belong to anyone? The questions ran within me and I urged them to disappear. Why deliberate over them, I am here, aren't I? I have no other world.[6]

Pola (Hammersfeld) Weinstein was rescued by a Polish family in Warsaw, while her mother survived on the Aryan side in Kraków. She was eleven when the war ended and well aware of her Jewish identity. The family had spoken Yiddish at home, and her grandparents, with whom she was close, were ultra-orthodox. From an early age she had been exposed to Zionist ideas; her father showed her pictures of the Land of Israel and read her Hebrew poetry. Pola, who had Jewish features, also possessed a strong Jewish consciousness. Her war experiences had been highly eventful, but she emerged from life among the Polish population on the Aryan side largely unscathed.[7]

2   Ibid., pp. 158–162.
3   Ibid., pp. 164–168, 181–187.
4   Ibid., pp. 168–170.
5   Ibid., pp. 261–279.
6   Ibid., p. 183.
7   Zvika Dror, ed., *Testimonies of Survival: 96 Personal Interviews with Members of Kibbutz Lohamei Hagetaot*, vol. 3 (Hebrew) (Tel Aviv: Ghetto Fighters' House and Hakibbutz Hameuchad, 1984), pp. 1001–1006.

She followed Christian customs in her rescuers' home but was not baptized and did not attend church because of her Jewish appearance. Nevertheless, she was quite attracted to Christianity and after the war went through an identity crisis in which she spurned Judaism, as she recalled in later testimony:

> I absorbed the Christian spirit, Catholicism, from the atmosphere in the [rescuers'] home. I became an ardent believer... I prayed alone at my bedside. I did not cross myself in public. At first I turned to God in my prayers. God is Jesus. I often asked for father to remain alive. But I felt that he would die. My guardians liked the fact that I was becoming a Christian. It delighted them to feel that they had succeeded in turning a Jewish soul towards Christianity. When the subject of my future came up after the war, they said: "Don't worry, if no one comes to take you, you will always be ours."[8]

Her mother's arrival after the liberation to claim her was not entirely a cause of joy for Pola. "I am no longer used to mother... It bothers me that mother is not a Christian like me. I try to persuade her to convert. Contrary to my custom, during the effort to persuade her I kneel demonstratively next to the bed and cross myself in front of her... I insist on my way and she on hers, and she registers me in a Jewish school that has opened." Her gradual acquisition of a sense of freedom and a shared expectation with her mother for the return of her father drew them closer. However, it was only later, when she met survivors of the death camps and learned of her father's death, that her prayers to Jesus tapered off and she gradually forsook Christianity.[9]

Aliza Penski, who had survived in a convent (see Chapters Six and Ten), was also fortunate to have her mother, who had survived on the Aryan side, arrive to claim her after liberation. As they left the convent, her mother asked, using her name from home, "Alinka, are you happy that now we will always be together again?" "Yes, mother," she replied, "but call me Krysia" — her Christian name — and she asked whether she would be able to pray at home. Giving her a sad look, her mother said only, "Yes, we will talk about it." This reply disturbed her, because she knew she was a Jew and that Jews do not attend church. Like Pola, Aliza too waited in mute expectation for her father to return and found consolation in prayer. She genuflected for hours in the house as she prayed. No one in the family said anything to her about it, but she did not dare ask to attend church. Her mother, who had grown up in a

8   Ibid., pp. 1023–1024.
9   Ibid., pp. 1031–1032.

traditional Jewish home, also kept silent about her Christian customs, but Aliza sensed that this was the calm before the storm. Aliza knew that her mother loved her, but felt that the long period of separation had created a barrier between them. They spoke little. Aliza continued to wait for her father to return, but finally realized she was waiting in vain. She then plucked up the courage to ask her mother if he had been killed because he was a Jew. Her mother nodded that it was so and her eyes welled up with tears. That same day Aliza recalls, she went to pray in church but no longer felt the well-being that had suffused her after praying in the convent. Gradually she forsook Christian worship, a development that was aided by the patience shown by her family, who let time do its work. In later years she explained that her Christian fervor had dissipated after she learned about the death of her father, for whom she had prayed.[10]

Toward the end of the war, Nina Drucker's Polish guardian (see Chapter Two) placed her in a convent. When the war ended, Nina, who was in sixth grade in school, understood that something momentous had occurred, but could not fully fathom how the events might affect her. However, the nun who looked after her and knew her true identity, explained the situation to her and said she should now return to her own people. Nina refused. In later testimony she explained that Christianity and the Polish identity she had acquired gave her a feeling of security, that she had only bad memories of the Jews, and that she felt good among Christians. As her parents had perished, the convent returned her to her Polish guardian who began to search for Nina's relatives; thus Yeshayahu Drucker (no relation) arrived and urged her to accompany him to the children's home in Zabrze. She did not want to go with him, she said in her testimony, because she did not want to relinquish her Christian faith. Finally, with childlike naïvety she decided that, like a missionary, she would go with Drucker and convert the Jews. Nina was among those who adjusted quickly to the conditions in the Jewish children's home, but nevertheless found it wrenching to abandon her Christian belief, which, as it turned out, was saturated with antisemitism. Although she no longer attended church, deep inside she was contemptuous of everything that symbolized Judaism, a repulsion she continued to feel long afterward, as is seen in testimony she gave more than twenty years later:

> I think that a repulsive element in Judaism is the externality of the people... There were unpleasant-looking Jews there... There was one

10  Testimony of Aliza Penski-Chayut, YVA, 0-3/2544.

*shammash* [synagogue attendant] who for me was a repulsive symbol of Judaism. In the Christian religion, irrespective of whether it is positive or negative, all the rituals have an aesthetic appeal. The paintings, the music, the prayers — everything is artistic and well-ordered, and that is impressive. And suddenly the Jews in the synagogue are shouting and there is no harmony in their prayers. That was a crude, repulsive contrast. If I hadn't seen things like that, events might have turned out differently. But for me the Jewish religion that I saw in the synagogue and in the person of the shammash stood for what was ugly in Judaism.[11]

In addition to their recoiling from Jews and things Jewish, some of the children suffered from the trauma of abandonment. A child who had been placed in the custody of a Christian family by parents or other relatives who had then disappeared felt abandoned, even if at some level he understood that they had acted to save him. Moreover, some of the children had been abandoned under harsh conditions, and harbored a lingering resentment toward their family. It is not surprising, then, that after having been given a home and refuge by compassionate Christians and growing accustomed to their new surroundings, they refused to go with relatives who appeared after the war, no matter what inducements they were offered.

Regina Motyl was about seven when she was given shelter by a pious and poor Catholic family, and she stayed with them until the end of the war (see Chapter Two). Her guardians loved her and treated her like their own daughter, even though she says she was not an easy child. She had undergone many ordeals, including abandonment, before reaching the family. Her father sent her and her brother, who was four years older, from their hiding place to find refuge with Christian acquaintances. Their wandering in the icy winter weather in search of shelter is a story of elemental survival. Her brother left her to fend for herself, because she slowed him down, and she never forgave him. After being given shelter by the Catholic family and adjusting to her new surroundings, her only wish was for her whole family to be annihilated without trace and obliterated from memory, so she could embark on a new life as a Christian after being baptized by her guardians. After the war she learned that her brother had survived as a shepherd in a village. Other relatives also appeared, and with Drucker's help took her from her rescuers against her will. Far from feeling close to her brother or her other relatives, Regina hated them for severing her from her benefactors. The relatives found it difficult to

---

11 Testimony of Noa Libes (Nina Drucker), OHD, (68)13.

cope with her, and not wanting to coerce her, they returned her to the Christian family before they left Poland.

In the meantime, her uncle — her father's brother — returned from the Soviet Union and again with Drucker's help, removed her from the guardian family for a second time and placed her in the children's home in Zabrze. She did not integrate well there and tried to escape. For a long time, until she reached France, Regina was considered one of the most difficult girls in the children's home. Years later, when she herself was a mother, she tried to explain her crass antisemitic behavior as a girl:

> I did not want to be a Jewess. The Jews are a filthy, inferior people and I had suffered enough for being Jewish. I became a Christian and was unwilling to return to that [Jewish] people... If the world is built so that Jews have to suffer, and I have the opportunity not to be a Jewess, why go back to Judaism? Maybe a girl like me was also influenced by the stories about the Jews being exploiters and speculators who love money, cheaters who suck the blood of the Christians.[12]

The converted children's adherence to Christianity and abhorrence towards Jews were the major obstacles in restoring them to Jewish society, a situation compounded by their situation as orphans. Most of these children had lost both parents, and their expectation of any relatives was that they would provide them with a warm home and take the place of the dead parents. However, this was rarely the case, and the children were deeply disappointed. What usually transpired was that the relatives — uncles, aunts, perhaps older brothers and sisters — after removing the child from the rescuers' custody (or having that done for them by the Koordynacja or Drucker), took the first opportunity to place him or her in an institution. The children naturally tended to be profoundly hurt by this behavior, which also undermined their faith in adults and hindered their integration into the new society.

At the same time, it must be remembered that in almost every case the relatives themselves were indigent refugees or demobilized soldiers who were in the midst of a difficult process of rehabilitation while seeking to embark on a new life. Most of them wanted only to leave Poland and establish a new family in place of the one that had perished. In these circumstances, they lacked both the forbearance and the economic ability to give their young relatives the warm home for which they craved. However, this objective state of affairs had little effect on the children's feelings: too young to understand their

12 Testimony of Rivka Yisraeli. [(Regina Motyl), (68) 17.

relatives' situation or the shattering experiences they too had endured, the children felt unwanted and became hostile and alienated.

Hanna Mordechowicz was left by her parents with a farm family in return for payment. After the war, distant relatives located her but did not take the trouble to reclaim her, imposing that task on the Koordynacja instead. Its emissaries lured her from the rescuing family with the promise that she would meet her father in Łódź. This placed a tremendous burden on the caregivers in the children's home, who had to cope with Hanna's bitter, inconsolable despair when she discovered that she had been lied to and that her father was no longer alive. Her despair was even greater because her relatives did not visit her in the children's home. The ties between them were severed and Hanna continued to hold a grudge against them for many years. Long afterwards, she acknowledged that she hated them for their behavior, and refused to speak to them even as an adult.[13] Hanna's reaction to the anguish she suffered when her relatives spurned her in her time of need, after she learned that she had been orphaned, was not unusual.

Yosef Sliwa, who also lost both his parents, was removed by relatives from the convent that rescued him and for a time lived with them. However, owing to their dire economic straits and other problems, they lacked the means and the mental fortitude to raise the boy. They placed him in a children's home of the Central Jewish Committee and afterward transferred him to a children's kibbutz, prior to immigration to Israel. They believed that his future would be assured there and that he would have a better life than in Poland. (They themselves remained in Poland but did not fare well.) Despite their good intentions, Yosef never forgave them for placing him in the children's home and not adopting him. In testimony a quarter of a century later, when he himself was a father, he said:

> What they did to me was not right. In my opinion, they should have taken me under their protection after they removed me from the convent and given me a feeling of home, like their son. But they thought differently, and it is possible that they could not handle the situation. I could not forgive them. They were the closest family I had at that time. It was my mother's brother... There were economic reasons and there were personal reasons, and their economic condition was serious. I expected my uncle to take me in and give me the warmth of a home that I lacked all along... When I came to them I had a bad feeling. I was the

13  Testimony of Hanna Hausler (Mordechowicz), OHD, (68) 59.

only survivor from my whole family, and they could have helped with big things and little things, but they did not. That stuck in my memory and it pains me to this day; I cannot forget it.[14]

After the war, Miriam Perlberg, who had lost both parents and was hidden by Poles in return for payment, found herself in a Polish orphanage. A distant relative discovered her whereabouts and moved her to a Jewish children's home. Before leaving Poland, the relative assured Miriam that she would do everything to have her join her in her new home, but she did not keep her promise. In the meantime, Miriam learned, to her surprise, that her uncle — her mother's brother — who lived in Belgium, was sending someone to bring her to Brussels. Miriam arrived at her uncle's home happy and eager. At last a genuinely close family: at last a home, she thought. She wanted her new family to ask her about what she had been through, but instead they questioned her about why she had not returned to the Jewish faith immediately after the liberation but had continued to pose as a Polish girl. Of the reception she encountered in her uncle's home, for which she held out such high expectations, she later wrote with disappointment: "How was I supposed to explain it? How could I say that for me, being a Jewess meant constant exposure to mockery, derision and antisemitic remarks? That to be a Jew meant suffering, persecution, and death?" After all the ordeals she had suffered, she had to listen to her aunt's offensive comments about her unbecoming "Polish" behavior. To make matters worse, shortly afterward her relatives told her that they were placing her in a Jewish children's home; she again became a forsaken orphan.[15]

The orphans who survived in Poland and those who were repatriated from the Soviet Union were housed in the network of children's institutions that were established after the war throughout Poland: in the children's homes of the Central Jewish Committee, the Koordynacja, the religious groups, and the children's kibbutzim of the Zionist youth movements. In practice, the task of rehabilitating the children and restoring to Judaism those who had been baptized, devolved on the educators in these institutions. The majority of the children who went through this educational system afterwards reached Palestine via the Bricha organization and illegal immigration routes and were absorbed into the new country of Israel through Youth Aliyah.

In contrast to the residents of the children's homes of the Koordynacja and at Zabrze, who for the most part had lived with Christian families,[16] the

14  Testimony of Yosef Sliwa, OHD, (68) 48.
15  Perlberg-Shmuel, *This Girl Is Jewish!*, pp. 70–71.
16  Koriski, "The Zionist Koordynacja," p. 260.

composition of the children in the other institutions was not homogeneous. Each child had his own distinctive biography. Some had survived on the Aryan side under an assumed Christian identity, others had hidden in a variety of places or in the forests. From the beginning of 1946, their numbers swelled with the arrival of the repatriates from the Soviet Union. Most of the children who went through these institutions possessed a clear Jewish awareness and had had no association with Christianity; on the contrary, they equated Christianity with the hostile Gentile world which had discriminated against them, persecuted them, and caused them untold suffering. In such circumstances, it was inevitable that the children who continued to follow Christian customs, such as wearing a crucifix, praying, and attending church, would find themselves in confrontation with the others in the institution.

In terms of atmosphere, the children's homes of the Central Jewish Committee were probably the best suited for the children who had had a Christian background. This is because Polish was the dominant language and culture in these institutions, and the educational orientation was secular and assimilationist, the aim being to integrate the children quickly and at any price into the Polish society to which they had become accustomed.[17] The teachers in these institutions did not view with equanimity the fact that some of the children still adhered to Christianity. However, their superiors instructed them that there was "no need to use a hard hand to set them back on the right path." The problem should be dealt with individually, in personal conversations. If the child wished to attend church on Sunday or pray to Jesus in the morning and evening, he should be allowed to do so. The teachers, most of whom were inexperienced and did not know how to deal with problems like this, were particularly cautioned not to shame the children publicly.[18] However, the problem lay not with the educators but with the children who possessed Jewish awareness and were intolerant toward their Christian-influenced peers.

Lena Kuchler, whose children's home in Zakopane (see Chapter Seven) housed a group of girls who survived on the Aryan side and in convents, describes their alienated behavior in the wake of harassment by the older boys, who tore the crucifixes off their necks. Kuchler defended the girls and reprimanded the boys, telling them that the girls must be given freedom and left alone, explaining to them that "it will take them a long time to get over it."[19]

17  Moshe Kol, *Holocaust and Revival* (Hebrew) (Tel Yitzhak: Hamidrasha Haliberalit, 1985), p. 97.
18  Miriam Hochberg (Marianska), Peleg, "I looked after survivor children," pp. 8–9.
19  Kuchler-Silberman, *My 100 Children*, pp. 202–204.

The children's kibbutzim, managed by the youth movements, received a small number of children who clung to Christianity amid a large majority who were repatriated from the Soviet Union and others who had spent the war in forest hiding places, without being compelled to forsake their Jewishness. These institutions followed a Zionist-oriented educational policy, ideologically opposed to the homes run by the Central Jewish Committee. The youth movements aimed to disengage the children from Polish culture and the Diaspora, as part of their preparation for life in Palestine. Thus their curriculum included Hebrew and subjects related to the Land of Israel, combined with folkloristic elements such as Hebrew songs and group dancing. As long as they were on Polish soil, these communal groups were of a largely temporary character, and the children did not attend Polish state schools. Everyone waited eagerly to leave for Eretz Israel.[20] The children communicated amongst themselves in their accustomed languages — Yiddish, Polish, and Russian. Yiddish, the dominant language, grated on the ears of the children who came from an assimilated Polish background, but they had to adjust quickly to the Jewish atmosphere that prevailed in the kibbutzim. Anyone who showed elements of Polish Christianity was the butt of derision, intolerance, and even physical harassment at the hands of those who detested Christians.[21] This small minority in the midst of a proud Jewish majority eventually adjusted to the new Jewish atmosphere and after leaving Poland gradually shed their Christian customs.[22]

The educational orientation of the Koordynacja children's homes was similar to that of the kibbutzim, but because the Koordynacja children were younger, aged thirteen and under, and in many cases had arrived unwillingly from a Christian background, complex and unanticipated educational problems arose. These children needed special treatment to rehabilitate them physically and restore their mental equilibrium before anything could be done in terms of their Jewish identity. Some of them were chronically ill, some suffered from long-neglected skin diseases which required urgent treatment. They had to be liberated from night fears and persecution phobias, and be weaned gradually from their Christian guardians, who missed them and

---

20  On the establishment of the children's kibbutzim in Poland and their distinctive way of life, see: Nessia Orlowicz-Reznik, *Mother, Can I Cry Now?* (Hebrew) (Tel Aviv: Sifriat Poalim, 1964).

21  Ibid., pp. 183-195.

22  Moshe Frank, *To Survive and Testify*, p. 82.

could not easily part with them. Only then could their demonstrative Christian piety be addressed.[23]

As it was clear that the youth movements could not provide the personnel needed to care for these children, the Koordynacja was compelled from the outset to discard some of its declared principles and recruit teachers from outside the movements' ranks. Some lacked formal pedagogical training or knowledge of Judaism, but volunteered to undertake the difficult mission and did so steadfastly.[24] It was mainly the first educators who formulated the educational method in the Koordynacja institutions, learning by trial and error. The best known among them were Chasia Bornstein-Bielicka, Mordechai Binczuk (Bahat), Hela Leneman and Roza Landau.

Chasia Bielicka, who in March 1946 established one of the first two Koordynacja homes in Łódź, was born in Grodno. A Gymnasium graduate, she was a member of Hashomer Hatza'ir from her youth. During the war she was active in the underground with Chaika Grossman in Bialystok, and afterward helped rehabilitate the movement and establish children's kibbutzim, and she also worked with the Bricha organization. She viewed the mission to create the Koordynacja children's home as a challenge and volunteered for it, even though she was not a teacher by profession. In later testimony she explained her motives: "I felt I was getting involved in something difficult, but responsible and close to my heart. I felt a need to help the little children... I remained alone and was lacking a mission, and the children were always close to my heart. In the ghetto, too, I worked with a group of children from the movement. I thought and felt that if I were to devote myself to these children I would be like their mother, and maybe together we would return to life."[25]

Bielicka worked with the children for about a year and a half. A few months after she established the children's home, she accompanied the first group of older Koordynacja children, the Geulim group, on the Bricha route to Germany and the DP camps. From there, still led by Bielicka, they reached Palestine with the illegal immigration organization, and were then interned by the British in Cyprus. Finally, in August 1947, they arrived in Kibbutz Gan Shmuel. Bielicka was replaced in Poland by Mordechai Bahat, another Hashomer Hatza'ir activist.

23  Neshamit, "Coordinating Child Rescue," pp. 117, 121, 141.
24  David Shirman, "Management of Homes for Redeemed Children," in Shmuel Bornstein, ed., *Studies in the Redemption of Jewish Children from Christians in Poland after the Holocaust* (Hebrew) (Ghetto Fighters' House, 1989, pp. 39–46).
25  Testimony of Chasia Bornstein-Bielicka, OHD, (68)26.

Bahat, who was born in Nieśwież, White Russia, had a movement background similar to Bielicka's; unlike her, however, he spent the war years deep inside the Soviet Union, where he was able to study in a Russian pedagogical institute which had been evacuated from besieged Leningrad. Repatriated to Poland in the summer of 1946, he immediately became active in the Hashomer Hatza'ir movement. With his pedagogical training he was assigned to work with the Koordynacja children and accepted the task without being aware of its implications. In later testimony he said, "The problems that arose in this work were new to me. I was familiar with a different type of education: movement education, school education, but what I encountered resembled neither. When I reached the Koordynacja in Łódź, the pattern was already set."[26] Like Bielicka, Bahat spent a lengthy period with the Koordynacja children. At the end of 1946, he and Yaakov Gissis led a group of about eighty of them from Poland to France, remaining with them for about two years. Bahat looked after the younger children, Gissis the older ones. In September 1948, at the height of the War of Independence, the two brought the group to Israel and placed them in the care of Youth Aliyah.

The director and chief educator of the second Koordynacja children's home in Łódź, which was intended primarily for very young children, was Hela Leneman. She established the home and worked in it for a considerable period, aided by the teachers Susanna Shor and Cyla Kaminska. All three had previous educational experience in orphanages in the Soviet Union and in children's kibbutzim in Poland. However, their work with the Koordynacja children posed a very different pedagogic challenge. Baruch Kaplinsky, the only Youth Aliyah emissary then in Poland, paid frequent visits to the Koordynacja children's homes and discerned the singular educational problems faced by the teaching staff, but was unable to help. In a report to his superiors he wrote: "A very difficult problem exists there, of redeemed Catholics and antisemites. There are children who rush outside and call out loudly: 'Catholics help, the Jews want to take us to Palestine.' This is a difficult problem to solve. To that end an Educator with a capital E is needed."[27]

In addition to caring for the children physically, the staff had to overcome their alienation and mistrust of adults, as well as find practical methods to enhance their Jewish identity. As we saw, many of the children were brought to the homes against their will, by deception and enticement. Child-

26　Testimony of Mordechai Bahat, OHD, (68)20.
27　B. Kaplinsky, Report on Visit to Children's Homes in Poland, February 10, 1947, CZA, S75/1760.

ren in the Koordynacja homes frequently tried to escape back to their Christian guardians, perhaps abetted by the rescuing family; some of the escapees were never found again. Children who had become attached to the Christian family that had rescued them, expected visits from them in the children's home, and when these failed to materialize felt betrayed and broke into fits of crying. The children who arrived from convents were generally disciplined, but in a submissive manner manifested in passive behavior and a tendency to form insular groups with other convent children. They found it very difficult to interact with children from a different background and some of them at first had altogether no idea what they were doing among Jews.[28]

In large measure, the children's demonstrative adherence to the Christian faith and its rituals reflected their refusal to accept their severance from a world in which they had felt secure. Accordingly, this was not the educators' primary concern as they tried to help the children's integrate into their new surroundings. The overriding problem, which necessarily preceded any attempt to restore their Jewish identity, was how to win their trust. Bielicka describes the situation:

> Entering the girls' room one evening, I saw that they were all kneeling and praying. It was a moving sight. I asked them to go to sleep and decided to talk to them, but not that evening. I did not study child psychology, but I had intuition. I had two types of children. There were those who did not believe in anything, not in people and not in God. It was extremely difficult to restore their belief and their love. They were in despair. However, I did find the way to the heart of the children who believed in something. I understood that if I deprived them of what they believed in, I would only break their spirit and not strengthen them.[29]

On this issue, Mordechai Bahat adds: "My goal was to gain the children's trust. Often I made a pact with them and said to them that I always tell the truth, and the children tested me quite often. By this means I wanted to advance to the real goal of their reeducation. They experienced a crisis of trust toward adults after having experienced the worst in life. I did not argue with them about matters of faith before acquiring their trust. I held back, even though it upset me very much."[30]

28  Testimony of Chasia Bornstien-Bielicka, (68)26.
29  Ibid.
30  Testimony of Mordechai Bahat, OHD, (68)20a.

The children's complex problems demanded a personal approach, with minute attention paid to each child to address his particular needs. However, this was not always possible in the circumstances, with teachers often having to deal simultaneously with dozens of children. In extreme cases, children who resisted entry into a home were usually placed with foster families in the initial stage, where they received more attention and domestic warmth, before being brought to the children's home. Still, these were exceptional cases.[31] The educational staff discerned the children's sensitivities and took note of their special problems, but found it difficult to impart an atmosphere of security and stability, not only owing to their lack of experience but also because of the constant arrival of new children and the chronic shortage of teachers. The few educators in the Koordynacja framework had to make a supreme effort of devotion to the children under impossible conditions. Bahat, then unmarried and in his early thirties, describes his experience in the first period:

> I went to sleep late after a strenuous day of work and felt as though the whole world was spinning around me. I was not sure I could go on. The work hours were unlimited and you had to forgo a private life. We were volunteer counselors and worked without pay. We received only pocket money, which was barely enough for occasionally going out. We were given food and lodging at the site. One of the conditions was that we had to live in the home.[32]

Bielicka, who was also unmarried at the time, provides a similar account: "Our family grew, and when a new child arrived, the door would be shut. The children became despondent. I had to give all my time to the new children and neglect the group as a whole to some extent. Barely would I finish cracking one hard nut when two others appeared in his place."[33]

In addition to each child's specific problems, there were large age disparities between them. Most of the children under Bielicka's care were seven to twelve years old, but some were of kindergarten age. As the only teacher for a group of dozens of children, she decided intuitively to divide them into mixed groups of different ages and have the older children look after the younger ones, like brothers and sisters in a large family. She was then able to devote more time to the particularly problematic children, who needed

31 Arye Sarid, in *Mission to the Diaspora*, pp. 90–91.
32 Testimony of Mordechai Bahat, OHD, (68)20a.
33 Chasia Bornstein-Bielicka, "Returning to the Bosom of their Nation," in Dror Levy, ed., *Book of Hashomer Hatza'ir*, vol. II, p. 322.

more attention.[34] The age gap remained large even after the children's homes were institutionalized, but efforts were made to meet everyone's educational needs. A year after the home established by Bielicka opened, and after it had already sent six groups to Palestine, twenty-five children were still living in the facility, divided almost equally into elementary school and kindergarten age. A few of the older children attended the city's Hebrew school, while others received private lessons in the home. The younger children attended a kindergarten in the home itself. Seven girls looked after this small group, four of them as teachers. Roza Landau, an experienced teacher, managed the home and was the educator of the older children. The kindergarten group was under the care of Dr. Claudia Kirzner, a physician, who was assisted by Sima Bek and Jadwiga Dek. Despite the overcrowding — the home had only six rooms, and shabby furniture — the staff worked hard to bring about integration among the children and create a pleasant atmosphere.[35]

Weaning a child from his Christian faith and customs was a protracted process, not to be undertaken until he had adjusted to his new home. Antisemitic outbursts at moments of crisis by children who had been converted made it clear that this was a highly sensitive issue that required time and patience. Yet probably no one at the time fully grasped how deeply their Christian education had become imprinted on these children, and consequently how much time would be needed to erase it. It should be stressed that the Koordynacja from the outset adopted a tolerant educational approach and the teaching staff was at pains to avoid angry confrontations with the children over their Christian beliefs. No attempt was made to remove the crucifixes the children wore, and they were allowed to pray quietly without being mocked. The teachers addressed the situation sensitively, offering the children alternatives to Christianity.[36] Bahat describes the essence of the educational activity in the Koordynacja children's homes:

> The educational line was Zionist-pioneering. The activities were conducted in the style of the youth movements and included learning Hebrew songs, talks about the Land of Israel, scout activities, parades, workshops, handicrafts, and Israeli dances. The most fruitful talks took place in the evenings in small groups, in which the children talked about what they endured in the Holocaust. Their harsh life experience left them

---

34 Testimony of Chasia Bornstein-Bielicka, OHD, (68)26.
35 B. Kaplinsky, Report on Visit to Koordynacja House in Łódź, March 31, 1947, CZA, S75/1760.
36 Neshamit, "Coordinating Child Rescue," p. 139.

very suspicious. In an effort to gain their trust, we tried to tell them the truth and avoided making promises that would be hard to keep. In the ceremony of welcoming the Sabbath we had them dress festively and we lit candles, served a festive meal, and sang Shabbat songs.[37]

In practice, this approach turned out to be too rational to produce the hoped-for results quickly, as Bahat himself acknowledges:

It was very difficult to remove from their hearts and minds what they had absorbed during the period of the war against the Jews. Most of them did not want to be Jews, yet found that some people wanted to send them by force to a land with which they had no connection. They wore crucifixes and continued to genuflect in prayer every evening. As non-religious people, we found this difficult to cope with. They were attracted to the Christian religious rites. The main problem of the Koordynacja home was to educate the children in Judaism and to settle in the Land of Israel. That was a difficult task and on many occasions we despaired of achieving the goal. Our approach was difficult, because we could not offer them anything religious in place of Jesus. This lasted a year, two years, and more.[38]

In their efforts to restore the children's Jewish identity the educators did not flinch from delving into their past. At moments of crisis they took them aside and got them to talk about their parents in order to stimulate identification with them, in the hope that they would want to follow in their footsteps as Jews. Even though education in the Koordynacja children's homes was basically secular, traditional Jewish holidays were observed, with special emphasis on Passover and Hanukkah, and the children took part in preparing the celebrations. However, the results were not always positive. In the holiday-eve gatherings, the sight of the candles sometimes generated negative emotional reactions. Thus, some children came to the first Passover *seder* still wearing a crucifix around their necks, and at the sight of the matza and the wine some of them burst into tears and refused to touch the matza, which they had been told was made with the blood of Christians.[39] On the other hand, the Hanukkah celebrations evoked, at least for some of the children, happy memories from home. Bahat describes the Hanukkah festival at a Koordynacja home:

37  Mordechai Bahat, "Redeemed Children on their Way to Israel," in Shmuel Bornstein, ed., *Studies in the Redemption of Jewish Children*, p. 96.
38  Testimony of Mordechai Bahat, OHD, (68)20a.
39  Testimony of Leibel Koriski, OHD, (68)15a.

The preparations began two weeks before the holiday. The party was held in the presence of all the members of the Koordynacja director-ate and the rescuers who worked in the field... After the candle-light-ing ceremony the children put on a play about the Maccabees and the Hanukkah miracle. Finally we all danced together, the children, their [Jewish] rescuers, and the members of the directorate. After the party a few children came up to me and admitted that the evening had brought back memories of the holiday at home, and they acknowledged their Jewishness.[40]

Bielicka did not try to destroy the children's Christian faith, but to super-impose a different faith upon it. "Because I was not religious," she said in testimony years later, "I could not get them to believe in God, so I got them to believe in good people; and instead of believing in Jesus, brought them gradually to belief in the Land of Israel and the Jewish people."[41] But when she was about to leave Poland with her wards, she found that they were by no means mentally prepared for this move. On the eve of their departure she assembled them to inform them of their imminent journey and asked them to pack their things. The children were appalled. Some burst into tears and asked to go back to their Polish rescuers; the convent children begged to be returned to the convents, and prayed quietly. Bielicka paints a grim picture of the atmosphere:

It was a hard evening. The children did not fall asleep in bed after lights out. I heard choked crying from the beds. I knew that in the morning I would face a serious problem on the way to the train. I cannot forget that evening, how each child sat on his bed with his little bundle of sou-venirs. This one had a photograph of the *goya* [Gentile woman], another had a chain with a crucifix, a third had a keepsake of some kind that he received as a farewell gift from someone dear to him. Each of them packed his souvenirs. It was a moment of extraordinary emotion, part-ing with every rag that reminded them of the ties, and the farewell from the Gentiles.[42]

Sara Neshamit, who escorted a convoy of Koordynacja children to the border on the way to Palestine, recalls her parting from one of the "antisemitic" girls,

40 Mordechai Bahat, "Redeemed Children on their Way to Israel," p. 96.
41 Testimony of Chasia Bornstein-Bielicka, OHD, (68)26.
42 Ibid.

316 • *At the Mercy of Strangers*

who had become attached to her: "She took a picture of the Holy Mother out of her bra and handed it to me, saying: We are parting, but I want you to know that I will remain a Christian, because the Holy Mother saved my life. But you were good to me, so please accept this image from me."[43]

The educational method adopted toward the "Christian" children in the Zabrze home was basically the same as in the Koordynacja institutions. This was somewhat surprising, given the disagreement between the religious groups and the secular Zionist youth movements over the question of religious education for the survivor children — the dispute which had kept the Mizrahi movement out of the Koordynacja.[44] In practice, though, there was little difference between the education received by the Koordynacja children and the children who were under the protection of the religious groups. Indeed, although the rabbis of the Committee of Religious Communities insisted on a strictly orthodox way of life at the Zabrze facility, the atmosphere there was actually quite liberal. Girls and boys were not separated and the boys were not made to wear *kipot* (skull caps.) The pedagogic line at Zabrze was laid down by Nehama Geller, herself non-religious, although she appreciated that the children should receive a traditional education. Pedagogically, she was opposed to the idea of demanding that the children observe all the religious precepts, not least because of their exposure to Christianity. Drucker, who was an influential figure at Zabrze, was not especially religious either, even though he was a military chaplain, and he relied completely on Geller's judgment and supported her approach.[45] Not all the rest of the staff, including the teachers, were observant Jews. Some of those who were religious, such as David Hubel, tried to draw the children toward Jewish tradition, but others were far from observant.

The education at Zabrze was Zionist-traditionalist, manifested primarily by Sabbath observance. The boys attended synagogue, and on Sabbath eve the children and teaching staff gathered for the traditional meal around a table on which a white tablecloth was laid. Hubel recited the blessing over the wine without insisting that the children wear a head covering. The idea was to follow a traditional way of life in order to evoke in the children memories of the parental home and so return them to their roots. David Danieli (see Chapter Two), who was a ward in the Zabrze institution, describes the renewed encounter with his Jewish heritage:

---

43  Neshamit, "Coordinating Child Rescue," pp. 140–141.
44  Testimony of Yeshayahu Drucker, OHD, (68)28a.
45  Testimony of Yeshayahu Drucker, OHD, (68)28a, c.

On the eve of the Sabbath, I remembered Shabbat as it was at home. I looked at the two flames of the candles and it was as though I was hypnotized. And I was considered the toughest boy in the institution. I never cried. I remember my eyes growing misty, then getting up from the table and going to my room, where I burst into tears. I have to say, to Hubel's credit, that he did not rush after me and did not try to calm me down. I cried for about two hours and got up a different person. I had cast off some hidden burden, and after that everything felt good.[46]

On Shabbat, children and teachers ate together around fully-set tables and food was served that reminded them of home. For holidays they were given new clothes, and by such means were gradually drawn closer to Judaism. Drucker, who spent Sabbaths and holidays in the children's home, took his meals with the children and told them stories of Jewish life, creating a family atmosphere.[47]

The major emphasis was on Zionist rather than religious education. The home was decorated with national flags, and in addition to the religious holidays, important dates in Zionist history — such as the birthday of Theodor Herzl, the founder of political Zionism, and of the national poet Hayim Nachman Bialik — were also marked, and accompanied by performances. Here, too, as in secular Zionist homes, the children learned Hebrew and the geography of Israel. But zealousness for the Land of Israel was not as intense at Zabrze as in the Koordynacja institutions, because of Zabrze's ties with *Haredi* (ultra-orthodox) circles. As we saw (Chapter Nine), Rabbi Solomon Schonfeld from Britain supported the Zabrze facility, and had the cooperation of those in charge of the facility. They did his bidding when he arranged for children to be sent to religious families and institutions in Britain instead of Palestine.[48]

As in the Koordynacja institutions, the children at Zabrze were also weaned from Christianity slowly, cautiously, and without rancor. One of the "antisemitic" girls who clung to Christianity later noted that until she left Poland she was repelled by the sight of orthodox Jews with side curls and wearing long black clothing. Only after reaching France did she begin gradually to shed her antisemitic ideas and her Christian beliefs.[49] Kaplinsky, the Youth Aliyah emissary who visited the Zabrze home, was amazed at Nehama

46 Testimony of David Danieli. OHD, (68)53.
47 Testimony of Noa Libes (Nina Drucker), OHD(68)13.
48 Testimony of Yeshayahu Drucker, OHD, (68)28b.
49 Testimony of Rivka Yisraeli (Regina Motyl), OHD, (68)17.

Geller's educational achievements and noted in his report her special method to restore the children to Judaism. "She believes that without Zionism it is impossible to restore the children to the bosom of their nation. Instead of the Catholic deity she has to give the children a different deity to believe in. That other deity is Zionism." [50]

## On the Way to Eretz Israel

The great exodus of Jews from Poland began in the spring of 1946 and was accelerated following the Kielce pogrom on July 4 of that year. The children's kibbutzim of the youth movements, including the Koordynacja children and those at Zabrze, were the first to leave, having been accorded the highest priority. At the end of May, a first group of Koordynacja children and a few children's kibbutzim set out for Germany on Bricha routes.[51] In August 1946, a group of children and youth from the Zabrze institution left for France on the train organized by Rabbi Herzog (see Chapter Eight).[52] In September, Akiva Levinsky of Youth Aliyah in Europe arrived in Poland with the "Plan of the Two Thousand," which aimed to bring 2,000 children to France using visas provided by the French government. The organization's original plan had been to take the children to France as a last transit point before they went on to Palestine. France was then an important center both of Zionist activity and for the illegal immigration movement. It was from French ports that the large immigrant ships set sail, carrying thousands of children within the Youth Aliyah framework. Explaining the plan to the leaders of the Zionist youth movements in Poland, Levinsky said:

> We want our children to arrive in France legally, both psychologically and politically. France is the land of liberty, and we will be able to get along well there… Each movement will have its own home. We will establish Hebrew schools and joint workshops for all the movements. To implement the plan we need teachers, counselors, and [administrative] personnel. It may be that there are no longer two thousand children in

50  B. Kaplinsky, Report on Visit to Children's Homes in Poland, February 10, 1947, CZA, S75/1760.
51  Shlamek, Leaving Poland (letter from Poland to Germany), June 5, 1946, Hashomer Hatzair Archives (HHA), (2)30.2.
52  Goldshlag, *Rescue Mission*, pp. 80–81.

the movements. We will try to exert influence on the CJC [Central Jewish Committee]. No time must be lost.[53]

With the flight of the Jews from Poland in the wake of the Kielce pogrom, the youth movement leaders, in coordination with the Bricha organization, decided not to wait for the formal finalization of the arrangements to take the children out legally, as was requested by Youth Aliyah. Instead, they moved most of the children under their care to Germany on the Bricha routes, while only about 1,200 of them reached France in 1946–1947.[54]

The majority of the Koordynacja children were taken to DP camps in Germany. Toward the end of 1946, when Youth Aliyah began to organize special homes, most of them were moved to the Dornstadt camp, which was one of the twelve children's centers in the American Occupation Zone.[55] Only a fraction of the children, about eighty, reached France in the "Plan of the Two Thousand" project, and were initially housed in an ancient castle, Mont St. Anne, near Limoges in the south of the country.[56] In contrast, nearly all the Zabrze children were sent to France, where most of them were accommodated in two temporary children's homes established by Hapoel Hamizrahi. One was in Strasbourg, under the management of Meir Weissblum, the other near by in Schirmeck, under Y. Spinger, both of them Hamizrahi movement activists who had worked to restore children to Judaism in Poland and arrived in France together with their wards.[57]

Most of the Koordynacja children whose parents were still living were reunited with them in Germany, leaving mainly the orphans in the temporary homes. Of the 450 Koordynacja children who arrived in Dornstadt at the end of 1946, about 300 were still there six months later.[58]

---

53 Minutes of meeting with Akiva Levinsky in Łódź, September 21, 1946, CZA, S75/1760.
54 According to a Bricha report of April 3, 1947, the organization removed 7,000 children from Poland in the period from July 1945 to the beginning of 1947. Most of them were taken to DP camps in Germany. See Cohen, *Operation "Bricha,"* p. 469, Appendix XI; on the removal of the children from Poland, see also: Meta Planter, Polish Children's Project, March/April 1947, CZA, S26/1317; B. Kaplinsky report on Poland, *Pages — Europe* (Hebrew), Youth Aliyah Bureau, Jerusalem, [Summer 1947], CZA, 984.
55 Michael Zelinger, Problems of the Children and Youth, November 13, 1946 (Hebrew), CZA, S75/4655.
56 Testimony of Mordechai Bahat, OHD, (68)20b; Bahat, "Redeemed Children on their Way to Israel," p. 97.
57 Kalman Binyamini to Youth Aliyah Bureau, Jerusalem, [Summer 1947], CZA, S75/1903.
58 Michael Deshe, "The Koordynacja Camp in Dornstadt," *Diary of a Jewish Agency Delegation* 4 (Hebrew), April 8, 1947, Haganah Archives, 32/114.

320 • *At the Mercy of Strangers*

All the children and adolescents organized in the youth movements were placed under the supervision of Youth Aliyah, and were to be integrated into the land-settlement movement in Palestine. However, the Koordynacja children, who were not affiliated with any movement, posed a problem for Youth Aliyah. Unlike the children's kibbutzim, which were identified with specific youth movements, the Koordynacja was an anomalous body, and precisely because so many different movements were involved in its creation, the end result was that the Koordynacja children bound for Palestine were without movement "parents."

In the politicized situation of the time, when movement affiliation was a defining factor, the Koordynacja children could not remain for long in such a vacuum. The struggle for their souls was already being waged behind the scenes when preparations were under way to leave Poland. The representatives of the various movements on the Koordynacja directorate knew that the children would follow their madrichim — their group leaders — so each movement tried to ensure that its personnel would accompany the children. As the first group prepared to leave for Germany, representatives of Mapai (the dominant party in Palestine) and of the youth movement Hanoar Hatzioni on the Koordynacja directorate, tried to prevent Chasia Bielicka, a Hashomer Hatza'ir activist, from escorting the children. However, Hashomer Hatza'ir, which had assigned its best people to the Koordynacja homes, balked at this and insisted that Bielicka, the founder of the first Koordynacja children's home, lead the first group bound for Palestine. In the end, a madrich from Hanoar Hatzioni, Yonas Guler, also joined Bielicka as the group's co-leader.[59] This pattern was repeated six months later, when Mordechai Bahat, who was chosen to lead his group to France, was joined by Yaakov Gissis from Noham (Noar Halutzi Meuhad), another Mapai-affiliated youth movement.[60]

To regularize the anomalous situation of the Koordynacja in the organizational structure of Youth Aliyah, the latter's emissaries in Germany formed an ad hoc committee consisting of representatives of the Koordynacja movements — Dror, Noham, Hashomer Hatza'ir, and Hanoar Hatzioni — and two of its own senior officials. Its task was to deal with the problems of the Koordynacja children on their way to Palestine.[61]

---

59  Testimony of Chasia Borenstein-Bielicka, OHD, (68)26, see also: Michael Deshe to David Omansky, April 24, 1947, CZA, S75/1907.
60  Testimony of Mordechai Bahat, OHD, (68)20b.
61  Michael Zelinger, Problems of the Children and Youth, November 13, 1946, CZA, S75/4655.

The children at Dornstadt were under the care of three Youth Aliyah emissaries — the poets Michael Deshe and Anda Pinkerfeld-Amir, and Ruth Allon, the wife of Yigal Allon, the commander of the Palmah — the commando force of the Haganah (later an Israeli deputy prime minister) — who empathized with the children's distinctive problems. They also approved of the Koordynacja inter-movement framework and did all they could to preserve it, even though, understanding the realities of the Yishuv and its methods of integrating newcomers, they had doubts about its future. In April 1947, after the first eighty children had set sail on the illegal immigrant ship "Theodor Herzl," Deshe wrote to David Omansky, a key Youth Aliyah activist in Palestine:

> The Koordynacja, which you have undoubtedly heard about, is a kind of commercial agreement between four "firms," meaning youth movements, to keep the redeemed (ransomed) children from Poland together. This agreement is not all that clear and detailed. For example: until when, and where, will the children be kept together — only until their maturity, or will they also create joint projects? Many questions with no answers. As long as the children were in a [DP] camp in Germany, these questions were not very meaningful… Of course, below the surface the madrichim, willingly or perhaps also not so willingly, steered their education according to their movement ideology… Many of these groups have already decided to make their way to Hashomer Hatza'ir kibbutzim. Well, our privileged moment came, too, and we sent the first group to Eretz Israel. That group is now, we believe, in Cyprus… It is headed by Chasia Bielicka from Hashomer Hatza'ir, an excellent madricha who has a great influence on the children, and Yonas Guler from Hanoar Hatzioni. Before their departure the two promised us that they would do everything possible to preserve the group's integrity and that in the Yishuv they would become a Koordynacja *garin* [nucleus group] that would settle in the Land of Israel. At the farewell event the children, too, promised solemnly to remain together and establish a joint [land-settlement] enterprise to be called "Olelot" — the name of the children's home in Germany. Nevertheless, I am deeply concerned about the fate of this group. Even an inkling of a split could cause the disintegration of the whole group. If that happens, everyone will then blame everyone else for the bad beginning, and everyone will plead righteousness. Accordingly, I request that you concern yourself about the group's fate even before it arrives in the country.[62]

62  Michael Deshe to David Omansky, April 24, 1947, CZA, S75/1907.

Omansky, a member of Kvutzat Geva and the representative of Hever Hakvut-zot, a land-settlement movement affiliated with Mapai in Youth Aliyah, was no stranger to the integration process of young people. In his reply he reminded Deshe of the Palestinian reality:

> In your letter to me you touched on one of the questions that has no solution in the Yishuv. We are well aware of the existence of the Koordynacja from Poland... But we are also aware that the Koordynacja children have not stayed the course in other places, and are even less likely to do so here... Apparently you have somewhat forgotten the situation here. If it is still possible for Hanoar Hatzioni and Hashomer Hatza'ir to be part of the same institution overseas, that is absolutely out of the question in the Yishuv, even if the children themselves should wish it to be so. After all, what are the places of [immigrant] absorption? Do they not belong to the various land-settlement streams? And do the absorption institutions not belong to the different streams? Clearly, no movement will agree to its members being educated in a different movement... And what movement here will forgo its members? Regrettably, your demand-request is unrealistic and cannot be realized.[63]

The fate of the Koordynacja was actually sealed even before the children reached Palestine. The final stage of the struggle over movement affiliation began with the arrival of the first group at the youth villages in the British detention camps in Cyprus. Amid the prevailing gloomy atmosphere, Bielicka decided to put the issue to the senior Youth Aliyah officials there — Hanoch Reinhold (Rinott), the director of the Youth Village, and Hans Beith, the head of Youth Aliyah, who was then visiting the Cyprus camps. In the circumstances, the decision was to eliminate the Koordynacja framework in the Cyprus camps and allow each child to join the movement of his choice. Most of the children decided to join Hashomer Hatza'ir.[64]

The story of the Koordynacja in Germany was repeated in France, with various movements, including Hamzrahi, trying to gain control of the children. Joseph Burg (later an Israeli cabinet minister), who was then an emissary in France for Hamizrahi, demanded that Youth Aliyah not wait for the children from Poland to reach Palestine, but begin already in France to classify them according to their home religious background in order to determine whether they should be directed to secular or religious education. In

---

63  Michael Omansky to Michael Eisenstadt (Deshe), May 13, 1947, CZA, S75/4655.
64  Bornstein-Bielicka, "Returning to the Bosom of their Nation," pp. 342–343.

this connection, Burg wrote to Akiva Levinsky: "We think the Koordynacja children should also be classified... As you know, the Koordynacja homes are not party-based or wholly non-religious. Even though Hamizrahi in Poland terminated its cooperation with the Koordynacja for political reasons at a certain time, there are a large number of children with a definite religious background in the Koordynacja groups, and it is thus urgent to classify them."[65]

In the end, the Koordynacja children remained without a supportive movement in their rigid and zealous movement-dominated temporary homes in France. At first the personnel who arrived with them from Poland had to look after them by themselves in an unfamiliar environment. Like the youth movement homes, the Koordynacja children's homes in France were under the supervision of the Youth Aliyah office in Paris, but as they were hundreds of kilometers from the capital, Youth Aliyah officials visited them only infrequently and the organization provided only meager assistance. At the end of 1947, a Youth Aliyah official in France tried to move the Koordynacja children to Pouges-les-Eaux, closer to the center of the country, where the Noham movement's children's home was located, with the aim of unifying the two groups. The initiative failed, both because the leader of the Koordynacja group, Mordechai Bahat, vehemently opposed it and because the children, too, objected to the plan and resisted it fiercely. An attempt to transfer Bahat to a Hashomer Hatza'ir children's home was also unsuccessful.[66] The official who was apparently behind this move, Yohanan Gertner, a senior Youth Aliyah emissary in France, had not been enthusiastic about the Koordynacja from the outset. In a report to Youth Aliyah headquarters in Palestine about the movement-run children's homes in France, he added the following: "I don't know whether you have detailed information about the Koordynacja matter. The idea is undoubtedly worthy, but little remains of the initial good intentions. In the meantime, every movement is thinking about the most appropriate methods to win over the Koordynacja children. And the bad intentions on all sides [are] in the meantime the main reason that this body is still in existence."[67]

The Koordynacja framework in France lasted until the children immigrated to Israel in 1948. Bahat and Gissis then placed them in the hands of

---

65  Joseph Burg and Aharon Becker to Akiva Levinsky, February 27, 1947, CZA, S75/1902.
66  Testimony of Mordechai Bahat, OHD, (68)20b.
67  Hans [Yohanan] Gertner to Youth Aliyah Department, Jerusalem, March 24, 1947, CZA, S75/1902.

Youth Aliyah, which disbanded the group and classified the children by age. Those aged fourteen and under were sent to the Ben Shemen Youth Village, and the older children were given the choice of joining a *hevrat noar* (youth community) in either Kibbutz Merhavia or Kibbutz Ein Harod.[68]

## Integrating the Children into Israeli Society

A useful parameter for assessing the Christian-influenced children's acceptance of their Jewish identity and their integration into the new surroundings is their evolving attitude toward Christian symbols. The children's severance from Poland and its culture, and their mingling with a large body of children having a clear Jewish awareness, was undoubtedly a major factor in loosening their attachment to Polish culture and to Christianity, but was not in itself definitive. They continued to speak Polish for a long time afterward, though, like the other children, they also willingly learned Hebrew. Externally, they were indistinguishable from the others, both in their behavior and in terms of the Zionist spirit inculcated in them by the madrichim, and they looked forward eagerly to moving to Palestine.[69] Nevertheless, there was something palpably different about them, manifested, for example, in their desparate clinging to their Christian names. After Chasia Bielicka's group had been in Germany for nearly a year, had become assimilated among children with a different background, and appeared to accept their Jewish identity, Bielicka tried to change their Polish names for Hebrew ones. After persuading them to make the change, she held a special ceremony, and the children threw a scroll containing their Polish names into a bonfire. However, the attempt ultimately failed because some children had objected to the idea all along and many of them afterward reverted to their Polish name.[70]

The children's insistence on retaining their Polish name and their rejection of a Hebrew name — which in some cases at least, was actually their original name from home — underscores the potency of their emotional bond with their Christian past and their continuing recoil from Judaism. Despite their longing for the Land of Israel and their readiness to endure the trials of illegal immigration, inwardly they were still caught up in their past.

68  Testimony of Mordechai Bahat, OHD, (68)20b.
69  Michael Deshe, "The Koordynacja Camp in Dornstadt, *Diary of Jewish Agency Delegation 4*, April 8, 1947, Hagana Archives, 32/114.
70  Testimony of Chasia Bornstein-Bielicka, OHD, (68) 26.

Bielicka constantly sought ways to free them from this trauma. In Cyprus she organized a collective project to compile a pamphlet of memoirs. The children were asked to write about their experiences in the war and afterward, until their internment in Cyprus. The response was enthusiastic. Nearly all of them, including the most reticent and introverted, wrote down their story in an effort to unburden themselves of the harsh memories and oppressive feelings.[71]

The girls' changing attitude toward their crucifixes is a story in its own right. In the children's homes in Poland they had worn the crucifixes with pride. After leaving Poland and integrating with other children they still wore them, but now hidden under their blouses. Their difficulty in parting with this ultimate symbol of their attachment to Christianity is illustrated by the story of a group of girls who survived in convents and were taken from Łódź to the children's home in Blankenese in the British Zone of Occupation in Germany. Here they were under the charge of the educator Hanna Dichter, who was aware of their past. In an effort to draw them closer to the Jewish world, she told them in personal conversations that while their parents had placed them in a convent to ensure their survival, in their hearts they had prayed that after the war they would return to being daughters of the Jewish people. After she won their confidence, the girls asked her privately what to do with their crucifixes. She suggested that they collect them in a box and give them to a priest in Nazareth after their arrival in Palestine. The girls removed the crucifixes and placed them in a box, but not before crossing themselves.[72]

As we saw, the majority of the youngsters who went through the children's institutions were placed under the supervision of Youth Aliyah in Palestine. The obvious question in this regard is how much the Youth Aliyah staff — which at the time was the most experienced and best organized mechanism for integrating and educating Diaspora youth — knew about the special problems of the children with a Christian background and whether they were properly prepared to receive them. Their comments, as quoted in previous chapters, make it clear that the officials in charge of bringing the children to Palestine and seeing to their integration knew about the difficulties that had been involved in their removal from their non-Jewish rescuers. However, neither the senior educators of Youth Aliyah, who met the children on their

---

71 Bornstein-Bielicka, "Returning to the Bosom of their Nation," p. 344; "Geulim" group pamphlet, Kibbutz Gan Shmuel Archive.

72 Yitzhak Tadmor, ed., *The Cherries on the Elbe: The Story of the Children's Home in Blankenese* (Hebrew) (Givat Haviva: Yad Yaari, 1996), p. 90.

way to Palestine, nor the emissaries who worked with them, fully grasped the psychological hurdles faced by these children.

The emissaries of Youth Aliyah and of the land-settlement movements who met the children in Poland and in the DP camps amid the large stream of children making their way to Palestine, were mainly occupied with administering the education and welfare systems in the DP camps and in the Cyprus detention camps. True, they also assisted the madrichim and the teachers who worked with the children in preparing curricula and in teaching certain subjects, such as Hebrew, geography of the Land of Israel, and the Bible. However, because they were few in number compared to the scale of the task, their personal contact with the children was largely superficial, as one senior emissary, Michael Zelinger, acknowledged at a conference of emissaries in Germany: "We do not penetrate deep enough in the individual handling of the children. Only rarely do we manage to look into their sad eyes. We see group upon group of children, but what we do not see is the child himself and the problem of being orphaned."[73] This is probably one reason that the emissaries' reports about their educational work with the survivor children refer only occasionally to the special problems of the children with a Christian background. Another reason is that these children blended in with those from other backgrounds, particularly the repatriated children from the Soviet Union — the overwhelming majority — so the emissaries did not notice the differences, although their difficulties and scholastic achievements are sometimes mentioned incidentally in a general discussion of the children's welfare.

Michael Deshe, the Youth Aliyah emissary, who coordinated the educational activity at the Dornstadt children's camp which housed the largest group of Koordynacja children in Germany, describes how the children were organized, their integration into the camp's education system, the subjects they studied, and their extracurricular social activities. He also notes that although many of them did not know Yiddish, their cultural and educational level was satisfactory, their knowledge of Hebrew was not among the lowest, and they never stopped asking when they would be going to Palestine. However, his detailed notes are silent about their attachment to the Christian world from which they were wrenched, or about their specific problems of adjustment to the new Jewish surroundings.[74]

---

73 Michael Zelinger, Problems of the Children and Youth, November 13, 1946, CZA, S75/4655.
74 Michael Deshe, "The Koordynacja Camp in Dornstadt." *Diary of Jewish Agency Mission 4, April 8, 1947,* Haganah Archives, 13/114.

The Hashomer Hatza'ir emissary, Yosef Lobman, an experienced teacher who looked after children from his movement and was sent to France by Youth Aliyah, wrote a comprehensive report noting the problems faced by these children and the physical and behavioral imprint left by their harsh experiences. He distinguishes between the children who were rescued by Christians and the others, identifying the former by their alienation from Jewish culture and the antisemitism they had absorbed: "There are many who were redeemed from convents and Christian homes. Few remember the *aleph-bet* they learned as children. Some of them were raised in a nationalist Catholic atmosphere and even absorbed hatred of Jews." However, the educational doctrine he sets forth in his report does not suggest any special method for drawing these children closer to Judaism. In his perception, their problems are no different from those of the other children who underwent the brutal traumas of the Holocaust: "These are the same youngsters we got to know in Eretz Israel when we took in the children of Teheran and Transnistria."[75]

In contrast, the Youth Aliyah religious emissary Kalman Binyamini (later a professor of psychology at the Hebrew University of Jerusalem), who worked with children and adolescents of Hapoel Hamizrahi in France, among them those who had arrived from Poland in the train organized by Rabbi Herzog, emerged quite optimistic from his first meeting with the children, who by then had been in France for almost a year. His report to Youth Aliyah headquarters noted: "For the most part, the children and youth were brought to the training farms in Poland from forests, places of hiding, convents, and Christian homes. Today it is difficult to discern their past in them. They are Jewish Jews, and the difficulties of adjustment and behavior are already behind them. The homes are decorated in the style of the Land of Israel, and in the clubs are pictures, wall newspapers, and articles, just as we have in our youth clubs."[76]

A discussion of the integration of the children who were rescued under an assumed Christian identity, and the long-term effect of their Christian background, lies beyond the scope of this book, but it assuredly merits a separate study, from both the historical and more cogently, the psychological viewpoint. Apart from the people who were close to them and looked after them, few considered what the children had endured as they re-entered Jewish society. Some were absorbed in a Youth Aliyah framework, others joined their family in Israel or abroad, while a few remained in Poland. Numerous

---

75   Yosef Lobman, The Children's and Youth Houses in France (Hebrew), November 2, 1947, CZA, S75/1904/1.
76   Kalman Binyamini to Youth Aliyah Bureau, Jerusalem, [Summer 1947], CZA, S75/1903.

testimonies describe their difficulties in adjusting to Jewish society, but as yet no comprehensive study of the subject has been carried out. It is certainly not a coincidence that the first and only article on the subject written in Israel is by the educator Binyamin Gruenbaum. Gruenbaum, the son of Yitzhak Gruenbaum, one of the Zionist leaders of Polish Jewry and later the head of the Jewish Agency's Rescue Committee, was in charge of the integration of the first Koordynacja children who arrived in Palestine; he was their teacher for three years in Kibbutz Gan Shmuel, and accompanied them throughout their adolescence.[77]

Even though the present study is about the rescue of children under an assumed Christian identity and their restoration to Jewish society, it would be incomplete without addressing their initial stages of integration in Israel. Thus, to conclude, I have chosen to discuss the integration of Chasia Bielicka's Geulim group, the first Koordynacja children to reach Palestine. They arrived on the illegal-immigrant ship "Theodor Herzl;" were deported to Cyprus by the British mandate authorities and returned to Palestine at the end of August 1947, after four months in detention camps, as part of a group of 500 orphans who were given immigration priority by the British as a goodwill gesture.[78]

To begin with, the group reached the state-to-be when the struggle for its existence was at its height and the physical and educational problems of integration facing Youth Aliyah were unprecedented. Indeed, of the more than 30,000 survivor children who had passed through Youth Aliyah hands by 1952, nearly half arrived between 1945 and 1948.[79] In fact, Youth Aliyah first encountered the special problems of survivor children while the war was still raging, well before the arrival of the large numbers of orphans from the camps in western Europe and Cyprus in 1947–1948. The problems had already cropped up in 1943, with the arrival of the Teheran Children, some 800 children and adolescents who reached Palestine overland from the Soviet Union via Persia, and the more than 600 orphans from Romania who arrived the following year after surviving deportation from the region of Transnistria.[80]

77  Binyamin Gruenbaum, "The Impact of the Catholic Religion on Jewish Children," in B. Gruenbaum, *Words and Heart* (Hebrew) (Tel Aviv: Sifriat Poalim, 1976). The article was first published in the education journal of the Kibbutz Ha'artzi movement in, *Ofakim*, A/41 1958. See also: Flora Hogman, "The Experience of Catholicism for Jewish Children During World War II," *Psychoanalytic Review*, 75, 4 (Winter 1988).

78  Nahum Bogner, *The Deportation Island: Jewish Illegal Immigrant Camps in Cyprus, 1946–1948* (Hebrew) (Tel-Aviv: Am Oved, 1991), pp. 139–146.

79  Bar-Gil, *Youth Aliyah*, p. 22.

80  Ibid., pp. 18–19.

Nevertheless, Youth Aliyah did not, even in the light of these cases, modify the educational principles it had adopted since its inception in the 1930s.

Those principles involved severing the children from their Diaspora past and "remolding" them in the culture of the Land of Israel through "self-realisation" and a personal revolution to be accomplished through agricultural settlement and manual labor. Neither did Youth Aliyah reconsider its existing frameworks of activity. Thus, the youth groups in the kibbutzim and in the youth villages were meant to provide not only an educational framework but also a replacement for the home and family the children had lost. However, no special attention was paid to the special educational needs of the Holocaust children, still less to those who arrived with a Christian background and lacked a clear personal identity. Personal rehabilitation was intertwined with national rehabilitation. The doctrine of Youth Aliyah held that the individual would forge a new Jewish-Zionist identity by mobilizing for the national revolution within the "educational environment of the kibbutz or in the cooperative community of the youth village." The child was required to undergo a radical cultural transformation and assume a new identity manifested symbolically by acceding to an explicit demand to change his foreign name to a Hebrew one and by discarding the past.[81] Psychological rehabilitation was to be achieved not by excavating the past but by burying it. There is evidence that the teachers were instructed not to talk to the children about their past or about their war experiences, but to focus on their future in Israel. This orientation was given expression by a Youth Aliyah madrich, Matityahu Shelem, in a message to the emissaries who worked with the youngsters: "They go through moments of great happiness and moments of bitter disappointment, which reverberate within the minds of the young people and set their course of life for a lengthy period. At this time the madrichim should not probe too deeply into their past, but on the contrary, they should lend an ear to the heart's present pounding. If the emergent pulse of life reaches their ears, they will naturally hear echoes from the past as well."[82]

At the end of August 1947, after a journey lasting a year and a half, the first thirty Koordynacja children from the Geulim group reached Kibbutz Gan Shmuel, still under the leadership of Chasia Bielicka, and after joining Hashomer Hatza'ir in Cyprus. She entrusted them to their new Youth Aliyah madrich, Binyamin Gruenbaum. The group, whose average age was fourteen,

81 Ibid., pp. 195–200.
82 Matityahu Wiener (Shelem), "The Transition Period for New-Immigrant Youth" (Hebrew), in *Letter to Emissaries*, 1, Bureau of Children and Youth Aliya, May 1947, p. 18.

consisted of eighteen girls and twelve boys. Most had been rescued by Christian families and convents. In order to preserve their social cohesion despite the age disparities, Kibbutz Gan Shmuel and the Youth Aliyah directorate worked out a special agreement under which they would be given a three-year training period, of which two years would take place in the kibbutz educational institution, where they would form a separate class. At the end of the two years the conditions were extended for another year — a year more than other children their age received in Youth Aliyah. The extra year was granted by the Youth Aliyah directorate at Gruenbaum's behest. The group, he said, must be given special consideration because of the children's distinct educational needs arising from their past ordeals and their sensitivities. In addition to a curriculum designed specifically for them, every effort was made to integrate the group into the kibbutz children's society in terms of living quarters, social activity, and work, in order not to draw distinction of status between them and their peers.[83]

Upon the group's arrival in Gan Shmuel, Bielicka apparently briefed Gruenbaum about their past and the educational process they had undergone on the way to Palestine. Gruenbaum, an experienced and unconventional teacher, watched the behavior of his new wards with a discerning eye before deciding on his pedagogic approach. Externally, they seemed to be as healthy and happy as other children their age. But from the outset he noticed that they were different from the first youth groups that had been educated at Gan Shmuel and that their outer gaiety was a cover for an inner nervous emotionalism due to a lack of self-confidence. Moreover, any affront, real or imagined, generated bitterness, hidden tears, and a feeling of victimization. From the first, it was clear to Gruenbaum that an especially sensitive approach was required and that it was essential to be receptive to each individual's distinctive problems. His initial impressions produced the following analysis:

> The experience of the years has not yet been erased... The youths are afloat on a sea of internal contradictions. A general explanation of the objective reasons for the personal tragedies and earnest probing in private conversations can liberate the youths from an onerous mental oppression that disturbs them ceaselessly, distorts the image of their world, and interferes with their new life... Their autobiographies can be an ex-

---

83 Binyamin Gruenbaum to Youth Aliyah directorate on duration of training period for the Geulim group, September 28, 1949; Yohanan Gertner to Benny Gruenbaum, October 10, 1949, Gan Shmuel Archive.

cellent opportunity for this. Against this background the madrich will speak and explain the roots of the phenomena as broadly as possible.[84]

Gruenbaum put his ideas into practice. His approach in the first stages of the integration process was more tolerant and less demanding than was customary in the youth groups of the time. To facilitate the children's adjustment, he was lax in discipline and even allowed himself to give some lessons in Polish, so the youngsters could express themselves freely. This approach was a radical departure from the educational norms espoused by Youth Aliyah at the time. Two months after the group's arrival in the kibbutz, an inspector from Youth Aliyah arrived to see how its integration was proceeding. She was displeased by Gruenbaum's methods and said so in a talk with him and in her report:

> The method of the madrich is to ease the difficulties of adjustment of this special group. All of them were raised by Christian families or in convents. As they were rooted in the Polish culture and language, the madrich was less stringent in demanding that they switch to Hebrew. Some of the lessons take place in Polish(!), and Polish is the language the children speak among themselves... I felt a lack of attention, concentration, and order in the classroom. When I remarked on this, I was told that this too is part of the method of easing things at the start. My impression is that the educational regime of Benyo [Gruenbaum] is not the answer to the problem of the Geulim group, but I did not get into an argument about it, because they are about to move to a different regime.[85]

Gruenbaum did not reject the educational goals of Youth Aliyah. On the contrary: he was a demanding teacher, zealous in instilling in young people the values of personal, social, and national responsibility. However, upon encountering this exceptional group he grasped immediately that their "re-education" required unconventional methods. At the same time, he accepted the Youth Aliyah concept according to which the surrounding society should take an active part in the youngsters' education. Accordingly, he shared the group's special problems with the kibbutz members. Six months after the group's arrival, Gruenbaum wrote an article explaining the difficulties involved in imparting Jewish cultural concepts to youths aged fifteen and sixteen who had been assimilated into Polish culture and society. This could not be accomplished quickly: any such attempt would be superficial. Like the madrichim abroad, he too believed that destroying their cultural universe without pro-

---

84  Binyamin Gruenbaum, "First Impressions" (Hebrew), in *Alim* 25–26 (1947/1948).
85  Ruth Birk, Report on Visit to Gan Shmuel (Hebrew), November 18, 1947, CZA, S75/2389.

viding something new in its place — something more than just a promise that "in another year or two they will absorb Jewish culture" — would only undermine the little self-confidence they possessed. In practical terms, this meant not pressing them to take a Hebrew name instead of their Polish one, or not insisting that they speak Hebrew before being able to express themselves freely in that language. "If we succeed in creating the conditions in which [the children] will be able to discard the burden of the memories that weigh them down and reclaim, even to a small degree, their childhood years, with that, even with that alone, we will have fulfilled our task in this first stage of integration," he wrote.[86]

After the children had adjusted to the kibbutz and their studies were proceeding smoothly, Gruenbaum discovered that beneath the cover of integration they continued to harbor antisemitic notions, manifested outwardly by a lack of interest in clearly Jewish subjects such as Bible and stories from the *shtetl*. At the same time, they developed a cult of the *sabra* (Israeli-born child) and the sabra ethos. Gruenbaum found that they more easily identified with Israeli children than with Yiddish-speaking youths from the Diaspora. Nevertheless, he decided not to give in, and deliberately chose to teach them stories written by Y.L. Peretz, a Polish-born Yiddish writer (1852–1915), in order to impart through them the universal human values of Diaspora Jewry. He also utilized every opportunity to talk to them about the special problems of the Jewish people. The results seemed to be encouraging. After a year and a half in Gan Shmuel, the group had acquired a fund of knowledge in Jewish subjects and its members could articulate their identification with the Jewish people and its past and talk about building their future based on the values of Jewish and Hebrew culture, including Diaspora culture. Their derisive attitude toward Diaspora Jewry had disappeared. But Gruenbaum still had the feeling that it was all external, sheer intellectualization. His apprehensions on this score were confirmed one day during an outing. As they drove in pouring rain through Galilee landscapes that reminded them of the Polish countryside, the group, to Gruenbaum's astonishment, spontaneously broke into singing Polish songs and kept it up for the entire drive. "We love the Land of Israel conceptually, but [we love] Poland without thought or explanation — we just love it," one of the girls told him afterward.[87]

86  B. Gruenbaum, "Geulim," in *Words and Heart*, pp. 131–134.
87  Binyamin Gruenbaum, "Development of Jewish and National Awareness in a Youth Group from Poland" (Hebrew), in *Letter to the Madrich*, Bureau of Children and Youth Aliya, January 1950.

Four years after the children were restored to Jewish society, nearly three of them spent in the kibbutz framework during the turbulent period of the birth of the State of Israel, Gruenbaum summed up astutely the achievements of the education which these boys and girls had received, after a childhood spent in Christian families and convents amid the ravages of war:

> I do not delude myself that the deep connection to Poland and to everything related to it has been uprooted and is gone for good. Indeed, I doubt that this connection will ever be completely uprooted … That connection is apparently intertwined with memories from the war and being orphaned, which will remain with these youths throughout their lives. Accordingly, it is enough for us to try to shape their consciousness and their outlook so that they will be able to control their lives and determine their behavior; and as for their memories — suffice it for us if they do not interfere with their lives.[88]

88  Ibid.

# Conclusion

The Nazis' "Final Solution," aimed at eradicating the Jewish people in Europe biologically and culturally, doomed the children to extinction in order to prevent the nation's resurgence. Indeed, in the systematic implementation of this policy the children were the first to be targeted. If the Germans tried to deceive some of the adults into believing in the illusion that they might survive by working efficiently to further the war effort, in the case of the children there was not even the pretense of such an effort. This is attested to horrifically in the notorious children's Aktions — in which the children were hunted down savagely, torn from their parents' arms, and transported to the death camps — which were among the most barbarous manifestations of the Holocaust. Nothing more vividly reflects the horror and the uniqueness of the Holocaust phenomenon, at both the national and universal level, than the attempt to eradicate the children absolutely. Anyone who searches for the slightest signs of compassion in the Nazi attitude toward Jewish children as children — an innate element in human civilization — will search in vain. For the Nazis, the Jewish children were not children but little Jews, and as such marked for death.

In the struggle for the lives of the children in the face of extermination, all those involved — murderers, victims, bystanders — displayed both the basest and the highest aspects of human nature. The possibility of rescuing children from the Nazi tidal-wave of destruction that swept away the Jewish communities in German-occupied Europe depended on the willingness of their Christian neighbors to shelter and hide them. Clearly, the number of Jewish children who were rescued in each of the occupied countries is a faithful reflection of both the attitude of its Christian inhabitants toward their Jewish neighbors and their moral standards in the face of the evil that descended on large segments of the population in this period of brutalized relations between human beings.

The fact that the number of Jewish children who found refuge amid the Christian population in Poland and survived was so small, is due above all to the deeply-rooted antisemitism among broad sectors of Polish society, and the

336 • *At the Mercy of Strangers*

very few Poles who were prepared to take the risk of rescuing Jews. Certainly the exceptionally harsh conditions of the Nazi occupation of Poland, including the threat of execution for anyone who concealed Jews, hindered their rescue. Nevertheless, more children could have survived, even in Poland, if the majority of the Christian population had been able to shed the residues of its attitude toward the Jews in the face of the common enemy and show less indifference toward their fate. The proof of this lies precisely in the difficulties that accompanied the rescue of the pitifully few children who managed to escape from the ghettos and find refuge under an assumed identity among Christian families and in orphanages and convents. The major problem was the unwillingness of the surrounding population to give the rescuers moral support and not denounce them to the German authorities. The fact is that however tenaciously the Nazi occupiers pursued their racial doctrines, they would have had little chance of discovering hidden children solely on the basis of racial features, without the aid of the local population. Thus the greatest fear of the children and their rescuers was that their Christian neighbors would denounce them. Even adults with a broad life experience found it difficult to function in the atmosphere of hostility and anxiety surrounding the Jews who hid among the Christian population in Poland, still more the children who were cut off from their parents and were at the mercy of strangers.

Standing out like beacons in this dark night of history are those few Christians, mainly women, from all classes of Polish society, who dared to swim against the current, ignore the prevailing antisemitic atmosphere, and open their homes and their hearts to those friendless children who escaped the clutches of death. They risked their lives and the lives of their loved ones to rescue Jewish children, and shared their meager fare with their wards. In many cases their acts of rescue reached the most transcendent level of devotion and sacrifice, reflecting, like the glint of pure crystal, love of humanity, mercy, and compassion, at a time when these qualities seemed to have vanished from the face of the earth.

The problem of the survivor children did not end with the conclusion of the war; indeed, it arose in all its acuity immediately after the liberation, when many of the orphaned children had no one to look after them. The effort to care for the solitary children, first by individuals who themselves had just emerged from the catastrophe of the Holocaust, and afterward by the organized Jewish establishment — whether by individual communities or at the national level, such as the network of orphanages that was established as the highest Jewish priority, even before the arrival of help from the Jews of the free world — attested powerfully to the public responsibility of the remnants of Polish Jewry immediately after liberation. Simultaneously, a search began for the children who remained in non-Jewish hands, with the aim of restoring them to their heritage. One thing the survivors agreed upon was that whatever their personal ideology, the place of these children was back in the Jewish fold.

The difficulties — emotional, economic, religious — of reclaiming the children from their Christian rescuers arose in all the liberated countries, and Poland was no exception. However, probably no other Jewish community in Europe was as determined to return the children to their origins as the remnants of Polish Jewry. The firmness of purpose demonstrated by those who redeemed the children from their Christian rescuers, even if this sometimes entailed crossing a thin ethical line, must be seen against the background of the period and viewed as a reaction to the residues of the Polish past: the acrimonious relations that existed between Jews and Christians in the Holocaust period and afterward.

The establishment of the Koordynacja organization to ransom the children, within the framework of which a special education system was created to meet the needs of the children who had been severed from their nation, was a unique phenomenon in the self-rehabilitation process of the surviving Jews in Poland.

The necessity to hide for a protracted period in the Christian world under an assumed identity, an intolerable burden for adults and still more for children, made many children recoil in disgust from their Jewish identity, which they saw as the cause of all their suffering. It is not surprising that many of them could not stand the pressure and sought to be free of it by formally adopting their new Christian identity, thus hoping to shed their perceived inferior status. This effort was usually unsuccessful, resulting in a split identity that they could not shake off and that would bedevil their lives for years to come.

The difficulties these children experienced in trying to readjust to the new Jewish society were unanticipated and emerged only during the integration process. Their anguish, particularly powerful in the orphans, was mitigated primarily by a small number of devoted youth leaders ("madrichim") and educators who volunteered to live with the children, care for them, and support them in their difficult moments. No institution had trained them to cope with the acute problems of the orphan children. It was only thanks to their deep empathy for the children, fused with sheer common sense, that they managed to ease the children's return to the Jewish nation. Most of these madrichim remain unknown. It is to be regretted that the lesson of their work was not learned at the time and that the Youth Aliyah organization, which was in charge of absorbing and educating most of these children, did not consult with the madrichim about how to approach these children in order to facilitate their integration into the new Jewish society.

# Sources and Bibliography

## Archival Sources

*I. Yad Vashem Archives (YVA)*

JM, Microfilm

2619, Walk-Natanblut, Anna, *Ci, co przeżyli*

3636, Kaczmarzyk, Magdalena, *Pomoc udzielana Żydom przez Zgromadzenie SS Albertynek w czasie Wojny Światowej II*

M.20, Archive of Dr. Abraham Zilberschein, Geneva
  22, Minutes of a meeting of the Committee for Children of the World Jewish Congress

M.31, Righteous Among the Nations

M.49, Collection of Documents from the Jewish Institute, Warsaw, ŻIH
  Oliwa, Franciszka, *Dom ocalonych dzieci w Otwocku*

O.25, Zilberberg Collection, Archives of the Polish Underground Research Institute, London
  89, *Sprawozdanie Kościelne*, June 1st 1941—July 15th 1941

O.3, Yad Vashem Testimonies

O.6, Poland Collection
  11, Domanus, Adela, *Historia jednej żydowskiej dziewczynki, z czaso okupacji Warszawy*

O.33, Testimonies, Diaries, Memoirs
  760, Wróbel-Goldberg, Luba, diary

938, Kaplan — Halberstadt, Diary of a teacher in an orphanage (Polish)

1376, Excerpts from a letter from the director of D.D. Zabrze, February 1948

P.20, Dr. Zerach Warhaftig Collection

### Testimonies

| | |
|---|---|
| O.3/4057 | Altman, Sonja |
| O.3/5568 | Altshuler, Yonah |
| O.3/5737 | Avrutzky, Hana |
| O.3/5732 | Batista, (Rozen) Hana |
| O.3/2221 | Blim, Avraham |
| M.31/239 | Boczkowska, Zofia and Podoshyn (Baron) Hanka |

| | |
|---|---|
| M.31/3550 | Bombas, family file |
| M.31/558 | Czartoryska, Helena |
| O.3/4059 | Czesinsky, Yaakov Avraham |
| O.3/1647 | Dembinski, Jerzy |
| O.3/3249 | Drucker, Yeshayahu |
| M.31/3674 | Elbinger, Martha and Rogala, Marianna |
| O.3/2544 | Fink, Fajga and Hana |
| M.31/402 | Gold (Menshynski), Sara and Wislocka-Milkowska, Maria |
| M.31/4071a | Goren (Winter), Martha |
| O.3/694 | Greenwald, Michal |
| O.3/1872 | Horn, Zosia |
| O.3/5708 | Hoter, Bela |
| O.3/2541 | Kahane, Berta |
| O.3/3408 | Kartoz-Gil, Anina |
| O.3/1859 | Kelber, Alexander |
| O.3/4071 | Klein, Miriam |
| O.3/2824 | Krener, Teresa |
| O.3/3109 | Kyslowitz (Brik), Dora |
| O.3/3540 | Lev, Joseph |
| O.31307 | Lubliner, Tamara |
| O.3/4152 | Lustigman (Zlotnik), Rivka |
| O.3/2557 | Oldak, Apolonia |
| O.3/6745 | Or-Ner (Zilber), Magdalena |
| O.3/4816 | Pawlowski, Grzegorz (Griner Jakub Hersz) |
| O.3/3410 | Penski-Chayut, Aliza |
| M.31/3255 | Reiwitz, Michal |
| O.3/2734 | Ryba, Golda |
| O.3/5538 | Sarel, Alexander |
| M.31/4394 | Sendler, Irena |
| O.3/4751 | Shchori (Rosenblatt), Hana |
| O.3/1863 | Seinfeld, Adam |
| O../2716 | Thau, Miriam |
| M.31/3496 | Tishler-Lekach, Marsha |
| O.3/3122 | Tokarski, Katya |
| M.31/1929 | Wąsowska-Renot, Eugenia |
| O.3/4062 | Weinstein, Zvia |
| O.33/1376 | Weiss (Kokotek), Fela |
| M.31/4298 | Winnik, Eugeniusz; Wisocki (Lipszyc), Bracha |
| M.31/3009 | Wodnicka-Dębska (Rozner), Adama |

*II. Oral History Division (OHD), Institute of Contemporary Jewry, Hebrew University of Jerusalem*

4.      Bricha (Organized Escape) and Holocaust Survivors
68.     Redeeming Jewish Children from Poles after the War

**Testimonies**

(68) 20       Bahat, Mordechai
(68) 26       Bornstein-Bielicka, Chasia
(68) 48       Brener (Shein), Jadwiga and Brener, Liber
(68) 53       Danieli (Danielski), David
(68) 28       Drucker, Yeshayahu
(68) 27       Fleischer-Zilber, Devora (Marysia)
(68) 34       Gvirtzman, Avraham
(68) 22       Harari (Hoterer), Eliezer
(68) 59       Hausler (Mordechowicz), Hana
(68) 24       Hochberg-Peleg, Miriam (Marianska)
(68) 17       Israeli, Rivka (Motyl, Regina)
(68) 60       Jozek (Leichter), Shoshana
(4) 15        Kahane, David
(68) 21       Kaplinsky, Baruch
(68) 49       Karski-Kongis, Bernard
(68) 32       Katz, Binyamin
(68) 15       Koriski, Leibel
(68) 45       Krivos, Pinhas
(68) 50       Lederman, Sara
(68) 13       Libes, Noa (Drucker, Nina)
(68) 1        Mazeh, Alfred
(68) 10       Sarid, Arye
(68) 42       Sliwa, Joseph
(68) 41       Zeidenberg, Pesach

*III. Beit Lohamei Hagetaot (Ghetto Fighters' House) Archives (BLHA)*

Koordynacja Files
      790/BL
      798/BL

## IV. Central Zionist Archives (CZA)

S26    Jewish Agency Rescue Committee
S75    Department for Immigration of Children and Youth
C2     Office of the World Jewish Congress, London
44     Minutes of meetings of the Jewish Agency Executive
JI/7264 Minutes of executive of the National Council
5612   *Farn Yiddishn Kind* (Koordynacja journal), November 1946

## V. Haganah Archives

114  Ephraim Dekel Collection
     Ha'apala (Illegal Immigration) Project, Information Center
     35, Microfilms from Jewish Historical Institute, Warsaw 24.85–25/50
     44.8–19, 24.58

## VI. Hashomer Hatza'ir Archives (HHA)

(2) 32.2 Correspondence with Poland

## VII. Kibbutz Gan Shmuel Archive

Geulim Group

## VIII. Mordechai Shatner Family Archive

## IX. Archiwum Żydowskiego Instytutu Historycznego (AŻIH) (CKŻ. WO)

Sprawozdanie wydzial opieki nad dzieckiem C.K. Ż w P. na rok 1946
5518, Ewa Goldberg, Moje wspomienia z pobytu u Siostr Sercanek

## X. Givat Joint Archives (GJA) (Jerusalem)

AJDC Activities in Poland
     12B/C–61.034
     125B/126A

# Memoirs, Diaries and Documents

Altbeker Cyprys, Ruth, *A Jump for Life: A Survivor's Journal from Nazi-Occupied Poland*, New York: Continuum, 1997.

Arad, Yitzhak, Gutman, Yisrael and Margaliot, Abraham, eds., *Documents on the Holocaust*, Jerusalem: Yad Vashem, 1988.

Arczynski, Marek and Balcerak, Wieslaw, *Kryptonim "Zegota": Z dziejów pomocy Żydom w Polsce 1939–1945*, Warsaw: Czytelnik, 1983.

Ashkenazy-Engelhard, Halina, *I Want to Live* (Hebrew), Tel Aviv: Moreshet and Sifriat Poalim, 1976.

Atzmon, Shlomo, *I Won the Bet; A Story of Survival of a Jewish Child* (Hebrew) Tel Aviv: Moreshet, 1992.

Avinun, Sara, *Rising from the Abyss: An Adult's Struggle with her Trauma as a Child in the Holocaust*, Hod Hasharon: Astrolog Publishing House, 2005.

Barlas, Chaim, *Rescue in the Holocaust*, (Hebrew), Tel Aviv: Ghetto Fighters' House and Hakibbutz Hameuchad, 1975.

Bartoszewski, Wladyslaw and Lewin, Zofia (eds.), *Ten jest z ojczyzny mojej*, Kraków, Znak, 1969.

——, *Righteous Among Nations: How Poles Helped the Jews*, London: Earls Court Publications, 1969.

Ben-Shem, Reuben, "Excerpts from a Warsaw Ghetto Diary" (Hebrew), Massua, 10, 1982, pp. 33–51.

Berman, Adolf Abraham, *From the Days of the Underground*, (Hebrew), Tel Aviv: Hamenora, 1971.

——, *In the Place Where Fate Sent Me* (Hebrew), Tel Aviv: Ghetto Fighters' House and Hakibbutz Hameuchad, 1977.

——, "Jews on the Aryan Side," in Yitzhak Gruenbaum, ed., *Encyclopaedia of the Jewish Diaspora: Poland series, Warsaw*, vol. I, pp. 685–732 (Hebrew), Jerusalem, 1953.

Bielicka-Bornstein, Chasia, *One of the Few* (Hebrew), Tel Aviv: Moreshet, 2003.

——, "Returning to the Bosom of their Nation," in Dror Levy, ed., *Book of Hashomer Hatza'ir* (Hebrew), Merhavia: Sifriat Poalim,1961, vol. II, pp. 316–345.

Blumenthal, Nachman and Kermish, Joseph, eds., *Resistance and Revolt in the Warsaw Ghetto; A Documentary History* (Hebrew), Jerusalem: Yad Vashem, 1965.

Bornstein, Shmuel, ed., *Studies in the Redemption of Jewish Children from Christians in Poland after the Holocaust* (Hebrew), Ghetto Fighters' House, 1989.

Breslav, Shmuel, "Poles and Jews," *Yalkut Moreshet* (Hebrew), vol. XI, (1969), pp. 103–107.

Breznitz, Shlomo, *Memory Fields,* New York: Knopf, 1993.

David, Janina, *A Touch of Earth: A Wartime Childhood,* New York: Orion Press, 1969.

Dekel, Ephraim, *Survivors of the Sword* (Hebrew), Tel Aviv: Ministry of Defense Publishing House, 1963.

Dror, Zvika, *Testimonies of Survivors: 96 Personal Interviews from Members of Kibbutz Lochamei Hagetaot* (Hebrew) Tel Aviv: Ghetto Fighters' House and Hakibbutz Hameuchad, 1984.

Erlichman-Bank, Sara, *In the Hands of the Impure* (Hebrew), Tel Aviv: Ghetto Fighters' House and Hakibbutz Hameuchad, 1976

Ezer-Olitzky, Chena, *Fabric of Life: Interviews with Survivors who were Children in the Holocaust* (Hebrew), Tel Aviv: Gvanim, 2006.

Frank, Moshe, *To Survive and Testify* (Hebrew), Tel Aviv: Ghetto Fighters' House and Hakibbutz Hameuchad, 1993.

Fried-Blumenkrantz, Lea, "Lilka the Convent Girl" (Hebrew), Edut, 10 (1994), pp. 71–83.

Friedländer, Saul, *When Memory Comes,* New York: Farrar, Straus and Giroux, 1979.

Garfunkel, Leib, *The Destruction of Kovno's Jewry* (Hebrew), Jerusalem: Yad Vashem, 1959.

Glowinski, Michal, *The Black Seasons,* Evanston: Northwestern University Press, 2005.

Goldshlag, Yitzhak, ed., *Rescue Mission* (Hebrew), Jerusalem, 1947.

Grayek, Stefan, *The Struggle: Polish Jews 1945–1949* (Hebrew), Tel Aviv: Am Oved, 1989.

Gruenbaum, Binyamin, "Development of Jewish and National Awareness in a Youth Group from Poland" (Hebrew), in *Letter to the Madrich,* Bureau for Immigration of Children and Youth, January 1950.

——— , "First Impressions" (Hebrew), in Alim 25–26 (1947/1948), pp. 38–39.

Grzybacz (Gazit), Shlomo, "Into the Bosom of my Nation" (Hebrew), *Yediot Beit Lohamei Hagetaot,* Bulletin, 20 (1958), pp. 59–65.

Gutenbaum, Jakub and Latala, Agnieszka, eds., *The Last Eyewitnesses: Children of the Holocaust Speak,* vol. 2, Evanston: Northwestern University Press, 2005.

Guz, Leon, *Targowa 64,* Warsaw: Czytelnik, 1990.

Hochberg-Marianska, Maria and Grüss, Noe, eds., *The Children Accuse,* London: Vallentine, Mitchell, 1996. See also Peleg.

Hochberg, Miriam (Marianska) Peleg, "I Looked After Survivor Children" (Hebrew), *Yediot Yad Vashem,* vol. 8–9 (1956), pp. 12–13. See also Peleg.

Ishai, Moshe, *In the Shadow of the Holocaust; Memoirs of a Mission in Poland 1945–1946* (Hebrew), Tel Aviv: Ghetto Fighters' House and Hakibbutz Hameuchad, 1973.

Jaromirska, Leokadia, "Bogushia," *Yalkut Moreshet,* English Edition, vol. 3 (Winter 2003), pp. 94–131.

Kahane, David, *Lvov Ghetto Diary,* Amherst: University of Massachusetts Press, 1990.

———, *After the Flood* (Hebrew), Jerusalem: Mossad Harav Kook, 1981.

Kermish, Joseph (ed.), *To Live with Honor and Die with Honor: Selected Documents from the Warsaw Ghetto Underground Archives "O.S." (Oneg Shabbath),* Jerusalem: Yad Vashem, 1986.

Klonicki, Aryeh, *The Diary of Adam's Father,* Jerusalem: Ghetto Fighters' House and Hakibbutz Hameuchad , 1973.

Klukowski, Zygmund, *Dziennik z lat okupacji Zamojszczyzny,* Lublin: Lubelska Spoldzielnia Wydawnictwo, 1958.

Kol, Moshe, *Holocaust and Revival* (Hebrew), Tel Yitzhak: Hamidrasha Haliberalit, 1985.

Koriski, Leibel, "The Zionist Koordynacja for the Rescue of the Children in Poland 1946–1949" (Hebrew), *Gal-Ed,* vol. 7–8 (1985), pp. 253–261.

Kranzler, David and Hirshler, Gertrude, eds., *Solomon Schonfeld: his Page in History,* New York: Judaica Press, 1982.

Kubovy, Aryeh L., "The Silence of Pope Pius XII and the Beginning of the Jewish Document," *Yad Vashem Studies* VI (1967), pp. 7–25.

Küchler-Silberman, Lena, *My 100 Children,* New York: Souvenir Press, 1961.

———, *The Hundred to Their Borders* (Hebrew), Tel Aviv: Schocken, 1969.

———, *We Accuse: Testimonies of Children from the Holocaust* (Hebrew), Merhavia: Sifriat Poalim, 1963.

Kuper, R. Irit, *At the Edge of the Forest* (Hebrew), Tel Aviv: Hakibbutz Hameuchad, 1977.

———, *As Everything Passes,* (Hebrew), Tel Aviv: Hakibbutz Hameuchad, 1980.

Levin, Avraham, *From the Notebook of the Teacher from Yehudiya* (Hebrew), Tel Aviv: Ghetto Fighters' House and Hakibbutz Hameuchad, 1969.

Levin, Yitzhak, *I Immigrated [to Palestine] from Specje* (Hebrew), Tel Aviv: Am Oved, 1947.

Lidowski, Eliezer, *The Spark has not been Extinguished* (Hebrew), Tel Aviv: Association of Partisans and Ghetto Fighters in Israel, 1987.

Livneh, Zalman and Weiner, Yeshayahu, "Movement in Ruins," in Dror Levy, ed., *Book of Hashomer Hatzair* (Hebrew), vol. II, Merhavia: Sifriat Poalim, 1961, pp. 279–301.

Maslowska-Sobol, Janina, "Children Speak" (Hebrew), *Yediot Beit Lohamei Hagetaot*, 21(1959), pp. 93–94.

Meed, Vladka, *On Both Sides of the Wall*, Tel Aviv: Ghetto Fighters' House and Hakibbutz Hameuchad, 1972.

*Mission to the Diaspora 1945–1948* (Hebrew), Tel Aviv: Yad Tabenkin and Hakibbbutz Hameuchad, 1989.

Neshamit, Sara, "Coordinating Child Rescue in Liberated Poland" (Hebrew), *Dapim Leheker Hashoa V`Hamered* [Pages on the Study of the Catastrophe and the Revolt], vol. 2 (1952), pp. 116–148. See also Shner-Neshamit.

Opoczyński, Perec, *Sketches from the Warsaw Ghetto* (Hebrew), Tel Aviv: Ghetto Fighters House and Hakibbutz Hameuchad, 1970.

Orlowicz-Reznik, Nessia, *Mommy, Can I Cry Now?* (Hebrew), Tel Aviv: Sifriat Poalim, 1964.

———, "Shomeri Children's Home" (Hebrew), in Dror Levy, ed., *Book of Hashomer Hatza'ir*, vol. II, Merhavia: Sifriat Poalim, 1961, pp. 311–316.

Pawlowski, Grzegorz, (Jakub Hersz Griner), "Moje zycie," in *Tygodnik Powszechny*, 15/16 (1966), pp. 339–371.

Peleg, Miriam (Marianska) and Peleg, Mordecai, *Witnesses: Life in Occupied Kraków*, London: Routledge and Kegan Paul, 1992. See also Hochberg.

Perechodnik, Calel, *Am I a Murderer? Testimony of a Jewish Ghetto Policeman*, Boulder: Westview Press, 1996.

Perlberg-Shmuel, Miriam, *This Girl Is Jewish!* (Hebrew), Haifa: Shurot, 1997.

*Report of Activity for the Jewish Central Committee in Poland, January 1, 1946–June 30, 1946* (Yiddish), Warsaw, 1947.

Ringelblum, Emmanuel, *Polish-Jewish Relations During the Second World War*, Jerusalem: Yad Vashem, 1974.

———, *Diary and Notes from the Warsaw Ghetto: September 1939—December 1942* (Hebrew), Jerusalem: Yad Vashem and Ghetto Fighters' House, 1992.

Samet, Shimon, *I Came on the Morrow: A Journey in Poland, 1946* (Hebrew), Tel Aviv: Leinman, 1946.

Schoenfeld, Joachim, *Holocaust Memoirs: Jews in the Lvov Ghetto, the Janowski Concentration Camp, and as Deportees in Siberia*, Hoboken: Ktav, 1985.

Schonfeld, Solomon, *Message to Jewry*, London: Jewish Secondary Schools Movement, undated

Schweiger-Blady, Adina, "On the Aryan Side of Warsaw" (Hebrew), Edut, 4 (1989), pp. 43–72.

Sendlerowa, Irena, "Ci ktorzy pomagali Żydom," *Biuletyn Żydowskiego Instytutu Historycznego, (BZIH)*, 45/46 (1963), pp. 234–247.

Shner-Neshamit, Sara, I Did Not Find Rest (Hebrew), Tel Aviv: Ghetto Fighters' House and Hakibbutz Hameuchad, 1986. See also Neshamit.

Sliwowska, Wiktoria, ed., *The Last Eyewitnesses: Children of the Holocaust Speak*, vol.1, Evanston: Northwestern University Press, 1997.

Slomczyński, Adam, *Dom ks. Boduena 1939–1945*, Warsaw: Panstowy Institut Wydawniczy, 1975.

Smólski, Wladyslaw, ed., *Za to grozila smierć: Polacy z pomoca Żydom w czasie okupacji*, Warsaw: Instytut Wydawniczy Pax, 1981.

Szulkin, Michal, "Sprawozdanie z działalnoscie Referatu dla Spraw Pomocy Ludnosci Żydowskiej przy Polskiego Komitetu Wyzwolenia Narodowego," in *Biuletyn Żydowskiego Instytutu Historycznego,(BZIH)*, 3(79) (1971), pp. 75–90.

Tadmor, Yitzhak, ed., *Cherries on the Elbe: The Story of the Children's Home at Blankenese* (Hebrew), Givat Haviva: Yad Ya'ari, 1996.

Tenenbaum, Benjamin, ed., *One of a City and Two of a Family* (Hebrew), Merhavia: Sifriat Poalim, 1947.

Turkow, Jonas, *After Liberation* (Yiddish), Buenos Aires: Association of Polish Jews in Argentina, 1959.

———, "Children of the Ghetto" (Hebrew), *Dapim; Studies of the Holocaust and Jewish Resistance*, vol. 1, pp. 256–265, Tel-Aviv, 1969.

———, *The Glorious Children of the Ghetto* (Hebrew) Tel Aviv: Eked, 1982.

Warhaftig, Zerach, *Refugee and Survivor: Rescue Efforts During the Holocaust*, Jerusalem: Yad Vashem, 1988.

Wiener (Shelem), Matityahu, "The Transition Period for New Immigrant Youth" (Hebrew), in *Letter to Emissaries*, Bureau for Immigration of Children and Youth, May 1947, pp. 17–28.

Zaderecki, Tadeusz, *Under the Rule of the Swastika in Lvov: The Destruction of the Jewish Community Through the Eyes of a Polish Writer* (Hebrew), Jerusalem: Yad Vashem, 1982.

Żeminski, S., "Kartki dziennika nauczyciela w Łukowie z okresu ukupacji hitlerowskiej," *Biuletyn Żydowskiego Instytutu Historycznego,(BZIH)*, 27 (1958), pp. 105–122.

Ziemian, Joseph, *The Cigarette Sellers of Three Crosses Square*, (Hebrew) Tel Aviv: Moreshet and Sifriat Poalim, 1968. [English edition: London: Vallentine, Mitchell, 1970]

Zuckerman, Yitzhak, *The Polish Exodus* (Hebrew), Tel Aviv: Ghetto Fighters' House and Hakibbutz Hameuchad, 1988.

Zylbersztajn, Stella, *A gdyby to bylo wasze dziecko?* Łódź: Oficyna Biblofilow, 1994.


# Research Studies — Books and Articles

Bar-Gil, Shlomo, *Youth Aliyah Policy and Activity in the Absorption and Rehabilitation of Holocaust Survivors 1945–1955* (Hebrew), Ph.D. thesis, Hebrew University of Jerusalem, 1995.

Bartoszewski, Wladyslaw, "Some Thoughts on Polish-Jewish Relations," *Polin, A Journal of Polish-Jewish Studies*, vol. 1 (1986), pp. 278–287.

Bauer, Yehuda, *Out of the Ashes: The Impact of American Jews on Post-Holocaust European Jewry*, New York: Pergamon Press, 1989.

——, *Flight and Rescue: Brichah*, New York: Random House, 1970.

——, "Joint Distribution Committee (JDC)," in Yisrael Gutman, ed., *Encyclopedia of the Holocaust*, vol. 2, New York: Macmillan, 1990, pp. 752–756.

Ben-Sasson, Chaim Hillel, *Jewish History in the Middle Ages* (Hebrew), Tel Aviv: Am Oved, 1962.

Berenstein, Tatiana and Rutkowski, Adam, *Assistance to the Jews in Poland 1939–1945*, Warsaw: Polonia Publishing House, 1963.

Bogner, Nahum, *The Deportation Island: Jewish Illegal Immigrant Camps on Cyprus, 1946–1948* (Hebrew), Tel Aviv: Am Oved, 1991.

——, "The Convent Children: The Rescue of Jewish Children in Polish Convents during the Holocaust," *Yad Vashem Studies*, vol. XXVII, 1999. pp. 235–285.

Cohen, Asher, *History of the Holocaust: France* (Hebrew), Jerusalem: Yad Vashem, 1996.

Cohen, Yohanan, *Operation "Bricha," Poland 1945–1946* (Hebrew), Tel Aviv: Zmora Bitan, 1995.

Czerniawski, Irit, "The Polish Righteous Among the Nations — Statistical Aspects" (Hebrew), *Dapim Lecheker Hashoa ve`Hamered* [Pages on the Study of the Catastrophe and the Revolt], 14 (1997), pp. 339–365.

Datner-Spiewak, Helena, "Institucje opieki nad dzieckem i szkoly powszech-ne Centralnego Komitetu Żydow Polskich w latach 1945–1946," *Biuletyn Żydowskiego Instytutu Historycznego, (BZIH),* 3/119 (1981), pp. 37–51.

Dequeker, Luc, "Baptism and Conversion of Jews in Belgium 1939–1945," in Michman, Dan, ed., *Belgium and the Holocaust,* Jerusalem: Yad Vashem, 1998, pp. 235–271.

Dobroszycki, Lucian, *Survivors of the Holocaust in Poland,* New York: M.E. Sharpe, 1994.

Dvorzetsky, Mark, "The Jewish Child During the Holocaust" (Hebrew), *Yediot Beit Lohamei Hagetaot,* 21 (1956), pp. 85–91.

——, "Psycho-Sociological Problems of Jewish Children Hidden by Non-Jews in the Holocaust" (Hebrew), *Dapim Refuiim Aleph,* vol. 25 (1966), pp. 3–9.

——, "Children with No Childhood" (Hebrew), *Tefutsot Hagola,* 1–2 (1972), pp. 162–172.

Engel, David, *Between Liberation and Flight: Holocaust Survivors in Poland and the Struggle for Leadership, 1944–1946* (Hebrew), Tel Aviv: Am Oved, 1996.

Fein, Helen, *Accounting for Genocide: Victims — and Survivors — of the Holocaust,* New York: Free Press 1979.

Fijałkowski, Zenon, *Kosciól katolicki na ziemiach polskich w latach okupacii hitlerowskiej,* Warsaw: Wydawnictwo "Książka i Wiedza", 1983.

Fogelman, Eva, *Conscience and Courage: Rescuers of Jews During the Holo-caust,* New York: Cassell, 1994.

Frącek, Teresa, "Zgromadzenie Siostr Franciszkanek Rodziny Maryi w latach 1939–1945," in *Kosciól katolicki na ziemiach Polski w czasie II wojny swi-atowej,* vol. 10, Warsaw, 1981.

Frenkel, Yuval, "The Activity of Monsignor Angelo Roncalli" (Hebrew), *Yal-kut Moreshet,* 59 (April 1995), pp. 109–136.

Friedman, Philip, *Roads to Extinction: Essays on the Holocaust,* New York: Jewish Publication Society, 1980.

——, *Their Brothers Keepers,* New York: Holocaust Library, 1978.

Garlinski, Józef, *Poland in the Second World War,* London: Macmillan, 1985.

Gawrys, Cezary, "Turkowice — śmierć i ocalenie," *WIĘŻ, 4(342) (1987),* pp. 4–42.

Gelber, Yoav, *Jewish Palestinian Volunteering in the British Army During the Second World War,* vol. 3, *The Standard Bearers* (Hebrew), Jerusalem: Yad Yitzhak Ben-Zvi, 1983.

Goldberg, Jacob, *Converted Jews in the Polish Commonwealth* (Hebrew), Jerusalem: Zalman Shazar Center, 1985.

Gross, Jan Tomasz, *Polish Society under German Occupation: The Generalgouvernement, 1939-1944*, New Jersey: Princeton University Press, 1979.

Gruenbaum, Binyamin, *Words and Heart* (Hebrew), Tel Aviv: Sifriat Poalim, 1976.

Gutman, Yisrael, *The Jews of Warsaw 1939-1943: Ghetto, Underground and Revolt*, Bloomington: Harvester Press, 1982.

———, *The Jews in Poland after World War II* (Hebrew), Jerusalem: Zalman Shazar Center, 1985.

———, "Polish Jewry in the Holocaust" (Hebrew), in Bartal, Yisrael, and Gutman, Yisrael, eds., *Polish Jewry: The Broken Chain Through the Ages*, vol. 1, Jerusalem: Zalman Shazar Center, 1997, pp. 451–506.

Gutman, Yisrael and Krakowski, Shmuel, *Unequal Victims: Poles and Jews during World War II*, Bloomington, Indiana University Press, 1986.

Hogman, Flora, "The Experience of Catholicism for Jewish Children during World War II," *Psychoanalytic Review* 75(4), (Winter 1988), pp. 511–532.

Keren-Patkin, Nili, "Jewish Children Salvation Projects in France," (Hebrew), *Yalkut Moreshet*, 36 (1983), pp. 101–150.

Kermish, Joseph, "The Activities of the Council for Aid to Jews ("Żegota") in Occupied Poland," in Yisrael Gutman and Efraim Zuroff, eds., *Rescue Attempts During the Holocaust*, Jerusalem: Yad Vashem, 1977, pp. 367–398.

Kless, Shlomo, "Rescuing Jewish Children in Belgium", *Yalkut Moreshet*, 37 (1984), pp. 129–142. (Hebrew)

Kloczowski, Jerzy, "The Religious Orders and the Jews in Nazi-Occupied Poland," *Polin, A Journal of Polish-Jewish Studies*, vol. 3 (1988), pp. 238–243.

Korbonski, Stefan, *The Polish Underground State; A Guide to the Underground 1939-1945*. New York: Hippocrene Books, 1981.

Krakowski, Shmuel, *The War of the Doomed: Jewish Armed Resistance in Poland, 1942-1944*, New York: Holmes and Meier, 1984.

———, "Losses of Polish Jewry during the Holocaust — Statistical Estimate" (Hebrew), *Studies on the Holocaust Period*, vol. 2 (1981), pp. 231–237.

———, "Relations Between Jews and Poles during the Holocaust — New and Old Approaches in Polish Historiography," *Yad Vashem Studies*, vol. XIX (1988), pp. 317–321.

Kubiak, A, "Dzieciobójstwo podczas okupacji hitlerowski," *Biuletyn Zydowskiego Instytutu Historycznego, (BZIH)*, 17/18 (1956), pp. 61–105.

Kurek, Ewa, *Your Life Is Worth Mine: How Polish Nuns Saved Hundreds of Jewish Children in German Occupied Poland*, New York: Hippocrene Books, 1997.

Kurek-Lesik, Ewa, "The Condition of Admittance and the Social Background of Jewish Children Saved by Woman's Religious Orders in Poland from 1939–1945," *Polin, A Journal of Polish-Jewish Studies*, vol. 3 (1988), pp. 244–275.

———, *Udzial Żenskich Zgromadzeń zakonnych w akcji ratowania dzieci żzydowskich w Polsce w latach 1939–1945*, częśc II, Żrudla i opracowania, Ph.D. dissertation, Katolicki Uniwersytet Lubelski, (KUL) 1988.

Lestschinsky, Jacob, *Crisis, Catastrophe and Survival*, New York: Institute of Jewish Affairs of the World Jewish Congress, 1948.

Litwak, Joseph, "The JDC's Contribution to the Rehabilitation of Jewish Survivors in Poland 1944–1949" (Hebrew), in Benjamin Pinkus, ed., *Eastern-European Jewry from Holocaust to Redemption, 1944–1948*, Sde Boker: Ben-Gurion Research Center, 1987, pp. 334–388.

Madajczyk, Czeslaw, *Hitlerowski terror na wsi polskej 1939–1945* Warsaw: Panstwowe Wydawnictwo Naukowe, 1965.

Mahler, Raphael, *Jews in Poland between the Two World Wars* (Hebrew), Tel Aviv: Dvir, 1968.

Marrus, Michel R. and Paxton, Robert O, *Vichy France and the Jews*, New York: Basic Books, 1981.

Meltzer, Emanuel, *No Way Out: The Politics of Polish Jewry 1935–1939*, Cincinnati: Hebrew Union College Press, 1997.

Mendelson, Ezra, "Polin" (Hebrew), in Tsur, Jacob, ed., *The Diaspora: Eastern Europe*, Jerusalem: Keter Books, pp. 169–211.

Michlis, B. Joanna, "Who Am I? Jewish Children's Search for Identity in Post-War Poland 1945–1949," *Polin, A Journal of Polish-Jewish Studies*, vol. 20 (2007), pp. 98–121.

Michman, Yosef, "The Problem of Jewish War Orphans in Holland" (Hebrew), in Gutman, Yisrael, and Drechsler, Adina, eds., *She'erit Hapletah 1944–1948: Rehabilitation and Political Struggle*, Jerusalem: Yad Vashem, 1990, pp. 187–209.

Oliner, Samuel P., and Oliner, Pearl, M., *The Altruistic Personality: Rescuers of Jews in Nazi Europe*, New York: Touchstone, 1992.

Paldiel, Mordechai, "Fear and Comfort: The Plight of Hidden Jewish Children in Wartime-Poland," in *Holocaust and Genocide Studies*, 4/6 (1991), pp. 397–413.

Pat, Emanuel, *Jewish Children Back to Life* (Yiddish), New York: Yiddisher Arbeiter Komitet, 1949.

*Pinkas Hakehilot: Encyclopedia of Jewish Communities — Poland* (Hebrew), seven volumes, Jerusalem: Yad Vashem, 1976–2000.

Pinkus, Chasia, *From Four Winds: Rehabilitation of Immigrant Youth* (Hebrew), Jerusalem: Hasifriya Hazionit [Zionist Library], 1971.

Prekerowa, Teresa, *Konspiracyjna Rada Pomocy Żydom w Warszawie 1942–1945*, Warsaw: Panstwowy Instytut Wydawniczy, 1981.

———, "Żegota," in Israel Gutman, ed., *Encyclopedia of the Holocaust*, vol. 4, 1990, pp. 1729–1731.

———, "The 'Just' and the 'Passive'," *Yad Vashem Studies*, vol. XIX, 1988, pp. 369–377.

Redlich, Shymon, "Szeptycki and the Jews During World War II" (Hebrew), *Shvut*, 13, 1989, pp. 7–17.

Sarid, Levi Arye, *Ruin and Deliverance: The Pioneer Movement in Poland Throughout the Holocaust and During its Aftermath 1939–1949* (Hebrew), vol. 2, Tel Aviv: Moreshet, 1997.

Shlomi, Hana, "The First Stages of Organizing the Jews in Poland at the End of World War II" (Hebrew) *Gal-Ed*, vol. 2 (1975), pp. 287–331.

———, "Activity by Polish Jews to Renew Jewish Life in Poland" (Hebrew), *Gal-Ed*, vol. 10, 1987, pp. 207–225.

Spector, Shmuel, *The Holocaust of Volhynian Jews 1941–1944*, Jerusalem: Yad Vashem, 1990.

Stopnicka Heller, Celia, *On the Edge of Destruction: Jews of Poland Between the Two World Wars*, New York: Columbia University Press, 1977.

———, "Poles of Jewish Background — The Case of Assimilation Without Integration in Interwar Poland," in Joshua Fishman, ed., *Studies on Polish Jewry 1919–1939*, New York: YIVO, 1974, pp. 242–276.

Tec, Nechama, *When Light Pierced the Darkness: Christian Rescue of Jews in Nazi-Occupied Poland*, New York: Oxford University Press, 1986.

Turowicz, Jerzy, "Polish Reasons and Jewish Reasons," *Yad Vashem Studies*, vol. XIX, 1988, pp. 379–388.

Van Den Wijngaert, Mark, "Belgian Catholics and the Jews during the German Occupation 1940–1944," in Dan Michman, ed., *Belgium and the Holocaust*, Jerusalem: Yad Vashem, 1998, pp. 225–233.

Wolman, Leib, "Jewish Children in Europe after World War II" (Yiddish), *YIVO Bletter*, 33 (1949), pp. 84–94.

Zielinski, Zygmund, "Activities of Catholic Orders on behalf of Jews in Nazi-Occupied Poland," in Otto Dov Kulka and R. Mendes-Flohr, eds., *Juda-*

*ism and Christianity Under the Impact of National Socialism,* Jerusalem: Historical Society of Israel and Zalman Shazar Center for Jewish History, 1987, pp. 381–399.

# Index

"Theodor Herzl" (illegal-immigrant ship) 321 328
Three Crosses Square 104 109 110 112
Torah veAvodah movement 255 256
TOZ (Jewish Society for the Protection of Health) 122
Transnistria 327 328
Treblinka 26 36 40 115 134
trials 272–76 300 [legal procedures]
Trojanowski, Jan 91
Trzaskalska, Kazimira 125
Turkow, Jonas 106 126 132 200 202
Turkowice 143 144 158–59 161–62 172 173 179 283
Tykocin 270

Ukraine, Ukrainians 16 19 21 22 23 24 33–34 45 52 62 71 74 79 82 143 184 188 277
army units 24
Ukrainian national movement (OUN) 23
Umschlagplatz 121
underground. *See* Poland: underground
Unger, Moshe 237
Uniate (Greek Catholic) Church 33 148 149 153 176 180
Uniate Studite order 176 179–80
Union of Polish Patriots (ZPP) 232
United Nations 217
United Nations Commission on Human Rights 218
United States 188 206 207 218 222–23 224 225 234 235 242 243 250 255 256 263
UNRRA (United Nations Relief and Rehabilitation Administration) 185 220
Urbanowicz, Father 30

*Va'ad haHatzalah* (Rescue Committee of the Orthodox Rabbis in America) 194
Van Roey, Cardinal 214
Vatican 33 210–11 212 214
villages, villagers 32 38 45 49 53 54–55 60 62 64 73 74 99 111 112 144 151 158 186 188 190 191–92 195 197 198 199–200 231 238 249 251 257 259 262 266 271 293 303. *See also* farmers; peasants
Vilna 237 238
Volhynia 38 53 143 183 186
Volksdeutsche 23 27 47 62

Walęga, Janina 47
War of Independence (Israel) 310
Wargon-Grayek, Utta 229
Warhaftig, Zerach 225 256 283 291
Warsaw Ghetto 22 25 26 27 39–41 42 44 46–47 48 55 56 67 69 80 82–83 85 96 99 100–104 106 111 113 133–36 145–47 232. *See also* ghetto, ghettos
Warsaw 17 22 25 30 39 40 42 n. 9 44 46 48 51 55 59 61 63 64 69 74 99–113 117 118 120 121 122 125 126–27 128 129 130 131–32 133 135 136 137 144 146 153 154 161 170 173 175 176 179 185 192 194 195 202 203 204 224 225 226 227 229 233 234 235 242 248 255 258 264 267 272 273 278 279 300
Municipality 27 121 135 147 204
Warszawiak, Sara. *See* Avinun Sara
Wąsowska, Eugenia (Sister) 28 278 n. 47
Wędrychowska, Zofia 125
Weiner, Shaike 237
Weinstein, Pola (Hammersfeld) 300
Weissblum, Meir 319
Werba 186
White Paper 221
Wieliczka 72 195
Wierbowa, Wanda 122